Interpreting Court Song in Uganda

Eastman/Rochester Studies in Ethnomusicology

(ISSN: 2161–0290)

Ellen Koskoff, Founding Editor
Eastman School of Music

Damascus Kafumbe, Series Editor
Middlebury College

Recent Titles

*Faith by Aurality in China's Ethnic Borderland:
Media, Mobility, and Christianity at the Margins*
Ying Diao

Performing Arts and Gender in Postcolonial Western Uganda
Linda Cimardi

*Intimate Entanglements in the Ethnography of Performance:
Race, Gender, Vulnerability*
Edited by Sidra Lawrence and Michelle Kisliuk

*Walking with Asafo in Ghana:
An Ethnographic Account of Kormantse Bentsir Warrior Music*
Ama Oforiwaa Aduonum

The Kecak and Cultural Tourism on Bali
Kendra Stepputat

Songs for Cabo Verde: Norberto Tavares's Musical Visions for a New Republic
Susan Hurley-Glowa

*New York Klezmer in the Twentieth Century:
The Music of Naftule Brandwein and Dave Tarras*
Joel E. Rubin

*Tuning the Kingdom:
Kawuugulu Musical Performance, Politics, and Storytelling in Buganda*
Damascus Kafumbe

*Listen with the Ear of the Heart:
Music and Monastery Life at Weston Priory*
Maria S. Guarino

Music, Indigeneity, Digital Media
Edited by Thomas R. Hilder, Henry Stobart, and Shzr Ee Tan

Interpreting Court Song in Uganda

Musical Meaning, Power Relations, and Political Life

Damascus Kafumbe

UNIVERSITY OF ROCHESTER PRESS

Copyright © 2025 Damascus Kafumbe

The eBook edition of this book is available under the Open Access License CC BY-NC-ND. Open access publication of this book was made possible through generous support from Middlebury College and the Pabst Steinmetz Foundation.

Some rights reserved. Without limiting the rights under copyright reserved above, any part of this book may be reproduced, stored in or introduced into a retrieval system, or transmitted, in any form or by any means (electronic, mechanical, photocopying, recording or otherwise).

First published 2025

University of Rochester Press
668 Mt. Hope Avenue, Rochester, NY 14620, USA
www.urpress.com
and Boydell & Brewer Limited
PO Box 9, Woodbridge, Suffolk IP12 3DF, UK
www.boydellandbrewer.com

Our Authorised Representative for product safety in the EU is Easy Access System Europe - Mustamäe tee 50, 10621 Tallinn, Estonia, gpsr.requests@easproject.com

ISBN-13: 978-1-64825-122-1 (hardback); 978-1-64825-048-4 (paperback)
ISSN: 2161-0290

Library of Congress Cataloging-in-Publication Data
Names: Kafumbe, Damascus, author.
Title: Interpreting court song in Uganda : musical meaning, power relations, and political life / Damascus Kafumbe.
Other titles: Eastman/Rochester studies in ethnomusicology ; 16.
Description: Rochester : University of Rochester Press, 2025. | Series: Eastman/Rochester studies in ethnomusicology, 2161-0290 ; 16 | Includes bibliographical references and index.
Identifiers: LCCN 2025009571 (print) | LCCN 2025009572 (ebook) | ISBN 9781648250484 (hardback) | ISBN 9781805433330 (pdf) | ISBN 9781805433323 (epub)
Subjects: LCSH: Music—Political aspects—Uganda. | Songs, Ganda—Political aspects—Uganda. | Songs, Ganda—Uganda—History and criticism. | Uganda—Court and courtiers. | Uganda—Politics and government.
Classification: LCC ML3917.U33 K33 2025 (print) | LCC ML3917.U33 (ebook) | DDC 782.42096761--dc23/eng/20250305
LC record available at https://lccn.loc.gov/2025009571
LC ebook record available at https://lccn.loc.gov/2025009572

A catalogue record for this title is available from the British Library

Cover image: Ludoviiko Sserwanga singing to the accompaniment of the Kiganda tube fiddle (*endingidi*) at the Uganda Museum. Photograph by Damascus Kafumbe.

Cover design: riverdesignbooks.com

To the memory of Albert Muwanga Ssempeke (ca. 1930–2006), Ludoviiko Sserwanga (ca. 1932–2013), Ssaalongo Kiwanuka Matovu Deziderio (1924–2015), Ssaalongo Paulo Kabwama (1923–2020), and Semeo Ssemambo Ssebuwufu (1959–2015) for teaching me everything I know about Kiganda court music

Contents

Acknowledgments		ix
Note on Translation, Transliteration, and Orthography		xi
Prologue: Songs, Stories, and Strategies		xiv

Part I: Foundations

1	Political Landscape, Court Music, and Research Collaborators	3
2	Research Methods and Approaches to Lyrical Interpretation	20
3	A Multi-Epistemological Framework: Discourses and Canons	32

Part II: Songs about Political Engagement, Criticism, and Commentary

4	"The Handsome Catch a Slight Squint": False Praise	51
5	"Fair-Skinned": Flattery, Deceit, and Satire	60
6	"As He Plucked Them": Greed and Selfishness	69
7	"Householder": Mourning and Ridicule	79
8	"Federalism": Manipulation, Exploitation, and Reciprocity	87

Part III: Songs about Leadership and Responsibility

9	"Unadvisable Kayemba": Advice and Caution	105
10	"He Has a Lot on His Mind": Deliberation and Animosity	115
11	"Gganga Had a Narrow Escape" or "They Chopped Off His Fingers": Punishment and Mercy	128

Part IV: Songs about Loyalty and Duty

12	"I Would Have Given You a Large Haplochromis": Regret and Appreciation	143
13	"The Flutists' Legal Case": Lament and Uncertainty	158

14	"The Little Lion": Power and Selfishness	175
15	"The King Is a Lion": Reverence and Love	188

Part V: Songs about Mutuality and Cooperation

16	"Mawanda Loves His Men" and "They Show Each Other Stumps": Love, Unity, and Reciprocity	205
17	"Baamunaanika Hill": Genuine Praise	214
18	"We Love the Supreme Man Exceedingly": Love and Respect	224

Part VI: Songs about Conflict and Loss

19	"Ssematimba and Kikwabanga": War and Fate	241
20	"Poland": War and Imperialism	254
21	"The Battle of Nsinsi": Civil War	261
22	"Let Me Plod with a Stick Close to Kibuuka": Disagreement and Invocation	269
23	"The Pebble Is Breaking Me": Mortality and Spirituality	281

Author Interviews   293

Works Cited   295

Index   301

Acknowledgments

First, I am forever thankful to the Almighty God for blessing me with the wisdom, collaborators, and resources with which I have carried out and completed this project.

No words can express the debt of gratitude I owe my dear wife, Betty, and my sons, Joshua, Jonathan, and Joseph, for their support throughout the process of researching and writing this book.

Interpreting Court Song in Uganda would not exist without the experiences and knowledge of the composer-performers who generously shared their versions of court songs as well as many of the stories presented throughout the book's pages.[1] To these artists I am forever grateful: Albert Muwanga Ssempeke, Ludoviiko Sserwanga, Ssaalongo Kiwanuka Matovu Deziderio, Ssaalongo Paulo Kabwama, Albert Ssempeke Bisaso, Ssaalongo Ssennoga Majwala, Semeo Ssemambo Ssebuwufu, and Mukasa Kafeero.

Many thanks also to the research collaborators who interpreted the court songs in this manuscript: Edward Ssebunnya Kironde, Harriet Kisuule, John Magandaazi Kityo, Jimmy Ssenfuka Kibirige, Jessy Ssendawula, Steven Mukasa Kabugo, and Peter Kinene.

I am deeply indebted to my long-term collaborators Kabenge Gombe, Waalabyeki Magoba, Francisca Nakachwa, Jessy Sendawula, Jimmy Ssenfuka Kibirige, and Peter Kinene for their assistance with transcribing, translating, and analyzing the Luganda interviews on which this book's narrative is based.

Deep thanks to the following Middlebury College student research assistants and collaborators for helping to refine and produce this book: Emma Binks, Annie Beliveau, Elizabeth Cady, Vaughan Supple, Angelina Como-Mosconi, Brett Sorbo, and Ryo Nishikubo.

I am also grateful to all the students enrolled in my courses at Middlebury College who engaged with some of the content of this book. These courses include African Music and Dance Performance, African Musical Lifestyles, African Soundscapes, Approaches to Music Inquiry, Music Ethnography, Music in World Cultures, Performance Lab-Afropop, Performing Arts and

---

1 For other versions of the songs these musicians performed for this project see Anderson 1968; Cooke 1996, 1998; Kubik 1998, 2010; Tracey and Tracey 1998; and Wachsmann 1953.

Community Engagement in Uganda, What in the World Is Music?, and World Musical Instruments.

Special thanks are owed to the Pabst Steinmetz Foundation and Middlebury College for funding the research for and publication of this book; to the editorial staff at the University of Rochester Press; and to outside readers for helping to get the manuscript published.

I am grateful to Katherine Scott and Joyce Li for copyediting, Marilyn Bliss for indexing, and Bernice Cheung for proofreading this book.

An alternate version of chapter 11 has appeared in the edited volume *Ubuntu: A Comparative Study of an African Concept of Justice*, edited by Paul Nnodim and Austin Okigbo (Leuven University Press, 2024). Excerpts from the prologue and chapter 1 appear in my contribution to a revised version of the Society for Ethnomusicology 2023 President's Roundtable, "Tell Me a Story: Translating Experience into Ethnography" (forthcoming in *Ethnomusicology* 69, Fall 2025).

Note on Translation, Transliteration, and Orthography

I have extracted some of the text in this narrative from the "Note on Translation, Transliteration, and Orthography" section that appears in my first book.[1] I conducted most of the research on which this book is based in Luganda, the language of the Baganda people or natives of Buganda, and my first language. Buganda is the largest kingdom of Uganda located in the country's south-central region. It is the homeland of the Baganda (plural for Muganda), who speak Luganda and use the adjective *Kiganda* to describe their cultural customs and practices.[2] Transcribing Luganda interviews and translating them to English was a complicated process that required the assistance and expertise of multiple Ugandan research collaborators and participants. Attaining accurate and idiomatic English translations demanded that I weigh between using literal and free translations. At first, I aimed to adhere to the Luganda's syntactical order without necessarily considering the idiomatic expressions of American English; however, this approach often resulted in awkward translations that would have made little sense to readers, and it became clear to me that this particular exercise in translation required a freer, more sensitive approach. Thus, toward the end of editing this book, I embraced that my translations ought to prioritize conveying the intended meaning of the text and presenting its idiomatic quality rather than seeking literal correctness. Taking cues from Mirela's observations about different kinds of translations, I extensively modified phrasing, substituted words, and tailored content to different cultural contexts.[3] This process allowed me to account for the wide range of meanings and idioms present in the Luganda transcriptions. I am confident that the English translations featured in this book accurately represent the ideas that my research collaborators expressed

---

1   Kafumbe 2018, xvii–xviii.
2   For a more detailed discussion of the kingdom's history, see Kafumbe 2018, xxi–xxviii.
3   Mirela 2024.

in Luganda interviews, which is one of the primary goals of this study. I do not include Luganda transcripts of quoted text.

The Luganda texts featured in this book are song lyrics, proverbs, and key terms related to the main themes of the book. Throughout the manuscript, Luganda words and phrases appear in italics except for proper nouns (names of ensembles, groups, places, clans, institutions, organizations, and so forth) and song titles. It is my hope that including Luganda song lyrics and proverbs will give the reader some insight into the translation process I have described. Luganda speakers will quickly notice that although my presentation of Luganda text attempts to follow contemporary writing conventions, some of the song lyrics barely adhere to the rules of Luganda grammar.

In addition, some meanings are only implied, and I explain these subtleties in the analysis that follows the song lyrics. I encourage readers to join me in reading the song lyrics as poems and the proverbs as riddles, as doing so allows for a deeper appreciation of my research collaborators' artistic creativity and stylistic diversity, which enrich the text's literal and nonliteral meanings. For improved readability, my treatment of song titles does not fully follow standard usage. I present the titles in roman type and in quotation marks, and their English translations precede the Luganda song titles, which appear in parentheses. Similarly, key Luganda terms appear in parentheses and are preceded by their English translations. However, in my presentation of song lyrics and proverbs, the Luganda text precedes its English translation, which appears in parentheses.[4]

In some instances, Luganda terms have initial vowels *a*, *e*, and *o*, which may indicate articles or prefix forms of infinitives in the case of verbs. However, I omit these initial vowels when I use English articles before most noun stems; keeping them would both be redundant and result in confusing, awkward wording. I capitalize all Luganda titles preceding proper names, and I treat some names of musical instruments and other performance materials as proper names, in which case I use initial uppercase letters and italicize the terms to distinguish them from other types of proper names.

Readers interested in pronouncing the Luganda text in this book should bear in mind that like other Bantu languages, Luganda is tonal—thus the meanings of words and phrases depend on the relationship between tone and pronunciation. Luganda vowels *a*, *e*, *i*, *o*, and *u* are pronounced "ah," "eh," "ee," "oh," and "oo," respectively. Double vowels create longer sounds, and *i* rarely follows *y* when the latter is preceded by a consonant (*y* is regarded as both a consonant and a semivowel). Luganda consonants include *b*, *c*, *d*, *f*,

---

4   Many of the proverbs presented in this book or their variations also appear in Walser 1982, which I have consulted extensively.

g, h, j, k, l, m, n, p, r, s, t, v, w, y, z, ny, and *ŋ*, which has a velar nasal sound similar to the sound at the end of the English word "ding." Pronunciations of consonants depend on the vowels that follow them. These pronunciations, coupled with the tonal range and length of the vowels, shape the tonal character of words, which in turn determine their meanings.

The sounds of consonants also depend on their various combinations. For example, double consonants indicate stressed and longer approximant sounds. The *ny* combination may act as a syllable and as a nasal consonant, while the *ky* digraph sounds like the consonant *c* (pronounced "ch"), although *c* has a shorter sound than *ky*. Therefore, double vowels usually follow *c*, while a single vowel follows *ky*. When *ky* appears in a closing syllable of a word, it normally has a short sound. Although the combination *ggy* and *jj* may sound similar, some Luganda speakers pronounce them slightly differently. *Ggya* can sound like "gea" in the English word "gear," while *jja* sounds like "ja" in the English word "jar." Finally, the consonant *r* sounds similar to the consonant *l*.

Prologue

Songs, Stories, and Strategies

This book critically examines twenty-one songs from the essential repertoires of selected royal court musicians of Buganda. It draws on two decades of research activities to demonstrate how song can be wielded as a tool for promoting mutually beneficial relationships. The research activities include extended performance and research collaborations with court composer-performers; their accounts of the repertoires' origins and meanings; lyrical analyses by a group of Ugandan citizens who interpret the songs through the lens of national politics; my own analysis of both the repertoire and research collaborators' contributions; and my consultation of the work of scholars from various fields. In court musicians' explanations of the stories and meanings behind their song repertoires, they relay enthralling tales of how the Baganda people have traditionally served, supported, admired, advised, praised, evaluated, and challenged royals and non-royals. Non-performers who interpret the songs then reframe them, diverting from their historical purposes and highlighting their connections to current national political realities in Uganda and beyond. Most of their interpretations engage with universal themes that pervade both personal and official spheres of life. Problematizing the relevance of historical royalist lyrics to twenty-first-century national politics, interpreters and I show how court songs live in a dialogue with contemporary Ugandan political life.

Through these activities, and within past and present contexts, we find unique perspectives to the myriad hidden meanings related to power relations, which surface via lyrical interpretation. These meanings are embedded in daily interactions among common people as well as between leaders and subjects. Some of the meanings are difficult to articulate in written word because the full affective texture of the court songs I examine does not come just from their lyrics but also from the process by which composer-performers re-create them. The musicians' improvisatory presentations depend on the mood of their performance environment and theatrical abilities, and they occur in a nonlinear order. The songs' meanings also depend on the stories that have trickled into, formed around, and defined the songs since time immemorial. The songs are passed on to new generations, and their meanings undergo various levels of abstraction such as renaming characters and recontextualizing events. In this sense, the broader Kiganda storytelling tradition I describe in the following pages provides a framework for discourse wherein new signifiers can come to represent previous ones, which then allows meaning to branch off in many analytical directions. The multiplicity of meanings that I allude to throughout this book refers to the all-encompassing interpretive possibilities that are typical of oral tradition.

Throughout the book I foreground the perspectives and political experiences of composer-performers and interpreters, an approach through which I bridge the gap between researcher-centered analysis and the unique knowledge of Ugandans who contribute to the project's overall narrative. Essentially, these research collaborators are my co-analysts, and it is by this orientation that we reach the insights we do about the court song repertoire that *Interpreting Court Song in Uganda* investigates, thus achieving a more informed understanding of Ugandan political life. The project uniquely assumes a discourse about power via song, but it is also a journey through the interpretation process premised on the argument that meaning is not singular, static, and monolithic but dynamic and multivalent. In this sense, we come to understand many hidden meanings related to power relations behind Kiganda court songs.

A Story and Song about Harvesting White Ants in Buganda

During a fieldwork trip to Uganda a few years ago, a research collaborator and interviewee, Peter Kinene, shared with me a story that served as a focal point of the research that informed this book. He explained how, since time immemorial, white ants have been important insects in Buganda. Kinene also noted that in the twenty-first century the insects are so valuable that they are used as a substitute for tax and a delicacy for making paste and sauce. Moreover, harvesting them is a source of employment and of dowry, and sharing them is an act of love and care. As a child growing up in Buganda, Kinene enjoyed seeing white ants appear at the beginning of the rainy season, particularly after an evening downpour. The morning sunshine would hit the anthills, priming the ants for leaving the hills in the evening. If the sunshine did not hit the hills, the ants would stay inside, making it impossible to harvest them. Consequently, their skin continued to grow hard and they appeared with wings in the next season. Kinene's favorite type of ant was called *ennaka*. Small and dark with snow-white wings, these ants never built anthills but instead did their breeding underground. Harvesters of the ants engaged in complementary tasks. They would delay or accelerate the harvesting process as they wished. To delay the ants' leaving their colonies, harvesters simply blocked the hill exits for as long as they needed. And to accelerate harvest, they still blocked the exits, but they also sprayed the colonies with water in the evening to simulate rainfall and cause the ants to go aboveground the following day. An important step in the harvesting process was to construct a sort of enclosure around each hill, using sticks or reeds, and to dig a small collection hole for the ants.

Next, the harvesters lined the collection hole with a young banana leaf that either the sun or a saucepan had rendered flexible. The leaf had to match the size of the hole. The harvesters then took pieces of spear grass and aligned them with the anthill exits, creating pathways that led directly into the collection hole. They also placed a thin, translucent banana leaf at the front of the collection hole to allow light to filter through the collection setup and to act as a sort of beacon for the ants. After the setup was complete, the harvesters removed blockades to the hill exits, and the ants began to leave. Once a significant number of ants had left the hill, the harvesters once again blocked the entrances to the hill so that the ants were unable to return. Those that had managed to escape from the collection hole congregated among tree roots, and the harvesters collected them again when possible. Once the collection hole was filled up, the harvesters removed the ants in batches and placed them inside containers for later processing. They harvested the ants in September and October, accompanying themselves with the song "The Harvester of White Ants" ("Omussi w'Enswa"), which features the following lyric or its variation:

> *Omussi w'enswa; anaalyanga ku mukuyege*
> The harvester of white ants; he or she will always eat termites
>
> *Omussi w'enswa; nnaalyanga ku mukuyege*
> The harvester of white ants; I will always eat termites[1]

Taking Cues from the Story and Song

Different themes in Kinene's story drew my attention to various strategies that would be applicable to my ethnographic experiences. The process of harvesting white ants—requiring as it does both an in-depth understanding of the ant's relationship with the environment and an appreciation for the environment's effect—was particularly useful. The relationship in question is evident in harvesters' use of various tools to reproduce the effects of sunlight and rain to trick the ants into leaving the hill whenever they want them to. The process speaks to the importance of connection, not just among people

---

1 Kinene interview, December 16, 2019.

but with the environment. Without a strong grasp of the context within which the ants live, effective harvesting may not be possible. However, with an understanding of the relationship between the ants and their environment, one can successfully harvest them with consistency and relative ease. Harvesters build the importance of this relationship into the process of harvesting white ants outright.

Kinene's story also highlights the benefits that come from collaboration. It demonstrates that even though hard work is important, it does very little if done in solitude. In other words, success is not an individual achievement but the outcome of community and collaboration. The story reminds us that true success draws on harnessing a mutually respectful social contract and an immersive experience. Similar to the process of harvesting white ants, creating *Interpreting Court Song in Uganda* was not a solitary deed but a process of building relationships. From data collection to research collaborators' analyses, the process depended on our respective and cooperative work as researchers, composer-performers, interpreters, analysts, commentators, and student research assistants. By engaging in various complementary tasks, we harvested a rich collection of voices and perspectives. *Interpreting Court Song in Uganda* became a culmination of numerous engagements, experiences, and interactions, all of which extended beyond my early studies with experts in Kiganda music and dance, training in ethnomusicology, extensive research on Kiganda royal court music, and collaborative work with several individuals.

Furthermore, the uses of white ants that Kinene describes show how the harvesting of the insects has a wide-reach impact, intersecting with the social and economic life of many Baganda. They function to both produce and preserve kinship, which reflects further on their investment in interconnectedness. Kinene's description of harvesting white ants embodies the importance of both dedication and interdependency, not only in the methods people use to harvest them but also in the ways in which they use them after the fact. This complex process further prompted me to reimagine the song "The Harvester of White Ants" in a way that highlights how the harvesting procedure emulates reciprocity at every stage of its existence. Knowledge of the process was key to the construction of meaning in both the song and my ethnographic work.

Kinene's story and the lyrics of "The Harvester of White Ants" also highlight the benefits that come from industriousness, dedication, and making the most of opportunities. The lyrics tackle the themes of the benefits of hard work and seizing opportunities, painting a picture of success through the motifs of ants and termites. While these insects are traditional food of Buganda, they also represent values of determination and success, themes that one of my research collaborators, Semeo Ssemambo Ssebuwufu, stresses in his interpretation of "The Harvester of White Ants" when he notes:

> The song means that the person who harvests white ants is also able to find and eat termites . . . In terms of seasonality, termites usually appear before white ants. So someone who does not go to catch white ants will not get both ants and termites.[2]

In Kinene's own interpretation of "The Harvester of White Ants," he expands on Ssebuwufu's focus on the seasonal relationship between termites and white ants by explaining that one could miss the opportunity to harvest if one allows the ants to grow too hard-skinned. This perspective further highlights reciprocity in the relationship that the white ants in Kinene's story have with their environment, as it shows how they behave differently depending on the occurrences around them. Ssebuwufu and Kinene give us more tools to interpret "The Harvester of White Ants." Their complementary perspectives underscore the collective and dynamic meaning-making process that is at the heart of the lyrical interpretations featured in this book. Furthermore, Ssebuwufu's and Kinene's perspectives shed light on how the one who takes the initiative in a chore such as harvesting white ants can gain added benefit from it, that is, enjoying the additional benefits of termites. Underlining the importance of hard work, this belief reminds us that if one engages in challenging field activities, one might reap gains beyond what one originally expected.

Beyond Fieldwork and Beyond an Ethnomusicological Study

I conducted ethnomusicological fieldwork with the primary goals of becoming more knowledgeable about the relationship between court songs and political life in my native kingdom and country and of documenting key aspects of its rich musical culture. However, my hard work was to result in lifelong relationships with members of my research community, advanced professional development, and a publication that is more than an ethnomusicological project. The songs featured in *Interpreting Court Song in Uganda* are simultaneously musical, philosophical, political, and social texts. The songs' subject matter and accompanying stories prompt further critical engagement regarding their connections to power relations and political life in general. The notion of *reimagining* or *recasting* these songs stands at the heart of their performance, analysis, and interpretation. People—composer-performers, interpreters, analysts, researchers—and their worldviews shape

---

2   Ssebuwufu interview, June 10, 2013.

the songs' meanings and relevance as they apply new ideas to them via analysis and performance. In this vein, *Interpreting Court Song in Uganda* performs a reimagining or recasting of its own, as its collective analysis aims to inspire new meanings by bringing timeless lyrical themes to life in present-day contexts. The book is at once an academic text, an ethnographic work, and, importantly, a practice in storytelling, interpreting, and reimagining. Similar to the collaborative story time by the fireplace I present in the following section of this prologue, the book's narrative captures the process of inventing new characters, new ideas, and new philosophies that germinate from the tales it tells. With this, *Interpreting Court Song in Uganda* challenges us to expand what constitutes an ethnomusicological study in the first place and how such a study might be produced.

Storytelling and the Tale of Njabala

My foundational experiences as a child participating in storytelling sessions with my family also informed how I approached the study and representation of the songs and stories featured in this book. Like many Baganda children growing up in my native kingdom, Buganda, I looked forward to visiting my grandparents because they told stories and taught us how to tell them. Most storytelling sessions took place after dinner and featured collective music-making by the fireplace. Here we shared tales that instructed, corrected, rebuked, and inspired us. The stories we shared addressed a wide range of topics, including the risks of traveling alone at night and interacting with strangers; the importance of collaboration and division of labor; the benefits of hard work and good time management; being in the right place at the right time; extending kindness and assistance to those in need; visiting members of one's extended family regularly; and honoring parents and elders. By engaging with these topics, we unearthed the hidden meanings embedded in Kiganda stories. Each storytelling session—highlighting the value of learning from one another—felt like a reenactment of the Kiganda proverbs, *Amagezi muliro; bwe gukubulako okima wa munno* (Knowledge is like fire; if you lack or run out of it, you fetch some from your friend) and *Amagezi gakuweebwa munno* (Knowledge is given to you by your friend). Here, "fire" means fire in one's hearth, "your friend" can mean one's neighbor, and "knowledge" can be interpreted to mean "good advice."

I still recall the storytelling session when I first heard my grandmother narrate the tale of Njabala. The session opened with her asking each of us to share something personal about our day or week so she could curate a set of stories for the evening. After everyone spoke, she began narrating the story. According to her version, a woman gave birth to a daughter and named her Njabala. Njabala was so beautiful that every man in her village desired to have her as a wife. Being the only daughter of a single mother, she received a lot of pampering. Consequently, she became a lazy girl and could not do any task by herself. For every task Njabala would call on the mother to help her out. The mother would immediately respond to the daughter's call. Unfortunately, Njabala's mother soon died, which forced Njabala to find a marriage partner. But as a married woman she could not perform any chores. Njabala's weakness made her husband quarrel with her each time he returned home. His frustration in turn made Njabala feel restless and regretful, and she cursed her mother, who had not prepared her for adulthood. She would do so by singing,

> *"Jangu maama, gwe wankuzanga ekyejo*
> Come, Mother, it is you who spoiled me
>
> *Buli kye nkola, omusajja takyagala*
> Whatever I do, my husband does not like it
>
> *Ne bwe njoza engoye, agamba nti sizitukuza*
> Even when I wash clothes, he says that I do not make them clean."

As Njabala was still desolate and confused, her mother's spirit would appear and begin doing Njabala's chores while she sang the following:

> *"Njabala Njabala*
> Njabala, Njabala
>
> *Njabala, tolinsaza omuko, Njabala*
> Njabala, do not let my son-in-law ever find me, Njabala
>
> *Abakazi balima bati*
> Women dig like this
>
> *Njabala, tolinsaza omuko, Njabala*
> Njabala, do not let my son-in-law ever find me, Njabala
>
> *Bwe batema nga bawala*
> They dig as they till
>
> *Njabala, tolinsaza omuko, Njabala*
> Njabala, do not let my son-in-law ever find me, Njabala
>
> *Ensukusa basimba*
> They plant banana suckers
>
> *Njabala, tolinsaza omuko, Njabala*
> Njabala, do not let my son-in-law ever find me, Njabala
>
> *Olusuku balutemera*
> They plow the plantation

Njabala, tolinsaza omuko, Njabala
Njabala, do not let my son-in-law ever find me, Njabala

Bitooke babisalira
They prune the banana plants

Njabala, tolinsaza omuko, Njabala
Njabala, do not let my son-in-law ever find me, Njabala

Bikata babitema
They make mounds

Njabala, tolinsaza omuko, Njabala
Njabala, do not let my son-in-law ever find me, Njabala

Malagala babyala
They implant stems

Njabala, tolinsaza omuko, Njabala
Njabala, do not let my son-in-law ever find me, Njabala

Bijanjaalo basiga
They plant beans

Njabala, tolinsaza omuko, Njabala
Njabala, do not let my son-in-law ever find me, Njabala."

"Mounds" and "stems" refer to planting potatoes. Njabala's mother did her daughter's chores and sang while Njabala was looking on with folded hands. Friends of her husband noticed this and tattled on Njabala, telling her husband that a spirit was performing her duties for her. Not believing this, he sought to find the truth himself and prepared to spy on Njabala. One day, as the spirit of Njabala's mother was busy helping her with chores as usual, the husband arrived. He was shocked to see the skeleton of Njabala's mother digging. This prompted him to whip Njabala severely and to divorce her afterward. These events marked the end of their marriage.

After narrating this story, my grandmother asked me and the other children to comment on its potential morals and applications, suggesting that our responses would help her know whether the tale had resonated with us. Each of us ascribed various interpretations to the tale's meaning, and we did not move on to the next story until everyone had shared his or her interpretation, which was an integral part of our collective discourse. According to one family member, the story demonstrated how happiness founded on laziness is very short-lived. Another one shared that it reminded him of how it is easier and better to teach and correct children when they are still young. Yet to another family member, the story had two main lessons: what befalls one when one knows it is coming robs one of little; a person cannot be liked by everybody. My response to the prompt highlighted the importance of learning by doing and empowering the learner, both of which have been core principles of my research engagements.

Taking Cues from the Tale: Structuring the Book

The overall structure of *Interpreting Court Song in Uganda*'s narrative utilizes storytelling techniques that Baganda use in oral tradition and expression, including repetition, variation, dialogue, and extemporization. The book has six parts, the first of which features three foundational chapters. Chapter 1 ("Political Landscape, Court Music, and Research Collaborators") presents pertinent background information on political life in the Kingdom of Buganda before and after its 1966 abolition, Buganda-Uganda relations, and connections between politics and lyrical interpretation. The chapter further introduces the main characters we encounter in the book's narrative, including court music composer-performers, interpreters, and other research collaborators. It also interrogates the history of gender and court music performance in Buganda. Chapter 2 ("Research Methods and Approaches to Lyrical Interpretation") engages with the key themes of my research methods and approaches, including lyrical interpretation, collaborative research, court song, musical analysis, power dynamics, and ethnography. Chapter 3 ("A Multi-Epistemological Framework: Discourses and Canons") presents a discussion of the key theoretical discourses and canons with which this book engages and their relevance to the study's multi-epistemological framework. This discussion covers a variety of topics, including representation, Kiganda song, meaning, power relations, history, and temporality.

Parts 2–6 draw on the ideas that came from my conversations with the composer-performers and interpreters of the court songs presented throughout the book. A diverse set of themes emerged when we looked at the song repertoire's content, its background stories, lyrical interpretations, and analyses of all these elements together. These themes provide the structure and frame the language of part 2 ("Songs about Political Engagement, Criticism, and Commentary"), part 3 ("Songs about Leadership and Responsibility"), part 4 ("Songs about Loyalty and Duty"), part 5 ("Songs about Mutuality and Cooperation"), and part 6 ("Songs about Conflict and Loss"). In addition to providing different angles on power relations and serving as the backbone of my theorization of these relations in chapter 3, these themes draw out the complexity of lyrical meaning and highlight the collective meaning-making process that is central to sociopolitical life in Uganda.

In addition, my use of a song-based chapter format within each of these parts emerged from some of the points that court musicians raised in our interviews. Respecting their preference, I treat each song in a separate chapter. The chapter titles highlight the themes set forth in the songs. Thus, chapter 4 ("'The Handsome Catch a Slight Squint': False Praise"), chapter 5 ("'Fair-Skinned': Flattery, Deceit, and Satire"), and so on.

Each chapter in parts 2–6 explores the history of the song it focuses on and what the work's lyrics reveal about power relations in Buganda and Uganda. Within the chapter, composer-performers primarily provide insight into the relevance of Kiganda court songs to Buganda's political past before the twenty-first century, while interpreters focus on the repertoire's significance in twenty-first-century Uganda. I structure these song-based chapters with a generic progression: (1) a background story about the song that the chapter examines, often narrated by the performer; (2) analysis of this background; (3) discussion of the song's sonic or stylistic elements and presentation of its lyrics in Luganda and English; (4) an analytical summary of the lyrics; (5) interpretations of the lyrics by non-performers; (6) critical analysis of these interpretations; and (7) a conclusion. This structure allows me to prioritize the voices of my research collaborators, whose opinions make up the analytical bulk of *Interpreting Court Song in Uganda*. In this way we collectively engage with the critical political perspectives that one might find in modern-day Uganda. Only seldom does the book stray from this format, and these variations are slight. For example, chapter 16 discusses two songs rather than one, and chapter 23 features commentary from only one interpreter.

Finally, although all song-based chapters feature analyses and summaries of their lyrics, I also include their full transcriptions and translations (these are supplemented with audio recordings on the book's companion website). As already pointed out, these transcriptions and translations are integral to this book's interpretive approach, which requires readers to perform their own interpretations of the song lyrics presented in it. Readers may jump between chapters as they see fit for their own purposes, but I strongly suggest that they read part 1 chronologically and in full so that they can contextualize the songs they encounter in the following parts. This will give readers and listeners a fuller appreciation for the power and hidden meanings that these songs hold.

Online Material

Supplemental audio material for this book can be found on the book's companion website, http://hdl.handle.net/1802/38496.

Part I
Foundations

I

Political Landscape, Court Music, and Research Collaborators

The Kingdom of Buganda, located in south-central Uganda, has somewhat unclear origins, but historians suggest it originated from Bantu clans dating back to around AD 1000. According to oral tradition, Kato Ruhuuga, from the neighboring Kingdom of Bunyoro, became the first hereditary leader of Buganda in the early fourteenth century, later taking the name Kintu. Buganda grew significantly between the fourteenth and fifteenth centuries, and by the eighteenth to the nineteenth centuries had expanded to include areas of the Bunyoro Kingdom. Its strategic location on the northern shores of Lake Victoria, fertile soil, and ability to absorb foreign influences contributed to its becoming the strongest kingdom in the region. The nineteenth century brought Arab traders, who introduced Islam, followed by Christian missionaries: first Anglican (1877) and then Catholic (1879). These religious influences set the groundwork for colonial rule.

When Uganda became a British protectorate in 1894, the British implemented indirect rule through Buganda's existing power structures. The Uganda Agreement of 1900 was crucial, giving Buganda "special status" within the protectorate and recognizing traditional institutions, including the monarchy. This agreement held great symbolic meaning for the Baganda people. Between the 1900s and 1950s, tensions grew between colonial administrators and the Buganda government. One significant conflict led to the 1953 arrest and exile of Buganda's king, Sir Edward Muteesa II (r. 1939–1966), by Governor Andrew Cohen, who wanted to integrate Buganda more closely into Uganda's structures. This exile severely destabilized Buganda's sociopolitical hierarchy until the king's return in 1955.

Uganda gained independence in 1962, with Muteesa II becoming the country's first president. Apollo Milton Obote, a member of the Lango ethnic group, became his executive prime minister. However, conflict soon arose between Muteesa II's conservative supporters and Prime Minister Milton Obote's Uganda People's Congress. In 1966, Obote ordered the national army under Idi Amin to attack the king's palace, forcing Muteesa II into exile in Britain, where he died in 1969. In 1967 Obote imposed a new republican constitution that terminated both the federal system and the country's kingdoms, leading to Buganda's becoming politically moribund for decades.

The post-independence period saw rapid political changes. For example, Idi Amin (president 1971–1979) initially gained Baganda support by returning Muteesa II's body to Uganda, but he never reinstated the monarchy. After Amin's overthrow, several short-lived presidencies followed, including those of Baganda leaders Yusuf Lule and Godfrey Binaisa. Yoweri Kaguta Museveni seized power in 1986 after a military campaign based in Buganda. In 1993, President Museveni's government restored the formerly abolished kingdoms, allowing for the enthronement of Ronald Mutebi II as king. However, the federal system established by the 1900 Agreement, which had given Buganda considerable autonomy, was never restored.

Contemporary Buganda retains its cultural significance but has less of its original political power, which now primarily rests with Uganda's central government. The Baganda still recognize the king as their leader—the apex of Buganda's sociopolitical hierarchy, which is grounded in the intertwined institutions of kinship, clanship, and kingship. This structure, along with the kingdom's division into eighteen counties, continues to be an important feature of sociopolitical organization in the region.[1]

Kiganda Court Music in Postcolonial Buganda

Despite the destruction that the attack caused on Buganda's main court in 1966, some court musical instruments survived. The musicians who were able to escape carried surviving instruments with them and protected them until President Museveni and his administration restored the kingship under King Ronald Mutebi II in 1993. But the government's refusal to reinstate the federal status of previously abolished kingdoms further weakened Buganda's court music institution. During the abolition of the kingship, performances of standard court songs in royal contexts rarely occurred, for the main court was not functional and the kingdom had no reigning king.

Between 1967 and 1993 and following Buganda's restoration, efforts to revive standard court songs led their performers to present them in the context of national politics rather than in their historical royal contexts. As a

---

1   Kafumbe 2018, xxiv–xxviii.

result, the musicians performed the songs in ways that did not limit their lyrics to these contexts. In fact, the content of many standard court songs became widely applicable to a variety of national political situations, with their performers playing key roles in these settings. Still, the songs were in popular decline, which weighed heavily on these dedicated court performers. Given the importance of their songs' lyrical content in both Kiganda philosophy and day-to-day life, these artists were eager to share with me, a Muganda ethnomusicologist, their versions of the court songs they had learned and performed for decades. Moreover, they wanted these songs to be accessible to many people in hopes that they might be able to revive their art form.

Some of the factors responsible for the decline of Kiganda court songs at the time of my research (2000–2020) included the precarious position in which Kiganda court music had been since the restoration of Buganda in 1993. Although surviving court composer-performers attempted to carry on the legacy of court music, they faced an uphill battle against twenty-first-century musical alternatives such as pop and electronic music and the greater disinterest of the younger generation in maintaining tradition. Most young people lacked knowledge of Kiganda court songs and its importance within the culture of Buganda and the nation of Uganda and thus had limited knowledge of their own history. Some even framed these songs as something just for the elders, and hence they did not make efforts to keep the repertoire relevant to modern demands.

Musicians' efforts to carry forward court music traditions and practices were also undermined by infrequent opportunities to perform as a result of the tense relationship between the central government of Uganda and the country's different kingdoms. Consequently, these musicians began to perform court songs in non-royal contexts, a trend that prompted the older generation that had once listened attentively to these songs with the goal of learning and applying the lessons in their lyrics to instead focus on the entertaining aspects of the repertoire's performances. Now, while entertaining the masses, the musicians were also contributing to other sectors of society by providing political perspectives and boosting the economy. Such roles underscored the extent to which their songs were still part and parcel of life in Uganda. *Interpreting Court Song in Uganda* joined the court music specialists I worked with in arguing that court songs were too significant and integral to the people's lives to vanish entirely. Some research collaborators even equated the relationship between these songs and political life in Buganda to that of the snail and its shell: the snail grows by creating a new shell; its existence depends on this new, larger shell.

A major obstacle to resuming the regular performance of court songs was the growth in popularity of foreign media and technology. The extent to which mass media introduced foreign cultural products and traditions into preexisting local culture, including traditional musical arts, is documented in Gerhard Kubik's work.[2] Here, a push and pull between the new and the old is inevitable. As Kofi Agawu points out, even as many traditional elements of African music remain omnipresent, others are either reincorporated with or replaced by new elements, like pop music and electronic production.[3] Although Buganda's main royal court still featured court songs during the research that underlies this book, these performances were rare. When they occurred, they were often supplemented with music played on stereo systems and other forms of modern technology, which detracted from the improvisatory aspects and analog musical instruments that had historically accompanied court song lyrics. This arrangement furthered the songs' decline by pressuring the royal court, one of the final enduring bastions of tradition, to adopt modern tendencies. These developments remind us of J. H. Kwabena Nketia's observation that traditional music thrives when we preserve it in changed contexts rather than avoid such change as if it will infect the music.[4] Moreover, the developments echo Michael Bakan's definition of tradition as "a process of creative transformation whose most remarkable feature is the continuity it nurtures and sustains."[5]

Buganda-Uganda Relations

As previously mentioned, Uganda's government in 1993 declined to reinstate the federal structure created by the 1900 Agreement that had granted Buganda substantial self-governance during colonial rule. Consequently, while Buganda maintains its cultural importance today, it possesses reduced political authority compared to its historical position, with most power now concentrated in Uganda's central government. Neil Kodesh indicates that the kingdom's officials began to use European monarchical social norms implemented during colonial rule to present a royalist history of Buganda's past that emphasized the role of kings as social actors.[6] This may have resulted in the current understanding that the king is a solitary ruling figure rather than an extension of the people, a relationship that was, at one time, negotiated within the royal court music institution. Derek Peterson notes that new ideas introduced during the colonial period influenced an emerging

---

2   Kubik 2010, 32.
3   Agawu 2016, 41.
4   Wiggins 2005, 74.
5   Bakan 2007, xxviii.
6   Kodesh 2010, 3.

East African ethnic patriotism, where nationalist groups throughout the region presented themselves as new social formations in contrast to what they insisted were derelict, defective ethnic groups of the past.[7] This mindset was evident in Uganda's earlier postindependence leaders, including Prime Minister (later President) Milton Obote and his contemporaries.

Beyond the national government's abandoning traditional political institutions, Uganda also witnessed a social and moral shift. Mikael Karlström's work shows that during the postindependence period, kinship and clanship structures became less important as the moral and social structure of the Baganda began to deteriorate.[8] Politically, this tension between tradition and modernity has persisted in the present day. Although in 1993 the Uganda national government restored traditional political institutions that Obote had abolished in 1967, the people were wary of letting kings amass too much political power and popularity. Accordingly, the national government confined them to being "cultural leaders" and limited the number of large events that they could participate in. In the case of Buganda, these events provided key performance opportunities for court music performers, as some people saw court music as an expression of the halcyon days of the Kiganda kingship. Others believed that the national government was limiting the heavy promotion and revival efforts of court song performances because as an extension and affirmation of the kingship, they could feed into calls for Kiganda autonomy, which would pose a threat to the central government. The inherent connection between court musicians and the king meant that these artists were also subjected to the same anti-royalist treatment under the national government.

Political Conundrum and Lyrical Interpretation

The current political regime in Uganda has been in power since 1986 when President Museveni rose to lead the country. His reign has corresponded with the relative political dominance of the party that backs him, the National Resistance Movement (NRM). These two constants have provided the backdrop for the various political movements and structural changes that have occurred over the years. One of these major changes by President Museveni was the reinstatement of the traditional kingships in 1993. The arrangement partly secured his support from the kingdoms and ultimately helped him defeat the incumbent ruler, Apollo Milton Obote. However, having only restored the rulers of the kingdoms as cultural figureheads,

---

7   Peterson 2012, 15.
8   Karlström 2004, 598.

this move failed to truly fulfill President Museveni's initial promise to the kingdoms, and many Baganda continue to criticize him for this issue today. Additionally, he dissolved the party system, which resulted in a format where national political candidates ran as individuals, unattached to any party affiliation. The official, government rhetoric of the time declared that the system was a way for candidates to be elected on personal merit rather than party affiliation.[9]

This system ended in 2005, when a national constitutional referendum in favor of a multiparty political system was passed. The final set of major changes within the political system were the abolishment of presidential term limits in 2005 and the abolishment of presidential age limits in 2017. Several sources posit that these standards were overturned to allow President Museveni to continue running for office.[10] Now, without these limitations, it is uncertain whether any leader's rule in Uganda will be able to end through the peaceful transfer of power. In recent years, opposition movements have gained increasing traction as dissatisfaction with the government continues to grow. Alternative political parties have been on the rise, although they only hold a minority number of seats in parliament. Some Ugandans have felt that the government has become increasingly secretive and unresponsive to their needs, whereas others have raised concerns about its use of violence and intimidation tactics at polling sites as well as a growing intolerance for dissenting views.[11] Criticism for the administration has also heightened internationally. This is the political conundrum that most of the research collaborators featured in this book navigate and comment on in their interpretations of court songs.

Court Composer-Performers of the Songs Featured in This Book

The versions of court songs that appear in this book were performed or composed by Albert Muwanga Ssempeke (ca. 1930–2006), Ludoviiko Sserwanga (ca. 1932–2013), Ssaalongo Kiwanuka Matovu Deziderio (1924–2015), Ssaalongo Paulo Kabwama (1923–2020), Albert Ssempeke

---

9   "Constitution of the Republic of Uganda," ULII (Uganda Legal Information Institute), December 31, 2023, https://ulii.org/akn/ug/act/statute/1995/constitution/eng@2023-12-31.

10 "Uganda Profile—Timeline," *BBC News*, May 10, 2018, https://www.bbc.com/news/world-africa-14112446.

11 "Yoweri Kaguta Museveni," *Britannica*, https://www.britannica.com/biography/Yoweri-Kaguta-Museveni.

Bisaso (b. 1979), Ssaalongo Ssennoga Majwala (b. 1953), Semeo Ssemambo Ssebuwufu (ca. 1959–2015), and Mukasa Kafeero (b. 1971). Ssempeke, Sserwanga, Deziderio, Kabwama, and Ssebuwufu had long-standing connections to the Kiganda court music institution and served as resident musicians in the kingdom's main court in Mmengo during the reigns of King Daudi Ccwa II (r. 1897–1939) and Muteesa II. They remained faithful to the kingship throughout its dissolution between 1966 and 1993 and returned to the Mmengo court to perform there occasionally after the kingship's restoration in 1993. Majwala and Bisaso performed in the Mmengo court only after the restoration. Although Kafeero never served as a resident musician in the main court, he lived and performed at the Wamala royal court in the late 1970s and 1980s. In the following paragraphs, I present brief biographies of these musicians along with the titles of the songs they contributed to this book.

Mukasa Kafeero (b. 1971)

A musical historian and custodian of knowledge on various aspects of Kiganda royal court history, Mukasa Kafeero performed four of the songs discussed in part 2: "The Handsome Catch a Slight Squint" ("Empujjo Zikwata Balungi"); "Fair-Skinned" ("Kabirinnage"); "As He Plucked Them" ("Bwe Yazimaanya"); and "Householder" ("Nnannyinimu"). Kafeero learned a lot about royal court life during the 1970s. At the time, he was living in the Wamala royal court of King Ssuuna II (r. ca. 1824–1854), where he was raised by his grandmother. During that time Kafeero became acquainted with every department of the Wamala court, learning many songs in the court music repertoire. By living in the court and listening to narrations of royal histories, he became familiar with the lives and reigns of Kings Kamaanya (r. ca. 1794–1824) and his son Ssuuna II.[12] The sparse, conversational nature of the performances of the four songs he presented during our interview in 2005 reflects some of the ways that important information has been passed down via oral performance historically in Buganda. These performances particularly provide insight into the improvisational, even haphazard, method by which Baganda composer-performers bring new songs to life and re-create preexisting ones.

Semeo Ssemambo Ssebuwufu (ca. 1959–2015)

A talented xylophonist, Semeo Ssemambo Ssebuwufu was particularly unique among the musicians I interviewed for this book because he was

---

12   Kafeero interview, July 28, 2005.

the only one who had served as a court page (*omusiige*) within the royal court in Mmengo. Ssebuwufu shared that his family nominated him for a court page position when he was a little boy, during the administration of King Muteesa II. Ssebuwufu's father, the court music performer Yowaana Maswanku Kalyagonja, submitted the names of Ssebuwufu and his younger brother Musisi for the position of page from their primary clan, the Elephant (Njovu) Clan. The musicians' paternal uncle Antanansi Nnakuzaabasajja, also a court musician, helped considerably with their appointment process. Nnakuzaabasajja served as the head of the Players of Seventeen to Twenty-Two Slab Xylophones (Abaakadinda). Playing this instrument was one of the duties of the Elephant Clan. Ssebuwufu and his brother played the xylophone at the Mmengo court until the national government bombed it in 1966 and were among the few court pages and residents who survived the event. When I interviewed Ssebuwufu for this project in 2009 and 2013, he was performing Kiganda court music at social events and working as an instrument-making instructor at Kyambogo University, where he taught for four decades until his retirement in 2012.[13] Ssebuwufu contributed the following songs to this study: "Gganga Had a Narrow Escape" ("Gganga Alula") or "They Chopped Off His Fingers" ("Baamutemako Engalo"), "Mawanda Loves His Men" ("Mawanda Ayagala Abasajja Be"), and "Baamunaanika Hill" ("Akosozi Baamunaanika").

Albert Muwanga Ssempeke (ca. 1930–2006) and Ludoviiko Sserwanga (ca. 1932–2013)

Although it was not unusual for siblings to serve in the royal court at the same time, Albert Muwanga Ssempeke and Ludoviiko Sserwanga were the only two sibling court performers who simultaneously lived into the reign of King Ronald Mutebi II (r. 1993–present) and the beginning of the twenty-first century. For this project Ssempeke performed four songs: "I Would Have Given You a Large Haplochromis" ("Nandikuwadde Enkejje Entulumba"), "The Flutists' Legal Case" ("Omusango gw'Abalere"), "The Little Lion" ("Akawologoma"), and "Let Me Plod with a Stick Close to Kibuuka" ("Ka Nsimbe Omuggo awali Kibuuka"). Sserwanga also performed four songs: "They Show Each Other Stumps" ("Balagana Enkonge"), "Baamunaanika Hill" ("Akosozi Baamunaanika"), "We Love the Supreme Man Exceedingly" ("Ssaabasajja Tumwagala Nnyo"), and "Ssematimba and Kikwabanga" ("Ssematimba ne Kikwabanga").

Ssempeke and Sserwanga first began playing Kiganda musical instruments when they were about nine and seven years of age, respectively, when they

---

13   Ssebuwufu interview, June 4, 2013.

were still in elementary school. A man named Dawuda first introduced them to Kiganda music through records. He would travel to their village every Sunday with a gramophone to play music in people's homes for ten cents a song. The brothers were enthralled by Dawuda's presentations, which were seminal in their choice to pursue musical careers. Whenever the brothers heard that a resident in their native Lutengo-Naggalama village had hired or hosted court performers, Ssempeke and Sserwanga could not resist going to see them. They often attended performances by the Musicians of the King (Abadongo ba Kabaka), a court group that featured singers and players of bowl lyres, tube fiddles, notched flutes, gourd shakers, and various types of drums. The brothers would spend the day or night at any of the group's performances, listening closely and learning their instrumental and vocal performance styles. In the early 1940s, Ssempeke and Sserwanga met a court flutist named Kibirige, from whom they first learned and mastered the Kiganda notched flute (*endere*). He later acted as one of their sponsors, taking them to the Mmengo royal court, where he introduced them to other experienced performers.[14]

At the court Ssempeke and Sserwanga initially learned several tunes and techniques from these experts by simply listening to and watching them perform. Later they would join in their performances. Whenever these musicians were hired to perform at social events such as weddings outside the Mmengo court, Ssempeke and Sserwanga would accompany and sit with them, flutes in hand. When the court musicians played a song that the brothers knew, they would request to play along. It was easy for Ssempeke and Sserwanga to perform along because they had acquired their flutes from professional musicians, who had tuned them appropriately. At the end of the performances, before the professionals returned to the court, sometimes they would promise to secure Ssempeke and Sserwanga future performance opportunities at the Mmengo court. Eventually these professional musicians sponsored the brothers to join the court. When Ssempeke officially began performing at the Mmengo court in the early 1940s, he was about twelve years of age and had dropped out of school after third grade. The early death of his parents forced him to support himself and his younger siblings, including Sserwanga. In the court, the brothers were part-time performers and primary members of the Flutists of the King (Abalere ba Kabaka), a flute and drum ensemble. However, they would mingle with and learn from members of other court ensembles whenever they could. For instance, they often visited performers in Abadongo ba Kabaka. Part of what enticed them to observe other ensemble members was the uniqueness of each group's musical repertoire. On occasion, Ssempeke and Sserwanga would add their

---

14 Ssempeke interview, July 11, 2005.

flutes to whatever song other ensembles were playing. Over time they grew quite close with many musicians who performed at the Mmengo court prior to its attack in 1966.[15]

Following the crisis and the subsequent exile of King Muteesa II, Ssempeke and Sserwanga continued to perform outside the court setting with their private group, Siblings in Love (Abooluganda Kwagalana). After his time at the court, Ssempeke went to work at the Uganda Museum in Kampala as a resident musician. While there he had the opportunity to learn and play the Kiganda bow harp (*ennanga*) under the guidance of Evalisto Muyinda, a senior court musician. This opportunity was particularly special for Ssempeke because he had always loved the sound of the instrument and had attempted to learn it years before in the Mmengo court. He worked at the museum for twenty-eight years, retiring in 1994.[16] I met and interviewed him between 2000 and 2006, during which time he was giving private music lessons at the Uganda National Theatre and performing with Abooluganda Kwagalana. I interviewed Sserwanga between 2006 and 2013.

Albert Ssempeke Bisaso (b. 1979)

Son of the famed court musician Albert Muwanga Ssempeke and nephew of Ludoviiko Sserwanga, both discussed earlier, Albert Ssempeke Bisaso took after his father and uncle, working as an on-demand performer at social and political events inside and outside the court. He explained that because of his father's busy performance career, Bisaso was primarily raised by his maternal grandparents. He first began playing Kiganda musical instruments when he was around nine years old. His choice to pursue Kiganda court music performance was a conscious decision through which he intended to preserve the work and legacy of his father. Bisaso's father taught him much of what he learned during his early years, but later he learned from other relatives, his paternal uncle Sserwanga and his brothers.[17]

Bisaso continues to work for a living as a performer and a music instructor, and he plays various musical instruments, including the Kiganda bowl lyre (*endongo*), tube fiddle (*endingidi*), xylophones (*amadinda* and *akadinda*), bow harp (*ennanga*), flute (*endere*), and animal horn (*eŋŋombe*). He also plays musical instruments from other ethnic regions, including the bow harp from northern Uganda (*adungu*), the trough zither from Kigezi (*inanga*), and the lamellaphone or thumb piano from Teso (*akogo*).[18] After

---

15 Ibid.
16 Ibid.
17 Bisaso interview, September 14, 2003.
18 Ibid.

the deaths of his father and uncle, Bisaso and some of his siblings have taken up the crucial role of continuing the legacies of Ssempeke and Sserwanga. Because Kiganda court music was so ingrained in the lives of these two men, Bisaso's continuation of their practice has made him, in essence, a historian. I interviewed Bisaso between 2000 and 2004, and he performed two songs featured in this book: alternate versions of both "Ssematimba and Kikwabanga" ("Ssematimba ne Kikwabanga") and "The Battle of Nsinsi" ("Olutalo olw'e Nsinsi"). These songs were also performed by some of the other musicians discussed in this section.

Ssaalongo Kiwanuka Matovu Deziderio (1924–2015)

Like most of the other court composer-performers presented in the preceding sections, Ssaalongo Kiwanuka Matovu Deziderio was introduced to and subsequently became fascinated with Kiganda music at an early age. His uncle Matyansi Kibirige Baazibumbira introduced him to the tube fiddle (*endingidi*), and from then on he was determined to master the instrument. Around 1937, Deziderio began performing at weddings after learning various songs from his uncle. These types of performances enabled him to meet King Muteesa II later in his youth. Deziderio and Muteesa II met at a wedding in Kabasanda, where the former had attended the event to sing and play the tube fiddle (*endingidi*). The two were the same age, and Muteesa II—whose father, King Daudi Ccwa II, was the king of Buganda—was a mere prince. Muteesa II attended this event as an honored guest, to which he had traveled with accompanying attendants in his father's car. After listening to Deziderio's skillful performance on the tube fiddle, the prince called him over and asked if he wished to be a performer in his father's court. Deziderio, who could not believe his good fortune, quickly agreed to see what the job was like. However, he loved playing at weddings and knew that the court administration barely allowed resident musicians to perform extensively outside the court, so he decided to continue as a wedding performer for the next few years. Eventually in 1950, by then a young man, he took a position at the Mmengo royal court. His primary role as a tube fiddle player and singer was within Abadongo ba Kabaka, one of the court ensembles mentioned earlier. Deziderio performed at the Mmengo court until the 1966 attack.[19] I interviewed him between 2005 and 2006, during which time he performed the four songs he contributed to this book: "Federalism" ("Federo"), "The King Is a Lion" ("Kabaka Mpologoma"), "Poland" ("Polanda"), and "Unadvisable Kayemba" ("Kayemba Nantabuulirirwa").

---

19   Deziderio interview, July 15, 2005.

Ssaalongo Paulo Kabwama (1923–2020)

The musical career of Ssaalongo Paulo Kabwama began with the tube fiddle (*endingidi*), which he first played in 1939 while performing court songs. Kabwama's father, Kayondo, a court musician who served King Daudi Ccwa II and his heir, King Sir Edward Muteesa II, paved the way for the young musician to join the court. Although a magnificent artist in his own right, Kabwama served as only a part-time performer in the royal court, meaning that he did not live there full-time, unlike the musical pages. He was not satisfied with mastering only one instrument, so he made it his goal to study with skilled musicians who played instruments that were new to him. Once he discovered that someone played his instrument extraordinarily well, he would observe, imitate, follow, and meet religiously with him to learn his skill. Like many of his contemporaries, he learned through participation, imitation, and absorption, among other indigenous learning styles.[20] Although Kabwama did not talk very often or openly with his parents about his interest in Kiganda instruments, his drive and talent were so pronounced that they were able to recognize it, and soon enough his parents began to connect him with other players.[21] I recorded Kabwama's interview in 2005, during which time he performed the song "He Has a Lot on His Mind" ("Alina Bingi By'Alowooza") for this project.

Ssaalongo Ssennoga Majwala (b. 1953)

Ssaalongo Ssennoga Majwala first encountered Kiganda music during his childhood, through playing his father's drum. Later he became an expert on the various types of Kiganda drums (*baakisimba* or *embuutu, empuunyi, engalabi,* and *nankasa* or *namunjoloba*). In addition, he learned how to play other Kiganda musical instruments such as gourd shakers (*ensaasi*), xylophones (*amadinda* and *akadinda*), animal horn (*eŋŋombe*), bowl lyre (*endongo*), and bow harp (*ennanga*). Although Majwala never performed in the court before the 1966 political crisis discussed earlier, he played these instruments at many occasions involving royals both inside and outside the Mmengo court following the restoration of Buganda's kingship in 1993. Over the course of his professional career, he learned a significant portion of the court music repertoire from some of the aforementioned musicians.[22] He also maintained an active research career and served as a music lecturer at Kyambogo University until 2018. Majwala continues to work with the

---

20 For a detailed discussion of these styles, see Wiggins 2005, 74.
21 Kabwama interview, July 20, 2005.
22 Majwala interview, September 22, 2003.

Uganda National Examination Board and teach part-time at Kyambogo, where he judges arts festivals and events. I initially interviewed Majwala and recorded the two songs he performed for this project in 2003: an alternate version of "The Battle of Nsinsi" ("Olutalo olw'e Nsinsi") and "The Pebble Is Breaking Me" ("Akayinja Kammenya"). In subsequent years I attended and documented various public events at which Majwala performed these songs.

Gender and Court Music Performance

This book's discussion does not feature any female court instrumentalists and singers because these roles in Buganda have historically been men's. The court composer-performers introduced in the previous section, all of whom are men, noted during our interviews that before 1966, female drummers did participate in a few private court rituals, such as twin initiations, which selected royals attended.[23] According to Ssempeke, some of these rituals had restricted attendance, and even the official court musicians were not invited to be part of them.[24] Women primarily served as dancers, accompanying the music of male singers and instrumentalists. They were critical to court performance, as they helped engage audience members visually, challenging them to use as many of their senses as possible in experiencing performances.[25] Their movements both illustrated the subject matter of the corresponding songs and emphasized certain aspects of the music; in other words, these women were an entertaining force that enhanced the quality of performances.[26] Part of the reason women's musical roles were limited in this way was that culturally it had been inappropriate for them to play any musical instruments whatsoever. This custom had originated long ago when women were restricted to the domestic sphere. They generally did not spend much time outside their homesteads, where they maintained the household and raised their children while their husbands went out in public and worked to earn a living.[27]

Sylvia Nannyonga-Tamusuza reveals that one of the reasons women generally did not play the drums is that they were believed to lack the physical endurance necessary to properly drum for long periods.[28] The

---

23 Sserwanga interview, July 15, 2005.
24 Ssempeke interview, July 12, 2005.
25 Ibid.
26 Ibid.
27 Sserwanga interview, July 15, 2005.
28 Nannyonga-Tamusuza 2005, 15.

irony of this belief is that dancing, the performance role to which women were typically regulated, often required more strength and endurance than drumming.[29] Such limitations and general expectations for modesty and demureness among women were the values that formed the basis for the traditions of modern Buganda regarding male and female roles within the court. However, these traditions have faded significantly as late-twentieth-century social developments have continued into the current era. In fact, women's musical roles have continued to broaden since the mid-1950s. It has not been uncommon to see women performing in public with musical instruments. Sserwanga recounted that during the celebrations that marked King Sir Edward Muteesa II's 1955 return from exile in the United Kingdom, huge throngs of people lined the streets to rejoice. Everyone in the area, except for the court staff members, showed up to take part in the festivities. Many of the participating musical troupes included both male and female instrument players, and a smaller number was made up solely of women. They were able to actively participate in the celebration of their king, not only as Baganda but also as musicians.[30]

Nannyonga-Tamusuza further shows how today gendering and gender norms continue to weave themselves into even the lives of seemingly inanimate musical or sound objects. Accordingly, many Baganda consider certain drums as male and others as female, with the two types kept together so that the male drums will always protect the female.[31] The projection of gender norms onto these sound objects indicates the importance of their role in society. For example, performances of *baakisimba*—a music and dance genre—separate drumming and dancing parts along male and female lines. Aspects of *baakisimba* performance—including costumes, dance movements, drum sounds, and interaction with the audience—are all partially defined by their relation to constructed gender identities.[32] As suggested earlier, the male-female binary determines who can and cannot play the drums. Nannyonga-Tamusuza maintains that historically, women's not being able to play the drums is a restriction that men uphold, whereas women generally see no issue with beating the drums themselves. She argues that because the cultural significance of the drum is so strong, denying women the right to play it effectively denies them of their right to be Baganda.[33] As Buganda continues to develop and encounter different ideas on gender, more and more women have begun playing drums. They are no longer passive in accepting

---

29   Ibid.
30   Sserwanga interview, July 7, 2005.
31   Nannyonga-Tamusuza 2005, 64.
32   Ibid., 1.
33   Ibid., 147.

gender roles and are redefining themselves as agents of cultural change in a way that challenges public perceptions of their weakness or subordination. This increase in female autonomy and involvement in the musical sphere has brought more unique voices and varying perspectives among the Baganda. As society increasingly welcomes women into the realm of instrumental music, the responsibilities, rituals, and expectations of the domain will continue to change and grow.

Other Research Collaborators

Interpreters of the court songs discussed throughout this book include Edward Ssebunnya Kironde, Harriet Kisuule, John Magandaazi Kityo, Jimmy Ssenfuka Kibirige, Jessy Ssendawula, Steven Mukasa Kabugo, and Peter Kinene. I share minimal personal information about these interpreters to protect them from any backlash for exercising their voice about sensitive political matters. In some of their commentaries, they often point to a handful of current Ugandan cultural and national leaders, including General President Yoweri Kaguta Museveni as well as members of his cabinet such as Major General Minister Kahinda Otafiire; and two of President Museveni's major political opponents, Honorable Activist Robert Kyagulanyi Ssentamu (also a music artist popularly known by his stage name Bobi Wine) and Colonel Dr. Kizza Besigye. Cultural leaders include Buganda's King (Kabaka) Ronald Mutebi II (r. 1993–present) and Prime Minister (Katikkiro) Charles Peter Mayiga. I must stress that the political views featured in the interpreters' commentaries, which they shared willingly, are not my own. My analysis of these views only seeks to clarify interpreters' opinions, which may seem to digress at times.

I transcribed, translated, and analyzed the Luganda interviews on which this book's narrative draws with some input from the following long-term Ugandan collaborators: Kabenge Gombe, a drummer and choir conductor, Mushroom (Butiko) Clan leader, retired lecturer, Kiganda culture historian, and Luganda specialist; Waalabyeki Magoba, a journalist, creative artist (actor, scriptwriter, producer), Luganda author, radio presenter, and Kiganda culture consultant; Francisca Nakachwa, a music teacher and practitioner; Jessy Sendawula, Jimmy Ssenfuka Kibirige, and Peter Kinene, all three of whom were among the aforementioned interpreters. These colleagues made invaluable contributions to *Interpreting Court Song in Uganda* and its development.

I also refined and produced this book with input from numerous Middlebury College student research assistants and collaborators, including Emma Binks, Annie Beliveau, Elizabeth Cady, Vaughan Supple, Angelina

Como-Mosconi, Brett Sorbo, and Ryo Nishikubo. These students first took my ethnomusicology courses, and many were eager to apply their newly acquired knowledge and skills. Their roles included editing the project's prose for style, brainstorming broader conceptual and structural issues such as chapter sequencing, and analyzing translated interview transcripts as well as sonic and extra-sonic elements of the songs discussed throughout this study. These, among other roles, occasionally involved contributing new text that was based on my original research and preexisting ideas. Binks and I edited the first draft of the English translations of the interviews I conducted in 2019 and 2020. In the early stages of assembling the book, Beliveau worked with me to analyze these translations and those of interviews I had conducted between 2000 and 2015. We identified and grouped conceptual themes within court song lyrics and composer-performers' biographies. Cady, with whom I coproduced the film *Drum Making as a Way of Life in Southern Uganda*, collaborated with me to edit all interview translations and assemble the first draft of the manuscript. She also acted as a sounding board for my ideas about the draft's themes and assisted with summarizing content from pertinent secondary sources. Supple served as a developmental coeditor, providing feedback on the thematic and structural content of the second draft of the manuscript. He also copyedited the draft's narrative and offered substantial input on the analysis of the sonic elements of the songs I discuss. Como-Mosconi copyedited the book's third draft. Sorbo assisted with secondary research and copyedited the final draft, suggesting ways to revise the prose for concision. Nishikubo and I collaborated on fleshing out the extent to which the interpreters featured throughout the book reimagined Kiganda court song repertoire in contemporary political contexts. Drawing on my notion of *recasting the song*, he extensively commented on and theorized various interpretations of lyrical meanings in the first draft of the manuscript. His engagement with interpreters' commentaries via this idea enhanced the theoretical tone of this project, which would have turned out differently without Nishikubo's input.

Focus of the Book's Narrative

Throughout my research with the song composer-performers and interpreters who contributed to this study, we prioritized the lyrical content of court songs. Interactions with these research collaborators led me to the realization that a more sonically oriented study would bring our discussion away from Kiganda worldviews and the cultural importance of the court songs under investigation. However, I perform some light musical analysis to highlight key connections between the sonic and extra-sonic elements of the songs, including the extent to which stylistic elements mark themes of power relations that emerge in the lyrics. Indeed, the lyrics and their political meanings are the focus of the book's narrative. This focus aligns with another suggestion that research collaborators gave to me regarding underscoring the practical applications of the lyrics' meanings, particularly their relevance to social relations. In this spirit, *Interpreting Court Song in Uganda* takes an approach to engaging with music slightly different from that of many ethnomusicologists.

2

Research Methods and Approaches to Lyrical Interpretation

Since 2000, I have been looking at the lyrics of the court songs presented in this book over and over, still confounded by their meanings. Some days, a song will mean one thing to me, and the next it will mean another. Similarly, some of my research collaborators' lyrical interpretations occasionally seem to conflict. This is exactly the point, as this book's interpretive process depends on its alternate, conflicting interpretations. I seek to harmonize these interpretations in the wider framework of the project, as they are simply *entangled* with one another. I propose that seemingly contradictory statements are not irreconcilable but represent a greater need for interpretation on the reader's part. Showing how a single analysis may not necessarily negate or supersede the other, for example, I embrace the differences or variations in presented interpretations and stories. As I demonstrate, conflicting narratives allow a fuller mosaic of meaning to emerge from the analysis of the songs and their historical as well as current contexts. *Interpreting Court Song in Uganda* also values how the veracity of these narratives lies in their applicability to everyday life rather than their factual correctness.

To explore these conundrums, I encourage readers to take their time with the full transcriptions of the song lyrics I include throughout the book and to enjoy the process of wrestling with what the stories in and around them mean. It would be difficult to simply absorb and integrate these views, and readers will actively grapple with this tension. And yet, we open ourselves to new ways of ideating when we embrace, not avoid, such analytical discomfort. Understanding this approach to interpretation requires an appreciation of the Kiganda worldview, specifically the idea that contradictions (*tension*) are opportunities (*fertile ground*) for new interpretive possibilities (*resolution*). This philosophy, as we shall see later in the book, permeates other aspects of Kiganda life, including musical and dance performances with rich stylistic variation and that rely on the integration of different parts that seem contradictory but harmonize. I further implore readers to consider any logical tension that the interpretations of the songs and stories in this book present in the scope of the Kiganda oral tradition I discuss earlier in which the content of stories can morph depending on the speaker and his or her performance. In this sense, the art of retelling stories does not concern itself as much with maintaining factual "correctness" as with conveying meaning and perspective.

Because the life of Kiganda songs depends on the interaction of their meanings via the interpretive process, a curious and analytical readership will add to the meanings of the songs discussed in this book and thus contribute to the continuity of a long-standing tradition. Indeed, readers' personal interpretations will enrich the mosaic of meaning that this book documents. Many of the musicians who performed and composed the songs and told many of the stories presented here have passed away in recent years. They were the honorable custodians of these repertoires and belong to the last generation of Buganda's resident royal court musicians. This book enshrines their names and contributions to that legacy. First, these artists bring their perspectives to life through intimate renditions of their musicianship, lyricism, and worldviews. Second, rather than homogenizing and codifying their spirits, *Interpreting Court Song in Uganda* saturates them with vitality, allowing the reader to become an interpreter in tandem with them. Thus, even as the royal court musicians of the older generation pass away, their spirits live on. Each interpretation and each reimagining will reignite the songs these artists composed or performed and the stories they told.

With all these ideas in mind, I define *lyrical interpretation* as a method of creative renewal that infuses vitality into court songs. This outlook allows interpreters and analysts to play with a collection of meanings rather than hold on to a single narrative. In turn, the interpretive process extends the life of the songs by allowing new versions to proliferate from them. That is, the interpretation process serves to renew each song's life, to highlight its relevance to contemporary contexts, and to help us discover truths and myths about present-day situations. As I argue throughout the book, the court songs under examination are not stagnant memorabilia from another time. Rather, they are cultural and political documents that have endured for centuries and continue to inspire curiosity about the respective role of the individual and the community. By surveying and engaging with a wide range of voices and perspectives, one will learn to appreciate these songs and their accompanying stories more fully—as extensions of their composer-performers, interpreters, and contexts, as well as rich sources for the development of this book's theories. Overall, *Interpreting Court Song in Uganda* challenges the typical notion that meaning is singular, static, and monolithic.

Working with Composer-Performers

Before moving to the United States for my graduate studies in 2004, I studied and performed Kiganda music with most of the composer-performers featured in this book, who also became principal participants in my research about the royal court music genre. Working closely with these artists provided me with multiple opportunities to master a variety of Kiganda musical instruments and their associated court song repertoire. In the early 2000s, I apprenticed and performed (as a singer and drummer) with Albert Muwanga Ssempeke (ca. 1930–2006) and Ludoviiko Sserwanga (ca. 1932–2013) and their performing group, Siblings in Love (Abooluganda Kwagalana) at many events in Kampala. The group also featured Albert Ssempeke Bisaso (b. 1979), Ssempeke's son, with whom I performed in another ensemble in the early 2000s. Ssempeke and Sserwanga were my primary Kiganda court music teachers, and I owe most of my knowledge about the subgenre to them.

These and related events partly inspired me to research Kiganda court music during my undergraduate studies at Makerere University and later during my graduate studies at Florida State University. Similarly, observing performances of court songs in ethnic and national contexts allowed me to appreciate their relevance to political life in Uganda. In the mid-2000s I attended events at which Ssaalongo Kiwanuka Matovu Deziderio (1924–2015) and his Badongo Dancers group performed some of the songs discussed in this book. I would later hire him and the group to perform at my wedding reception in 2006. Performing court music and attending events at which it was being performed offered me rare insights into the varied political and contextual meanings of Kiganda court songs. In other words, these extended engagements prompted me to make important connections between the lyrical content of the songs and the power relations within Uganda. The familiarity I gained with the songs' political themes informed how I conducted research with the selected group of non-performers who served as the interpreters in this project.

I recorded some of the songs analyzed in parts 2–6 in 2003 and 2004 as part of my research on the continuity and change of the Kiganda royal bow harp (*ennanga*).[1] The study consulted solo performances by Ssempeke, Bisaso, and Ssaalongo Ssennoga Majwala (b. 1953). In 2005 and 2006 I recorded additional songs during the research I carried out for a project that focused on the historical role of royal court musicians during the reign of King Sir Edward Muteesa II (r. 1939–1966). Building on my previous research on Kiganda royal court music, the project consulted solo

---

1 Kafumbe 2004.

performances of songs by Ssempeke, Sserwanga, Deziderio, Bisaso, Majwala, Ssaalongo Paulo Kabwama (1923–2020), and Mukasa Kafeero (b. 1971).[2]

Working with Interpreters of the Songs' Meanings

In the fall of 2019 and the spring of 2020, I returned to Buganda with court song recordings I had made and analyzed between 2003 and 2015. I identified a set of research collaborators, introduced the recordings to them, and asked them to reinterpret the repertoire's lyrical content over several days, working with a different interviewee each day. Song interpreters included long-term colleagues or collaborators and a few individuals whom those collaborators introduced to me during the 2019 and 2020 research trips. In deciding my research group, I selected individuals who could provide a variety of perspectives on connections between the lyrical content of Kiganda court songs and political life in Uganda. I also ensured that all interviewees had an in-depth understanding of Buganda and Uganda's political landscape and that they were fluent speakers of Luganda, the language in which I conducted most of the research for this book. The research collaborators included a medical student, a preschool teacher and activist, a popular music artist, two secondary-school English literature teachers, a traditional music artist and farmer, and a secondary-school art teacher and Luganda teacher as well as songwriter and poet. These participants' varied experiences helped prompt a richer narrative where a wider variety of perspectives on power relations could shine through. This variety also helped reveal new insights into the relevance of historical repertoire to political life in twenty-first-century Uganda. In this way the interpreters, like performers, would become co-analysts, offering viewpoints to complement the lyrical analysis of this book.

By positioning interviewees as central actors in analyzing Kiganda court songs, *Interpreting Court Song in Uganda* embraced an interpretive approach that primarily came from these individuals' commitment to promoting indigenous agency, and secondarily from voices in scholarly discourse. This approach required that I continuously build trust with them throughout the research process. It also required me to spend a considerable amount of time in the interpreters' communities, exploring the realities and experiences that informed their analytical lenses. Some of this context was not obvious at first glance, and understanding it required me to develop familiarity with the spaces that my interviewees inhabited. If I had not generated good rapport with interpreters, I would not have been able to detect

---

2   Kafumbe 2006.

certain vital political undertones. This was also true in relation to the subtle inequalities of power that existed among certain groups, including kin, sexes, and genders. On many occasions, I deferred to interpreters on the most practical and nuanced evaluations of the song lyrics in question. My extended time in the field confirmed that Ugandan permanent residents were indeed better positioned than I was to decipher the nuances of the songs and to take a lead in analyzing them. These interpreters inhabited the spaces in which these songs have been historically composed and performed, and this meant that they had unique insights into the relevant sensibilities and conceptions associated with the repertoire's lyrical content. Their active participation in analysis allowed them greater autonomy over the representation of their own ideas and resulted in the repertoire's being grounded in a broader cultural context. By prompting participants to freely explore power dynamics in personal and communal spaces via the interpretive process, I sought to account for important aspects of their lives in my representation of those ideas. Many remained open to the multitude of analytical possibilities that the songs made available to them, which in turn made them more self-aware of the uniqueness of their respective contributions.

During interviews, no two interpretations of a single song were similar, and in many cases a single interviewee provided multiple interpretations of a song. Even when interpreters discussed common topics, their interpretations varied greatly, as each contained details of their individual lives. Given their extended involvement in the meaning-making process, these interviewees were not simply subjects of study: they were *co-analysts* who brought their creativity and experiences to the interpretive process and cultivated meaningful reflections on the song's subject matter. They detected and commented on power relations, not only as a series of abstract ideas but as extensions of their day-to-day life. For example, in her interpretation of the song "We Love the Supreme Man [King] Exceedingly" ("Ssaabasajja Tumwagala Nnyo"), discussed in chapter 18, Harriet Kisuule noted,

> The same was true of President Museveni at first, when he had first come from the bush war. However, as the Baganda say, *Ekiwoomereze ekitata, kizaala enkenku* (Constant sweetening leads to stale beer spoiled by the lack of sorghum ferment). *Enkenku* comes about when the banana juice fails to ferment properly and therefore fails to make a good beverage. This ruins the brewing process and creates a liquid that is stale and spoiled, having not fully completed the fermentation cycle. Anyone who drinks this stale beer will notice its flaws immediately. They might complain to the brewer, who, though he began with a good purpose, did not fully see the process through and as a result has ruined what he initially tried to create. The same is true of President Museveni. The power that came along with ruling distracted him from fulfilling his initial promises to the people. He

has lost focus and turned against the interests of his people. As a result, there is a great amount of political tension, and the people are now willing to support opposition figures like Bobi Wine. They are disillusioned, frustrated with President Museveni's inability to deliver. He lost focus, and in turn the people's love for him subsided.[3]

In John Magandaazi Kityo's interpretation, he recognized the complexity of power relations between composer-performers of political songs and their audiences, noting,

> The ability to communicate a message to listeners is a God-given gift. However, sometimes this gift can come with troubles. If a performer sings a song that unflatteringly references the leader, they will be summoned to the CID (Criminal Investigations Directorate) offices to explain themselves. The CID officers must then listen to the song in question to try and parse out the intention behind it. This ability to instinctually understand the meanings of songs is another quality gifted by God. So, on the whole, the relationship between singers and leadership is one that can be fraught with tension and ultimately relies on the ability to communicate and interpret subtle signals.[4]

As research collaborators wove their lived experiences and emotions into the songs they analyzed through unique anecdotes, perspectives, and digressions on the repertoire's lyrics, they simultaneously brought them to life and expanded their network of meanings. Many used the songs' lyrics as a mechanism for speaking to future audiences in intimate and transformative ways such as suggesting new possibilities for how people should live and relate to one another. As such, their interpretations and the meanings they derived from the songs were applicable to power relations as they might manifest in global contexts. Interpreters recombined conceptions to imagine potentialities beyond the original intentions of the songs' lyrics. Indeed, this project benefited from each interviewee's intimate familiarity with the cultural context, subject matter, and language of the court songs I was investigating. The perspectives of Ugandan interpreters on these songs constitute one of the key elements of this study that makes it accessible to a wider audience.

---

3 Kisuule interview, December 21, 2019.
4 Kityo interview, December 14, 2019.

Ethical Considerations and Interpretive Process

I was always mindful of institutional review board (IRB) protocols while collecting data for *Interpreting Court Song in Uganda*. Before carrying out research for my 2016 study on the historical role of royal court musicians during the reign of King Sir Edward Muteesa II (r. 1939–1966), I submitted a procedure for research activities involving human subjects to the Florida State University IRB office. The office determined that my study was exempt, with no further IRB review and approval required to publish my findings. Furthermore, I considered my own biases, specifically how my prior knowledge of Kiganda court music could unproductively impact research activities related to this project. I was also mindful of potential ethical concerns that would arise from this project's focus on works performed or composed by artists I had worked closely with as teachers, band mates, associates, colleagues, and research collaborators.

Moreover, documenting interpreters' comments on power relations required that I pay special attention to ethical issues, that I explain to interpreters the nature of this project, the implications of their participation, and my intent to publish their responses. It also required a close focus on issues of privacy, as many of them discussed politically sensitive topics. For some, commenting on such topics necessitated trust that only came with time as we built rapport. As interpreters became increasingly comfortable in our conversations, they were more willing to get outside of their comfort zones and explore different dimensions of political life. With all these and other related issues being discussed, I began conducting formal interviews. I obtained verbal and written consent to both record and publish participants' responses at the start of each session. Throughout our conversations, I inquired about their level of comfort with commenting on political issues and guaranteed anonymity if necessary. Given this project's focus on meaning and interpretation, most interview sessions focused on lyrical content. Much of the process of exploring different flows of power in Kiganda court songs centered on open-ended interviews. I would play recordings of songs to interpreters, review Luganda transcriptions of the songs' lyrics, and then ask the interviewees to comment on the pieces in relation to political life in Uganda. Some participants would also comment on possible applications of the lyrical content, transforming the songs from mere historical texts to frameworks for interrogating the notion of power relations. This variety of activities promoted a rich discourse about the songs' connections to political life.

Similarly, supplementing song recordings with transcriptions of lyrics allowed commentators to closely study the repertoire we discussed and to deeply reflect on its relevance to power. Some noted that both audio recordings and written text helped them better understand and engage with the nuances of the lyrics. Moreover, combining dialogue, transcript reviews, and listening sessions minimized the anxiety associated with providing commentary. This strategy allowed for a more dynamic and engaging process of meaning-making, one that naturally encouraged participants to reflect on and discuss issues that were closer to their hearts in a relaxed environment. Because most interviews lasted for several hours, I offered interpreters breaks, which allowed for greater concentration and less fatigue over the course of our conversations. These moments also enabled participants to reflect on additional topics they wanted to discuss, to think more deeply about certain details, and to ask me questions. Their feedback on my interview style and questions proved helpful and prompted me to make constructive changes in subsequent sessions. Although I would incorporate new topics that previous interpreters had raised, I still encouraged subsequent interviewees to discuss topics that they felt most comfortable with. Participants' continued feedback on my interview techniques also helped to refine my ability to use accessible and relatable language during conversations.

Discovering and Discussing Power Relations

I encouraged the interpreters to consider a broader, more fluid notion of power and to discuss all topics that they found worth pursuing. However, where necessary I gently prompted respondents to draw on their lived experiences as well. Our discussion topics ranged from the historical functions of the court song repertoire and the songs' associated performance contexts to the repertoire's applicability in various twenty-first-century political situations. Research collaborators theorized about the different and sometimes competing power relations that mark their lives. Their responses also touched on wide-ranging aspects of political life, including government policy, civic responsibility, and cultural shifts. In this way, the songs they were interpreting provided them with tools to critically examine power dynamics as they appeared in the world around them. The songs also enabled them to communicate their personal views about power while relating the lyrics to modern political life. Interview sessions were a time for exploration, reflection, and joint study as we sought to understand how the themes and messages of the songs apply to both the micro- and macropolitical levels. Although each song offered its own unique set of themes that prompted specific topics of discussion, fresh themes arose during our conversations and listening sessions. I incorporated many of these themes into the organization of the book.

It is important to note that many of the participants' interpretations of court songs feature biased views, including allegations, controversies, and accusations. For example, many participants suggest that Uganda's political scene is dominated by men, yet the government has more women in cabinet posts than many other African countries. Others evaluate political leaders and their policies on the basis of personal preferences and political positions. Where possible, I supplement the presented evidence with additional sources in order to promote a richer dialogue about power relations. Although it is essential to analyze my interlocutors' views critically, I believe my primary responsibility as a researcher is to accurately represent those views. Therefore, rather than attempt to confirm the validity of their perspectives on political life in Uganda, my analysis focuses on what those viewpoints reveal about power relations.

Defining Court Song

My definition of court song repertoire in this book is grounded in the fact that the social rule of the court has historically extended beyond its walls. In this sense, court performers have served as mediators between these interior and exterior spaces. This dynamic was evident in the work and role of the king's private harpist (*omulanga*) or bow harp (*ennanga*) player before Uganda's national government launched a military operation on Buganda's Mmengo royal court (*olubiri*) in 1966 and subsequently abolished all the kingdoms in 1967.[5] Some people speculate that the bow harp player's title might have been derived from both the name of his musical instrument (*ennanga*) and the verb *okulanga* (literally, "to announce"). Others argue that his ability to foretell events informed listeners to take appropriate action. As Majwala pointed out, within the court the harp player entertained and advised the king and other royals. He was the only one permitted to point out the king's faults and correct him.

The harpist would also occasionally leave the court and travel among the various communities of the kingdom. During his travels he performed songs for the masses that informed them about court affairs. In response, the masses would tell him whatever problems they were facing because they knew he held a close relationship with the king. They knew that he could facilitate change, so they eagerly shared their stories with him, whether they sought him out themselves to tell him a specific problem or he overheard them talking about problems during his travels. The harpist would note all

---

5   For a more detailed discussion of the political events of 1966 and 1967, see chapter 1.

the issues that were on the people's minds, such as famine or poor infrastructure, and then would return to the court to compose songs with which he could deliver this information to the king. He spent a lot of time composing and preparing these songs for the leader, experimenting with lyrics and delivery methods until he reached a combination that communicated the message effectively.

The rapid rise of foreign media and technology during the twentieth century resulted in a decline in the court harpist's power and importance. As people began using devices that enabled near-instant communication, this traditional channel of communication between the masses and their king became increasingly obsolete.[6] The harpist and other musicians' movement back and forth between the court and its exterior not only enabled them to acquire fresh material for the songs that they used to deliver news and communicate important information but also shaped the identity of those songs.

Most of the court songs I selected for this project are part of a standard repertoire that musicians have historically composed and performed for court events and passed down from generation to generation. A few are original compositions by individuals who have served in the court. Taking cues from the contributions of these musicians, my analysis defines court song broadly—as a cover term for works with lyrics that make direct reference to court life and royal politics as well as songs that, although composed in and performed by court musicians outside the court context, make no direct reference to these topics.

One such example is "He Has a Lot on His Mind" ("Alina Bingi By'Alowooza"), which engages with the distress of contemporary politics by invoking a previous period in Ugandan politics (this song is discussed in chapter 10). The song comments on the prior dissolution of Buganda and suggests that the kingdom's leader is preoccupied with its affairs, but these themes only become apparent with knowledge of the background story that accompanies the composition. Thus, the performer's implicit reference to the themes leaves room for the lyrics to be applicable to other sociopolitical contexts.

Similarly, "Ssematimba and Kikwabanga" (discussed in chapter 19) recounts the tragedy of two brothers who died in battle before they could enjoy the goats they were saving to eat later. The song serves as a lesson to be thankful for each living moment and not to count one's chickens before they hatch. The composition's background story reveals its connections to Kiganda royal politics—the two brothers in question were Baganda warriors whom King Ssuuna II (r. ca. 1832–1857) appointed to go to war.

---

6   Majwala interview, September 22, 2003.

Another song that does not distinctly refer to royal politics is "Poland" ("Polanda"), which recounts some of the events of World War II (see chapter 20). Its background story reveals that court performers, as representatives of the people, composed the song in response to Buganda's decision to send troops to fight in the war. This context provides insights into how some "court songs" use global events to refer to power dynamics in Uganda's political spheres. As a result, "Poland" suggests the universal nature of political conflict.

"The Battle of Nsinsi" ("Olutalo olw'e Nsinsi") also makes no direct reference to Buganda. The song narrates a very violent conflict at a place known as Nsinsi (see chapter 21). Highlighting the tragedies of war and the ubiquitous nature of violence, the song's background story discloses a historical conflict between Buganda and one of its neighboring kingdoms, Bunyoro. In a related fashion, the lyrics of "Let Me Plod with a Stick Close to Kibuuka" ("Ka Nsimbe Omuggo awali Kibuuka") focus on marital and family conflict (see chapter 22), but the song's citation of Kibuuka, the Kiganda deity of battles, suggests his role in various Kiganda sociopolitical contexts, including royal ones. Furthermore, the performer of "The Pebble Is Breaking Me" ("Akayinja Kammenya") represents the spirit of a deceased person, who compares the world of the living with that of the dead (see chapter 23). This song's focus on the effects of death, including its ability to take leaders, makes it relevant to various social and political domains. It is these compositions' indirect reference to court, royal, or kingship affairs that qualified them as court songs.

As mentioned previously, this study also analyzes performances of original songs that were composed by court musicians outside the court, in non-royal contexts. These included "Federo," or "Federalism" (see chapter 8), which a single former court artist composed in the early 1990s and presented with his private performing group in many national political contexts. The song's lyrics deal with subjects such as corruption, inequality, imperialism, and conflict in contemporary Uganda. They specifically protest against the Ugandan national government, accusing it of bureaucratic decisions that lead to the unjust suffering of its people. "Federalism" is an ideal composition for the post-1993 period, which has seen some former court artists engage with national politics through fresh compositions that draw on their deep knowledge of Kiganda politics and musical practices. Compositions like "Federalism," appropriate for broader political discourse, have become commonplace at campaign events, during which artists use them to advise the masses, impact how they choose candidates, and shape political leaders' perspectives on policy. The label "court song" is appropriate for songs such as "Federalism" because their creation is partly inspired by composers' and performers' experiences with royal politics and expertise in court musical idioms.

Power Dynamics and Ethnography

As a touch point among the various relations mentioned in previous sections, this book is both a research study and political act, as it weaves itself into the ongoing conversations about power that permeate every level of Ugandan society and the world at large. My many years of performing Kiganda court songs, participating in their various performance contexts, discussing them with court composers and performers, and listening to stories and commentaries about them all contributed to my realization that power relations was a recurring theme across the repertoire. This realization prompted me to revisit the court songs I had documented between 2003 and 2015 and to explore what their current interpretations might reveal about power in present-day Uganda. As an overall framework for the manuscript, I remained sensitive to how power relations dictated my interactions with all participants in the research that informed this book. As an ethnomusicologist, analyst, and interpreter, I was responsible for faithfully and ethically conveying my research collaborators' ideas. Despite our shared positions as Baganda and citizens of Uganda, these participants were more informed about political life in Uganda than I was because I live outside the country indefinitely and only return to conduct research or visit family. Therefore, they were responsible for guiding me in the research process.

Power dynamics also shaped the circumstances surrounding my participation in some of the performances of the songs discussed in this book. For instance, in the same moments that I was acting in my role as a researcher by seeking to understand the nuances of the songs through participating in their presentation, I was also in a subordinate position to the experienced court music experts I worked with. In my practice under these artists, who generously shared these essential repertoires, I became their student and protégé. Then, even as I became a student, I also became plugged into the relations of power that characterize the role of court musicians. This arrangement was similar to that of my interaction and collaboration with my own students (see chapter 1). My voice joined many others' voices in contributing to the nation's political and social discourses. In this way, this book's discussion of power relations is an integrated narrative of my analysis and that of my research collaborators. I am not simply an observer but a node in a series of densely layered networks of power. This layering emphasizes the complexity of my own sociopolitical position and sheds light on this book as a living, active contribution to these networks of power.

3

A Multi-Epistemological Framework

Discourses and Canons

No single theory can encapsulate the diversity and entanglement of the narratives presented in this project, and so its overall conceptual framework draws on the various strategies of my research process. These include returning to the field with my recordings of court songs, sharing them with a selection of new research collaborators, soliciting their interpretations with a focus on power relations, and representing these interpretations to the reader. Accordingly, the framework considers how these commentators cast court songs in a new light. That is, how they apply the historical purposes of the songs' lyrics to current contexts, which then assign them new meanings in the national political sphere. In these contexts, *Interpreting Court Song in Uganda* treats Kiganda court songs not only in terms of the ethnic group with which they are primarily associated, the Baganda, but also in terms of the broader national Ugandan polity. As suggested in previous chapters, it is within this polity that the songs assume a myriad of meanings. In addition, this study's conceptual framework engages with ideas from my research community and within multiple canons, advancing, challenging, and building on the work of scholars across different fields. A broader multi-epistemological framework captures the complexity of the varied songs, stories, analyses, and lyrical interpretations and meanings that appear in this book. I study these texts not as individual narratives but as parts of a collective discourse that extends beyond the boundaries of a single coherent narrative.

Representation

Academics' overly pedantic methods often lead researchers to overwrite and misconstrue the priorities of the communities we investigate, resulting in misleading and misrepresenting studies. For example, the typical authorial voices we prioritize subsume research collaborators' perspectives, limit our capacity to represent them appropriately, and make our work inaccessible to readers. These and other trends arise from colonial approaches, which have finite applicability. Representation in ethnomusicology is a critical issue because studying and translating culture is a process tied to the relations of power that exist between two parties. Philip Ciantar observes that even amid the processes of collaboration and translation, one is always tethered to and shaped by these power relations as they appear both between and within different societies and subcultures.[1] As Beverley Diamond shows by citing missionary accounts of indigenous music in North America, colonial and assimilationist frameworks only serve to obscure and misrepresent interpersonal interactions rather than illuminate them.[2] In a related fashion, Kofi Agawu draws our attention to how Western ethnomusicological discourse overemphasizes certain functions of music-making when documenting the role of music in African society. This results in generalizations that are incomplete at best and entirely misleading at worst.[3]

With these points in mind, *Interpreting Court Song in Uganda* joins other projects attempting to dismantle colonial practices, particularly those projects that suggest ways through which our research methods and approaches could undergo a deliberate decolonial shift. Following Elizabeth Mackinlay, I embrace "a refusal to get caught up in the desire to document, deconstruct, and 'disseminate' in academic servitude to coloniality."[4] Furthermore, I build on Liz Przybylski's suggestion to listen "deeply," "widely," and "personally,"[5] as well as Sara Hong-Yeung Pun's proposal to conduct research "*with*" indigenous communities "rather than *about* them."[6]

Accordingly, I reject a prescriptive approach to analysis, instead taking cues from participants in my research and remaining sensitive to their priorities in the book's interpretive process. With a focus on song, combining both cultural and sonic experience, this work emphasizes the intellectual value of listening and seeks to avoid using the Western hegemonic mode of

---

1 Ciantar 2013, 30.
2 Diamond 2013, 158–159.
3 Agawu 2016, 36.
4 Mackinlay 2012, 16.
5 Przybylski 2012, 14.
6 Pun 2012, 11.

listening. Dylan Robinson identifies this as "hungry listening," a mindset that prioritizes acquiring sonic information over absorbing tangible spiritual truth.[7] Reckoning with these notions, this book's approach, methodology, and content encourages a dynamic, multivalent, and growing engagement with meaning. My analysis and methods prioritize and take cues from my collaborations *with* research collaborators rather than my authorial hand. That is, I represent their stories and analyses, such as lyrical interpretations, on their own terms and downplay appealing to the aesthetic preferences of academia. As such, rather than positioning research collaborators as subjects of study, I foreground their voices and perspectives in the meaning-making process. By decentering my authorial voice, I seek to underscore direct dialogue between my research community and the readership of this work.

As a project based on the type of decolonial thought described, *Interpreting Court Song in Uganda* acknowledges that knowledge production in a global context is asymmetrical. In global history, this concept has been conflated by settlers to mean that particular cultures that manifest distinct physical embodiments of power dynamics and thus social functions and mores are essentially irreconcilable because of these differences. This mistaken concept laid the foundation for European colonialism in Africa. Building on work that challenges this concept, *Interpreting Court Song in Uganda* attempts to diverge from the hegemonic discourses of Western culture and neoliberalism. As Nic Cheeseman and others have written, these discourses tend to sustain the inaccurate notion that Africa's history since the 1960s has been a story solely of conflict.[8] Imani Sanga stresses that resisting this generalized identity is necessary for African nations to participate fully in the global sphere and that this aspiration is a prerequisite for beginning the work of balancing the uneven distribution of power between the Global North and the Global South.[9]

Interpreting Court Song in Uganda celebrates, delineates, and preserves the distinct culture of Buganda as it is documented and expressed through the beauty, complexity, and uniqueness of the kingdom's court songs. In this exploration, the project seeks to transcend the limited identity that has been imposed on Africa by the West via hegemonic discourse. Inspired by Bode Omojola's examination of songs that evoked the motivations, hopes, and frustrations of subalterns that drove the various independence movements of African nations, *Interpreting Court Song in Uganda* advocates for cultural pride, freedom, and reimagining as keystones in both the creation

---

7   Robinson 2020, 38.
8   Cheeseman et al. 2015, 96.
9   Sanga 2008, 80.

of ethnomusicological works and in the representation of the cultures they document.[10] As Judith Lynne Hanna and William John Hanna indicate, numerous anti-colonial independence movements in the twentieth century illustrated that cultural liberation was necessary to achieve political liberation.[11]

Broadly speaking, my research methodology adopts an approach that addresses the colonial dynamics that striate ethnomusicology as a field. Even though I address the historical repression of indigenous voices and perspectives and challenge conventional research practices that promote mechanisms for historically violent systems of power, I am equally aware of the fact that colonial approaches remain a systemic issue that must be addressed on a larger scale than any single study can undertake.

Kiganda Song

The songs explored in this book are part of a larger genre known as Kiganda songs. According to Andrew Cooke and James Micklem, Kiganda songs are composed and performed in Luganda, a tonal language consisting of long and short syllables, the ratio of their lengths being roughly 2:1. The songs use two basic tones ("low" and "high") and an additional tone that results from combining the first two.[12] Francis Katamba and Peter Cooke note that the concept of pitch in relation to these tones is a relative matter: a low tone only must be lower than the high tone that immediately precedes it. Furthermore, because most phrases tend to be said with a falling pitch, a high tone at the end of a phrase may be lower than a low tone from the beginning.[13]

As Cooke further points out, most notes in Kiganda songs relate to textual phrases, but the songs also contain some unrelated notes that are believed to enable greater flexibility and improvisation.[14] Cooke and Micklem also observe that the structure of performances of Kiganda songs can be infinitely repetitious and often can feature numerous verses, both standard and improvised, and performances are not limited to a specific length.[15] When performed by several individuals, Kiganda songs follow a cyclical structure, and the chorus will be used at the same point in each cycle. Soloists can sing

---

10   Omojola 2009, 291.
11   Hanna and Hanna 1968, 42.
12   Cooke and Micklem 1999, 49.
13   Katamba and Cooke 1987, 53.
14   Cooke 1994, 476.
15   Cooke and Micklem 1999, 49.

at any point and will sometimes overlap their singing with the chorus, using a different pitch to differentiate their parts.[16] Solo performances, such as those of the song versions in this book, typically have a through-composed structure.

Cooke breaks down the components of Kiganda song texts or lyrics in the liner notes that accompany a CD album that Albert Muwanga Ssempeke (ca. 1930–2006) recorded during his visit to Edinburgh University as the music faculty's first African musician in residence in 1988. Cooke describes: (1) "'Nuclear' texts" that act as the backbone or foundation of the song and give it its "identity"; (2) generic phrases that may be used in a vast array of different songs or contexts; (3) historical "utterances" that have been passed down and disseminated through the greater musical discourse of Kiganda music (these serve to "reinforce" the song's theme by linking it back to signifiers in its earlier renditions); (4) newer idioms that are introduced by the song's current performer; (5) improvised commentary that relates to "recent events" or other contemporaneous elements of the performance; and (6) a general and consistent affirmation of "obeisance to the Kabakaship." (Kabakaship is derived from the term *kabaka*, which is the title for Buganda's king).[17]

Lyrics of Kiganda songs serve many purposes. As Sylvia Nannyonga explains, by providing social commentary, humor, and layered meanings, song lyrics act as a method of public communication whereby performers can make statements that would not be acceptable in other contexts.[18] Solomy Katasi Dungu reminds us of how the lasting impression of these messages depends on how music interacts with emotion. According to her, music exists in the minds of composers and listeners, not only as sound but as a collection of "images, ideas, ideals, thoughts, and emotions."[19] It is this amalgamation of concepts and feelings that enables the music's interpretability, as each new interpretation draws on these same base ingredients to create a unique set of associations. This point reinforces Cooke's observation that Kiganda songs are living monuments to Buganda's history, as the nature of Kiganda musical sound is veritably enduring.[20] From its rhythmic principles to its timbral character, Kiganda sound functions as an expression of the Baganda people in every aspect.[21] Although stylistic choices and sonic arrangements may change with the sociopolitical climate of Buganda, the core repertoire of the kingdom's music remains the same, thus embodying a strong Kiganda

---

16 Cooke and Micklem 1999, 50.
17 Cooke 1988.
18 Nannyonga 1995, 183.
19 Dungu 1993, 20.
20 Cooke 1996, 443.
21 Ibid.

tradition. This arrangement is consistent with Agawu's conclusion that in African societies, music's close association with people themselves relies on the ostensibly unchanging nature of its foundational elements—language, texture, structure, rhythm, and timbre.[22] Consequently, even as songs and dances become reimagined, each new performance will retain certain aspects of the lyrics and choreography.

The discussion of instrumental music is beyond the primary scope of this book, but it should be noted that the songs presented here can be performed instrumentally, and many of them feature instrumental accompaniment to the singing. As Lois Anderson recalls, the Baganda refer to all their instrumental music as songs, in part because song is considered to have emerged from and originated in the human voice.[23] Indeed, many songs are instrumental interpretations of song melodies. Agawu references Peter Cooke and Klaus Wachsmann's research on the xylophone music of Uganda when he attests to how African performers conceptualize instrumental music as "wordless songs, songs whose words are not nonexistent but have been relegated to a strong supplementary function."[24] Agawu's and Cooke and Wachsmann's work highlights how, though instrumental songs might lack lyrics, their performers often express their textual elements through the intonations of instrumental sounds. For the Baganda, this is possible because Luganda, their language, is tonal, which allows words to be implied by instruments.[25] In Lisa Gilman's research on gender, performance, and politics in Malawi, she argues that although lyrics are important for expressing meaning during performance, they represent only certain aspects of a song's complete meaning.[26] These observations, especially those on the relationship between instrumental and vocal music, suggest that many African instruments are capable of capturing certain tonal and vocal qualities, including intonation, and that vocals and instruments simultaneously play a key role in defining a song's meanings. After all, Kiganda instruments are fashioned to recreate the peculiarities of the voice, so it would be inaccurate to conceptualize them as separate accompaniments.

Joseph Kyagambiddwa's writing on the origins, construction, playing techniques, and styles of Kiganda instruments offers additional insights into how the Baganda conceptualize the relationship between vocal performance and instrumental accompaniment and how they derive meaning from this relationship. When we examine the visual transpositions of Kiganda song

---

22 Agawu 2016, 49.
23 Anderson 1968, 153.
24 Agawu 2016, 30.
25 Cooke and Wachsmann 2003, 11.
26 Gilman 2007, 19.

compositions, it becomes apparent that their semantic content is inextricably linked to certain melodic patterns. For example, lyrical texts are broken up into syllables, and each syllable is associated with a specific note in accordance with its emphasis. A melody is created as the lyrics flow, which can then be transferred from vocal to instrumental performance. Because lyrical and melodic patterns are intimately related, specific words and phrases become inseparable from purely instrumental performances. Melodic phrases even affect the way that instruments are referred to, such as the names for the wooden xylophones (*amadinda* and *akadinda*) played by multiple musicians, which are "mere sound imitations: ding dang."[27] These and other practices speak to the broader conception of song in Buganda as both a vocal and instrumental praxis, ultimately rooted in text and the oral transmission of meaning.

This connection between vocals and instruments—which forms the foundation of Kiganda song—is also prominent in nonmelodic instruments. Most prominently, Kiganda drums are conduits for speech because they contain various permutations of rhythmic emphasis and verbal patterns. As Kyagambiddwa confirms, the *mbuutu* drum "does not merely sound but speaks."[28] This possibility for speech demonstrates that the drum is much more than an instrument to beat and that its sounds can be interpreted subjectively by various listeners. Moreover, there are hundreds of playing styles associated with the *mbuutu* drum, each of which requires its own terminology.[29] Different types of drums carry responsibility in expressing meaning through speech. For example, some drums are tasked with voicing certain clan slogans or melo-rhythmic beats with associated textual phrases (*emibala*) at public events and gatherings.[30] This practice further demonstrates the centrality of text in song, since these recitations are not only nonverbal but also nonmelodic, meaning only the rhythmic patterns of rhetoric will sound.

While much of the text that is "spoken" by instruments is based strictly on specific phrases and expressions, there is also flexibility in the sentiments communicated by certain instruments. For instance, the harmonic tunings of the Kiganda bow harp (*ennanga*) are permanently fixed, but those of the Kiganda bowl lyre (*endongo*) are free, meaning that players can improvise with their own sense of tonality.[31] This difference in agency and creative freedom between certain instruments resembles the fluctuations between

---

27 Kyagambiddwa 1955, 115.
28 Ibid., 113.
29 Ibid., 113.
30 Ibid., 114.
31 Ibid., 106, 108.

fixed speech and conversational spontaneity that the Baganda experience in everyday life. While Kiganda musical artists must often draw from centuries-old musical motifs, they are also able to express their own personalities in a performance if the occasion allows for improvisation.

For many Kiganda instruments there is a general rule of practice that vocal singing must accompany the performance. Instruments such as ground bows (*ssekitulege*) and flute (*endere*) quintets must include vocals, since the texture they produce creates room for vocal lyrics to weave into the very fabric of the performance. Examining the performance logistics of the bow harp, we can appreciate that its music fulfills three separate yet intertwined responsibilities: *okunaga* (literally, "to initiate"), *okwawula* (literally, "to split"), and *okuyimba* (literally, "to sing"). The first two are instrumental, played by the hands, but when they are performed, the audience "can hear the voice part mysteriously looming up," demonstrating how these musical components are inseparable.[32] The human voice and the instruments that accompany it illustrate a mutual relationship in which both elements are not only equally important but reinforce each other. This concept of mutuality remains prominent throughout most Kiganda performance practices and their various contexts. For example, in performances featuring xylophones (*amadinda* and *akadinda*), each instrument is assigned to a group of performers who play separate, interlocking, complementary parts.[33] The marriage of these two parts creates melodic linearity and rhythmic cohesion. Members of each group of performers play off each other, listening for cues and falling in sync rather than reciting a memorized sequence of notes in a rigid manner. The relationship between these players epitomizes mutuality in its most balanced and conversational form, and the various elements of musical sounds (rhythm, texture, harmony) produced are the result of this reciprocity.

Musical Meaning

This study treats each court song "as a form of speech utterance," drawing on J. H. Kwabena Nketia's idea that song and speech are nearly the same phenomenon, given their analogous qualities and functions in social communication in African societies. As a result, the themes of these songs tend to reflect and elaborate on the concerns of "a community or the social groups within it," which are then equally disseminated through both simple and complex social rituals.[34] As mentioned previously, the songs examined

---

32   Ibid., 106.
33   Ibid., 115.
34   Nketia 1975, 189.

here are living works, constantly blooming and being reborn each time they are performed, heard, and interpreted. Each song is ripe with hidden meanings that can be assigned, drawn out, expanded, revitalized, and applied by performers, listeners, and interpreters.

My interpretive approach considers a wide range of perspectives on meaning in African music. These include Tony Langlois's idea that music serves as a stage for the actualization of meanings, which in turn transform the political and social dynamics in which that music is being performed.[35] This is related to the way I draw on Greg Barz's observation that experiencing musical performance begets the formation of new meanings.[36] I also follow Kwasi Ampene's discussion of how lyrical meanings might be part of a broader network of meanings, including those associated with musical instruments, performance regalia, and other "verbal art forms."[37] Ampene further stresses that meanings depend on the contexts in which musical arts are performed and the rhetorical devices employed.[38] These observations are pertinent to my discussion of the role context plays in the complex meaning-making process.

Meaning in African music, according to Nketia, exists as a series of modes and perspectives rather than as one static and unitary concept. Accordingly, one must examine the multitude of statements, interpretations, and relationships associated with musical performance and practice.[39] Moreover, one must treat these elements as fundamental aspects of the way musical meanings take shape rather than as tangential details.[40] Nketia further emphasizes the primacy of context in meaning-making, noting that many African societies define their song repertoires by their "contextual function" and by the ways the content of those songs might apply to specific social purposes. He reiterates that Africans select songs for a variety of vocations and social situations (recreation, work, war, rites), which are themselves variable depending on the mood or content of the occasion. In this regard, choosing themes and lyrics simultaneously depends on the feeling of the moment and any preheld expectations that precede the event. But again, these moods, expectations, and social needs can change, and performers will be flexible to use songs with specific themes that happen to feel appropriate for their given contexts. For example, songs about death may not be restricted to funeral

---

35 Langlois 2009, 224–225.
36 Barz 2001, 107.
37 Ampene 2020, 13.
38 Ampene 2021, 534.
39 Nketia 1962, 5.
40 Ibid.

rites; in fact, they might inevitably be appropriate for recreational contexts. Thus, "the themes of songs are not rigidly compartmentalized."[41]

As already established, the court songs explored in this book, which belong to the larger genre of Kiganda songs, feature lyrics that contain multiple meanings, at times layered into a single repeated utterance. David Pier points out that the full extent of lyrical meaning in Kiganda songs is often only discernable to those who have a deep knowledge of Kiganda idioms, history, and mythology, a phenomenon he describes as "deep Luganda."[42] This notion aligns with Omojola's conclusion that the semantic ambiguity of songs has a loosening effect on meanings which have been cemented in social and political spheres.[43] Sylvia Nannyonga-Tamusuza reminds us that some Kiganda songs are rich with ambiguity and the possibility of multiple meanings because the Baganda tend to use innuendo and "hidden language" to discuss scandalous topics.[44]

Another factor that may account for the multiplicity of meanings in Kiganda songs is the singers' tendency to draw on the personal experiences and attitudes of the audience.[45] In fact, performers sometimes choose to structure songs in ways that allow listeners greater interpretive freedom by, for example, ending them without a clear resolution.[46] These instances, among others, highlight the heterogeneity that may be at the heart of a given song. They further imply the primacy of interpretation in musical performance, not only to draw out a song's core meaning but also to creatively actualize new potentials for understanding it.

Power Relations

This project is interested in the extent to which power shapes social interactions and how research collaborators relate those interactions to the meanings they derive from the court songs discussed in the subsequent chapters. My analysis problematizes how power relations are a foundational element in the creation and broader relevance of the songs. Music, possessing universally acknowledged affective power, is a medium through which we can express the emotional quality of power relations. The Kiganda court songs presented in this book have assumed this function for centuries, detailing

---

41 Nketia 1975, 203.
42 Pier 2017, 13.
43 Omojola 2012, 9.
44 Nannyonga-Tamusuza 2002, 138.
45 Ibid.
46 Ibid., 136.

relationships between family members, neighbors, king and subject, kingdoms, and more broadly, humans and their nonhuman surroundings. During precolonial and colonial times, in court performances individuals hashed out the power dynamics affecting their lives. As I explain in the previous chapter, musical performances by the king's harpist expressed the fundamental needs of local populations, which held both direct and indirect contact with the court. These musical ambassadors served the vital political role of assuaging tensions between ruler, subject, and other entities along the local power structure.

This study recognizes music's power in shaping politics through both direct and indirect means. At a broad view, it acknowledges Jack M. Barbalet's notion that superordinate and subordinate social actors recognize and, begrudgingly, accept their power relationship: the subordinate actor, depending on its influence, will moderate the political effectiveness of the superordinate actor; and the superordinate actor, which holds the power, will continue to repress, or dominate, the subordinate actor, depending on its power resources. Barbalet claims that this dynamic "has been regarded as paradoxical" because it requires the acquiescence and resistance of both actors.[47] He adds that power (or the level of *initiative* of the superordinate) and resistance (the level of *initiative* of the subordinate) cannot be calculated by the same metrics.[48] *Interpreting Court Song in Uganda* highlights references to colonial power structures as they appear in court song lyrics and their interpretations, as both isolated incidents and extensions of larger systems of violence. The project generates fresh insights into how political life in my research community, Buganda, is shaped by historical cultural exchanges and how the songs featured in it might serve as tools for challenging power structures rooted in colonial power dynamics. But the project also pays close attention to how court songs intervene in the formation of local power dynamics.

Interpreting Court Song in Uganda also considers Lisette Balabarca's claims that musical artists under totalitarian regimes accumulate this initiative by weaving signifiers of cultural resistance into their sounds, which can "only be understood by the subjugated group, but never by those who are in power."[49] Laudan Nooshin writes that when such a government is wrestling with the competing forces of "modernity and tradition," any hypocrisy or confusion in it that enforces social conduct will open a clear "opportunity for subversion."[50] With each of these articulations, we can understand sub-

---

47   Barbalet 1985, 531.
48   Ibid., 535.
49   Balabarca 2013, 81.
50   Nooshin 2005, 233, 242.

ordination (or *subalternity*, to use a postcolonial term) as an opportunity to harness resistance. Such is the basis of political engagement, criticism, and commentary (see part 2). As we shall see in chapters 4–8, when musicians represent subjected people, they can choose to direct their critique right back at the government, transmit it in "hidden language" to the general population, or employ some mix of both. Other artists might shy away from critiquing political institutions, although they still may deliver performances that subtly inspire conformity with or departure from social conduct.

As James Garratt says, not every musician whose music causes social disruption will have done so by playing overtly political material.[51] Various artists in the twentieth and twenty-first centuries fall along this spectrum, but resistance through music is a timeless phenomenon of power relations globally. The Kiganda court songs in this book belong to this universal notion, and the project builds on other studies that examine music's relationship to politics in other African political contexts. Mhoze Chikowero shows how songs and other forms of African music shape the political culture and atmosphere that establish the act of "African self-crafting," while Joseph Kaminski and Barbara G. Hoffman demonstrate how songs may challenge, maneuver, and affirm power structures in Ghana and Mali, respectively.[52] Gavin Steingo shows that the capacity for kwaito music to function politically within South Africa is not exclusive to "political music," which, depending on the individual's interpretation, can become strikingly apolitical.[53] Nomi Dave similarly indicates that songs by popular music artists in Guinea will remain vague about issues like political corruption and violence despite explicitly singing about social problems in society. As a result, musicians can sympathize with the struggle of average people without making themselves targets of the direct ire of the state.[54] Laura Lohman further describes how the Egyptian singer Umm Kulthūm's ability to present herself as apolitical enabled her to make her fundraising campaign for the rebuilding of Egypt's armed forces more sustainable in international contexts. Keeping the language in her songs vague allowed her audiences to interpret them freely. By providing this interpretive space, she gave her listeners greater opportunities to connect with her music, which drove them to make larger contributions to her cause.[55] These case studies confirm that the relationship between music and politics is not straightforward but is an extension of a variety of factors, including audience interpretation and social context.

---

51   Garratt 2018, 131.
52   Chikowero 2015, 5; Kaminski 2012; Hoffman 2017.
53   Steingo 2007, 23–24.
54   Dave 2014, 14.
55   Lohman 2016, 42–43.

Leaders may hold power over their subjects, but indulging in domination might lead to their demise. As Barbalet suggests regarding the relationship between superordinate and subordinate, the health of a nation depends on how rulers respect their deeply held responsibility to subjects. A ruler, whether a monarch, governor, or congressperson, also must balance responsibility to the ideals that bind a nation. Nooshin posits that nations historically concerned with strict, highly upheld spiritual principles require an effective leader who will simultaneously balance the following things: assuaging the public's desire for expanded civil liberties, appealing to religious authorities, stymieing dissent, and (specifically in postcolonial contexts) maintaining sovereignty while encouraging investment and cultural acceptance from nations abroad.[56] For such a strenuous leader, allowing music will inevitably arouse people's most deeply held passions and threaten the stability of the superordinate. One way to mitigate or soften a social upheaval is to listen and respond to the public. As Mukasa Kafeero shared during my fieldwork, one of the Buganda kings discussed in this book, Ssuuna II (r. ca. 1824–1854), adored music and frequently engaged in court performance. As a result, he was often praised for maintaining an active, trusting period in the kingdom's history. Seeing musical performance as more than just entertainment, Ssuuna II would frequently join court performers during royal ceremonies to make music with them, playing his whistle as part of their performances. Unlike his father, Kamaanya (r. ca. 1794–1824), he experienced music as an active, reciprocal, and intimate process of exchange, in this case between the king and his subjects. His music-making modeled music's role at the court as a uniter, an adviser, and a voice for those who were deprived of one. Beyond the counsel of his court performers, Ssuuna II's own musicianship had an impact on his philosophy of leadership and, thus, his rule.[57]

Such subordinates and superordinates cultivate trust, they form a sense of loyalty and duty to one another (see part 4), which challenges the notion, as political realists would have it, that power relations are only agreed on begrudgingly or that they are based on a fundamental skepticism of the opposing actor's desire to upend the other. Pointing to the Armenian composer Aram Khachaturian as an example, who worked within the Stalinist state, Marina Frolova-Walker indicates that it can actually be a natural choice for an artist to maintain dual commitments to the strength of the state and the cultural expression of subjected people.[58] Although such duality can be understood as a balancing act between two actors opposed to each other,

---

56 Nooshin 2005, 238.
57 Kafeero interview, July 28, 2005.
58 Frolova-Walker 1998, 362.

Khachaturian succeeded in aligning with Stalin's state slogan, "National in form, Socialist in content," by appealing to its respective "diversifying . . . [and] unifying tendenc[ies]."[59]

Interpreting Court Song in Uganda discusses the court musicians' skillful wordplay and the way it played a substantial role in easing the anger of King Kamaanya. Beyond simply flattering him, the musicians used this skill to elicit a great deal of respect and trust from the king. In turn, it allowed them to change his decisions and guide his thinking without his giving their motives a second thought. Far more powerful than brute strength, the musicians were not just mere entertainers but guided the kingdom toward success.

Loyalty and duty (the theme of part 4)— toward a nation, one's parents, or one's ideals— necessitates a deeper understanding of the mutuality and cooperation that guide human survival and cultural well-being. As a representation of and a vehicle for enacting change in power relations, song-making embodies mutuality and cooperation. Leila Qashu directs our attention to how group performance can function as a legal process where community members band together to address and resolve personal transgressions.[60] Qashu cites the example of the female performer Arsi Oromo singing in Ethiopia. Whereas a court setting would encourage definitive statements that prove the innocence or guilt of the transgressor and determine a punishment, processes like these involve a resolution dynamic that can heal subtler wounds and help community members reconcile their wrongdoing. In this sense, law, order, and justice are based in mutuality and cooperation rather than severity and finality, and as a result individuals may feel a stronger loyalty to a social fabric that respects their personal sovereignty and that sees transgression as not just a personal infringement but as a group wound.

This project recognizes the possibility of enacting violence as a reaction to encroachments on personal sovereignty: violent uprisings have happened against ruling classes worldwide to reinstill or establish new power dynamics, just as governments have committed outsized violence against their civilians. Embedded in several of the songs examined in *Interpreting Court Song in Uganda* are details of a Kiganda cognizance of mortality, both in the contexts of violent war and of the natural cycle of life. In the case of political institutions, death can also describe the end of a political term, of a king's rule, or the dismantling of a political party (see chapter 23). Today, the Kiganda court institution that once allowed political discourse to thrive and tensions between communities to be resolved has allegedly been put to rest by the central government of Uganda. *Interpreting Court Song in Uganda* responds to this circumstance by operating as much like an oral

---

59 Ibid., 363.
60 Qashu 2019, 249.

tradition as like a theoretical examination of power: it resurfaces the spirit of mutuality between king and subject, which has historically been maintained through musical activity, and it seeks to revive this maligned yet ever-conscious social fabric. The song discussed in chapter 11 demonstrates the long-lasting effects of conflict and violence and reminds the listener to avoid them. Characterized by the universal themes of justice, responsibility, and permanent trauma, the song is relevant to a multitude of sociopolitical contexts, old and new.

History and Temporality

As suggested earlier, assembling this manuscript has required understanding the differences of the presented historical narratives. Steven Feld acknowledges that to construct a historical account, one must first recognize the discrepancies between public and private discourses.[61] At the same time one should also understand that one's decision to include or exclude historical information impacts how this history comes to life in the present.[62] In approaching the histories of the court songs examined here, *Interpreting Court Song in Uganda* remains conscientious of the divisive potential of examining and writing about history. The project conceives of Ugandan history not as an objective and detached scientific process but as an explicitly subjective, creative, and transformative one. In the same vein, drawing on the work of Michel Foucault, this work considers the notion that those who study history must recognize historians' internal biases and personal discontinuities not as deficiencies of the work in question but as extensions of its historical relevance, because they provide a snapshot into the societal norms and expectations of the time.[63] Discrepancies or contradictions should not be dismissed; instead, we should examine them as critical elements of a text's construction. In *Interpreting Court Song in Uganda*, this challenge is compounded by the project's focus on oral tradition, an inherently subjective domain, as well as oral transmission, which is an inherently subjective act and process.

This book further addresses Beverley Diamond's observation that historical studies have tended to present the views of the indigenous people they study as timeless and ahistorical.[64] Many anthropologists and ethnographers view native people as being outside history and linear time itself.

---

61 Feld 2012, 8.
62 Ibid.
63 Foucault 1977, 157.
64 Diamond 2013, 155.

This assumption serves to dehumanize indigenous populations by relegating them to a time outside of time and imagines them as primitive precursors to the "modernity" of the Western world.[65] In response to this colonial ideology, *Interpreting Court Song in Uganda* affirms the complex ways that different cultures conceptualize time and history and acknowledges that the structures employed to understand the past, present, and future may alternatively complement, contradict, or remain completely disjointed from one another. This notion guides *Interpreting Court Song in Uganda*'s treatment of the often-contradictory accounts of composer-performers of the songs featured throughout the following chapters. Kiganda conception of history is more like that of other indigenous cultures in that it does not follow the strict linear model prevalent in Western cultures. From the standpoint of Diamond's framework, history is not presented as a consistent series of factual events but as sequence of heterogeneous iterations born from a bricolage of collective and individual experience.

Interpreting Court Song in Uganda's structure also reckons with concepts of temporality, in particular the relationship between the political past, present, and future of Buganda and Uganda. Imagining time as a fluid and multidirectional phenomenon guides this work, especially when relating the historical background of court songs to present and future power dynamics. As mentioned previously, each song-based chapter begins with a composer-performer's narration of the historical background of the song it investigates. This text provides context for the reader to understand my lyrical analysis as well as non-performers' interpretations, which problematize the song's relevance to the present and the future. Putting historical narratives in dialogue with contemporary issues and discourses challenges notions of history as a static and unchanging record, instead conceptualizing it in terms of its living and dynamic interactions with the present and the future.

The song-based structure of the chapters in parts 2 to 6 follows a multilateral approach, which accepts the aforementioned subjectivities and contextual contingencies that are inherent in history. Daniel Reed's work suggests that multidirectional interpretation, unlike linear narrative structure, aligns with, rather than contradicts, narrative consistency by recognizing the entangled and sometimes contradictory forces from which stories develop.[66] This approach is appropriate because of the nature of the works that this project deals with, as many of them are simultaneously song lyrics, stories, interpretations, and sociopolitical ideologies. Throughout the book these domains interlock, much like parts of musical works or ensemble

---

65 Ibid., 156.
66 Reed 2016, 21–24.

sections, offering an integrated, dialogic narrative without which this book would feel incomplete.

Extending the foregoing discussion and building on John Campbell's work, one of this book's guiding principles for studying oral traditions is to consider *nonliteral* meanings and contexts.[67] Some of the literal meanings of these songs historically carry social taboos, which composer-performers were often reluctant to speak about during our interviews. As a result, nonliteral interpretations are useful to imply these hidden truths. Faustine Adima cites a similar challenge in his study of the Lugbara people of northern Uganda.[68] Indeed, inconsistencies in historical account can make it difficult to present a succinct narrative. Furthermore, these discrepancies implicate the process of historical analysis as an intellectually legitimate form of study. In the same way that an analysis of a piece of literature or a painting might involve a creative analysis that positively impacts the form of a work, history is often a collective guessing game that takes shape with each retelling. By exploring and revitalizing various historical accounts, *Interpreting Court Song in Uganda* does not simply present the past as a strictly definable point; instead, it imagines a living entity whose representation and meanings morph and fluctuate as time goes on.

---

67 Campbell 2006, 84.
68 Adima 2004, 8.

Part II

Songs about Political Engagement, Criticism, and Commentary

Kiganda court songs, as a product of the royal court, are inextricably linked to the world of politics, leadership, and decision-making. In part 2 we focus on themes of political engagement, criticism, and commentary found within five court songs, all of which reflect the efforts of musicians to shape the political decisions of their eras, either by influencing the king or by speaking directly to the masses. This process draws our attention to the power and influence of court musicians in the political domain, and it emphasizes the unique strategies they deploy to wield this influence. Each chapter highlights specific methods court music performers have used to engage with and alter the political landscape around them. The first two chapters highlight how court musicians have influenced their king through such strategies. Chapter 4 demonstrates the theme of false praise by looking at how the musicians of the quick-tempered King Ssuuna II (r. ca. 1824–1854) used the song "The Handsome Catch a Slight Squint" ("Empujjo Zikwata Balungi") to offer insincere compliments that appeased him. Chapter 5 discusses the musicians' use of flattery, deceit, and satire in the song "Fair-Skinned" ("Kabirinnage"), which cunningly celebrated Ssuuna II's physical appearance. This song reminds us that mockery can be disguised as flattery to fool leaders with inflated egos.

The other three songs use direct criticism to confront political subject matters and address leaders, thus serving as creative conduits to express the sentiments of the Baganda people. Chapter 6 underscores the themes of greed and selfishness, focusing on court musicians' use of the song "As He Plucked Them" ("Bwe Yazimaanya") to criticize and challenge King Kamaanya (r. ca. 1794–1824) for his cruel and unusual behavior. A unique feature of this song is its use of cultural imagery. Chapter 7 examines the themes of mourning and ridicule via the song "Householder" ("Nnannyinimu"), which, after the death of King Ssuuna II, his musicians employed to criticize and celebrate the king's flawed but omnipotent rule and to express the somber emotions of his subjects. Chapter 8 focuses on the themes of manipulation, exploitation, and reciprocity in the song "Federalism" ("Federo"), which protests the Ugandan national government, accusing it of making bureaucratic decisions that have led to the unjust suffering of its people in the twenty-first century. These three songs take a more confrontational stance than the first two, demonstrating how criticism can be just as effective as praise in the realm of political action. The three songs embody lyrical criticism of governmental authority in a myriad of social and historical contexts. In a way, court musicians act as intermediaries between the king and his people, constantly balancing and stimulating this mutual two-way flow while simultaneously remaining a sovereign figure. As members of the royal court, not only are the musicians close to the king and his duties but they also exert their own form of authority by association. Between false praise and direct criticism, the five songs featured in part 2 illustrate that diverging performance methods influence social change, for better or for worse.

All five exemplify the power held by musicians in the royal court and, in a more universal sense, the power of music, art, and performance in the political domain. Yet the true power of these songs lies in their ability to be reimagined by multiple interpreters, who derive distinct meanings from each verse, lyric, and word. Some take a more traditional route in their interpretations, exploring the historical accounts and lived experiences of Baganda to understand the lyrics. Others find meaning through comparisons with the contemporary world, as the content of the songs under examination are equally applicable in the context of twenty-first-century political leaders and the interactions they have with the public.

4

"The Handsome Catch a Slight Squint"

False Praise

Originally composed for King Ssuuna II (r. ca. 1824–1854), the song "The Handsome Catch a Slight Squint" ("Empujjo Zikwata Balungi") illustrates false praise, a strategy through which his court musicians changed their political circumstances. The musicians used the song to assuage the vanity of the king, as its lyrics deceitfully praised Ssuuna II's handsomeness. Before performing his rendering of "The Handsome Catch a Slight Squint," Mukasa Kafeero (b. 1971) narrated its historical context as follows:

> Ssuuna II, having inherited his father Kamaanya's quick temper, enacted several wars; however, Ssuuna II was more successful than Kamaanya in achieving peace. He was also prone to rage that occasionally led him to enact violence, usually execution, against those who displeased him. Many of his subjects knew him as a man of festivities who took it upon himself to always celebrate with his people. Ssuuna II himself was a musician, and many believed that his support of court music might have been the strongest out of any of the kings of Buganda, evident from his active participation in certain performances; in fact, the only quality that appears to have rivaled the king's anger was his love of music. His reign witnessed great innovations in musical practice.
>
> From childhood, Ssuuna II loved performing music and was rather good at playing the Kiganda notched flute (*endere*). He played constantly, sometimes to the annoyance of his elders. They would chide him for ceaselessly playing the flute, commenting that one day it would disappear. Ignoring their admonishments, he named his flute Lumoonyere (Ceaseless). The name caught on, and soon people began calling anyone who was acting incessantly Lumoonyere, after the king's flute. Whenever young Ssuuna II's elders attempted to take and hide his flute, he would

simply whistle instead. His whistling was as incessant as his flute-playing, and he imitated its sounds well.

It was impossible to tell by sound alone whether Ssuuna II was playing the flute or just whistling, as such was the extent of his skill. After becoming king, however, it was no longer acceptable for Ssuuna II to play about with his instruments as he had done before. Instead, he now had court musicians who would play for his enjoyment. He never allowed anyone to whistle in his vicinity, as he considered whistling a marker of his childhood and perceived those who whistled in his presence to be mocking his former childlike behavior. Ssuuna II himself, however, continued to whistle. He became popular for adding his own improvisations to whatever drumbeats or musical parts performers would play at his court. The Baganda came to refer to this whistle as the giver (*oluwa*) because Ssuuna II, whenever he was enjoying music or organizing performances among his people, would use his whistle to give the players keys of songs; often, Ssuuna's whistle would initiate the tune.

During Ssuuna II's reign, around 1844, the first Arabs, led by a man named Ahmed Bin Ibrahim, came to Buganda. When they first arrived at his court, they presented Ssuuna II with many gifts, one of which was a woven tunic (*ekkanzu*). Because of this, some Baganda believe that Ssuuna II was the first Muganda to wear a cloth garment. To help him admire himself in his new attire, the Arabs also brought with them a mirror. Having never used a mirror before, Ssuuna II was startled to discover that he had a squint, or a lazy eye. For all his years, his subjects had often praised him for being handsome, and yet he did not understand how a lazy eye could possibly be deemed so. Angry that his court singers had lied to him, he called them to assemble before him immediately. He asked why they had mocked him and been sarcastic, flattering his vanity when in fact he had a squint. He ruled that Kkunsa, his rather infamous royal bodyguard (*omumbowa*) and prosecutor, should execute them for their insolence.

As he led the musicians away from Ssuuna II, Kkunsa pulled out his sword, eager to begin carrying out the sentence. But first, he ordered one of the musicians he was taunting to explain himself to the king. The man explained to Ssuuna II that what he had noticed in his eyes was not a squint. He added that the king was not cross-eyed and that the ugly, the lowly, or the common folk would never have what he had; rather, only the handsome and members of the royal family would catch Ssuuna II's particular feature. The man further explained that the feature distinguished the handsome royal from the masses, marking him as uncommonly handsome. This performer's words pleased the king greatly and eased his anger. As a result, he forgave the ensemble for their apparent transgressions. In the jubilation of having been able to save themselves from a terrible fate, the performers organized themselves at once and quickly composed a song. Accompanying themselves with the bow lyre, flute, and every other instrument they could muster, they began to sing, *Empujjo zikwata balungi* (The handsome catch a slight squint).[1]

Although monarchical leadership may seem to be an individualistic pursuit, the foregoing story shows that the Baganda people found successful leadership on the mutual rule of the king and his numerous aides. The relationship between Ssuuna II, the prosecutor Kkunsa, and the court musicians exemplifies this arrangement. Whereas Kkunsa seems to reflect the anger and rage of the king, the musicians represent the leader's more celebratory and forgiving attitudes. These aides serve as extensions of the king, revealing that leadership cannot be contained within a single body. In this sense, to lead is to become inundated in a series of relations that are inextricable from each other. This is especially true when considering how Ssuuna II's musicians respond to his anger. Rather than simply turning on each other and accepting death, they pursue a resolution that they think will satisfy the interests of the kingdom and themselves equally. To them, supporting the kingdom and themselves means supporting the office and duties of the king.

Ssuuna II's love of whistling demonstrates the extension of the king's engagement with music beyond pleasure, embodying an active, reciprocal, and intimate process of exchange. Additionally, it facilitates his participation in the performances of his court musicians, thus activating social fabric through which the king entwines himself with them. By engaging creatively with the process of producing song, the king is also taking part in conversing with the musicians, involving himself in the story-making process. Overall, Ssuuna II's musicality plays a profound role in his success as a leader.

Given the parallels between his and his father's temperaments, Ssuuna II's willingness to embrace the wisdom of the court musicians guides him to success. Beyond assisting court performers, his own musicianship has an impact on his philosophy and, thus, his rule. In addition, the musicians' skill with language plays a substantial role in easing the king's anger. Beyond being a useful tool for flattery, their skill garners them a great deal of respect and trust from the king. This allows them to change his decisions and guide his thinking without his giving their motives a second thought. Providing more than entertainment in the court, the performers and their songs influence the king's decisions, and thus all the kingdom's politics.

Kafeero's performance of "The Handsome Catch a Slight Squint" is very brief, featuring the line from which the song takes its title, which he performs without instrumental accompaniment. Lacking a clear melodic or rhythmic pattern, the performance seems to emphasize the song's text.

---

1   Kafeero interview, July 28, 2005.

The brief lyrics of "The Handsome Catch a Slight Squint" illustrate how musicians might manage a leader's temperament, influence his decisions during crises, and guide him to greater success. In doing so, the text creates a multiplicity of meanings, as leadership becomes a matter of cooperation and manipulation, influenced by the relative vanity or humility of leaders.

False Praise

Focusing on the theme of false praise, different interpreters dive into the lyrics of "The Handsome Catch a Slight Squint," commenting on how leaders may respond to the hypnotic adulations of people who try to appeal to them or to please their ears. In Jessy Ssendawula's discussion of the various principles of successful leadership, he hints at the intrinsically cooperative nature of King Ssuuna II's role. He explains how the cooperation was bimodal, as its success resulted from satisfying both the king and his musicians. It also allowed for various strategies to evade violence (creative manipulation of the king's insecurity, in this case). According to Ssendawula, lying is a legitimate political possibility, especially if it happens out of empathy for the greater populace:

> The song reassured and restored the lost pride of King Ssuuna II. In return, it saved the musicians from facing death at the hands of Kkunsa, the draconian captain of the guard. Thus, it achieved a multileveled victory: saving the lives of the musicians while soothing the king's insecurity and frustration. The song also cautions leaders against making decisions in anger. Leaders should focus on why their subjects behave the way they do and why they might put themselves at the mercy of their leaders. More generally, the song expresses a need for greater empathy and sympathy among the masses in that one of Ssuuna II's musicians lied to him to save the others. The song teaches us that a lie with good intentions is better than a truth that brings disaster. Soothsayers can praise authoritarian leaders, as long as the praises soothe those leaders and therefore help protect the masses.[2]

The king's extreme responses to the musicians' performances that Ssendawula highlights imply that a song can have a profound impact on every part of life in the Kingdom of Buganda. Ssuuna II never deemed the singers' words meaningless or ignored them entirely, but that he would execute his musicians for such an infraction demonstrates the immense power that the musicians held in political relationships. Court musicians were dangerous enough to be worth executing, especially if those in power believed that they were using their skill with ill intentions. This degree of musical importance extends into the present day, as Imani Sanga shows, with some

---

2 Ssendawula interview, December 28, 2019.

leaders recognizing that developing a coherent national identity depends on those who create music and the arts.[3] In this way musicians are more than entertainers, for their songs and performances also shape the laws, politics, culture, and social life of Buganda. Steven Mukasa Kabugo elaborates:

> Singers can make anybody feel beautiful, regardless of how flawed their appearance may be. Indeed, listening to their songs may make others feel as if it is impossible for ugliness to exist in the world. They can make any listener feel accepted and loved by other people. It is an unspoken rule that musicians rarely criticize a person's appearance during their songs. A more official rule is that performers who sing about taboo topics receive punishment. In fact, sometimes those singers are putting their lives at risk because the leaders consider certain subjects treasonous. Seeing their colleague in trouble, the court performers of Ssuuna II once sang, *Omusango gw'abalere gwegaludde, bantwale e Bbira gye banzaala* (The flutists' legal case has resurfaced, they should take me to Bbira, my birthplace).[4] Again, if a performer sang something against the king and the latter found out, the court soldiers would execute him for disrespecting the king.[5]

Here, Kabugo underscores that there are some subtler rules that court musicians and singers must follow. For example, their music must highlight the beauty of their leaders.

As John Magandaazi Kityo further highlights, musicians' voices can shape the self-perception of listeners and empower them. They have the capacity to reverse values, to make the ugly beautiful for the duration of the song "The Handsome Catch a Slight Squint," just as in other songs they bring dead characters back to life or make old practices new. In this way musicians can break down calcified binaries and restructure the way we think about the world.

> "The Handsome Catch a Slight Squint" encourages us to never lose sight of our self-worth. It allows people who are struggling to rebuild their self-esteem and be happy with their looks in the same way it made Ssuuna II's deformity appear handsome.[6]

In this sense, the court performers exaggerated Ssuuna II's beauty not with ill intent but with a desire to appease his lack of self-confidence, which was the emotional complex that drove him to make a rash decision in the first place. In this case, Ssuuna II was able to reclaim control over his almightiness, thus his role as superordinate, which allowed the cooperative fabric of the kingdom to continue.

---

3   Sanga 2008, 55.
4   See chapter 13 for additional details about this lyric and its themes.
5   Kabugo interview, December 19, 2019.
6   Kityo interview, December 14, 2019.

Whereas some earlier views have focused on the way music mediates between court musicians and the king, Jimmy Ssenfuka Kibirige interrogates how the king could have responded to the musicians' performance differently. This variation suggests that when leaders accept their shortcomings, they might gain public support rather than come off as weak or unauthoritative. This way of thinking would acknowledge that imperfection is ubiquitous and that a social contract between king and subject that allows for mistakes and misunderstandings could build a deeper sense of trust between political institutions and its participants. Although King Ssuuna II had a background in music and presumably appreciated and respected his musicians, his ego still caused him to act rashly. This personal limitation demonstrates that good leaders should not necessarily avoid complications but respond to them appropriately. Ssuuna II's court musicians successfully avoided the death sentence because they could respond quickly and suitably when a lapse in trust occurred. Kibirige stresses that leaders must emulate this ability:

> It can be difficult for leaders to accept satire, particularly when their subjects direct it at them. In recent times, a Russian government official visited Uganda. During his stay, he attended a theater production of *The Government Inspector*. The plot of the production revolved around the ineptitude and immorality of a small Russian village, which the Inspector General was due to inspect. The village devolved into a panicked mess as its inhabitants tried to cover up what they had done wrong. The Russian official, the chief guest at this performance, surprisingly enjoyed himself immensely, laughing loudly from the audience, despite the play's subject matter. Like this official, leaders should be tolerant or even enjoy satire directed at them in good faith. Ssuuna II, after receiving gifts from the Arab traders, looking into the mirror, and realizing that he was cross-eyed, could have laughed and accepted that the songs his musicians had composed earlier were jokes.[7]

When a leader has humility, it means that their ego is flexible—that it can bend without breaking. This is what leaders expect of their societies, that they will not crumble in the face of adversity. In turn, they ought to commit themselves to this very principle.

Extending his interpretation of "The Handsome Catch a Slight Squint" to a more contemporary setting, Kibirige relates to the ways in which today's leaders tend to pursue compliments and other forms of ego support. This dynamic speaks to the importance of thinking critically about the actions of one's peers before accepting them as genuine. In this way, "The Handsome Catch a Slight Squint" not only calls for manipulating language as a tactical strategy to assuage leadership but also speaks to the importance of mediating these relationships. In the same way that subjects (musicians) should avoid blindly following a leader,

---

7 Kibirige interview, December 18, 2019.

a leader should avoid blindly trusting them. A leader and subjects should challenge each other in a reciprocal way, allowing for their network of competing interests to create an informed perspective on a given situation:

> Most of today's leaders only want to hear praise such as, "Long live our man!" Their efforts to gain cheap popularity are in no way beneficial. By lowering the cost, they will have to pay it back somewhere else. In other words, it will cause them to suffer in another area. To successfully direct the country socially, politically, and economically, they need to be wise and avoid being easily swayed by others. However, this does not mean they should not listen to their subjects. On the contrary, listening to the people is one of the most valuable skills that leaders should have. Knowing when to pardon someone for what they have done, as Ssuuna II pardoned his musicians for writing songs about his faults, is critical for good leadership.[8]

Listening, as Kibirige states, is the key component missing in contemporary leadership. When leaders seek compliments that satisfy only themselves, they ignore the dynamics happening to their subjects. For instance, those who fill their courts, or cabinets, with yes-men will have no idea that people are plotting overthrows underneath their noses. If they do not listen, which Ssuuna II fortunately did, then they will be lied to not by their caring servants but by the deceitful subjects who pretend to be.

As Kibirige further suggests, leadership should be a mutual pursuit between leaders and their people. Leaders who think only for themselves miss an important principle of effective leadership, which is to wield themselves and their subjects as extensions of each other. They should recognize that as leaders they are no more than extensions of the will of the people they lead. The leaders are the groups they lead—they succeed as those groups succeed and feel joy as they feel joy:

> Contemporary leaders lack the insight to determine other's intentions and significance. They focus on their own gains and are willing to treat their subjects poorly, even though these subjects brought the leader to power. You brought him to glory, but in return he pushes you to the grass; he does not recognize your value. Most leaders believe themselves to be good, competent public figures, when in reality they are selling off the societies they serve. They have yet to realize that the value of a leader is not embedded in the quality of their appearance but in the quality of their service. Through good service, they themselves can also benefit because the people will reciprocate with effort and praise. If they deliver on their promises and lead uprightly, then all the praise they receive will be genuine.[9]

---

8   Ibid.
9   Kibirige interview, December 15, 2019.

Kibirige's interpretation highlights several qualities useful to modern leaders that Ssuuna II appears never to have possessed—namely, the humility to accept criticism, personal faults, and the limitation of one's own knowledge.

Whereas other interpreters have spoken about the importance of mutual assistance in the success of a leader, Kibirige's interpretation also speaks to the ways in which such assistance could result in manipulation and failure. This is a valuable addition to creating a nuanced understanding of the lyrics of "The Handsome Catch a Slight Squint":

> Even though some leaders might be competent at what they do, there will always be people who work for them solely for the purpose of gaining personal benefits. They try to manipulate the leaders' decisions to garner the best for themselves. They convince them that policies that benefit them personally are also the best for everyone else, using praise and a variety of other psychological tactics to achieve this goal. Among contemporary politicians, Bobi Wine seems to be suffering from this same problem. His supporters give him undue praise and overstate his caliber. It is unlikely that he will win the 2021 election. His bid for presidency has come up too early in his political career, which those around him unduly manipulate. He should have remained in his position in parliament instead. The likelihood of him winning is incredibly small because he is going up against President Museveni, who has spent thirty years figuring out how to stay in power. The odds are stacked against Bobi Wine as he is a political newcomer, raised in the ghetto, with a musical career that some use to discredit his competence as a "serious" politician. Furthermore, the incumbent regime will do anything to maintain its power. Those who oppose Museveni as an absolute ruler for life will die. There are many forces working against Bobi Wine, and it is unwise for him to think he can enact instantaneous change just because the public tells him he can.[10]

Kibirige is certain that "The Handsome Catch a Slight Squint" revolves around manipulation and ulterior motives, highlighting its connections to the situation of opposition leader, Bobi Wine, President Museveni's main political competitor. As the interpreter points out, we ought to be reasonable in estimating how much power the president holds, especially over his own aides and the masses, who dare not dissent against him.

Conclusion

Ssuuna II's court musicians originally created "The Handsome Catch a Slight Squint" as a form of clever flattery for political advantage. By

---

10   Kibirige interview, December 19, 2019.

composing lyrics that dishonestly praise the king's appearance, these musicians sought to improve their standing through strategic false admiration. The song has a rich potential of interpretability. First, within the specific time and place of its composition, the song would have been interpreted differently by the separate parties involved. For the musicians, the song was an expression of joy and relief, as well as a plea for forgiveness and mercy; for the executioner, the song was most likely another transparent lie, like the empty praises the musicians had earlier sung; for the king, the song was an affirmation of respect and approval from his subjects.

As we have seen in the preceding paragraphs, twenty-first-century Ugandans interpret "The Handsome Catch a Slight Squint" in multiple other ways, locating universal themes that have relevance in the political present as they were in the nineteenth century. Their seemingly at-odds interpretations amplify one another in facilitating a rich political dialogue. My research collaborators and I encourage such healthy political debate throughout this book, the former including people along different nodes of power relations who make measured decisions for themselves and those around them. If not for these multiple contrasting perspectives, we might miss the many intricacies that envelope political and social relations in favor of a singular, superficial narrative.

5

"Fair-Skinned"

Flattery, Deceit, and Satire

As we have already seen, music could quell the temper of King Ssuuna II (r. ca. 1824–1854), soothe his insecurities, and influence him to reconsider his decisions, and like "The Handsome Catch a Slight Squint," the song "Fair-Skinned" ("Kabirinnage") manipulated King Ssuuna II through flattery. Mukasa Kafeero (b. 1971), the performer of the song's version analyzed in this chapter, explained,

> Similar to "The Handsome Catch a Slight Squint," "Fair-Skinned" served to manipulate King Ssuuna II through flattery. The song built on the qualities of the king, mainly his vanity and physical imperfections, and its composers sang in mocking praise of the leader. They intended for the song's lyrics to flatter him and increase his self-confidence despite his personal impediments. In turn, the tongue-in-cheek composition served to amuse the harsh king and make him reconsider his decisions. Whereas Ssuuna II's father, Kamaanya, disliked music, and thus refused the benefits it could provide, Ssuuna II loved music and thus aimed to reap as much from it as he could.
>
> In addition to being cross-eyed, he also had short stature. Whenever Ssuuna II looked at men who were taller than him, he suspected that they despised him because he was short. However, his musicians reassured him that his height was not a disease; rather, it was his handsomeness that had hindered his height. They told Ssuuna II that his creator had spent extra knowledge and wisdom making him handsome and that being taller would fall beyond the creator's plan, potentially ruining his handsomeness. So they composed and performed a song titled "Fair-Skinned" to convey their admiration of his shortness. Mixing different idioms or variations (*ebisoko*), they averred that he would have grown tall, but his handsomeness had impeded him from doing so. Whenever the king heard the song, he would undo whatever poor decisions he had made. Excited and thankful for "Fair-Skinned," he would even instruct his officials to

serve the performers food so they could eat their fill. Ssuuna II's musicians sang these words: *Kabirinnage obulungi bwamulobera okuwanvuwa, Kabirinnage* (Fair-Skinned's handsomeness prevented him from growing tall, Fair-Skinned); *Kabirinnage omulungi gwe njagala* (Fair-Skinned, the handsome I love).[1]

Kings Kamaanya and Ssuuna II held music in different types of regard. The result of this difference between the two kings was not simply audible, as the presence of music in Ssuuna II's court also accompanied a philosophy of musicality that benefited the overall quality of his rule. It is as though the presence of song itself shaped Ssuuna II's relationship to the court, his kingdom, and the world. As we have seen, music could control his temper, calm his insecurities, and affect his decisions. The impact of his court musicians, ensembles, and their songs was profound.

Kafeero's performance of his version of "Fair-Skinned" is very brief, featuring his singing two alternating, cheerful phrases in low and high tonal ranges, respectively:

1 *Kabirinnage obulungi bwamulobera okuwanvuwa, Kabirinnage*
Fair-Skinned's handsomeness prevented him from growing tall, Fair-Skinned

2 *Kabirinnage omulungi gwe njagala*
Fair-Skinned, the handsome I love

These vocal lines carry a bouncy rhythmic quality that would allow for drum accompaniment. Kafeero notes that in the context of ensemble performances, singers often perform the phrases in a repetitious, call-and-response style.

On the one hand, King Ssuuna II interprets the lyrics of "Fair-Skinned" as a form of flattery. He takes his musicians' playful words to be genuine compliments, and his mood is lifted as a result. The words flip his understanding of their context, as they convince him that his stunted height is not a negative trait, a sign of weakness or disability, but a positive one, a sign of great handsomeness (line 1). On the other hand, the satirical tilt of the song reveals to other listeners that the musicians are in truth making fun of the king rather than complimenting him. This aspect, coupled with the king's own gullible response, allows the musicians to express a nuanced criticism of the leader's vanity, as they show that his shortcomings are both trivial, implied by the jovial tone of the song, and invisible to him. It is crucial here to recognize that the sarcastic interpretation is not the correct or better understanding of the song. Both the sarcastic and genuine interpretations are only possible through the other, and it is only when both interpretations are imagined simultaneously that the impact of the song comes to fruition.

---

1   Kafeero interview, July 28, 2005.

Flattery, Deceit, and Satire

A number of interpreters connect the lyrics of "Fair-Skinned" to current political and personal contexts via the themes of flattery, deceit, and satire. Their comments reshape how we might relate the past and the present more broadly. Harriet Kisuule's interpretation of "Fair-Skinned," focusing on flattery, emphasizes the importance of maintaining a sturdy sense of self that can endure the opinions and criticism of others:

> The song and its initial context demonstrate that when people blindly believe in what others tell them about themselves, it can often cause problems. People should take flattery with a grain of salt. If someone claims that another person is particularly good in a certain area, it benefits the latter to personally reflect on whether they possess the qualities mentioned before they accept the praise.[2]

Kisuule illuminates how vanity and its associated problems imply notions of ignorance and wisdom. She reminds us to only cautiously accept the words of others with caution and encourages us, instead, to recognize those qualities for ourselves.

Kisuule explores this point even further by applying this individual praxis to leadership in a macropolitical context:

> Is it true what they say about me? Know who you are and do not accept being misled by others. Accept who you are, the way you were created, so that you can better understand and overcome any challenges set before you. One time, President Museveni blocked the current King Mutebi II's tour of Kayunga district. Because of the widespread support for the king, it is likely that he could have secured some form of access to the area anyway, but he accepted the amount of control Museveni had over the situation and decided to back down for the sake of peace. He also considered the number of lives that would have been lost because of the tension between the Buganda and central governments. Like the king, Ugandan leaders should know their limits and responsibilities.[3]

This commentary bridges the gap between the micropolitical and the macropolitical and connects the past with the present. In the first case, Kisuule shows us how personal decision-making connects to politics at large by exploring how one's aversion to flattery manifests itself in national events, as with King Mutebi II's hesitancy to tour Kayunga. This demonstrates how the capacity of leaders to make measured, patient decisions will allow them

---

2 Kisuule interview, December 21, 2019.
3 Ibid.

to respond better to crises of leadership. Remaining clear-sighted in one's personal life will ensure they do so on a larger stage as well.

Steven Mukasa Kabugo relates "Fair-Skinned" to more intimate atmospheres, focusing on the impact of flattery and deceit on the lives of common people. According to him,

> Musicians have often used the lyric "Fair-Skinned's handsomeness prevented him from growing tall, Fair-Skinned" to soothe the nervousness of uncommonly short brides in Buganda and help build up their self-esteem before the wedding. Wedding performers couple this lyric with a variety of proverbs or sayings that appeal to the self-conscious women in order to reassure them that they hold value in the eyes of men and society in general. Such sayings include *Ssekaswa akampi kaava enswa empanvu* (The short white ant produced tall ones), *Omubi akira ebbanga* (An ugly person is better than none), and *Omumpi takaddiwa; takootakoota* (A short person does not grow old; she does not stoop). The general message of these sayings is that a woman should not fear being disrespected due to any faults in her appearance, whether being short, ugly, or cross-eyed, as was the case with King Ssuuna II. She should remember that society judges women on their ability to be good wives and mothers and generally believes that women who possess physical faults tend to be better spouses.[4]

Whereas the previous analysis of "Fair-Skinned" connects the micro- and macropolitical realms, Kabugo's interpretation of its use in a wedding context suggests that songs can be applied to realms outside the court setting. In this case, the song's use in the wedding is itself a moment of reinterpretation. Wedding performers provide brides-to-be with the idea that their physical appearances matter less as long as they are good mothers and wives. This framing flips the meaning of the song away from physical appearance entirely. Just as the previous commentaries have focused on flattery in terms of service as a leader, Kabugo's commentary focuses on the importance of service as a mother. In this way, "Fair-Skinned" undergoes a layered process of reading to serve the needs of those who seek to embrace it.

Jimmy Ssenfuka Kibirige's commentary takes a different tack, speaking to the ways people tune (as with instruments) the qualities and insecurities of their leaders to ensure the best experience for all.

> Flattery and deceit were two major problems in precolonial Buganda. Part of the reason they were so rampant was the linear inheritance of the crown. It was impossible for all the kings in line to be perfectly fit for leadership, meaning that they would often fall for flattery to ease their own insecurities about their rule. In Ssuuna II's case, his insecurities were about his appearance, though of course there is no correlation between

---

4 Kabugo interview, December 19, 2019.

appearance and leadership ability. He was more focused on his appearance than he was on being a good leader. So at the end of the day, the musicians lied to him and told him that it was his beautiful skin that had made him shorter. They simply told him what they believed he wanted to hear. But no leader can be perfect. Between charisma, looks, and the ability to effectively serve, there is always at least one area where a leader is lacking.[5]

Kibirige shows how assuaging Ssuuna II was like "re-tuning" him so that he could shift his focus to maintaining Buganda's prosperity. This point reminds us of the song "The Handsome Catch a Slight Squint" (discussed in the previous chapter), reviving the notion that leaders are always imperfect, so others must support them if they are to succeed. Again, Ssuuna II's musicians knew that calming his insecurities would help him focus on leading. This constant pursuit to overcome our fixations and pursue mutuality continues to be crucial to leadership today, as we still wrestle with our fantasies of individual perfection and self-sufficiency. Kibirige's interpretation allows us to understand how we might interpret the content of the musicians' song as well-intentioned, because they prioritize the welfare of the kingdom by extinguishing the king's emotional blockage.

Kibirige further produces an alternative to his previous thoughts, illustrating the ways in which musicians reapply these actions to satisfy themselves. Drawing parallels between the song "Fair-Skinned" and the Ugandan politician Full Figure, he explains how Full Figure used flattery to gain power for herself while allegedly feeding President Museveni's ego:

> Those who are close to President Museveni and eat off his proverbial plate lack the ability to serve effectively as civil servants because they only do what Museveni tells them to. More than this, they switch sides to whoever suits their needs the most. For example, the politician Full Figure, who originally worked for the People Power Movement campaign, quickly changed her tune and began working for Museveni instead. She even stole the movement's titular slogan, "People Power," and reclaimed it as a part of Museveni's image due to his time as a guerrilla liberator in the bush (the Ugandan Bush War). Her desire for more personal gain purely drove her decision to change sides. Museveni has now become her "fair-skinned" and indeed is in much the same situation as Ssuuna II. Both are too focused on themselves and not on their country. Museveni expects great praise for meeting the bare minimum requirements for his job, such as constructing roads or ensuring that all Ugandans have healthcare access. He is comparable to parents who refuse to pay for their children's schooling despite its being their responsibility to provide for them. It would be ridiculous to assume that it is the children's responsibility to find money to pay their tuition.

---

5   Kibirige interview, December 19, 2019.

Moreover, the fact that parents are paying for their children's school does not give them the right to treat them poorly or make them toil for the school dues. In other words, power and responsibility should not be a free check for oppression and extortion.[6]

Kibirige's view here does not contradict his previous one. Instead, it functions as an embodiment of the song's own message. It demonstrates two perspectives that conflict but serve as amplifications of each other: they could not have the same impact if their counterpart did not exist. Kibirige's analysis cannot be as nuanced and valuable as it stands if it is deprived of one of these views, as without one or the other, he would have a merely one-sided conception of the song. As suggested in the previous part of the book, differences and contradictions in history and interpretations of history, though appearing troublesome on the surface, present an important opportunity for further learning. For instance, Kibirige's multiple perspectives on "Fair-Skinned" are as much an indicator of his own wariness of the current national leadership in Uganda as it is a commentary on Ssuuna II.

As noted in chapter 1, Michel Foucault has written that those who study history must recognize that there is inherent value within a historian's personal biases and the discontinuities that may arise from them because they can provide insight into societal norms and expectations of the time.[7] In other words, the past shapes the present by setting the limits, preexisting conditions, and general possibilities for present action. However, Sarah Politz reminds us that the present can also distort the past by selecting from public memory the details that align best with the current regime of knowledge.[8] This process is evident in Kibirige's elaboration on how some current leaders are similar to Ssuuna II. As he demonstrates, flattery, deceit, and manipulation are all barriers standing in the way of those leaders' fully accepting their imperfections.

In his interpretation of "Fair-Skinned," Jessy Ssendawula expands on Kibirige's thoughts about deceit within the song by providing a modern example of a satirical song that performers have used to express the failings of President Museveni. He sings,

> "Dear Museveni, we are happy to receive you here in Gulu.
> The education is poor, communication is poor.
> There are no more virgins in Gulu.
> They were all raped by Kony.
> But all the same we are happy."[9]

---

6   Ibid.
7   Foucault 1977, 157.
8   Politz 2018, 30.
9   Ssendawula interview, December 28, 2019.

The composer of these lyrics employs tactics similar to those featured in "Fair-Skinned" to address the recent civil war in northern Uganda (Kony was the leader of the Lord's Resistance Army rebels). Moreover, other examples of contemporary Ugandan popular songs that Ssendawula provides further reveal how the methods of the past have come to life in the present, mirroring the approach of "Fair-Skinned":

> Such bitter satires bring to light the challenges of the community, just like popular music artist Ronald Mayinja's song "They [the issues that took you to the bush to fight] Are Repeating Themselves" ("Bizzeemu") and the popular music artist Eddy Kenzo's song "I Am Fed Up with Them" ("Mbakooye"). While "Fair-Skinned" used false praise to critique the king with sarcasm, these songs directly criticize the government. The composers and performers of "Fair-Skinned" designed the song to encourage the king to reward them. In this aspect, it is similar to the joint popular music artist song "We Stand with You" ("Tubonga Naawe"), which praised President Museveni during the 2015 presidential campaigns. Some of the musicians featured in the song were not in support of Museveni but wanted to flatter him into paying them. It is important for leaders to pay attention to the voices of musicians and learn to reflect on the tone behind their singing. If they misjudge the tone, they may miss learning about the problems afflicting society or their own personal weaknesses. Instead of fighting Bobi Wine and other popular music artists, Ugandan leaders could study the messages in their songs: "The Amount of Sugar Is Just Right" ("Kassukaali Ke Ko"), "Officer, I Do Not Fight with You" ("Afande Sirwana Naawe"), "Get Up" ("Situka"), "Freedom" ("Ddembe"), "Hand Him Over to Kyagulanyi" ("Mukwase Kyagulanyi"), and "We Shall Wear the Crown" ("Tuliyambala Engule"), all by Bobi Wine.[10]

Ssendawula explains how songs like these serve a dual purpose, bringing to light the problems of the community while also encouraging the leader to reward the musicians for their criticism disguised as praise. In his commentary we see how we cannot make sense of meaning through a single narrative. Instead, we must imagine it in terms of a fabric of competing narratives that intersect to create a dense, sometimes contradictory, web of shifting meanings.

Peter Kinene's interpretation of "Fair-Skinned" elaborates on the negative consequences of trusting the flattery of others in the modern age. While evoking some of Kibirige's thoughts about being wary of flattery, he also explores the dual meanings that such praise could hold:

> Folks should be wary of people who constantly try to flatter them, as it is those people who are most likely to cause them problems. They may

---

10 Ibid.

offer undue or insincere praise, causing the people they praise to believe that they are something they are not. They may build someone up only to watch them fall and delight in their failure, such as the men who attempted to assassinate King Kayemba (ca. 1690–1704) with a clay boat.[11] Therefore, it is best for people to be prudent and remain cautious of those who flatter them extensively. Even if such people are not trying to cause those they praise to fail, at the very least they are likely only looking out for the personal gains they can get from their actions. They praise people hoping that they will reward them without considering any of the consequences. Moreover, people do not always act in a way that reflects how they feel, especially when it comes to happiness. Those who are quick to laugh and praise others are not necessarily in agreement with them; they could easily be acting sarcastically or ironically. It is therefore important to question the motivations behind their actions to determine if they are genuine or not. People can smile at the faces of those they praise while planning their downfall in the same breath.[12]

According to Kinene, these dual meanings are not necessarily dishonest, but they could be misleading if one does not consider them thoughtfully. On this point he emphasizes the importance of recognizing subtlety in expressions, such as satire. That is, he provides a more meta-level perspective on the song that reveals how language and meaning often exceed linear understanding. He shows us that the sarcasm and irony hidden in a statement are not just *the* meaning of that statement but are *a* meaning, constituting no more than a piece of the multitudinous possibilities that we have yet to create.

Conclusion

The lyrics of "Fair-Skinned" demonstrate how Ssuuna II's musicians used satire to communicate multiple meanings in different ways, which allowed them to express themselves fully and with finesse while avoiding the consequences of their statements. The text and historical significance of "Fair-Skinned" make it a familiar and widely applicable expression of the complexities of interpersonal relations and the asymmetries of power, many interpretations of which contemporary commentators explore. The song has such longevity because it remains relevant to modern scenarios. Its brevity, memorable lyrics, and catchy melody underscore the way it can be repurposed as a form of

---

11 For the clay boat reference, see the song "Unadvisable Kayemba," discussed in chapter 9.
12 Kinene interview, December 16, 2019.

sociocultural expression in several contexts. In political settings the song can appeal to powerful leaders, but simultaneously mock them through the style of performance. In personal settings, it can serve as a comedic in-joke for singers and their audience. The fact that "Fair-Skinned" can be interpreted in different ways as either sarcastic or genuine makes it a useful sociopolitical device, and ultimately it acts as both criticism and flattery. Although its various understandings may seem contradictory at first, it is crucial to recognize that no single one is wrong. In this sense, one comes to evaluate interpretation based on its applicability rather than its "correctness."

6

"As He Plucked Them"

Greed and Selfishness

The song "As He Plucked Them" ("Bwe Yazimaanya") is an example of a technique different from false praise, which the court musicians of King Kamaanya (r. ca. 1794–1824), the father of King Ssuuna II, used to shape their political landscapes. Although these musicians seem to have composed the song in the confines of the court, it is likely that they did not intend to sing it to the king. Following his performance of the song, Mukasa Kafeero (b. 1971) narrated its background as follows:

> Kamaanya's subjects considered him an extremely unpleasant man (whose mind might have been deteriorating for some time) and the song was originally a response to one of his nastier habits: ripping out the beards of people who displeased him. In other words, "As He Plucked Them" chided the king. He was a member of the Grasshopper (Nseenene) Clan, which means that grasshoppers were his totemic insects. The king hated men with long beards because they reminded him of grasshoppers, and he would rip them out with his hands as if they were their wings. This is how his subjects came to call him Kamaanya (which means "Plucker"). That is, he earned the nickname from plucking out men's beards and claiming that he was plucking grasshoppers. In response to this habit, his court performers composed and performed a song. The musicians would also joke with one another in private that Kamaanya ate grasshoppers; however, nothing said in the court is ever truly a secret, and as the rumor spread, it eventually reached the king. The musicians' new song made him furious because it implied that he had eaten his clan totem, both major taboos in Buganda. Due to the song and rumors that the musicians spread about the king, he stopped his wild behavior. The belief that Kamaanya's action of "plucking grasshoppers" indicated his readiness to eat them had bothered him enough to halt his actions.[1]

---

[1] Kafeero interview, July 28, 2005.

This history contextualizes the reasons King Kamaanya's musicians composed the song "As He Plucked Them" ("Bwe Yazimaanya") and the relationships that subsequently informed its content. The Baganda are organized into over fifty patrilineal, exogamous clans (*ebika*). Every clan has a primary totem (*omuziro*) and a secondary totem (*akabbiro*), and it derives its name from the primary totem. A totem "may be a plant, an animal, a part of either one, or a non-living substance such as water from a special source or an inanimate object such as an awl." Clan members may neither injure nor eat these totemic species.[2] According to oral tradition, many theories exist as to how the totems came to be. One suggests that ancestors of some clans assigned totems as beings that had harmed clan members. Another theory posits that elders of certain families assigned totems. A third theory is that during a time when food was scarce, the first king, or *kabaka*, of Buganda, Kintu, ruled that certain families could not eat certain species, though the sources of this theory omit the specific reasons for this ruling.

I briefly and subtly join in the second half of Kafeero's performance of "As He Plucked Them." He alternates and repeats two vocal phrases that several musicians traditionally perform in a call-and-response style, with instrumental accompaniment. Kafeero performs the two vocal lines twice, with a slight variation the second time:

1 *Bwe yazimaanya bwe yazirya, tomuwa nseenene*
As he plucked them, he ate alone, do not give him more grasshoppers

2 *Bwe yazimaanya bwe yazirya*
As he plucked them, he ate alone

3 *Bwe yazimaanya bwe yazirya, tomuwa nseenene*
As he plucked them, he ate alone, do not give him more grasshoppers

4 *Bwe yazimaanya bwe yazirya, omulangira*
As he plucked them, he ate alone, the prince[3]

The formal simplicity and repetition of these phrases highlight the importance of the song's lyrical content. The lyrics show how Kamaanya's musicians delicately use language to challenge and stop his negative behavior, thus exercising their particular ability to wield political power. In this way the performers take an active part in shaping power relations. The power of their song comes not from criticizing the king for his behavior but from the way its lyrics give rise to interpretations as he and others continue to listen to it. In this sense, these lyrics become fertile ground on which different understanding grow and shift. The success of "As He Plucked Them" in altering Kamaanya's behavior

---

2   Kafumbe 2018, 1.
3   Kafeero interview, July 28, 2005.

demonstrates the effectiveness of songs as sociopolitical tools. More than other forms of oral literature, they are lasting and often appear innocuous, factors that allow singers to conceal messages that listeners might otherwise perceive as too subversive to those in power. "As He Plucked Them" is thematically relevant to family and friends, masses and politicians, and leadership and consensus, as the multiple interpretations discussed in this chapter confirm.

Greed and Selfishness

Interpreters of "As He Plucked Them" reimagine the song in a set of meanings that revive its central themes, greed and selfishness, within different and current contexts. Like the song's original performers, who demonstrated the composition's potential as a tool for enacting salient political change, many interpreters articulate the importance of responsibility and loyalty in leadership, reckoning with personal complexes like self-centeredness. Through a diversity of commentaries and perspectives, they reflect on the current moment and illuminate new truths. Rather than looking at the meaning of the lyrics of "As He Plucked Them" literally, Jimmy Ssenfuka Kibirige views the song as an apt tool for reflecting on the greed of contemporary leaders.

> The song is a representation of leaders who use their position as an opportunity to serve themselves rather than the people they lead. They take the power people grant them and use it to benefit themselves. They embrace greed, selfishness, and short-sightedness. Rather than planning carefully and establishing goodwill among the people for subsequent elections, they use their time in office for personal pleasures. When the time comes for reelection, they scramble to secure the support of the people they ignored for the entirety of their terms, begging for votes for fear of losing their treasured leadership positions.[4]

As a criticism of politicians who forget their responsibility to the people who bestow power upon them, Kibirige's reading of "As He Plucked Them" reminds us that some leaders may become blinded by their own power, ignoring the responsibilities that accompany it:

> Such leaders should remember that no leadership position is permanent and that their positions will not sustain them for life. As such, they should remember that their duty is to serve and should give others the same opportunity. Losing their positions is inevitable; therefore, they should spend their time in office establishing protocols that will ensure the success of the people and future leaders.[5]

---

4   Kibirige interview, December 15, 2019.
5   Ibid.

Harriet Kisuule demonstrates how "As He Plucked Them" can expose the lack of transparency of many leaders during and after their election campaigns:

> Leaders often gain the vote of the people by making specific promises during elections, only to fail to fulfill those promises by the time their term is over. In doing this, such leaders deprive the people of what they promised them, and thus fail their responsibility to the people. One can say the same for autocracy, where dictatorial leaders pose an obstacle to their people's prosperity. Autocratic leaders isolate themselves from the people and remain unconcerned about the well-being of their subjects. To use the language of the song "As He Plucked Them," they eat all of the grasshoppers alone. For instance, President Museveni remains isolated from others, gorging himself on grasshoppers. When the guerrilla war (the Ugandan Bush War) in Luweero ended and Museveni and Colonel Dr. Besigye (his private doctor during the war) rose to popularity, it seemed like they were one person. Quickly, however, Museveni turned against many of those who supported him, Besigye included, which is how he came to be Museveni's opponent in later presidential races. The two now consider each other enemies. That, again, is the danger of autocracy: rulers pick and eat their grasshoppers alone, and thus only recognize a responsibility to themselves.[6]

Kisuule reveals here that the lyrics of "As He Plucked Them" imply how becoming a leader is laden with the seductive potential to overconsume and isolate himself. In this light, leaders must remain aware of their civic responsibilities.

Jessy Ssendawula further discusses the notion of responsibility and uses it to describe the current leadership's methods for maintaining order and control:

> The content of the song speaks to the attitude of the National Resistance Movement government, which uses the military and police to suppress all opposition, even if the dissidents' actions are benefiting the country. If the opposition continues to threaten the government's power, they will not hesitate to pluck them like grasshoppers. The song also serves as a warning to leaders to only take what they can consume and utilize. This is because it is unreasonable to expect the people not to eat whatever leftover grasshoppers remain themselves. Contemporary leaders need to recognize when they should let go. They should not force people to adopt their ideologies and work instead to convince them amicably. This is because ultimately, their fealty is to the people. Therefore, they should align their actions with the best interests of those people.[7]

---

6   Kisuule interview, December 21, 2019.
7   Ssendawula interview, December 28, 2019.

By comparing Kamaanya's rule to the National Resistance Movement government, Ssendawula offers fresh interpretation on the idea of picking or plucking grasshoppers. Framing this metaphor as state political repression instead of individual greed may seem like a stretch, but it aligns with and reimagines previous interpretations of "As He Plucked Them," giving it a new vitality that might allow contemporary listeners to familiarize themselves with the song's history.

Shifting to a more individual framing, Peter Kinene explains how "As He Plucked Them" asks the listener not to forget their fellows when they achieve success, adding that this sentiment aligns with many Kiganda proverbs, including *Akatono kazza omukwano* (A small thing rekindles friendship or love) and *Akatono okalya ne munno; bw'akwata enkukunyi, anyigira ku kinkumu* (You eat a little thing with your friend; when he gets hold of a flea, he squeezes it on his fingerprint). Squeezing on a fingerprint means pressing between fingers in order to share with a friend. According to Kinene,

> The idea is that it is appropriate for friends to help each other with everything, sharing their joys as well as their hardships. It does no good for one to wait until one has amassed enormous wealth to share with one's friends, especially because wealth may never come. The man who gives three teaspoons of sugar to his friend every week is a better friend than one who gives fifty kilograms of sugar to his friend once. In other words, friends are to share even the little things, especially if they have struggled together. This idea applies to the way leaders treat their old comrades after entering office. Most of those who participated in the National Resistance Army war in the Luweero Triangle, for instance, have never received a proper reward for their efforts and the sacrifices they made for their country. Others no longer hold important positions in government even though many are still alive. Instead, they live desolate lives; the country they served has forgotten them. People need to remember those who struggled with them to achieve what they have.[8]

By connecting exchanges between two acquaintances to the behavior of the president and other political leaders, Kinene strengthens the argument about the relationship between seemingly apolitical matters and overtly political ones. In this sense, friendship seems to be a universal principle that stretches across micro- and macropolitical realms.

In his analysis of "As He Plucked Them," Edward Ssebunnya Kironde compares Kamaanya's self-centeredness to that of Uganda's current leaders. Expressing the opinions of the younger generation, Kironde states,

---

8 Kinene interview, December 16, 2019.

The song explores greed among leaders. Both Kamaanya and many current leaders of Uganda have a strong connection to war and conflict. By eating grasshoppers, the king is the only one who benefits from his actions. In contemporary Uganda, leaders mimic this selfishness. They constantly remind people of how they fought during the guerrilla war (Ugandan Bush War), and whenever someone questions the legitimacy of this claim, they pester the younger generation about whether their ancestors fought alongside the liberators. Overall, they might be the only ones who enjoy Uganda as "the pearl of Africa."[9]

By interrogating Kamaanya's intentions, Kironde further explains that "self-centeredness drove the king's decision to pull out the beards of the court musicians. The leader's selfish actions only acknowledged his own dislike of beards while ignoring the effect his actions would have on others."[10] Kironde then suggests parallels to that situation, explaining how some current leaders of Uganda, similar to Kamaanya, think only of their own lives when making decisions for their country.

> Museveni fought and appeared as a messiah who saved Uganda, the country's Moses. However, once in power, he was quick to turn into a pharaoh. He openly said he does not view himself as a servant to anybody and is answerable to none. The only people he works for are his grandchildren, having already acquired enough benefits for his sons and daughters throughout his rule. Even among other members of parliament, there is similar arrogance. Kahinda Otafiire, a military officer and minister of justice and constitutional affairs, is infamous for his arrogance and aggressive nature. Whenever people question his policies or views, he responds by arguing that he and others of his generation who fought in the bush war know what is best for Uganda, so no one should question them. Many leaders like him bury any opposition, believing that Uganda is their nation to rule, their nation to extort, simply because they fought in the war.[11]

Kironde's understanding of "As He Plucked Them" as an allegory of greed and selfishness in the present day shows us how the intentions of King Kamaanya match up with those of some twenty-first-century leaders and their sycophants. His Christian faith and knowledge of the Holy Bible allow him to connect the story of Moses and the pharaoh to that of President Museveni's political agenda, suggesting furthermore that selfishness is a universal problem in political leadership.

---

9   Kironde interview, December 19, 2019.
10 Ibid.
11 Kironde interview, December 19, 2019.

Kibirige continues that ineffective leaders affect the livelihood of those they rule over. To combat the sorts of negligence of duty that take place in these situations, he not only points out the shortcomings of those who, as leaders, are supposed to represent the very best of what their people have to offer but also comments on the public ramifications of their actions.

> Leaders, rather than feeling entitled to their positions, should recognize that their voters will not award them more time in office in the cases where they fail to plan or fully accomplish what they set out to do. The responsibility, therefore, falls on them to make the most of the time their voters allot to them. During that time, they should use their power to create more opportunities for themselves and the people, harnessing their connections at home and abroad to enact change. Though their efforts might not always be successful, the important thing is that they attempted to make a difference, as goes the saying, "Shoot for the moon. Even if you miss, you will land among the stars." Some of the leaders of today, however, never even bother to try, which is a true disappointment to the people. The leaders cry for more grasshoppers, and the people shout back, "As he plucked them, he ate alone, the prince," with eating alone signifying their greed. They do not recognize that eating everything within sight is not the way to solve hunger, for instance, because these are ongoing processes. Simply put, though one may have gorged oneself today, one will surely be hungry again tomorrow. The solution is to eat sparingly, to leave some food on the plate for the people.[12]

Kibirige's opinions about leaders' refusal to cooperate with their people highlight the importance of harnessing connections to enact change. Using eating alone as a metaphor for greed, he reimagines "As He Plucked Them" to fit current contexts. In the original story, plucking beards and eating grasshoppers might have little to do with greed, yet Kibirige's position speaks to how one might reimagine the song for contemporary Uganda. By interpreting it differently, its meaning takes on new forms.

Kisuule expands on this allusion by explaining the relationship between cooperation and success. She identifies cooperation as a critical skill for today's leaders:

> When opportunities come up, it is unwise to be selfish and take them all for oneself. It is impossible to achieve cooperation when some people wish for themselves better than they do for others. People will not help someone who is unwilling to help them. In other words, they will not stay with that person through both the good and the bad unless they know that the person would do the same for them. This dynamic even manifests at the village level, where those who never attend the funerals of others' family

---

12 Kibirige interview, December 15, 2019.

members are hard pressed to find anyone willing to attend the funerals of their own dear ones. The case is the same in higher politics. When leaders come down to hear the issues of their people, the people are unwilling to give them their support unless they are sure that the leaders will support them as well.[13]

Kisuule's commentary on cooperation also reminds us of the extent to which one's willingness to work with others and to reciprocate assistance drives one's success. In fact, the commentary recalls how Kamaanya's self-obsession led him to fail as a leader.

Kinene echoes Kisuule's interpretation by discussing the importance of selflessness and gratitude:

> These are two characteristics that both Kamaanya and the current political administration appear to lack. People often speak about selfish leaders as if they are gluttons. They unwisely and selfishly satisfy only themselves rather than sharing with their fellows as expected. They need to share with others what they have gained, hence the following Luganda proverbs: *Ono alya n'ono alya; ye mmere egenda* (This person eats and the other one eats; so the food moves); *Ono aleeta n'ono aleeta; ye mmere ewera* (This person brings and the other one brings; so the food is abundant). Another reason to share with one's fellows is that a person who does not share what he has with others will not receive any good wishes or favors from them. When a person rewards a fellow but keeps the lion's share for himself, for instance, the fellow will not wish that person well. They will only see that person for their selfish behavior.[14]

Here, Kinene articulates the importance of generosity when engaging with others and suggests an association between greed and gluttony. By drawing on Kiganda proverbs to analyze the selfish tendencies of leaders, he happens to be pursuing an indigenous interpretive mode whereby he melds the meanings of the proverb and song. This process works to reify and strengthen the criticism of greed as a social evil with grave political consequences. Thus, Kinene's interpretation is not simply a process of searching for and subsequently discovering meaning; instead, it is a process of creation where he can mix different ingredients to put a fresh spin on a timeless concept.

Steven Mukasa Kabugo also comments on selfishness by describing "As He Plucked Them" within the contemporary context of nepotism:

> The song not only displays the selfishness of King Kamaanya but also suggests that those who are selfish are unlikely to receive help in dire circum-

---

13   Kisuule interview, December 21, 2019.
14   Kinene interview, December 16, 2019.

stances, even from those closest to them. Potentially, an entire lineage or family could fail to find someone to bail them out of a difficult situation. People might laugh, saying, "As you plucked them, so you ate alone; I can't give you mine." This selfishness also extends to nepotism, which is common in Buganda and Uganda. Whenever someone comes into wealth, they look out for those they are related to first. This practice recalls the proverb, *K'ezaala; k'ekomberera* (A cow licks her own calf). While looking after one's own flesh and blood first is not necessarily a bad thing, the practice has broken up entire clans. The negative side of this arrangement is evident in another proverb: *Nnaasiwa mu kange, asiwa mu ka bukuku* (One who says "I will brew beer in my own trough" brews it in a moldy one). This proverb describes someone who only wants to share his fortunes with those for whom he is directly responsible, such as his immediate family. He is totally unwilling to help anyone else, no matter how big or small their trouble is. Everything he earns goes to his family, regardless of whether they deserve it or not.[15]

Like Kinene, Kabugo uses Kiganda proverbs to expand on the themes of "As He Plucked Them," but in this case he invokes and provides two perspectives on the concept of nepotism. Whereas the first proverb he presents simply describes how familial favoritism is prevalent in Uganda, the second one articulates the point at which this becomes nepotism, explaining that such behavior could result in one's ruin. Again, proverbs add a new dimension to the song's meaning, suggesting how multiple narratives can interlock to illuminate complex issues such as greed and selfishness.

Conclusion

The composition "As He Plucked Them" represents a distinct political strategy employed by court musicians serving King Kamaanya. The musicians strategically leveraged their artistic position to challenge the king's behavior. Rather than using flattery like those who served his son, these musicians composed "As He Plucked Them" as social commentary on the king's habit of yanking out men's beards. They circulated private jokes suggesting the king consumed grasshoppers—his clan's sacred totem—knowing such rumors would eventually reach him. This approach represents a calculated political maneuver, as the musicians deliberately created controversy that succeeded in modifying the leader's behavior. Their actions demonstrate how court performers can use their privileged position to indirectly influence

---

15   Kabugo interview, December 19, 2019.

royal conduct through creative criticism disguised as entertainment, effectively establishing boundaries for even the most powerful ruler.

The various interpretations of "As He Plucked Them" bolster one another and allow us to grasp the song's relevance in more familiar political contexts. As we have seen with some Kiganda proverbs, interpreting a song can happen along various modes, which can then generate new connections for listeners and readers. In music, as Denis-Constant Martin demonstrates, meaning is determined not by its sonic elements only but by the context in which they exists.[16] This allows for multiple interpretations to emerge, which requires us to accommodate ambivalences or contradictions in meaning; music, however, is better suited than other forms of expression to contain these challenges.[17] In other words, it is not the conception that is important but the multiplicity of connection that might also spawn from it—the proliferation of multiplicity itself.[18]

---

16 Martin 2013, 49.
17 Ibid.
18 See also Nannyonga-Tamusuza 2002.

7

"Householder"

Mourning and Ridicule

The song "Householder" ("Nnannyinimu"), written after the death of King Ssuuna II (r. ca. 1824–1854), directly criticized the deceased king and demonstrated the disillusionment of the public with his rule. Mukasa Kafeero explains,

> Ssuuna II, the subject of the song, reached an extent of megalomania in his later years. According to some sources, he visited a traditional healer and diviner, who prophesied several things: he would probably not die; even when he died, he would return to life soon; and if his people dared to cry for him following his death, he would not come back to life. Accordingly, Ssuuna II instructed his subjects to not cry for him but instead sing in the event he did die. His musicians composed songs in preparation for the event. However, the king failed to realize that the musicians would sarcastically cry for him when he died due to the unpleasantries of his reign. The musicians despised one of Ssuuna II's brothers, who had stolen goats from the town of Kyebando. At the time of the alleged activities, the king had not been to Kyebando for a long time, but his brother would go there and free the tethered goats from the people, claiming the king had sent him for the animals. However, he was in fact taking them for himself to eat them. So when he and the king died, the people were happy, noting that the person who had been eating their goats was gone. Ssuuna II's musicians composed a sarcastic lamentation song about these incidents.
>
> Ssuuna II's subjects sang "Householder" at his funeral to lament him but also to celebrate him, and it became the most popular of all the songs they performed during the funeral. Since his reign it has become customary for Baganda to perform this song to mourn a deceased king. Today's performers of "Householder" perform it at a slow tempo to reflect a mourning atmosphere, rarely accompanying it with drums. When they do accompany their singing with musical instruments, they play them

softly. The sarcasm of "Householder" is consistent with the contemporary practice of funeral dirge performances, featuring idioms that ridicule the dead for what they did while they were alive. Other times, these dirges will ridicule the living for their bad habits, including those who never attend funerals of their neighbors' family members or who rarely keep vigil. In such instances, the performers may rework the idioms and text of "Householder" to suit its performance contexts.[1]

"Householder" succeeds as a funeral song. Rather than prostrating itself to the late King Ssuuna II and affirming his successes blindly, it seeks to mourn through ridicule. It pays its respects by commenting on the leader's shortcomings and imperfections during his reign, showing all the ways that he could have improved his rule. It encourages mourners, in the face of the king's death, to consider their own personal shortcomings. It frames mourning as a multivalent affair, one that includes both respect and evaluation, and this allows a combination of perspectives to articulate the life and death of King Ssuuna II and to avoid the limiting gaze of a single interpretation.

Kafeero's vocal performance of "Householder" features complex winding melodic lines that explore the full range of his voice. The convention is that multiple singers perform these phrases in a dialogic, call-and-response style. Some of Kafeero's phrases share the same rhythmic motifs throughout his performance, an approach that makes the song sound repetitive.

1 *Nnannyinimu, nnannyini mateeka, owulidde?*
Householder, maker of the law, have you heard?

2 *Bw'owulira mpitaba nga mpitaba ggwe, ssebo*
When you hear me answer, I am responding to your call, sir

3 *Eee*
Yes

4 *Nnannyinimu, nnannyini buyinza*
Householder, principal of authority

5 *Ekimaze embuzi e Kyebando ssalambwa ly'e Wamala, Nnabulagala*
What has finished the goats in Kyebando is the puff adder of Wamala, Nnabulagala

6 *Ssalambwa lyannuma, lyandekera nkovu*
The puffer adder bit me and left me with a scar

7 *Buli erifuluma libojjamu nze*
Whichever snake comes out bites me

---

1   Kafeero interview, July 28, 2005.

8 *Eee*
Eh

9 *Naye alirimponya ndimuwa n'ensimbi*
But whoever relieves me of it, I will even give money

10 *Ekimaze embuzi e Kyebando ssalambwa ly'e Wamala, Nnabulagala*
What has finished the goats in Kyebando is the puff adder of Wamala, Nnabulagala

"Householder" thrives on having various meanings that seemingly contradict each other. While it articulates the sadness following the king's death and provides a somber tone of mourning, it also provides criticism for the dead king, ridiculing him for what he has done in life (lines 6–7), even giving reasons why his death might be a positive event (lines 5 and 10). As these two narratives unfold, the song simultaneously uses allegory to elude explicit affirmation of either of the meanings just described. In this way it becomes at once a tune of mourning, celebration, warning, criticism, and remembrance. "Householder" and the other songs discussed in part 1 originally utilized criticism as a political vehicle for enacting change and meeting public demands.

Mourning and Ridicule

Different interpreters of "Householder" share varied perspectives on the meanings of the song via the themes of mourning and ridicule. One of them is Edward Ssebunnya Kironde, who speaks to the sarcastic tone that is both present in the opening line and underpins the entire song. He notes, "The song's most notable theme is the sense of sarcastic mourning. The theme allows the performers to pay lip service to the death of their leader while using it as a way of expressing how pleased they are to no longer deal with the oppression he brought."[2]

Kironde also highlights how the voice of the musician functions as an extension of the people. For example, through an artful use of language and poetry, Ssuuna II's musicians capture the frustration and hurt that the king creates in a way that exceeds the basic purpose of articulating the masses' thoughts. That is, the musicians simultaneously express the people's frustrations while providing guidance and commentary on what leaders and their subjects might do to avoid failures in the future. Kironde notes,

> It is important to note that householder (*nnannyinimu*) is an honorific for either the king of Buganda or a landowner. Whatever that person says,

---

2   Kironde interview, December 19, 2019.

those he looks after should obey without question in part because he always has the final say. But sometimes a house head can be a dictator who ignores the opinions and well-being of others. The late President Idi Amin is a good example because he sought total submission from the people he ruled. "Householder" expresses the emotions of oppression that people under the rule of Amin and other despotic leaders experienced. The song also expresses the damage that such leaders impose on their subjects. It accomplishes these goals in a particularly poetic and beautiful manner, comparing a dangerous snake ("the puff adder of Wamala, Nnabulagala") to a dangerous and untrusted leader. Like the snake, he deserves to be struck over the head as soon as he appears. That is what Ssuuna II's people felt was justified at the time and many people feel the same way today.[3]

Kironde underscores how Ssuuna II's court musicians bridge the gap between past and present and the gap between life and death. In the first sense, they find a way to repurpose the mistakes of the past as information for the present, generating a road map of failures for leaders to avoid going forward. In the second sense, they resurrect the king through song by recognizing his life's presence, even after his physical death. By ridiculing his rule, they reaffirm his life and mold it to create a new path for the kingdom to follow. Kironde's example of the former Ugandan president Idi Amin provides a glimpse into the previous struggles surrounding freedom of expression. Peter Cooke and Sam Kasule write that during the reigns of Presidents Idi Amin and Milton Obote, educated Ugandans became political targets because the government feared anyone who could think critically.[4] For many of them, their focus shifted from maintaining their professional or academic endeavors to simply trying to protect themselves and their families.[5]

The same was true for performers of traditional music, which, as Andrew Tracey and Hugh Tracey confirm, had such strong ties to the king of Buganda, or *kabaka*. Because of this, after the 1966 attack on the Mmengo royal court and the king's consequent exile, many musicians stopped performing altogether or would only practice in secret.[6] For instance, trumpet bands so strongly evoked the kingship that simply being a member of one would result in the government's labeling the person as a royalist, thus an enemy of the state.[7] The uncertainty of vocation these individuals felt in

---

3   Ibid.
4   Cooke and Kasule 1999, 7.
5   Ibid.
6   Tracey and Tracey 1998, 5.
7   Ibid.

this era evokes the same uncertainty Ssuuna II's subjects felt, which helps to explain the continued affinity for "Householder."

Jessy Ssendawula remarks on how "Householder" suggests that poor leadership enables "snakes" of all sorts to damage the people. However, he focuses on the snake symbolizing the associates of the leader rather than the leader himself, stating:

> The crimes that Ssuuna II's brother committed against the residents of Kyebando are comparable to the many atrocities that officials who are close to the current president of Uganda commit. Many believe they are untouchable by the law. They argue and fight among themselves to the point where the president does not even bother stepping in to solve their disputes. Not even the pope appeases them. Like Ssuuna II, they remain unchecked and use their power to take money and land from others. All leaders should learn to discipline their constituents if they are looking to have a peaceful and harmonious rule. They should give respect to the property of the masses and uphold the law, regardless of their authority or relation to those who are in power.[8]

By speaking on the behavior of associates as a crucial factor in the success of a leader, Ssendawula shares that "Householder" is not just a lamentation and criticism of the king but a commentary on all the individuals who were involved in his rule, including advisers, family, friends, and even his subjects at large. The scope of the song far exceeds what is immediately apparent from the lyrics. Even if "Householder" seems to be solely about the king, the song is really about leadership, and listeners can apply it to any relationship predicated on guidance that we encounter in everyday life.[9]

Jimmy Ssenfuka Kibirige builds on these ideas in his interpretation, suggesting that the king was actually a victim of the referenced snake rather than being the snake. In this interpretation, the puff adder allegorizes the leader's associates, and as a result the leader risks being labeled as a snake because of this connection. The masses may compare a leader with the puff adder if he remains too slow in responding to its poisonous presence. Kibirige further explains:

> Titles such as householder (*nnannyinimu*) and principal of authority (*nnannyini buyinza*) are signifiers of authority, so the people who hold them are usually leaders. Many benefit from holding these titles, but some fail to realize they also come with responsibilities and challenges. In fact, misusing leadership positions can result in damaging repercussions. Every ill act that occurs during a leader's term comes back to rest on their

---

8   Ssendawula interview, December 28, 2019.
9   In Buganda, *nnannyinimu* is a title for both the king and the head of a household.

shoulders, as the lyric "Whichever comes out bites me" (*Buli erifuluma libojjamu nze*) poetically suggests. The venom from a snake's bite also infects and endangers the house head himself. For example, the way the people he leads perceive his rule can shift for the worse. They may come to see the leader as a snake himself, spitting venom and slithering away while they, those who once supported him, lose their faith entirely in his ability to rule them. The subjects may shy away from him, unwilling to invite him to events or be in his presence. The puff adder is therefore a symbol of corruption and evil, particularly those that the house head causes or is associated with. As soon as the people spot it, they try to dash it out with sticks and rocks. And yet, despite their fear of being associated with that snake, it often continues to survive.[10]

Kibirige's interpretation gives new life to this serpentine imagery, as the puff adder becomes intertwined with notions of corruption and greed. It exceeds its own meaning to take on a new one, a fusion of forms that results in powerful and fresh imagery for relating to the situation at hand.

Continuing with the song's connections and relevance to the twenty-first century, John Magandaazi Kityo's analysis of the lyric "The puff adder snake bit me and left me with a scar" reveals that it is primarily about anger and violence. Kityo says, "The puff adder symbolizes violence while the scar represents anger. In contemporary politics, the damage that violence and anger cause is apparent. The masses are usually ill-equipped to either constructively work through their anger or to defend themselves properly when their leaders turn violent."[11] Kityo connects the puff adder metaphor to contemporary violence and anger. In this way he reveals how the message of "Householder" might symbolize a particular kind of relationship rather than a situation. As with every other interpretation that we have seen, Kityo's analysis generalizes the song to apply it to a more philosophical understanding of conflict with a theoretical tilt. This analysis reveals how "Householder," or any song, might embody theory by way of interpretation.

Steven Mukasa Kabugo concludes the analysis of "Householder" in contemporary context by reminding the common people of the dangers that can potentially arise when dealing with a leader.

> For as much as the song derides Ssuuna II, his musicians waited to compose and perform it until after his death, a time when they were safe from the most severe repercussions. Therefore, it is valuable for people to be cautious around leaders and to obey them. Even when leadership creates undesirable situations that push their subjects into corners, the people are tasked with bearing them, remaining calm, and accepting the larger forces

---

10 Kibirige interview, December 18, 2019.
11 Kityo interview, December 14, 2019.

at play. Some leaders, like the puff adder, are fierce and quick to anger. Ssuuna II's musicians conveyed this sentiment but disguised their meaning to avoid offending him. The lyric "But whoever relieves me of it, I will even give money" was a treasonous statement, but they disguised its sentiments using figurative language. The song teaches listeners to be cautious of those who are in positions of authority or those who possess more power than we do. It does not just serve as a lesson to people who lived during times when kings could execute subjects who offended them. It is a message pertinent to the current political atmosphere. When a householder instructs you to do something, you should obey, act accordingly, and fulfill his wishes. Otherwise, he might finish you off, as we see in the lyric "What has finished the goats in Kyebando is the puff adder of Wamala, Nnabulagala."[12]

Kabugo reveals how interpretation can also shift the way we understand subtly conveyed meanings in a song. He returns to this notion of subtlety discussed in previous chapters, articulating the importance of indirectness when it comes to criticizing the king or any other leader. This perspective provides an alternative purpose for the allegory we find in "Householder." Where other interviewees focused on the puff adder's possible meaning, Kabugo remarks that the snake is truly a clever allegory that might not provoke a leader to react because the ridicule operates at such a subliminal level. In this sense, integrating mourning into ridicule can be an effective way to indirectly criticize political malpractice.

Conclusion

"Householder" emerged as a posthumous critique of King Ssuuna II's reign. Created after his death, this song openly expressed public disappointment with his leadership, allowing court musicians to directly voice criticisms that would have been dangerous to express while he was alive. This strategy highlights how musical expression can shift from coded or indirect criticism during a monarch's lifetime to explicit condemnation once the ruler can no longer exact punishment. The language of "Householder" reflects one of the essential elements of meaning in Kiganda songs, "deep Luganda," which David Pier defines as a vernacular language that relies on layered meanings to convey its message.[13] As is the case with this song and many others featured in this book, and as mentioned in chapter 3, only those with an in-depth understanding of Kiganda folklore, history, and idiomatic expressions may

---

12   Kabugo interview, December 19, 2019.
13   Pier 2017, 13.

recognize the richness of lyrical meaning.[14] This command of language reflects the musicians' keen sensibilities, as they succeed in pushing their criticism without creating so much of a controversy as to earn them severe punishment.

Indeed, the interpretability of "Householder" allows it to be continuously reinterpreted. Some interpreters compare the song with other derisive funeral dirges and use its lyrics to challenge contemporary leaders who neglect their subjects' grievances. Other interpreters speak to how the song processes a king's demise, balancing the change in power relations with difficult emotions associated with death. The song's relevance to the rise and fall of many leaders explains its longevity throughout several generations of the Baganda and other ethnic groups in Uganda. Through its mix of criticism, praise, regret, and hope, the song challenges the traditionally accepted purposes of funerary music. "Householder" allows for these and other creative applications of its meaning, and the subtlety of its critique lends performers plausible deniability if they are met with government retribution.

---

14   Ibid.

8

"Federalism"

Manipulation, Exploitation, and Reciprocity

Ssaalongo Kiwanuka Matovu Deziderio (1924–2015) composed the song "Federalism" ("Federo") in 1996. The composition was a musical response to various political events, most notably the National Resistance Movement (NRM) government's refusal to restore federalism in the 1995 constitution. Federalism had been a topic of heated debate in the national parliament since 1993, when President Yoweri Kaguta Museveni's administration restored all the kingdoms that the 1967 constitution had abolished. The Kingdom of Buganda pushed for the restoration of this system, but the national government ignored its demands. To draw the government's attention to the Baganda's disappointment in President Museveni's administration and to contest the government's decision, Deziderio composed "Federalism" and performed it at various social and political gatherings (including at my wedding in 2006) in hopes that he would spark change. Deziderio had this to say about the song after performing the version analyzed in this chapter:

> These lyrics indirectly express how federalism was generally a peaceful political arrangement in Uganda. In this system, every person had authority over their own area, whereas the republic system instituted after political independence in 1962 enabled some people to take advantage of others, abusing them and stealing their property. Federalism accounted for everyone, and therefore many people would support it today. Because of the system's eminence and likability, this song urges the national government to restore federalism. The song presents federalism not just as the people's agreement but also one through which God works, suggesting that animals also have federalism among them. Because every animal has its own niche, the hippopotamus (*envubu*) sleeps in water, not in the marsh (a type of wetland, *olusa*), while the sitatunga (a type of antelope, *enjobe*) sleeps in the marsh, but the two kinds of animals share the same feeding grounds, because they all eat at a meadow (*ettale*). After they eat their fill, each one returns home to where it sleeps. When this was a governmental

arrangement, people in the assembly or parliament would join forces while working in the same space. When they were done, everyone would clean up and return to their respective areas, the Kingdom of Bunyoro, the Kingdom of Busoga, the Kingdom of Ankole, and other regions that are not kingdoms. If Ugandans did so today, instability and conflict could be alleviated.

Before 1966, the national government collected one shilling out of ten taxed to give to the Buganda government in Mmengo, and this money helped the king greatly. Citizens paid twenty-five shillings every month, ten shillings as the king's tax and fifteen shillings as graduated or poll tax. Accordingly, a taxpayer received two receipts. Citizens also faced a land tax (*obusuulu*), which came after *oluwalo*, another form of land tax and from which the king often exempted some of his musicians. Beneficiaries never did communal work (*bulungi bwansi*) such as plowing, digging, or maintaining roads in their home villages. Paying land tax on one's land meant the government would not evict them from their plot. In fact, once someone paid land tax, no one bothered them. These arrangements defined the later years of the colonial and postindependence eras, during which the king of Buganda, Sir Edward Muteesa II (r. 1939–1966), was the president of Uganda. When the national government dismantled the kingship in 1966, they removed land tax, which Buganda has attempted to revive in recent years. Many Baganda long for a better tax system, as the current one seems to disproportionately benefit the national government at the expense of the region of Buganda. The government has expanded many tax funds to their limit, exceeding what average people are able to pay without relinquishing all of their earnings, yet some government officials fail to pay any.

King Mutebi II (r. 1993–present) once asked me to perform "Federalism" on Central Broadcasting Services (CBS, Buganda's central radio). The engagement was an opportunity to aid many people's understandings of the changes that Buganda and Uganda faced after 1966.[1]

As Deziderio demonstrates, "Federalism" is not just background entertainment for people to consume blindly. Rather, it is a veritable political commentary worthy of the public's attention. Deziderio's earlier performances of the song were themselves a part of the composition, which articulates why the federalist system is relevant to people's daily lives and choices.

Deziderio's performance of "Federalism" opens with the bow strokes of the tube fiddle (*endingidi*), which he plays rapidly in triple meter. Soon his vocals start up, continuing throughout the entire song without any substantial pauses. The tube fiddle part continuously fluctuates between three central notes with occasional glides that deviate from the norm. While this repetition is unchanging, it does not lock neatly into a structured pattern,

---

1   Deziderio interview, July15, 2005.

and as such, it lets the song be spontaneous. This balance between rehearsed and improvised performance is evident in the character of the lyrics, which are simultaneously declarative and emotionally charged. The balance in question lends itself to the nature of African music performance, in which no two performances of a piece ever sound the same. Dezidario adopts a chanting vocal style, which signifies the seriousness of the song's subject matter. The timbre of his voice is loud, impassioned, and even hoarse at times, conveying a sense of wisdom and experience. The singer begins each melodic phrase at generally the same pitch, only sometimes dipping up or down toward the end of the phrase. Through this use of repetition and continuity, his lyrics sound meditative and introspective, taking on an almost sacred quality. The texture of the song barely changes, maintaining the lead vocal melody against the busy accompaniment of the tube fiddle. Although there are only two elements of sound in the performance, the energetic sincerity of the voice coupled with the swift momentum of the tube fiddle creates enough rhythmic and polyphonic texture to feel full and dynamic. That the song is performed by only one musician strengthens the personal, diaristic nature of the lyrics. Although Dezidario conveys many different ideas, the lyrics' sonic quality is quite uniform, such that the performance becomes contemplative; at the same time, the singer spurts out the lyrics quickly, endowing the song with a sense of urgency that suits its political subject matter. Dezidario's lyrics are as follows:

> 1 *Nandigambye ntya, nga eyankwana yabula, nandigambye ani?*
> What would I say, when the one who wooed me disappeared, who would I tell?
>
> 2 *Kaakati olowooza otya, nga wankwana, nandigambye ntya?*
> How do you now think, when you wooed me, how would I say?
>
> 3 *Abange nga Katonda bw'abeera, nga Katonda bw'atuusa, olowoozanga*
> Friends, just as God assists, just as God fulfills, always think
>
> 4 *Abange nga Katonda bw'abeera, nange n'amala Ambeera, olowozaanga*
> Friends, just as God assists, if He can also assist me, always think
>
> 5 *Balisanga tubuusabuusa, nti okukkiriza kuba kwa bato, olowoozanga*
> They will find us doubting, as believing is for the young, always think
>
> 6 *Abange endowooza ya bonna, nga endagaano bw'ebeera, nandigambye ntya?*
> Friends, a consensus, just like an agreement, how would I say?
>
> 7 *Bannange okuva ku ndagaano ziri, okutuuka ku y'olwenda, zaakolwanga baki?*
> Friends, from the past agreements, to that of 1900, who drafted them?

8 *Abange okuva ku ndagaano ziri, okutuuka ku y'o lwenda, zaakolwanga nnannyinimu*
Friends, from the past agreements, to that of 1900, they were created by the householder

9 *Ate okuva ku y'olwenda, okutuuka ku za leero, zino za kanyoolabikya*
And from that of 1900, to the current ones, these are neck twisters

10 *Abasajja abaakola endagaano empya, bbaffe mwamusuula nnyo, mwamujooga nnyo*
The men who drafted the new agreement, you left out our husband, you belittled him a lot

11 *Omuntu okuliira ewa munno, w'otemedde n'otamuwa, ye muli alowooza atya?*
Feasting from another's place, butchering meat from there but you do not share with one, how would one feel?

12 *Abange mwandiridde za musolo, oluwalo lubeera lulwe, afunenga ky'alyako*
Friends, you could have embezzled graduated tax, and leave the land tax to him, so that he earns a living

13 *Na wano e Kampala, yalinga emu ku kkumi eriweebwa, nga nayo emuyamba era*
Even here in Kampala, it was initially a tenth of the collections, and it would benefit him

14 *Naye bambi zonna mwazigatta wamu, ez'oluwalo n'omusolo, ne mulya ne mwekkutira*
But sadly you consumed it all, land and graduated taxes, and you embezzled to your satisfaction

15 *Kaakati mukuba bibejjagalo, mukuba bibejjagalo*
Now you are belching, you are belching

16 *Kaakati mukuba bibejjagalo, n'omuto avuga mmotoka, ffe ababe tukomba vvu*
Now you are belching, even the young drive cars, yet we—his subordinates—are licking ashes

17 *Njagala mutuule wamu, mukole endagaano endala, federo mugizzeewo*
I want you to sit together, and draft another agreement, and reinstate federalism

18 *Endagaano ya bonna, federo mugizzeewo, y'endagaano y'oku nsi*
The collective agreement, reinstate federalism, it is the earthly universal agreement

19 *Era eyo ye ndagaano ya bonna, ne Katonda mw'akolera, olowoozanga*
And it is the collective agreement, and one through which God works, always think

20 *Kubanga yo enjobe esula mu lusa, enjobe esula mu lusa, olowoozanga*
For the sitatunga antelope dwells in a marsh, the sitatunga antelope dwells in a marsh, always think

21 *Bannange envubu esula mu mazzi, yo enjobe esula mu lusa, zigatta lwaliiro*
Friends, the hippopotamus dwells in water, yet the sitatunga antelope dwells in a marsh, but they share the dinning ground

22 *Bannange zigatta lwaliiro, zituuka ne zikutula, olowoozanga*
Friends, they share the dining ground, but they eventually split up, always think

23 *Ate era nga zigatta lwaliiro, zituuka n'ezawukana, olowoozanga*
And even though they share the dining ground, they eventually part, always think

24 *Naawe essowaani njagala okoze mu yiyo, n'omulala munno, nga mugatta lwaliiro*
I want you also to dip in your own plate, and your other friend too, while you combine the dining ground

25 *Ate temugamba nti ntemaatema mu bantu, ng'ebigambo bye mpulira, kuno kulongoosa*
And do not say that I segregate people, as I already hear, this is putting things right

26 *Abange Kampala omugamba otya, okumuggya ku bannyini ye, Mbarara n'omuleka?*
Friends, how do you suggest taking Kampala away from its owners, and leave out Mbarara?

27 *Bwe muba nga mwagala kulongoosa, byonna mwandibiggyeewo, ffena ne tubeererawo*
If you want to put things right, eliminate all, so that we all stay without

These lyrics describe the political shifts that shook Buganda after 1900, when British administrators indirectly weakened the power of the king. The lyrics also allude to the political and administrative injustices that the king has endured against Uganda's leaders during the postindependence and postcolonial eras, highlighting the corruption and manipulation that has developed in conjunction with their rise. "Federalism" generally expresses political frustration, disappointment, and a strong desire to return to a previous form of government. "Householder" (line 8) refers to the king; "neck twisters" (line 9) means disagreeable arrangements; "our husband" (line 10) is the king; and "licking ashes" (line 16) means reduced to poverty.

The song begins with a series of questions (lines 1–2) that appear to express the singer's confusion and disillusionment with his present position, suggested by the phrase "when the one who wooed me disappeared" (line 1). This phrase insinuates that betrayal or loss is at the root of the singer's bewilderment. Lines 3 through 4 serve to expand on this notion of loss by evoking the figure of God as one who would empower and strengthen the singer. It is as though Deziderio is calling to the Creator to strengthen him against the imminent foe he will face. This point suggests some sense of the danger that subsequent lyrics reveal.

After overcoming his disorientation and calling for God's support, the singer begins to explain his conflict at hand (lines 5–11). For example, he describes the agreements of the past, which the king, householder (*nnannyinimu*), made. However, in 1900, British settlers chose to sidestep the leader and make agreements without his input (lines 9–10). These agreements were not made in the name of the people, and the drafters were the sole beneficiaries. As the singer puts it, these new agreements and the people who wrote them "left out" the king (line 10), after "butchering meat from" his "place" (line 11). The ignorance of the king's sovereignty, as John Lonsdale documents, reflected racist and antiquated colonial values, which held that Africans had no interest in politics or citizenship, that they lacked unity or fraternity between different tribal groups.[2]

The connection between the king and his civilians is a recurring theme in Deziderio's narrative, as the singer depicts the king not as a separate appendage of the kingdom but as an extension and representation of its people. The performer does this by speaking of their mutual sufferings almost interchangeably. In lines 9 through 16, for example, Deziderio describes how, in 1900, the king lost his ability to decide on governmental matters. However, rather than simply depicting it as a political shift, the singer articulates this change as one that directly impacted people. It was not just the king who lost his position, but the people lost their representative voice. Furthermore, Deziderio highlights the notion of self-centeredness by explaining how today's leaders embezzle excessively, not even leaving enough resources for the king to live on. The lyrics describe them as "belching" (line 15), as though the riches they steal are a massive and undeserved meal. The singer explains how even the youngest of these leaders are rich enough to own a car, while the rest of the country can do no more than eat ashes (line 16), be reduced to poverty. Rather than using stories that emphasize the grandeur and opulence of the king's struggle, Deziderio employs anecdotes

---

2 Lonsdale 1992, 328, 348.

that shorten the distance between the king and his subjects, demonstrating how ordinary themes of human life also pervade macropolitical decisions.

Having focused on the post-1993 situation, Deziderio transitions to his proposal of reinstating federalism (lines 17–23). To convince us of this idea, he provides an anecdote in the form of a story. He explains how the hippopotamus and the sitatunga live in different spaces yet come to the same place to have their meals and drink their water (line 20). Through this parable, justice becomes something inherent and universal—reflected in the most fundamental laws of animal nature—and makes Uganda's current political system appear all the more unstable. Deziderio's description of the intricate mutuality between wildlife species leads us to imagine that human political systems could calibrate themselves to the proposed model. From the comparisons he makes, we come to see that a friend's betrayal is no less significant than a politician's greed. In the same way, the complementarity of species in the wild that Deziderio references is no less significant than the systems of mediation that constitute our governments. Both determine the function of a community, whatever form it might take.

As already suggested, the singer's language also exemplifies the blend of politics and life. He uses words like "earthly" to describe the benefits of federalism, emphasizing a philosophical stance of sentient connection to the land against the type of abstraction and idealism typical of Western republics. Just as this book analyzes meaning by collaborating the voices of various figures, this "earthly" style of federalist governance is reciprocal, a quality that people can only achieve if they listen to one another. For this to happen, what must exist is an open, responsive channel for communication between different levels of political life. This can only happen if the government comes around to creating the infrastructure for it. As Deziderio mentions, an extension of the scenario he describes would be far better than the current system because it would allow all parties to have the freedom to operate independently but encourage them to unite when necessary (lines 24, 26, and 27). Overall, his lyrics plead for the implementation of federalism in Uganda.

Manipulation, Exploitation, and Reciprocity

Various elements of "Federalism" make it interpretable in many different contexts. These include the song's plea for the implementation of federalism in Uganda. Acknowledging that a constitution is the absolute foundation for a proper federation, John Magandaazi Kityo comments on how some of Uganda's leaders have violated the charter, as they continually revise it to fit their own interests, paying no attention to the effects that this might have on the people. Given the frequency of these changes, many citizens have to seek out the details of constitutional rights from their leaders. Kityo explains this trend:

> Because of the constant changes to the constitution, many Ugandans are unaware of the rights the constitution provides them and because of this are unable to defend those rights effectively. If the public were more informed about their constitutional rights, the nation would be in a much better state because the population would have a better grasp of the leadership and laws that govern them. Instead, however, people put all their hopes in the president to solve their problems, even those that the constitution outlines and protects.[3]

According to Kityo, rather than relying on the unspoken pact of their relation, the people feel compelled to always seek out what they need from their leaders. The relationship fails to be mutual because leaders pretend that they only have the capacity to fulfill the bare minimum rather than taking on extensive and exhausting demands. Leaders consistently use the subjects' reliance on them to further manipulate and skew things in their own favor. These realities remind us that a federalist constitution is a covenant between leaders and subjects. Evident in its lyrics, "Federalism" becomes a commentary on the way leaders have sidestepped the constitution and replaced it with disagreeable arrangements ("neck twisters"). This framing shows how such betrayal of the people's interests has recurred throughout history.

To this point about following a constitution, Steven Mukasa Kabugo's lyrical interpretation stresses the importance of upholding one's word and maintaining formal agreements, and he cautions:

> When entering into an agreement or formal solution with another party, it is best practice to follow through and uphold the agreement as much as possible. If one party fails to implement the agreement in full and further fails to heed any sort of counsel, they will have to face God's judgment. Dishonoring an agreement in this manner results in several repercussions, the main one of which is becoming an unreliable hypocrite in the eyes of others.[4]

Kabugo highlights how political agreements intersect with social and personal agreements, arguing that they are relevant to the micropolitical and macropolitical realms.

Kabugo further clarifies that the personal encounters that influence one's conception of the world will ultimately impact those political encounters

---

3 Kityo interview, December 14, 2019.
4 Kabugo interview, December 19, 2019.

that one considers the exclusive "drivers" of political change in the past. In this sense, human nourishment will factor into political nourishment:

> People should do their best to avoid hypocrisy in any form. This is the case with those who claim they are advocates for federalism and yet infringe on the federal rights of others. They are hypocrites who need to learn how to respect others in the same way they want those people to respect their own rights. They should respect the principles of federalism, which is a system of governance that gives individuals autonomy over issues such as speech, religion, and marriage.[5]

Rather than restricting the song to a commentary on the movement at the macropolitical level, Kabugo demonstrates its relevance to the smaller points of interaction occurring between people within communities.

Picking up from Kabugo's point about the infringement of the rights of others, Peter Kinene's reading of "Federalism" gives examples of when the national government allegedly rejected an opportunity meant to help Baganda because it was not financially beneficial for themselves:

> Selfishness and taking from others what is theirs remains a prominent problem in Ugandan society. In the latter half of the twentieth century, Buganda launched a fundraising campaign for the rebuilding of the Kasubi tombs. The project was part of a broader program named the Brick (Ettoffaali), which was the brainchild of Buganda's current prime minister, Charles Mayiga. He visited various areas to collect funds. His office then used the funds to pay for the construction of a fence wall around the perimeter of the roughly fifteen acres of land on which the royal tombs are situated. The funds also supported the construction of the Masengere commercial building in Kampala, the erection of the Muganzirwazza commercial building in Katwe, and the founding of a television station. Unfortunately, the national government sabotaged the fundraising campaign because they were unable to tax and profit from the masses' donations. In other words, the national government soon realized that the funds that participants in the program were donating to Buganda to develop itself were nontaxable, so they ordered the halt of the program. They did not benefit directly from it. The national government needs to recognize that they should not deny things to others just because they themselves cannot gain from them. They should not take away the peace of others; instead, they should let their subjects keep what they have.[6]

Kinene demonstrates how the central government's behavior broke relations between leaders and the people they serve, evoking the image of the

---

5   Ibid.
6   Kinene interview, December 16, 2019.

leaders "belching" after embezzling to their hearts' content. These leaders belch not from satisfaction but from overindulging in pleasures. The belch appears to represent the contempt that Buganda's leaders hold toward their civilians, smug that their greed will have no consequences.

Jessy Ssendawula contributes to the conversation on "Federalism" by introducing the concept of regional rights. He stresses that national and regional powers must find a delicate balance that can inspire a harmonious Uganda. However, he notes that regions are currently struggling beneath the weight of the more powerful national government. His interpretation of "Federalism" speaks to the ways in which today's leaders exploit their positions of power to take advantage of the formerly independent states that it encompasses. Much like the new leaders the song references, some politicians appear to only think of themselves, embezzling to their "satisfaction," often at the expense of those whom they are meant to represent:

> The song holds particular significance as the former federal states continue to compete in developing the services and resources available in their own areas, as well as for the larger picture of regional balance. For example, the Kingdom of Bunyoro could take a larger part in the oil drilling that takes place in their region. The taxes it collects from the project could help to build roads and towns, while funding from the central government could fund projects such as improving health and education, helping schools and health centers to run better. Furthermore, federalism and greater state autonomy could help minimize the effects of corruption at higher levels of government, with local officials having bigger stakes in the fulfillment of the basic needs of their area. On the whole, it is truly time for federalism in Uganda. The song "Federalism" is . . . calling for a new agreement between the national government and the eight former federal states of Uganda to restore federalism. It expresses the unfairness of the current situation, where the national government feeds on all the resources of the federal states, while the states themselves languish in anarchy and poverty. The government does not even remit the tax it collects in areas like Kampala to the treasury of the associated federal state. Instead, it remits all tax to the national government. However, the song is not calling for disunity or secession. It is advocating for the respect of regional diversity and autonomy. It is promoting the idea that the central government should remain at the same "dining place" while the federal states retire to their own "habitats" after partaking in a meal together.[7]

Providing broader context to the song's commentary, Ssendawula describes how Deziderio's lyrics extend beyond criticizing colonialism

---

7   Ssendawula interview, December 28, 2019.

to criticizing human exploitation more broadly. At the same time, this interpretation emphasizes the mutuality between the king and his subjects. All at once, embezzling from the king's funds comes to mean embezzling from the masses, as the king and his people are extensions of each other. Thus, when the national government cheats, manipulates, or steals from the king, per Ssendawula's claims, his people suffer as well. This mutuality extends beyond just a shared vulnerability, however. It simultaneously represents the king and his subjects' united strength as violating the interests of one without incurring the frustration of the other.

Jimmy Ssenfuka Kibirige provides greater context for the reasons that some Baganda are proponents of regional rights in his interpretation of "Federalism." According to Kibirige, President Museveni manipulated the interests of the Baganda to benefit his own agenda, and as a result, he ruined any chance of a meaningful relationship between himself and the Kingdom of Buganda to whom he demonstrated his untrustworthiness. In much the same way, the Baganda's realization of his alleged hypocrisy made them unreliable in President Museveni's eyes, and many are unlikely to support him in any circumstance, even in those where his intentions might be benevolent. Kibirige explains, further, that the result is a loss on both sides, as each is compelled to overcome the other to achieve their goals:

> To a large extent, they feel the government has jilted them of their promised autonomy. Federalism was really a pursuit of the Baganda people. Buganda was the kingdom that most strongly advocated for its implementation because it wanted the recognition of its status as a sovereign nation that could run its own day-to-day affairs. This was the promise that Museveni made to the Baganda during his rise to power in order to earn their support. He knew that he would be unable to win the presidency without the total support of the Baganda. This event, though of the past, exemplifies how politicians lie for their own gain. Museveni made this promise because he knew that if the Kingdom of Buganda backed out of supporting him, other kingdoms like Busoga and Bunyoro might have done the same. Furthermore, Buganda historically holds a lot of the critical elements that determine Uganda's prosperity, such as the capital, Kampala, access to Lake Victoria, and the border with Tanzania. Museveni knew he could not afford to lose these components, so he made promises he had no intention of keeping.[8]

Kibirige's observations suggest that the president desperately grabs hold of power, hoping that the masses will allow him to keep it forever. As he does so, he continues to deteriorate the state of Uganda by parasitically absorbing resources, hijacking improvement initiatives, and jeopardizing the country's

---

8   Kibirige interview, December 19, 2019.

chances at any form of nationwide uplift. These two points demonstrate the impact of selfish leaders. Their pursuits come at the expense of a more profound and satisfying form of success. They are alone in an existential sense because they sacrifice reciprocity for security. They allegedly cheat and lie, injuring the masses so they can maintain their positions. Yet they remain in denial of loss, constantly hiding from their inevitable expulsion from power, which could come through death, or revolt, or election. They debase themselves, enslave themselves to power, pursuing a Sisyphean task of redundant maintenance, including a cycle of allegedly rigging elections, silencing opposition leaders, and lying to citizens. They become too caught up in their own world to be able to appreciate the one that is already here.

Deziderio explains that federalism is the "earthly" (universal) agreement, one that implies a natural reciprocity between rulers and subjects. Pushing the argument for greater regional autonomy, Kibirige provides further examples of regional inequality and identifies the factors that cause them, confirming that they are all connected to the abolishment of federalism (thus abolishment of active reciprocity):

> Federalism in Uganda has been a long debated, hotly contested subject that is still on the minds of many. Many have died because of it, and others are still dissatisfied with the state of federalism in the nation. Still, many are striving for regional balance, regional management, and regional access to opportunities. For instance, people used to board buses all the way from Kabaale to Kampala for a chance to receive a great education at Makerere University, which is currently in poor condition. In recent years, the population in the area surrounding the university has gotten so dense that the quality of life is beginning to suffer. The population distribution across the country has become so uneven because there is no access to proper higher education in many of the other regions. Indeed, there is a huge disparity between the resources available in poorer regions and a region like Mbarara, where President Museveni hails from and to which he allocates significant funding. Leaders are defying the constitution in order to get benefits and resources exclusively for their region.[9]

This perspective demonstrates how Uganda's modern leaders prioritize one type of reciprocity (leaders giving back to their home regions) at the expense of others (neglecting other regions). With this example Kibirige provides greater nuance to the criticism that the populace is currently leveling at some leaders. The king's responsibility to his people does not only extend to his mother's clan but applies to every clan in Buganda's court; however, the government allegedly does not replicate this same fairness. Furthermore, Kibirige's views show us that reciprocity is not an inherent benefit to all involved and thus is

---

9   Kibirige interview, December 15, 2019.

not always an ideal relationship to aim for. Instead, it is far more comparable to a way of relating with the world, an attitude that can be beneficial or injurious depending on the context of each application. This perspective illustrates how reciprocity is not the be-all and end-all of the song's message. "Federalism," Kibirige adds, seeks to mediate such reciprocities so that they might do less to infringe on the relationships of others:

> Federalism dictates that regions should receive an equal, appropriate share of funding and resources. However, at the ground level many regions remain impoverished. The privileged people suppress the voices of the underprivileged. Some resource-rich regions are in an unspeakable state because others have exploited the natural abundance of their resources. The independent management solutions that federalism enabled in the past could provide a resolution to some of these problems. However, much of the success of federalism in bringing about these sorts of changes relies on the discretion of individual leaders. Ideally, leaders should be advocating for their people, earning their trust, and finding ways through which those people can learn to find success. The reality remains, however, that once leaders find their own success, they are quick to forget the people who depend on them. They instead focus on gaining power and benefits for themselves and their families. Those that can find assistance from these leaders are able to do so purely because of family connections or personal profits for the leaders. This sort of leadership tears regions apart instead of strengthening them. It robs regions instead of building them.[10]

In this commentary Kibirige contrasts the preferable type of leadership, one where the leader seeks to support and reinforce the desires of the people, with the one we have today, where leaders frequently forget the people they lead and only think of themselves. This insight reflects the contrast that "Federalism" describes in its earliest lyrics, which juxtapose the "past agreements" of the king with the "neck twisters" of the post-1900 period, emphasizing the startling manipulation used by those drafting these new agreements. In particular, the song focuses on the fact that the agreements of today no longer reflect the genuine care that the king feels, as they now only fulfill the needs of those who draft them.

Kityo's reading of "Federalism" further suggests that the true root of regional inequality in Uganda is the national government's denial of citizens' rights and benefits. According to him, the national government intentionally wields interregional conflict to exploit everyone involved. In the past, the king would seek to resolve an issue by appeasing all parties, whereas leaders today merely use the conflict as an excuse to take more resources for themselves:

---

10   Kibirige interview, December 19, 2019.

Regions should be able to control the resources found in their areas. The government recently discovered oil in Bundibugyo. Naturally, the Banyoro, who live in that region, are looking to profit from this discovery and are now advocating for increased autonomy in the name of federalism. One could say the same thing of the people of Karamoja, who became strong proponents of federalism after the government discovered gold in their region. However, the current lack of federalism and stronger regional rights means that national government officials can reconcile the various intraregional quarrels over these valuable resources by taking those resources for themselves. Individual regions are unable to benefit from the minerals and raw materials in their areas; the government collects them all. Going to the president to plead for change in the system is of no use either, because he and his lackeys are the very people who institute and benefit from these predatory policies. The central government is still restricting the rights and benefits that it could afford to the people of Uganda.[11]

Kityo's interpretation reframes our understanding of the "agreement" that "Federalism" references by suggesting that government leaders do not necessarily support the "agreement" because they cannot exploit it. Their substantial power and influence allow them to intervene in other "agreements" for their own favor. This means that leaders do not solve the conflicts between regions but merely replace them with new frustrations toward the government. Furthermore, they also fail to identify and resolve root problems, as the government's alleged "parasitic" attitude only compounds the deprivation that often causes such conflicts.

Conclusion

As a political instrument, "Federo" functioned as Buganda Kingdom's unofficial anthem of constitutional resistance following the 1995 governmental rejection of federalism. The song served as a persistent public reminder of unfulfilled promises, transforming various performance spaces—from political gatherings to personal celebrations like weddings—into forums for expressing collective disappointment with President Museveni's administration. By circulating across diverse social contexts for years after its 1996 creation, the composition maintained political pressure long after the constitutional debate in question had officially concluded. Beyond mere entertainment, the song operates as a form of documented protest, preserving Kiganda federalist aspirations in cultural memory when formal political channels seem to fail.

---

11 Kityo interview, December 14, 2019.

"Federalism" activates the philosophical imaginations of its listeners, spurring various interpretations regarding the national government's policies. As mentioned earlier, numerous elements of the song make it interpretable in many different settings. These elements include its lyrical nonspecificity: although there is a precise political situation that Deziderio is referring to, he does not call out specific politicians. This allows the song to be applied to various themes, including spirituality, wildlife, justice, and authority, among other universal topics, with various interpretations. As such, the song's political position and philosophical stance do more than provide fodder for theorists and music aficionados to discuss. "Federalism" reshapes listeners' understanding of the world, aided by Deziderio's unique use of language and storytelling.

Part III

Songs about Leadership and Responsibility

Part III focuses on the themes of leadership and responsibility, particularly regarding the duties and methods of an effective leader. Here we discuss songs that criticize, praise, or otherwise explain Kiganda kingship and leadership at large by comparing exemplary contexts with preferable models of behavior. First, chapter 9 explores themes of advice and caution in the song "Unadvisable Kayemba" ("Kayemba Nantabuulirirwa"). This song acts as a lesson for leaders to heed the advice of others, detailing the conflict and hardship that can result otherwise, as demonstrated by the fate of the unadvisable King Kayemba (r. ca. 1690–1704). Chapter 10 discusses the themes of deliberation and animosity in the song "He Has a Lot on His Mind" ("Alina Bingi By'Alowooza"). Comparing the past with the present state of Buganda and its kingship, the song recounts the dissolution of the kingdom and the distress of contemporary politics. Chapter 11 focuses on the themes of punishment and mercy in the song "Gganga Had a Narrow Escape" ("Gganga Alula"), alternatively titled, "They Chopped Off His Fingers" ("Baamutemako Engalo"). "Gganga Had a Narrow Escape" regretfully recounts the story of a court musician who suffered a gruesome punishment for his misbehavior, lamenting his fate and wishes for a less severe penalty, simultaneously calling into question concepts such as justice and duty. Its alternate version, "They Chopped Off His Fingers," describes the same story but emphasizes the way that conflict, violence, and retribution can have lasting effects on a group of people. The story of the punished musician in question explores the more unsavory, harsh, and difficult challenges of the kingship, while also avoiding a zero-sum evaluation of punishment and forgiveness. As the three songs demonstrate, contemplation, judgment, and decision are all responsibilities of the king, who must constantly work to embody the collective conscience and consider what is best for his people.

All three songs featured in part 3 detail the personas, responsibilities, and influence of Baganda kings as well as their images in the public eye. By outlining different demands of leadership, not only do these songs offer an in-depth understanding of a king's duties, but they also serve as tools for upholding certain political standards. Their lyrics portray active, engaged, and busy kings, and in doing so, they dissect the precise components that constitute proper leadership. Whereas some of the featured songs celebrate outstanding examples of kingship, others denounce the failures and shortcomings of more faulty governance. The interpreters featured here apply each song's content to the political leaders of today and compare historical accounts to more contemporary realities. In the context of twenty-first-century politicians like President Museveni, each song offers a multitude of varying, sometimes contradictory lessons and meanings that are applicable to the current times. Through the process of reinterpretation, not only do interpreters discover new potential meanings behind the songs' lyrics, but they also come to view their contemporary surroundings in a completely new light. These interpreters use the songs as open dialogues on modern society, revealing the duties that political leaders have to their people and the responsibilities that all people have to their communities. In this way, they embrace an ongoing discourse between the past, present, and future, and they imbue the compositions with new life.

9

"Unadvisable Kayemba"

Advice and Caution

The song "Unadvisable Kayemba" ("Kayemba Nantabuulirirwa") explores the dynamics of power as well as the violence and tragedy that can arise from poorly managing these responsibilities. Such was the case with King Kayemba (r. ca. 1690–1704), who ignored the advice of others. According to Ssaalongo Kiwanuka Matovu Deziderio (1924–2015), the performer of the version of "Unadvisable Kayemba" analyzed here:

> Once, some of King Kayemba's staff prepared a boat for the leader as a gift. Built from clay, they designed it to dissolve and sink, hoping that he would drown while attempting to cross a lake. On his way to the lake, however, Kayemba came across a flutist playing a tune. He asked him the meaning behind the song. The man sang in reply, *Kayemba Nantabuulirirwa, olisaabala bwa bbumba!* (The unadvisable Kayemba, you will row a clay boat!) In a clay boat Kayemba would perish. The flutist then explained that the staff members the king was supposed to meet down the road had prepared a boat for him. He told him that it was made out of clay and that it was meant to murder the king. Shocked at the flutist's revelation, the king asked him to accompany him the rest of the way to the lake. The flutist played his instrument as the pair set off and traveled down the road. When they arrived at the lake, the welcoming party showed the king the boat they had prepared for his arrival. Kayemba, having just been briefed on the truth behind the boat, praised its beauty. Cleverly, he rejoiced at the gift, claiming that it was so wonderful and, in an act of generosity, the people who had prepared it should be the first to row it, so he instructed them to sit and row. The welcoming party hesitated, clearly nervous. They suggested that it was inappropriate for them to sit in a king's special boat. However, His Majesty insisted that it was fine to sit in it and row. Unwilling to break the taboo of the land by refusing a direct order from the king, the welcoming party climbed into the boat. As soon as they pushed off the shore of

the lake, the boat began to disintegrate underneath them. They fell into the water, drowned, and died. The assassins learned far too late that trying to deceive the king would result in serious consequences.[1]

Deziderio's account highlights how the king historically carries many responsibilities on his shoulders, including communicating, commanding, and deliberating. He must receive, contemplate, and evaluate information to disseminate to his people, and this process reveals his inner character and priorities.

Deziderio's performance of "Unadvisable Kayemba" lasts only a few seconds, with impassioned delivery and a subtle melody. Considering the piece's short duration and lack of instrumental accompaniment, this delivery relies on the lyrics' brevity:

1 *Kayemba Nantabuulirirwa, olisaabala obw' ebbumba!*
The unadvisable Kayemba, you will row a clay boat![2]

The opening phrase of the song's lyric describes the king, Kayemba, as unadvisable; the second warns him about rowing in a clay boat, implying that his inability to take advice will lead him to ruin (line 1). The conception of the king as unadvisable reflects the importance of mutuality in formulating the leader's relationships. Accordingly, the song argues for advisability as a crucial factor in a king's success. Kayemba's narrow escape represents the many obstacles that kings face as powerful leaders, and the assistance he receives from the flutist demonstrates the role that musicians have in not only guiding the king but in helping avoid obstacles through their unique capacity for foresight. Although the story articulates such sights as fantastical, magical even, the type of sight that the flutist demonstrates is not much different from the kind of sight that court musicians grasp due to the embodied aspects of their performances. The philosophy built into their music means that in many cases, they can perceive what the king and others cannot. They have a unique grasp on the intricacies of reciprocity, a familiarity that their expressive and communicative talent only strengthens. As such, the stories associated with "Unadvisable Kayemba" reflect the musicians' unique ability to channel the king's relations through their own experiences and talents, creating an interwoven field of conceptions that can cast the world of interpreters in several new and exciting ways. These interpreters' world takes on new life as they reimagine the song in the context of their unique experiences.

1　Deziderio interview, July 15, 2005.
2　Ibid.

Advice and Caution

The background and central message of the "Unadvisable Kayemba" extends into further discussion among interpreters, who use the song's themes of advice and caution to reflect on the role of leaders and the current political climate of Uganda. In his analysis of the song, Steven Mukasa Kabugo details one of the alternative versions of the death of King Kayemba, which highlights the prophetic role of singers. His version provides us a unique perspective on what might have occurred had Kayemba not listened to his musicians:

> Singers take part in prophecy. A singer is a prophet, and though some of the people he warns or teaches may not take him seriously, they might later live to regret it. Singers can compose songs that illuminate the future, but because some leaders never treat singers seriously, they tend to take their warnings or predictions for granted. This was the case with Kayemba. According to one version of the story behind the song, during his reign a court official had an affair with one of his wives. Other officials who were loyal to Kayemba urged him to divorce this wife, but he ignored their advice. Consequently, the minister who had the affair plotted to assassinate the king in order to be with the woman he desired. Kayemba died because he failed to heed the advice of those closest to him, an instance that court performers communicated by singing, "Unadvisable Kayemba will row in a clay boat."[3]

Although Kabugo presents a different context, we can still see how the musicians' guidance is crucial to deciphering the often subtle or unknown events of the surrounding world. Many musicians can sense danger when it arrives, through the crackles in the air and the prickles on their backs. Whoever is so unwise as to ignore their warnings may end up caught within the very torrent of obstacles that they warn against. In this sense, Kabugo's comment frames the narrative about the clay boat as a metaphor for the sorts of foolish mistakes a leader might make by not heeding the advice of others, especially if those others are particularly skilled at predicting the future. The clay boat is no longer a clay boat but a mirror for the hubris of leaders.

In another version of the story, which my research circles had not previously heard, John Magandaazi Kityo holds that King Kayemba created the clay boat himself:

> Kayemba's subjects referred to him as "unadvisable" because he never took counsel. This habit led to the king building his own boat out of clay. Ignoring the concerns of his fellows who sailed in wooden boats, Kayemba used his pottery skills to shape and dry a boat from clay. When he took the

---

3 Kabugo interview, December 19, 2019.

boat to the lake to sail, his fellows warned him once again that the boat he made would not carry him. Kayemba did not listen. As soon as he sat in the boat and rowed it into the water, the clay gave way and dissolved.[4]

Kityo explains the story's moral, positing that the boat was a product of the king's own creation, resulting from his dogmatic refusal to heed the advice of his wood-using peers. As a result, as soon as he rowed into the water, the boat dissolved and sank.

> The moral of this tale is that every person, no matter what position they hold in society, should listen to others' views. This can help save individuals from making costly mistakes by providing ideas for better courses of action. "Unadvisable Kayemba" communicates or expresses the rewards for caring about the perspectives of others. Nobody follows a straight path without first listening to the advice of others. Human beings are all flawed individuals, so it is best to collaborate with others rather than making decisions alone.[5]

With this, we see that arrogance is an obstacle to sound decision-making. As we have seen in the previous part, failing to extend one's listening beyond their self-counsel will sabotage one's reign.

Jimmy Ssenfuka Kibirige's interpretation of "Unadvisable Kayemba" extends this discussion on communication and arrogance to contemporary politics, emphasizing the necessity of being open to advice and criticism. In particular, he speaks on the importance of leaders who, unlike Kayemba, are "advisable," and he describes what happens when a leader fails to be advisable. Namely, he points out how leaders come to mirror tyrants as the masses breed opposition and expose their dogmatic and self-interested attitude:

> Listening to and abiding by the wishes of the people one serves is a worthwhile endeavor. As a leader, one should be open to criticism. Indeed, only the unintelligent or the nefarious will claim to see no weaknesses in their leader. Those who are unadvisables (*bannantabuulirirwa*) are people who are rigid and unyielding to advice. In instances where they ignore the advice of others and "sail in a clay boat," they may not survive, prosper, or progress. Failure to progress as a leader is often to the detriment of the subjects. Because no leader is perfect, all leaders should strive to listen to the voices of others to preserve the prosperity of their people. The critical aspect of this notion is that a leader needs to listen regardless of positive or negative connotation of others' words. Additionally, they should receive all advice in good faith. Today when subjects speak of the weaknesses of

---

4   Kityo interview, December 14, 2019.
5   Ibid.

their leadership, the leaders say that it is their subjects or advisers who do not understand them. This dismissal of the masses' opinion reflects poorly on the leadership, indeed. Because there is no perfect leader, "The Unadvisable" should not exist. This is to say that everyone should be open to advice because no one is perfect. One who chooses to be unadvisable is no better than a dictator and tends to breed opposition. Indeed, today there are many opposition groups in Uganda because leaders have denied people a meaningful audience.[6]

These views reframe "Unadvisable Kayemba" through the lens of twenty-first-century political conflicts. Kibirige tells us that the behavior of the arrogant king still exists today. Many leaders suffer from the same flaws that the song criticizes; it can serve as a helpful metaphor when analyzing any given political conundrum.

Echoing these sentiments, Edward Ssebunnya Kironde gives historical examples of the inherent need for counsel in effective, productive political leadership. He argues that greatness and advisability go hand in hand:

"Unadvisable Kayemba" reminds us that however great a leader might be, if he fails to embrace the advice of others, he will inevitably make a mistake. He will cause problems for his subjects if he does not respect the fact that he needs counsel. No leader can claim he does not need advice because even the greatest kings in history required counsel and had flaws. For instance, King David, whom the Holy Bible discusses and who made many mistakes, relied on his advisers. Today's leaders should embrace the fact that they need advice and engage in dialogue with their people. The leaders should remember that the people they serve are not perfect and that leadership roles require one to be exceptional and bear the weight of the troubles their subjects may face or cause. Every time a leader does not listen to advice, he is more likely to stray from the needs of the people and become oppressive. This is counterproductive for the leadership because anytime people are oppressed, they are likely to take action against the oppressive leadership in question.[7]

Drawing on biblical philosophy, Kironde articulates that good leadership demands collaboration more than individual proficiency. Thus, the song he analyzes becomes an argument for mutual and collective rule by presenting the king as no more than an extension of the people's desires.

Referring to the current political landscape, Harriet Kisuule's analysis frames "Unadvisable Kayemba" in terms of the relationship between opposing political parties and the ways criticism feeds into their capacity for improvement and self-correction. She argues that such mutuality is

---

6   Kibirige interview, December 15, 2019.

7   Kironde interview, December 19, 2019.

crucial to all leaders' success, as demonstrating a willingness to adapt to the public's desires will help them gain their favor. Furthermore, she reminds us that such practices will ultimately set an example for other leaders, guiding them to do the same and thus become more flexible and receptive in their own right. Kisuule even connects the story about Kayemba with the alleged struggles of President Museveni. While commenting on the importance of heeding counsel, she suggests that people should still be wary of what others offer:

> Leaders need to accept correction and direction, especially if they want to overcome problems. They should avoid emulating the current leadership, which often does not accept advice. Indeed, this is part of the reason why President Museveni faces so many problems. Accepting advice is the key to achieving success, and if the president focused on communicating with the masses and listening to their needs, the people would be much less eager to offer their support to other politicians such as Bobi Wine. Additionally, by accepting corrections, Museveni would become an example to other leaders who would in turn adjust their own leadership practices. Accordingly, in order for leaders and their opposition colleagues to work with one another effectively in conjunction with their subjects, both sides should listen to each other and accept criticism where necessary. They should be transparent, truthful, exemplary, spiritual, and flexible.[8]

Rather than evoking the initially amicable relation of a king and his musicians, Kisuule highlights how even antagonistic or competing relations, such as those between current politicians, might become mutually beneficial if involved parties learn how to maneuver them gracefully. As such, Kisuule reimagines "Unadvisable Kayemba" in a way that allows it to reflect a new commentary on political behaviors in the modern era and points to a new possibility for interactions among all politicians.

Another lesson that one can glean from "Unadvisable Kayemba," according to Kisuule, focuses less on adaptability and receptiveness and more on the specific circumstances of modern-day politicians. She argues that people should avoid being too eager to make the former opposition leader, Bobi Wine, president. Although he is a promising leader, they must keep in mind the repercussions of such an event and consider the possibility of backlash if Museveni loses. This advice speaks to the potential of violence against opposing politicians and highlights how a misstep could be risky for figures like Bobi Wine:

> People are too quick to accept things they believe are good for them without fully considering the ramifications of the decision. Take the example of the

---

8   Kisuule interview, December 21, 2019.

politician Robert Kyagulanyi Ssentamu (Bobi Wine), who is popular with the people. If Bobi Wine wins the upcoming 2021 presidential election, the incumbent President Museveni may try to use the army to keep him from taking office. The people's support may not be enough to protect Bobi Wine, and in that manner the people might be rushing ahead with their decision without thinking of what the consequences may be. Bobi Wine is an inspiring and a promising candidate, but people need to take things one step at a time. Furthermore, even though on the surface Bobi Wine appears good, as Museveni did as a young leader, the masses cannot predict what type of leader he will become. A man might admire a woman and wish to marry her because of her beauty, but what lies inside her heart might be ugly and cruel in contrast. Rushing into a scenario, whether in marriage or politics, carries large risks.[9]

Like the musicians discussed earlier, Kisuule is reading "Unadvisable Kayemba" as a cautionary tale reminding the people that despite the optimism felt at Bobi Wine's rise, they should not be so impulsive as to overthrow the existing order. This reminder reshapes the song's more explicit message to fit a new context entirely. Rather than focusing on its abstract themes, Kisuule repurposes the song's original lesson as a warning to the public who, due to their role in determining leadership, could forget to listen, much like Kayemba did.

Elaborating on the need for caution when accepting things from others, Peter Kinene's uses "Unadvisable Kayemba" to discuss betrayal and how enemies often come disguised as friends. In this light, he borrows the story of the death of King Sir Edward Muteesa II (r. 1939–1969) while he was abroad, arguing that existential threats and danger can come from anyone, including those whom one trusts. Accordingly, Kinene explains, one must remain vigilant in every interaction and avoid trusting blindly:

> People should remain cautious because not everything gifted from others is good and can be dangerous or deadly. For that reason, it is beneficial to retain some element of suspicion when accepting things from others. Even someone you consider family may be plotting your downfall. You may be working hard to support that person while he or she is digging your grave. Recently, there has been staged accidents and plane crashes where the cause of death is not from any collision, but the victims' blind trust in those around them. Such instances evoke the proverb, *Abataka nkwenge; gw'olya naye y'akutta* (Landowners are like parakeets; the one with whom you eat kills you). Sometimes, the person you may think of as your closest friend may be the one jealous of what you have, secretly competing against you or wishing you ill. The death of King Sir Edward Muteesa II illustrates the

---

9   Ibid.

closeness of one's enemies. The king died from poisoning during his exile in the United Kingdom, and the person who betrayed him was allegedly a fellow Muganda, a young maid who worked for him. The king's enemies manipulated her into putting poison in his beer. On November 19, 1969, the king's birthday, he asked the maid to bring him his usual nightcap following his celebration and enjoyment of the company of his friends. After enjoying his drink, he went to sleep. The next day by about five o'clock news had spread that the king was dead. The betrayal was rooted in the king's own people. So the enemy works through one's allies.[10]

In the proverb Kinene references, "landowners" refers to friends, and "kills" can mean "stab with a knife." His perspective expands on Kisuule's previous point by illuminating the importance of caution in interpersonal dealings. It speaks to the inconstancy of people's loyalties and articulates the power one's enemies can wield by accessing one's inner circle. Although the deaths of King Kayemba and King Muteesa II have different contexts, the baseline message of the story remains true: one's trust of others is only as strong as one's physical and situational awarenesses.

Kinene offers another instance of treachery prevailing in describing the duplicitousness and espionage that may occur in the Ugandan political sphere. He further expands on his previous point by relating it more generally to how politicians deal with conflict. Reducing the stakes here from death to political ascendency, he shows us how an unnecessary amount of trust might lead to one's downfall. For example, members of a political party might steal another party's ideas and apply those proposed policies themselves. Trust might result in a greater chance of betrayal or outmaneuvering, as crucial information might become available to those looking to do one harm:

> Another moral of "Unadvisable Kayemba" is to guard one's secrets carefully, because even information shared among friends can eventually end up in the ears of enemies. This is a common phenomenon during political campaigns. The government in power takes the ideas of the opposition movement and labels them as their own. For instance, one opposition leader campaigned on the promise of abolishing graduated tax. The government, hearing the idea and not wishing for the politician to win his seat, abolished graduated tax themselves and did not give the opposition politician any credit.[11] To this end, it is best to keep one's secrets close to avoid giving enemies advantageous information.[12]

Here, Kinene links the betrayal of a life-threatening situation to betrayal encountered in political contests. Ultimately, the song he analyzes enforces

---

10 Kinene interview, December 16, 2019.
11 For additional information about this issue, see Mutebi 2012.
12 Kinene interview, December 16, 2019.

the notion that life is imperfect and filled with people who might be dishonest about their intentions or desires.

To conclude his interpretation of "Unadvisable Kayemba," Kinene delivers a point about personal diligence and the satisfaction that it brings. In the context of leadership, he believes self-accountability is important because it prevents leaders from blaming others for their own shortcomings. His commentary about self-diligence highlights the importance of personal virtue in one's duties, suggesting that one who puts in effort and reaps rewards is more satisfied than one who gains from the efforts and exploitation of many:

> In politics and leadership, we should focus on performing the part assigned to us rather than having expectations about what others can do for us. In other words, each person should do his or her duty instead of relying on other people's efforts. Diligence is critical. In that breath, there is an ancestral proverb that says, "*Kange*" *kakira* "*kaffe*" ("It is mine" is better than "it is ours"). The logic behind this saying is that what one can call one's own is better than what a group can claim because the former is what one has personally earned. That is, something that is the product of one's own sweat and effort is better than what belongs to many. The proverb advises people to work for their own personal gain instead of depending on what many own communally.[13]

Kinene pivots away from the cautionary framing of "Unadvisable Kayemba" to focus on the effort that one can make to realize one's power in each situation, as the flutist in the opening story did in order to protect the king. This process shows us how the song might relate to the behavior and dedication of individuals to achieve social goals. In this sense, hard work operates less as a demand than as a way to advise others.

Jessy Ssendawula rounds out the contemporary commentary on "Unadvisable Kayemba" by drawing back to a bird's-eye view of the principal morals of the song. He emphasizes the importance of accountability and attention regardless of social status, relating, "The lesson of the song is that people should listen to, use, and respect the counsel of others to avoid encountering tragedy. Even when in a position of power, one should listen to the concerns of those who are of a lower position."[14] Here, Ssendawula encourages a more egalitarian and accepting method of rule, as he argues that mutual respect transcends social status. Furthermore, he points out the importance of accountability in similar situations, arguing that regardless of the leader, his subjects must hold him or her responsible and recognize the leader for both successes and failures. This expectation expands the focus of "Unadvisable Kayemba" to the general behavior of leaders, detaching from

---

13   Ibid.
14   Ssendawula interview, December 28, 2019.

the more specific focus on politicians. The song's lyrics come to represent leadership at all levels, whether it be an unofficial leadership among friends or a legally sanctioned one in government.

Conclusion

"Unadvisable Kayemba" operates as a musical case study on failed governance, using its narrative structure to document the consequences of rejected counsel. The composition employs King Kayemba's reign as historical evidence to deliver a broader political thesis about the proper exercise of power. The song's very title emphasizes its central theme by permanently labeling Kayemba as "unadvisable." Accordingly, it transforms a specific ruler's character flaw into a cautionary archetype. By memorializing this leadership flaw through music, "Unadvisable Kayemba" creates an accessible political philosophy that transcends literacy barriers.

In "Unadvisable Kayemba," Deziderio blends the topics of violence and political injustice present in the other songs he performed and contextualized. The story he tells, in comparison to the ones that interpreters of the song provide, illustrates how different types of knowledge are shared by various generations of Ugandans. Whereas Deziderio, a lifelong servant to the king, recounts King Kayemba's shrewdness, interpreters recount stories that portray some national government leaders as unadvisable and stubborn. Perhaps the differences in the two sides' approaches to leadership reflect the increased distrust in the national government that has come to define the lives of the commentators. Some interpreters use "Unadvisable Kayemba" as a platform for criticizing President Museveni, whose period of leadership of almost four decades has allegedly been met with issues of distrust and broken communication. Other commentators interpret "Unadvisable Kayemba" in the light of countless failures and frustrations of contemporary political regimes within other contexts. Although the song refers to a specific historical king, the sentiment remains truthful throughout time, as its lyrical content acts as a protest of oppression in general. The figure of the clay boat in "Unadvisable Kayemba" persists as a representation of the political issues that can destroy a leader and his people, yet the song also exemplifies how the conception of a song evolves in response to historical events.

10

"He Has a Lot on His Mind"

Deliberation and Animosity

The song "He Has a Lot on His Mind" ("Alina Bingi By'Alowooza") has historically been performed in court settings, even though it does not make direct reference to Kiganda court life and royal politics. In his discussion of the composition's background, the performer of the version discussed in this chapter, Ssaalongo Paulo Kabwama (1923–2020), notes that the song indirectly addresses the differences between the Kiganda kingship of the past and present, particularly under the current national government of Uganda. The singer adds that he views his musicianship as a gift with which he can in turn serve his king, a topic he further highlights through the lyrics that list the reasons for which he is thankful for the eight-stringed bowl lyre (*endongo*) that he used to accompany his singing.[1]

Kabwama opens his performance with a random plucking and fine-tuning of the bowl lyre (*endongo*). He then plays a complex, bouncy instrumental that interweaves two interlocking parts: a principal melody produced by the low-pitched strings of the bowl lyre and a secondary melody produced by the high-pitched strings. Shortly after, Kabwama begins to sing over the instrumental. Throughout his brief performance he uses a mellow but chant-like singing style and coarse timbre. Keeping his vocal part in a generally high register, Kabwama sustains the ends of most of the part's melodic phrases on one continuous note. Toward the end of the performance, he repeats the same melodic phrases, slightly altering them each time with different lyrics before he finishes. Overall, his performance has a bittersweet tone, both beautiful and solemn, and features a complex polyphonic texture:

1 *Abaalukola ddala, abasajja batukeerera nnyo*
Those who started this political journey, indeed, the men and the
  suffering their politics brought really dawned on us

---

[1] Kabwama interview, July 20, 2005.

2 *Olaba bigenderedde, ebyobufuzi bifuuse bya mpalana*
You see, as things progress, politics has turned into animosity

3 *Kati tugenderedde, kati ebyobufuzi bigenda bya mpalana*
Now we have progressed, now politics transpires as animosity

4 *Edda baagambanga, nti obufuzi babuyisa lwa ddembe*
In the past they used to say that governance is peaceful and fair

5 *Alina bingi by'alowooza, nnaabeera wano*
He has a lot on his mind, I shall dwell here

Okwagala kabaka n'antunuulira, owange nnaabeera wano
Loving the king as he notices me, my friend, I shall dwell here

6 *Endongo eno, yantuusa omufumbo w'atuuka*
This bowl lyre, led me to where the married reaches

7 *Endongo yange eno, okusooka ye mununuzi asooka*
This bowl lyre of mine, first of all, is the first liberator

8 *Endongo yange eno, yantuusa omufumbo w'aliira*
This bowl lyre of mine, led me to where the married dines

9 *Endongo eno, yantuusa omufumbo w'akwata*
This bowl lyre, led me to where the married touches

10 *Ka batukolere, abalijja balyogera ebirala*
Let them serve us, successors will say their own things

The opening lyrics of "He Has a Lot on His Mind" describe the deterioration of Buganda and Uganda (lines 1–4), showing us the tragedy of current trends through explanations of the animosity of national politics today. The song's lyrics also provide a considerable amount of autonomy to the musician's instrument. Kabwama claims that despite the bad state of the world, his musical instrument redeemed him by bringing him close to the king, whom the singer describes as "the married" in lines 6 through 9. In line 5, "dwell here" refers to the king's presence. Lyrics such as "This bowl lyre, led me to where the married reaches" (line 6), "This bowl lyre of mine, led me to where the married dines" (line 8), and "This bowl lyre led me to where the married touches" (line 9) also employ an active voice to describe the actions that the musical instrument takes, thus personifying the singer's bowl lyre. James Makubuya shows how similar personification abounds through the decoration of the bowl lyre, which its makers adorn with a goat fur tassel to clothe and therefore dignify the instrument.[2] The power Kabwama accords to the musical instrument is evident in his supplemental

---

2   Makubuya 2000, 144.

remark. The performer states that the only way the public recognized court musicians before the 1966 crisis was with their musical instruments.[3] In other words, it was the musical instruments themselves that held the ability to bestow the musicians the status associated with being court instrumentalists. The song "He Has a Lot on His Mind" thus reframes the instrument not merely as a tool for producing sound but as an actor that influences the musician himself.

In the lyrics of "He Has a Lot on His Mind" we also find the juxtaposition of suffering and respite, which demonstrates the reciprocity that forms the basis of the king's relationship with his musicians. In addition, we understand the rejuvenating effect that performance has on court musicians, as their ability to perform allows them a chance to earn new status at the court, to take on new versions of themselves by dedicating their lives to the kingship. Their relationship with the king is mutual. Rather than describing it as a duty or a responsibility, they describe it as a relief and palliative. Again, the singer implies that were it not for the musicians' intimacy with the king, he would be lost in the deterioration of the world just as many others already have been. The language that the performer uses to detail the king's court, describing it as where he "dines" (line 8) and where he "touches" (line 9) demonstrates that the relationship between them is more than merely functional, showing that just as the king's presence soothed the nerves of the musicians, the musicians soothe the nerves of the king. Their interaction thus constitutes a mutually therapeutic event, socially recuperative in that it provides both parties an opportunity to take joy in the other's care. The events of the subsequent context that Kabwama describes, though, swiftly crush this mutual relationship. This section of the song sheds new light on what Kabwama might be referring to when he describes the deterioration of things. This is most evident in the closing lyric (line 10), as the singer predicts the loss of mutuality that would occur if the kingship were to be removed. He notes, "Let them serve us, successors will say their own things."

Deliberation and Animosity

Various interpretations of "He Has a Lot on His Mind" referenced in this section wield the song's lyrics to articulate notions of deliberation and animosity. Among other topics, they discuss greed and selfishness, conflict and consensus, as well as truth and dishonesty. Harriet Kisuule's interpretation reminds us that when politics devolve into animosity, some politicians might use increasingly deceitful and immoral tactics to come out

---

3   Kabwama interview, July 20, 2005.

on top. She suggests that this is the case with the current political scene in Uganda, as we see with her description of some of the methods that politicians use:

> There is no truthfulness in politics—it is a dirty game. For a politician to make it to the top, he must be able to lie well and often. Many politicians have no regard for fairness and do not care about people as long as they are able to make it to the top. As a result, there is a lot of hatred and aggressive competition in politics. The politicians' focus is on maintaining their own position, making the acquisition of a maximum number of votes their top priority. This means that sometimes they enact policies that are either harmful or irrelevant to others. President Museveni, for example, cares mostly about making policies that are helpful to those who are members of the National Resistance Movement, his political party. However, he still pays attention to the feelings of the majority because he needs to ensure he will be able to get through reelection when the time comes. His tactics exemplify how politicians need to be patient and attentive listeners to best gauge public opinion before engaging in the decision-making process. Careful analysis of a situation is necessary before taking any political action.[4]

But Kisuule also specifically comments on one of the ways President Museveni has demonstrated his ability to listen to the people, particularly through his various projects and campaigns:

> He has devoted efforts to issues such as child education and immunization, educational infrastructure, and healthcare, which he approaches through a combination of reforms and funding. His general focus remains on understanding the struggles of the poor, common man before devising solutions for them. The people whom he helps in turn appreciate his assistance and praise his rule, allowing him to remain popular among the lower class.[5]

Kisuule's interpretation speaks to the breakdown in the mutual relationship between a leader and his subjects. Whereas this dynamic previously embodied processes of mutuality and reciprocity, the prevalence of manipulation now continuously undermines any attempts to reinstate them. Some leaders no longer consider themselves extensions of the people, instead viewing themselves as separate entities whose primary objective is to gain power that they can use for themselves. Moreover, they advertise their conduct as beneficial to the state, as John Lonsdale observes.[6] These dynamics demonstrate the relevance of "He Has a Lot on His Mind" in the

---

4 Kisuule interview, December 21, 2019.
5 Ibid.
6 Lonsdale 1992, 466.

context of today's politics. The descent into animosity evident in the song's lyrics comes to represent the deterioration of mutuality between the people and their politicians. At the same time, Kisuule's commentary differentiates between compassionate and self-serving types of attentiveness. When leaders are only inclined to do the bare minimum as a political strategy that sways the people to their side, it exposes that serving or assisting the people is not the primary goal of their policies. Instead, they are smokescreens to obscure their selfishness as benevolence.

Continuing Kisuule's description of political tactics, Edward Ssebunnya Kironde expands the discussion to include the methods that more minor, local politicians use as opposed to the major power players like President Museveni. He articulates the problem in politics as a multipronged dilemma, endemic in all political parties as a symptom of the broader system itself:

> There is no true democracy in Uganda. The ruling party has violated and changed the constitution on numerous occasions. First, they removed the term limits for presidency, then the age limits. When the opposition produces a sensible policy, the ruling government refuses to implement it on principle, even if it benefits the country. Everyone involved is a wolf in sheep's clothing and eventually caves to their desire for personal gains. They use the struggles they have faced to pad their campaign. For example, one opposition councilor searching for votes repeatedly leaned on a story of herself protesting and getting tear-gased alongside the opposition leader, Colonel Dr. Kizza Besigye, to craft her image and gain votes. Naturally, these personal struggles, though impressive, are not indicative of whether someone is a capable leader. Regular people go through similar struggles all the time, but none of them tries to use their struggles as an intrinsic justification for political gain. Furthermore, many of those political climbers fail to be effective civil servants. Betty Kamya, for example, a potential presidential candidate for one of the opposition parties, has not made a remarkable impact while in her current post. This demonstrates that self-serving and ineffective behaviors are not just problems limited to the current ruling party; they are endemic among the opposition as well. As a result, the opposition is struggling to make any real headway because the people recognize that they are no different in behavior than those already in power. Additionally, those among the opposition truly invested in improving the country suffer at the hands of those who have adopted self-centered behavior. Politicians like Bobi Wine who are looking to enact real change struggle because the people they depend on are constantly backcrossing them, unable to devote themselves to serving for the common good.[7]

---

7   Kironde interview, December 19, 2019.

By criticizing the current government's opposition candidates, as well as the president himself, Kironde shows us that the problem in Ugandan politics is not limited to the current administration, as even those who challenge it demonstrate a selfish disregard of their responsibilities. This aspect shows how the lyrics of "He Has a Lot on His Mind" might not intend to guide us toward a particular leader but toward a new mode of governance. In this way, the singer's dedication to the king becomes more than mere calls to switch loyalties from one leader to another but an affirmation of a new way of conducting politics. Rather than pursuing animosity by drumming up support for one side while cultivating dislike for another, the song proposes creating mutual and reciprocal relations between political actors; in other words, a philosophy of consensus where all parties are dedicated to each other rather than themselves. As Kelly Askew suggests, leaders need to recognize that their rhetoric will gain no ground if it fails to resonate with the people. Success of a state relies on the mutuality between the government and the people, meaning that those excluded from or spurned by the state are more likely to dissent. Although the government might like to think otherwise, citizens will not merely accept blind obedience.[8]

Having described some of the methods that politicians use to ensure their reelection, Kironde's analysis of "He Has a Lot on His Mind" also examines the challenges of global and intra-ethnic politics causing further deterioration of the existing political apparatus. She notes that the instances of deterioration that politicians do not directly cause but instead are the result of external or unexpected forces:

> Political affairs in Uganda are particularly complicated due to the country's ethnic diversity. There are more than fifty ethnic groups, all with different names, traditions, and cultures, in a population of less than fifty million people. This is one of the reasons why maintaining political balance in Uganda is difficult. Another reason is that sometimes the masses might better maintain the political balance without a particular person's leadership. However, that individual, wanting to remain in power, puts his or her own desires before the needs of the country.[9]

Given Uganda's diversity, conflicting desires, and intersecting beliefs, it is impossible to avoid disagreement or conflict. However, attaining peace does not mean erasing or ignoring inevitable conflict but instead means finding methods to respectfully reconcile differences in a stable framework. The problem is that this might not be the mindset of Uganda's current leadership. Kironde is encouraging people to take up an attitude of interactive maintenance rather than rhetorical proliferation. This perspective

---

8 Askew 2002, 12.
9 Kironde interview, December 19, 2019.

creates a new meaning from the language that the lyrics of "He Has a Lot on His Mind" use. The bowl lyre is a redeemer not because it erases conflict or failure but wrestles with it, lifts one out of it, eventually allowing one to overcome it. In the same way, the king does not cure conflict but thinks critically about resolutions. He maintains "a lot on his mind" because there is much to deliberate about, much to resolve. However, it is through this crucial process of overcoming political blockages that the agreements and disagreements that have passed through the kingdom might "liberate" themselves.

Peter Kinene reflects in his interpretation that leaders are more concerned about maintaining power than promoting peace. He suggests that if any politician has the choice between maintaining power and giving the masses a joyful rule, in most cases he or she will choose the former, engaging in cutthroat competitions. This mismanagement of conflict primarily results in losses for the people, as they are left stranded while their officials continue to bicker and hatch plots. Kinene cautions, "Though people may think politics is a game, today's politics are not. They are dangerous and can involve loss."[10] This perspective gives "He Has a Lot on His Mind" fresh relevance by reconstructing the meanings behind animosity and peace outright. It shows us that peace does not only refer to the lack of conflict but also speaks to the priorities of governance and how leaders place the well-being of their people before the well-being of themselves. The descent into animosity reveals a descent into disagreements founded not on an honest desire to help but on a desire to cause difficulties.

Kironde further accounts for the government's deterioration into animosity. His criticism of the government draws on far larger commentary regarding the circumstances of governance in Uganda. Managing conflicting interests, under ideal leadership, would already be incredibly taxing and barely manageable; however, when one places such responsibilities on the back burner, an already difficult job turns impossible:

> Leaders are also constantly on the lookout for betrayal, whether from within or beyond. Treachery is such a prominent feature of rule that many songs mention it. Leaders come to fear hypocrisy and are wary of fully trusting anyone. They must balance the forces within their own internal government as well as broader national and international tensions. For Uganda, that means balancing the Christians and the Muslims, the Baganda and the Banyoro people, alongside other more massive forces such as the United States, China, Russia, the United Kingdom, and the Middle East. Each group wants to have their say, particularly the ethnic groups of Uganda, which have their own ceremonial leaders but

---

10   Kironde interview, December 16, 2019.

lack true independence. To balance out all these needs is no easy feat. Indeed, sometimes the state of the government running our country seems more akin to a television drama than reality. People lose children, experience the effects of natural disasters, or die prematurely. They cry out to the government to help, but often it can be the government itself that is responsible for their troubles. Government officials are the highest criminals of them all.[11]

Expanding on the idea of disloyalty, Kironde adds,

> Leaders fear betrayal. The cutthroat nature of contemporary politics breeds the fear that any wrong move may result in the loss of one's power or lead to one's death. Thus, leaders frequently spend time on themselves, shuttling between self-serving actions and avoiding betrayal. Accordingly, they rarely focus their attention on the interests of the people, unless doing so aids their own purposes. Between the many opposing interests, national conflicts can become confused and disorganized chaos, as all parties are aiming for different outcomes with varied motives.[12]

From Kironde's viewpoint, the notion of deterioration that "He Has a Lot on His Mind" presents is far wider and more daunting in scope than was previously apparent. The animosity that the song describes is allegedly spread throughout both the government's foundations and its insecurities, leading it to fight against itself.

In addition to detailing the qualities and practices that create a poor and selfish leader, interpreters also articulate the qualities and practices that make a just and helpful one. Jimmy Ssenfuka Kibirige describes an effective leader as one who can handle the many responsibilities expected of them throughout the day by consolidating time and multitasking. Kibirige emphasizes the importance of quick and fluid thinking, making connections off hand even while doing something else, and producing solutions as quickly as problems occur:

> Because a leader always "has a lot on his mind," he should be able to do many things. Being a good leader requires the ability to think critically and multitask. There will always be obligations for a leader to fulfill throughout the day, such as community work or infrastructural projects. With such full schedules, leaders rarely have the time to sit down and think properly about the needs of their people. As a result, they need to be able to multitask and use the information they learn during their time among their people to devise their plans for serving them.[13]

---

11 Kironde interview, December 19, 2019.
12 Ibid.
13 Kibirige interview, December 18, 2019.

This method of adaptable leadership contrasts with that of many contemporary leaders in that the former often become engrossed in a single-minded obsession with their own self-preservation. While they are campaigning for themselves or passing laws to extend their power, they are ignoring their responsibilities to compartmentalize and expedite various actions. In "He Has a Lot on His Mind," the singer's love for the king is only possible given the king's drive and efficacy as a leader. As the lyrics demonstrate, he bears a lot on his mind, constantly thinking of ways to assist. However, he still makes the singer feel noticed and valued while doing so. This process demonstrates a dual relationship between intention and practice, highlighting that leaders must both enact and demonstrate care for their people, something that is allegedly missing in the national government.

Expanding on his previous commentary, Kibirige explores what happens when leaders fail to follow through on their proposed initiatives. This issue arises in the conflict between Buganda and Uganda, but it also occurs within the kingdom. Kibirige describes how some Baganda leaders have failed to follow through on an educational initiative and have instead contradicted their stated goals.[14] Whether the disconnect is between the government and the people or within a kingdom, the failures to enact policies might reflect the division that people face at an interpersonal level. The consequence of a lack of unity and thoughtfulness is that everyone suffers, as leaders waste resources on ineffective programs.

According to Kibirige's analysis, the supposed thoughtlessness of some current national government leaders speaks to the fact that the people's interests now only exist as an afterthought. These leaders seem to only care to the extent that the masses can reelect them, and thus they invest in projects that look and sound good but are wasteful and aimless. Kibirige challenges the claim that some initiatives of the kingship have been successful:

> Baganda leaders teach through the Better Education Less Labor project, among other social campaigns. These leaders, however, have yet to take this slogan to heart, as many are still putting their people into nonpaying jobs. They have mobilized the masses to make bricks, a labor-intensive job with poor pay, for instance. These sorts of employment strategies lack any creativity, and it is clear that they have not put much thought into generating a fresh, new solution for the general underemployment problem. There is still a lack of access to education across the country. In Buganda, there is the Kabaka Education Fund. It is a perfect demonstration of how leaders should take the time to create solutions for their people. There is also Muteesa I Royal University, Muteesa II University, Ccwa II Memorial College, and the Buganda at the Peak (Buganda ku Ntikko) project. These projects, which

---

14   Ibid.

highlight the legacies of previous kings' reigns, are the result of leaders who think, like the current King Mutebi II, and in turn provide the education that people need to find good jobs. They can find positions that have good pay and clear career opportunities, thanks to these projects.[15]

Here, we see how, despite the smaller amount of power that the kingdom wields, it is allegedly fulfilling its goal of helping the people far more effectively than the national government has. By thinking critically about a creative solution, the kingship has supposedly established a method that might present a lasting solution to the unemployment problem. The king's program is in no way perfect, but it allegedly still represents a positive shift in the Buganda government caring for civilians compared to the program that the national government produced. The phrase "He has a lot on his mind" becomes more than a description of how busy the king is, instead demonstrating the king's methodology whereby he does his best to fulfill his role to the extent of his power.

Echoing the sentiments of Kibirige, Kinene's interpretation expands on the ways a leader should attempt to serve his people. Kinene frames politics as a competition where one must sweat and exert oneself to achieve benefits. However, his interpretation of competition differs from that of other interpreters who have previously described competition negatively, as a cutthroat dynamic that buries the people's interests under an obsessive focus of winning elections. Kinene describes politics as competitive only in so far as it requires a constant process of exertion and self-overcoming. He therefore understands politics as a competition with oneself and one's predecessors. According to Kinene, the winner of the competition is the one who benefits the people the most, causing any new leader to be in a battle for growth, always seeking to improve and overcome the past to mark a brighter future:

> A good leader plans for his people and is always considering the best ways to transform them. Political activities are a competition; they are not just about sitting around and waiting for things to come to you, which is why leaders need to be planning constantly. As two Kiganda proverbs say, *Ebirungi biva mu ntuuyo* (Good things come from sweat) and *Atya omusana; talya bwami* (One who fears the scorching sun; does not become a chief). Leaders cannot earn their office without putting in some amount of work. They need to persist to achieve success, particularly within politics. Consider that those who dedicated themselves to serve the interests of the president are now serving as ministers. They were able to profit from their determination. Again, it is persistence that enables individuals to profit from their work.[16]

---

15 Ibid.
16 Kinene interview, December 16, 2019.

In the proverbs referenced, "sweat" refers to hard work, and "scorching sun" represents challenges. Kinene's interpretation of "He Has a Lot on His Mind" demonstrates the difference between animosity and competition. Where animosity defines the competition between politicians today, it does not necessarily mean that competition itself is an evil. In fact, one can consider healthy competition and hard work as a facet of thoughtful deliberation. In this sense, Uganda's problem today is not simply a structural issue that the electoral system allegedly creates but a philosophical one that people must wrestle with.

Today many politicians campaign on promises that they do not intend to keep. Like the people that the closing lyric of "He Has a Lot on His Mind" reference when Kabwama sings, "Let them serve us, successors will say their own things" (line 10), these politicians fail to do what others expect of them. Referencing a specific example of this phenomenon from President Museveni's rule, Kironde highlights how some politicians supposedly rely on dishonesty to achieve reelection and lie about policies to set an artificially improved image of themselves. However, in explaining this practice, Kironde also acknowledges that it is not always so easy to make decisions that benefit people in the long term while also pleasing them in the short term. As he illustrates with the current administration's decision to restructure the national curriculum, sometimes even a beneficial decision can lead to a great deal of backlash from those it affects. Thus, leaders with moral dilemmas may not have an ideal solution or a solution at all. Kironde elaborates on the idea that the phrase "He has a lot on his mind" (line 5) suggests these problems:

> President Museveni must engage in a delicate balancing act with the people. A vote is coming in 2021, so naturally he wants to appeal to the people as much as possible. However, some of the duties involved with being a leader are inherently unpopular among those people. Recently, for example, his government updated the national curriculum for secondary schools. Part of the changes the government made to the system included cuts to the number of subjects taught. The government scrapped some entirely while it merged others, such as commerce and entrepreneurship studies. It is less for the government to deal with, but at the same time it means that one out of every two teachers was cut. Naturally, while the curriculum may be better, it is quite unpopular due to the unemployment it caused. It is difficult to find a balance between long-term priorities and short-term popularity, but it is something that all leaders must grapple with.[17]

Although Kironde provides us with this more forgiving stance on imperfect leadership, he does not exonerate poor leaders for their failings,

---

17   Kironde interview, December 19, 2019.

affirming that such challenges are ubiquitous in politics. Instead, he is suggesting that a good or bad leader is determined by how well he manages, rather than eliminates, conflict. Kironde also sheds light on how the public often fails to acknowledge the difficulties of leadership, leading to greater stress as leaders are bombarded by criticism from all sides. Consequently, says Kironde, they fail in their duties as they dedicate their energies to overcoming the variety of other challenges they face:

> With all these factors to consider and try to balance, leaders always have too much on their mind. However, as soon as they make a single mistake, their subjects still ruthlessly attack them for it. The whole situation is a lot for one person to handle. Political opponents seek to undermine them at every step, and they are constantly in a battle between doing what is best for the country and doing what is most effective in garnering the favor of the people. Because of this, there is a high probability they will be unable to fulfill or will have to go back on several of the promises they made. Brexit sessions highlight the effect that the forementioned constant struggle has on leaders like Prime Minister Boris Johnson. When he appeared before the United Nations, giving a speech about robotic technology and its increasing prevalence, he seemed mentally exhausted and barely made any sense. Having to jump through all the hoops of Brexit really seemed to wear him down. One of the reasons that might have contributed to this stress was the competition he faced from the opposition parties. Democracy in the United Kingdom is quite strong, so unlike in Uganda it was expected that the opposition had a chance to properly challenge the incumbent leader. They have checks and balances that Ugandans do not.[18]

These dynamics further reframe the interpretation of the phrase "He has a lot on his mind." Kironde's comments draw a connection between overworked leaders and the deterioration of the government and politics. The former feeds into the latter because leaders become too drained to perform their duties effectively, and thus the government begins to collapse in on itself. At the same time, the latter feeds into the former as the animosity of politics drains leaders in the first place. "He Has a Lot on His Mind" therefore takes on a cyclic meaning, as its lyrics feed back on themselves and reinterpret each other all at once. A highlight of Kironde's commentary is the specific example he gives of a politician exhausted by the animosity among leaders.

---

18 Ibid.

Conclusion

"He Has a Lot on His Mind" maintains a tradition of royal court performance despite lacking explicit references to Kiganda court life or monarchical politics. The song is an indirect commentary on the evolution of kingship, functioning as a subtle political instrument that uses its seemingly apolitical lyrics to create a space for comparative reflection between historical and contemporary governance structures. Through "He Has a Lot on His Mind," Kabwama establishes a framework for examining how the institution of Kiganda monarchy has been transformed under Uganda's national government without requiring explicit criticism. In addition to affirming the singer's status and illustrating the role of royal court musicians in looking after the well-being of the king during particularly stressful times, "He Has a Lot on His Mind" addresses the differences between the politics of the king and those of the national government. It appears to criticize the electoral politics of the latter as a form that has "progressed" into "animosity," juxtaposing it with the kingship's redemptive, intimate, and mutual tendencies. However, the added commentaries, both from the song's performer and interpreters, recast its message to articulate far more than that.

Some interpreters understand the lyrics as a recognition of the king's thoughtfulness, while others read the song as a demonstration of all the stressors that contemporary politicians face, which consequently undermine their leadership. Through these competing interpretations, we see new ways to understand the song that extend from those previously imagined framings. The result is the constant revival of the composition through the extensive imaginations of those who encounter it. Each interpretation reflects a major shift in the song's meaning, its expression, and its philosophy, functioning as a celebration of the fertility that its text represents. It becomes immortal, preserved not in the static and frozen sense that we come to expect but in a living sense, constantly becoming new with every interpretative moment. These interpretations of "He Has a Lot on His Mind" demonstrate how court music can evolve beyond its original ceremonial function to become a vehicle for nuanced national political discourse. This process allows performers to address sensitive governance transitions through artistic expression rather than direct commentary.

11

"Gganga Had a Narrow Escape" or "They Chopped Off His Fingers"

Punishment and Mercy

The song "Gganga Had a Narrow Escape" ("Gganga Alula") tells the story of a royal court musician who was punished for his disobedience and inappropriate behavior in the court of King Mwanga II (r. ca. 1884–1888, 1889–1897). The subject matter of the song relates to the topics of discipline and correction within the royal court, both of which are examples of a two-way, reciprocal flow between the king and his subjects. To highlight Kiganda notions of justice, this chapter presents "Gganga Had a Narrow Escape" in two distinct iterations, each associated with a single performer. The alternative version is titled "They Chopped Off His Fingers" ("Baamutemako Engalo"). The song's interpreters listened to both iterations sequentially, so for purposes of brevity I hereafter refer to them iterations as "Gganga Had a Narrow Escape."

The performer of the first version, Ssemambo Ssebuwufu (ca. 1959–2015), shared this story about the song's history:

> Gganga was a virtuosic musician who played a bow harp (*ennanga*) in the royal court of King Mwanga II. Most of the staff in the royal enclosure were non-royals. According to court etiquette, they could not have sexual relations with royals. However, the king's daughter, Princess Nassolo, developed a secret romantic interest in Gganga and they ended up sleeping together, even though such an act was forbidden. Eventually, the king found out about the relationship through court officials. Although the punishment for this behavior was usually death, Mwanga II decided to spare Gganga's life because he was such a talented musician and a close

friend, instead ordering the administrators in charge of his case to find a suitable punishment for his crime. The officials reduced his punishment to a more minor enforcement of justice: they amputated Gganga's penis, which they deemed was responsible for the crime.[1]

This background underscores how, historically, the duties of the king of Buganda include more than contemplating and caring for his people. At times, he has to reprimand rule breakers and reinforce the status quo. This less savory aspect of leadership involves striking a delicate balance between punishment and mercy, which might be deemed justice when struck aptly. This arrangement is the subject of the song "Gganga Had a Narrow Escape."

During his performance of the song, Ssebuwufu sings to the accompaniment of a seventeen-slab xylophone called *akadinda*. Because the performance requires at least two musicians to play the instrumental part, I play with him. Ssebuwufu serves as *omunazi* (literally, "initiator") or player of the song's primary melody, while I act as *omwawuzi* (literally, "divider") or player of the composition's secondary melody. We sit on opposite sides of the xylophone and play alternating or interlocking notes, with each of our strikings comprising two notes separated by an interval of an octave. Ssebuwufu plays his initiator part on the beat, while I play my divider part on the offbeat. Together, our parts form isorhythms, and their interlocking allows for the parts to contribute equally to the realization of the song's overall instrumental melody, which supports Ssebuwufu's singing.

We begin performing the interlocking instrumental parts at a slow tempo and in triple meter, with Ssebuwufu starting with the initiator part before my divider part joins soon after. Our performance gradually increases in speed and intensity until we abruptly stop and deconstruct the piece halfway through the performance. Ssebuwufu then begins to play his initiator part again, this time at a much slower tempo than before. His vocal accompaniment joins in with the mix and ambles along with the initiator, instrumental, part for the rest of the song's performance, quietly yet consistently. He sings various lyrics to the accompaniment of this part for the rest of the performance, pausing a couple of times to reset the alignment of his instrumental and vocal parts:

1 *Ngalobikuggu yabba ennyama; yabba ennyama, baamutemako*
Partial Fingers stole meat; he stole meat, they chopped off his fingers

2 *Ngalobikuggu yabba ennyama; yabba ennyama, baamutemako*
Partial Fingers stole meat; he stole meat, they chopped off his fingers

---

[1] Ssebuwufu interview, June 4, 2013; see also Cooke and Wachsmann 2003, 18.

3 *Ngalobikuggu wuuyo ajja; wuuyo ajja, baamutemako engalo*
Partial Fingers, there he comes; there he comes, they chopped off his fingers

4 *Wuuyo ajja; yabba ennyama, baamutemako*
There he comes; there he comes, they chopped off his fingers

5 *Da da da da da da da da da*
Da da da da da da da da

6 *Ngalobikuggu yabba ennyama; yabba ennyama*
Partial Fingers stole meat; he stole meat

7 *Ngalobikuggu yabba ennyama; yabba ennyama, baamutemako*
Partial Fingers stole meat; he stole meat, they chopped off his fingers

8 *Ngalobikuggu yabba ennyama; yabba ennyama, baamu ...*
Partial Fingers stole meat; he stole meat, they ...

[*brief instrumental interlude*]

9 *Nnannyinimu omuwanvu, alimukwatako alikaaba, "yaaye!"*
The tall householder, whoever will touch him will cry, "*yaaye!*"

10 *Nnannyinimu omuwanvu, alimukwatako alikaaba, "yaaye!"*
The tall householder, whoever will touch him will cry, "*yaaye!*"

11 *Nnannyinimu omuwanvu*
The tall householder

12 *Baalimukubye emiggo, ne bamulekera engalo ezirya*
They should have flogged him, and left him with the fingers that he uses to eat

Ssebuwufu's singing has a mournful or somber tone that captures the emotion of the song's overall storyline. He emphasizes the significance of some of the textual phrases by repeating them, in varied ranges. His vocal phrases tend to follow a similar pattern, in which he starts out on high notes and descends to a lower range for the end of each phrase. He repeats the ends of some phrases verbatim but with a slight rise in intonation, as if reiterating a question. As he plays and sings, I mark the downbeat with a snapping or clacking sound that results from hitting my beaters together, a sound that also serves as a timeline for the overall rhythmic framework of the song for the second half of its performance. Overall, the complementarity of our instrumental parts and that of the xylophone parts and Ssebuwufu's voice has a mutual relationship. That is, these parts are not just equally important; there are also defined by each other's existence.

The lyrics of "Gganga Had a Narrow Escape" convey Gganga's sentencing through metaphorical language. "Fingers" (lines 1–4, 6–8, and

12) and "meat" (lines 1–2 and 6–8) serve as euphemisms for the male and female sexual organs, while "to eat" (line 12) is a euphemism for sexual acts.[2] "Householder" (lines 9–11) refers to the king, "touch him" (lines 9–10) means disturbing his peace, and "will cry 'yaaye'" (lines 9–10) suggests one will regret disturbing him. With this context in mind, the otherwise vague lyrics of "Gganga Had a Narrow Escape" illuminate its variety of meanings. Without this explicit context, however, interpreting the song will take various directions. It is important for us to note how the lyrics never explicitly blame or criticize the punishers' decision. Instead, the singer suggests alternate ideas for how the king could have punished Gganga (line 12). This process of advocating, rather than criticizing, is a delicate semantic balance that court music performers and subjects alike tend to consider when speaking with the king. Even the justification for the alternate punishment is indirect. Rather than saying that the king caused the "thief" to be unable to eat, it says that his punishers should have left his fingers because they made eating possible (line 12). The only active part of the lyric is the fingers, as they "allowed" the "thief" to eat. The basic meaning of the lyric remains the same; however, by using less causal language, these lyrics reflect criticizing the punishment rather than the king. Even the story of the song itself remains somewhat passive, as the description of the meat thief is an illusion to hide the true events behind the song. The closing lyric (line 12) suggests that the original performers of "Gganga Had a Narrow Escape" pleaded (on behalf of Gganga) for a less permanent punishment as well as a sentence that was not death, shedding light on the context of court judicial decisions.

Albert Ssempeke Bisaso (b. 1979), the presenter of the alternate version of "Gganga Had a Narrow Escape" titled, "They Chopped Off His Fingers," opens his performance with the rapid plucking of the bow harp (*ennanga*). This is followed by an instrumental featuring two parts that interlock in a manner like that of the xylophone parts described earlier. Bisaso plucks the strings of the bow harp with his thumbs and index fingers, and the two instrumentals quickly lock into a part that uses a consistent, swift tempo that he maintains throughout the duration of his performance. Following the instrumental introduction, his vocals soon follow, characterized by a mellow delivery while at the same time covering a range of different notes. Bisaso's voice fluctuates up and down in tonal range quite a bit before his performance ends very abruptly after the final lyric. Contrary to Ssebuwufu, Bisaso sings with more confidence, staying completely calm, as he sings the full version of "They Chopped Off His Fingers":

1 *Baamutemako engalo, tezadda*
They chopped off his fingers, they never returned

---

2   Ssebuwufu interview, June 23, 2009.

2 *Gganga alula; Nassolo, Gganga*
Gganga had a narrow escape; Nassolo, Gganga

3 *N'akyokooza Buganda ku zino engalo*
He provoked Buganda with these fingers

4 *Zino ezabbanga emmere*
These, which used to steal food

5 *N'akyokooza Buganda ku zino engalo ennene*
He provoked Buganda with these big fingers

6 *Nnaamukola ntya, mukama wange?*
What will I do about him, my lord?

7 *Abange, abange, abange*
My people, my people, my people

8 *Nagenda okulaba engalo gye zadda*
I went to see where the fingers went

9 *Yandiguze puliida, nawuliriza engalo gye zadda*
He would have hired a lawyer, to hold a hearing on the fingers' whereabouts

10 *Gganga alula; Nassolo, Gganga*
Gganga had a narrow escape; Nassolo, Gganga

11 *N'akyokooza Buganda ku zino engalo*
He provoked Buganda with these fingers

12 *Zino ezabbanga emmere*
These, which used to steal food

13 *N'akyokooza Buganda ku zino engalo ennene*
He provoked Buganda with these big fingers

14 *Oba weegaana, leeta ezo engalo, baazitemako*
If you are denying, show those fingers, they chopped them off

15 *Oba weegaana, leeta ezo engalo, baazitemako*
If you are denying, show those fingers, they chopped them off

16 *Engalo tezadda*
The fingers never returned

17 *Nnannyinimu omuwanvu, oyo gw'alikwatako alikaaba, "yaaye"*
The tall householder, whomever he will touch will cry, "*yaaye*"

18 *Abange, abange, abange*
My people, my people, my people

19 *Twagenda okulaba, engalo tezadda*
We saw that the fingers never returned

20 *Yandiguze puliida, n'awuliriza, engalo tezadda*
He would have hired a lawyer, to hold a hearing on their whereabouts, the fingers never returned

21 *Gganga alula*
Gganga had a narrow escape

22 *Nnaamukola ntya, mukama wange?*
What will I do about him, my lord?

23 *Gganga alula*
Gganga had a narrow escape

Bisaso's repetition of the lyric "Gganga had a narrow escape" (lines 2, 10, 21, and 23) highlights its importance to the identity of the song. The recurrence of this statement suggests the king's power and omnipotence, which his subjects never question. Bisaso also centers on the response that the royal court gave to Gganga's less-than-reputable behavior. Although Ssebuwufu's version describes this behavior, Bisaso's focuses far more on the process of deliberation that preceded the court's decision regarding Gganga's fate. In a couple of lyrics (lines 6 and 22), the singer asks the king what he should do, perhaps wondering what punishment would be best, given Gganga's crime. Other lyrics mention that Gganga should have hired a lawyer so that he could have a role in the deliberative process and fight for his freedom and life through his own means (lines 9 and 20). Throughout the song's narrative, we repeatedly hear of Gganga's fingers (lines 1, 3, 5, 8, 9, 11, 13–16, and 19–20), which remind us of the punishment he received: the amputation of his penis. The loss of fingers represents both the price Gganga paid for misbehavior and the compassionate way the court spared his life. We also hear of his crime (stealing food) in line 12. While Bisaso's overall take on the story of Gganga speaks to the deliberation and consensus that might go into the king's decisions, it is clear here that this punishment is not the sole decision of the king, as the song evokes many other figures that impact the trial's outcome. These include court musicians, who might have collectively struggled to save the life of one of their colleagues despite the risks of such an undertaking. Some historical sources posit that to avoid immediate death, the musicians composed "Gganga Had a Narrow Escape" and imbued it with indirect communication, complex hermeneutics, and subversive undertones which meant to sway Mwanga II to act differently.

Punishment and Mercy

Focusing on the themes of punishment and mercy, the following interpretations of "Gganga Had a Narrow Escape" or "They Chopped Off His Fingers" demonstrate the impact that conflict and violence as well as procedures of justice can have on both individuals and communities in the political realm. Peter Kinene's interpretation emphasizes how mercy is a crucial quality for leaders to have, reorienting the song under examination to focus on the perspective of the king, as he was ultimately the one who decided Gganga's fate:

> When resolving a conflict, a good leader first listens attentively and considerately to all sides involved before making an appropriate decision. When this fails to take place, incidents like that involving the Uganda Martyrs happen. There could have been another way of punishing those martyrs without killing them. Even though many Baganda honored them for their dedication, bravery, and martyrdom, their deaths resulted still from King Mwanga II's failure to listen. Therefore, they never shared in the glory they brought Uganda. Perhaps they would have been able to do things of even greater significance had he spared them.[3]

Kinene's mention of the Uganda Martyrs refers to events in Uganda between 1885 and 1887 that resulted in the execution by King Mwanga II of forty-five Christian converts. James Martin notes that Mwanga II felt that the influx of Christian missionaries in his kingdom, and Christianity at large, was challenging his authority. As more people began devoting themselves to God, the king interpreted this as disrespect toward the kingdom. He was also allegedly a pedophile, and when young Christian converts began rejecting his advances, he became determined to eradicate Christianity from Buganda, using violent tactics. This ultimately resulted in the burning of three Baganda Anglicans—Joseph Rugarama, Mark Kakumba, and Noah Serwanga—followed by the murder of an Anglican bishop, James Hannington. When Joseph Mukasa, one of the king's senior advisers and an Anglican Christian convert, criticized the leader for not offering Hannington the opportunity to defend himself, Mwanga II became enraged and killed Mukasa as well, transforming him into the first of the Uganda Martyrs. Mwanga II then turned his attention to the head of the court pages, Charles Lwanga, and even toward the many Anglican converts among the pages. What followed was an extended period of persecution that culminated in all their deaths as Mwanga II's men burned them alive.[4]

---

3   Kinene interview, December 16, 2019.
4   Martin 2011.

In referring to the Uganda Martyrs, Kinene highlights how punishment might vary depending on one's ability to think through a situation. Even though, according to Kinene, Mwanga II's advisers suggested that he do not kill the martyrs, he still called for their deaths. Regarding Gganga, on the other hand, when the king learned that the musician and his daughter had secretly become romantically involved, his closeness to the performer allegedly prompted him to avoid giving Gganga the death penalty. He probably listened to and considered the musician's plea, recognizing that despite his failure, he held no ill will and thus deserved clemency for his crime. Mwanga II exercised two different degrees of mercy here: none toward the Uganda Martyrs and at least some toward Gganga. Such variability suggests that rulers (even more brutal ones like Mwanga II) can find it in themselves to enact justice with compassion.

Jessy Ssendawula's interpretation of "Gganga Had a Narrow Escape" considers two more recent historical examples—the American bombings of Hiroshima and Nagasaki in Japan and the Rwandan genocide—which relate to the theme of the emotional and behavioral shifts caused by violence. Ssendawula demonstrates that pain does not end where it begins. Instead, it roots itself in the people and places where it occurs, spreading its tendrils to affect places and times that extend beyond its immediate environment. For example, an event like a war will have implications far beyond the events of the battle itself or the immediate population it affects. For generations after, the pain it creates can be ruminated on, persisting in the ripples of its inception. Ultimately, the violence of war impacts more indirect victims than we can imagine. Ssendawula expounds on this theme:

> War comes with long-lasting, gruesome effects that irrevocably alter the lives of those who experience it. One should consider the impact the bombing of Hiroshima and Nagasaki had on Japan, where the emotional aftereffects still impact people today. One should also consider the way the 1994 Rwandan genocide left devastating fear in its wake, to the extent that the Paul Kagame administration has banned reference to the event as well as the ethnic groupings of Hutu and Tutsi in schools. Similar effects are common among the people of northern Uganda, where the recent Lord's Resistance Army rebel war in Gulu has impacted people's lives for years on end. Considering all the damaging effects of war, leaders should try at all costs to avoid this senseless violence.[5]

The effects Ssendawula describes bring to the fore the notion of deliberation. In Ssebuwufu's and Bisaso's versions of "Gganga Had a Narrow Escape," we see how the singer asks listeners—including the king—what he

---

5 Ssendawula personal communication, April 8, 2020. For more information on the effects of the LRA rebel war, see Atim et al. 2018.

should do, encouraging them to reflect before deciding. By attempting to inform the king of the situation, the singer is perhaps providing him with a better outlook from which he can decide Gganga's fate. Ssendawula's interpretation suggests that smaller forms of violence still enact the same fundamental pain that massive wars do and that carelessly using violence as a form of justice might alienate a population from feeling that their leaders care about them.

Ssendawula shares his own version of the events of "Gganga Had a Narrow Escape" that slightly differs from Ssebuwufu's and Bisaso's renditions to provide tangible lessons to current leaders. He suggests that despite whatever justification a politician gives, violence will not erase political issues but will actually breed more issues for the society to deal with. In the case of Ssendawula's commentary, he points to war veterans as one instance of violence's effect, as their lasting wounds, physical and psychological, will require public support that reintegrates them into regular life. This process is very tenuous if one does not receive adequate support, and it may strain a government of its resources even further. Therefore, instead of believing that violence has no repercussions, Ssendawula argues that leaders should understand the reverberating, yet understated, impact of their political choices and should care for the population in this manner. Here, Ssendawula shares his alternate version:

> This song focuses on the aftermath of Gganga's narrow escape from death. His interrogators detained and punished him by chopping off his fingers before eventually releasing him. Having borne witness to his seemingly unwarranted punishment, the singer would have served as a witness for Gganga in a trial. However, Gganga took up a life of crime instead, using his disability against his fellow Baganda. Through manipulation, he stole from them repeatedly. The lesson that national government leaders should take from this song is that they need to take responsibility for victims of violence and war, particularly the needs of veterans who have fought for their country. People should not neglect their needs because doing so would force them to fight for survival and, as is the case with Gganga, pose a threat to the community. The very least the government can do is support them after the hardships they have faced.[6]

Ssendawula's points evaluate "Gganga Had a Narrow Escape" in terms of the song's effects. Rather than focusing on the scene of the story itself, the points center on what happens afterward and how one should endeavor to maintain some modicum of amicability during the story's aftermath. With Gganga, the kingship's oversight only made the problem worse, causing him to continue to "steal." With veterans, the laxity of twenty-first-century

---

6   Ibid.

leaders might lead to increased crime and poverty, as vulnerable soldiers face starvation or criminality as their only two paths to survival. Being unable to reintegrate also means that, for some, it is harder to hold a job, keep a house, or maintain healthy relationships. Both instances exemplify the importance of diligence when dealing with the precarious process of rehabilitation.

Steven Mukasa Kabugo ends the analysis of "Gganga Had a Narrow Escape" by explaining the lesson that young listeners should draw from it, especially during times of turbulence or political uncertainty. His approach differs from Ssendawula's thoughts in that Kabugo focuses less on ensuring accountability from the government for their own actions and more on the ways individuals themselves should behave to stay safe. He argues that the masses have a similar reciprocal responsibility to leaders, as they must equally take measures to protect themselves, even as leaders take steps to protect or uplift them. In the case of the song in question, Gganga had given in to his passions and failed to respect the conduct of the court. If he had followed Kabugo's advice, he likely would have saved himself and the king from trouble, and both would have been better off. This arrangement centers on the role of the subject in maintaining beneficial relationships with rulers. Kabugo comments:

> The story behind the song presents how some people died because of the political situation that was prevailing in Buganda—that is, from the ways they disrespected the king. The consequences these people faced show that the present youth need to be careful with their leaders and elders. When God ordains a householder (*nnannyinimu*), his subjects have to respect him and follow what he says, not only to be good citizens but also simply to stay out of trouble and ensure their own safety.[7]

Kabugo demonstrates the role a single figure can play in benefiting the community at large. In doing so, he provides nuance to Ssendawula's criticism of current leaders, suggesting that reducing political friction is a matter of personal conduct. This point further illuminates "Gganga Had a Narrow Escape" as a commentary of the actions that led up to Gganga's punishment. Rather than focusing on the sentence itself, this transformation drives us to reflect on its primary cause, forcing us to reconsider the dynamic between king and subject we might have at one time taken for granted.

---

7   Kabugo interview, December 19, 2019.

Conclusion

"Gganga Had a Narrow Escape" narrates the story of a court musician, most likely a harpist, who misbehaved in the royal court of Mwanga II and the punishment that followed. A literal reading of the song posits that the musician "stole meat" and had his fingers cut off as a result. According to this reading, the song is an indirect challenge to the harsh punishment. It suggests that the punishers of the "thief" should have left him his fingers because he needed them to eat. However, the singer does not reject the notion of punishment outright. Instead, he suggests a less severe form, validating the decision to punish while questioning the use of severe violence. In this sense, "Gganga Had a Narrow Escape" explores the question of accountability between the king and his people, not just in terms of the leader's capacity to extend punishment but also in the people's capacity to confront him. This arrangement is characterized by Kiganda notions of justice, which involves a reciprocal cycle of punishment and mercy.

Bisaso's alternate version of "Gganga Had a Narrow Escape," "They Chopped Off His Fingers," highlights the authority court musicians have historically held in some outcomes of legislative decisions. Court musicians have historically had the power to change the king's mind and alter his decisions, as exemplified by the lyrics of many songs discussed in this book. The song in question is therefore a reminder to the performers and civilians to always act on the power that they have to ensure the best outcome for their people. "Gganga Had a Narrow Escape" transforms an individual's punishment into a broader lesson about court etiquette and power dynamics. The song also preserves institutional memory about appropriate behavior within royal circles, using one musician's experience as a teaching tool for subsequent generations of performers. By memorializing this specific incident, the composition establishes boundaries for court musicians, demonstrating how artistic proximity to power carries both privileges and significant risks.

Characterized by the related themes of punishment and mercy as well as the universal topics of justice and responsibility, the two versions of "Gganga Had a Narrow Escape" analyzed in this chapter relate to a multitude of sociopolitical contexts, as demonstrated by the unique views of the interpreters featured in the chapter. At first glance, the song might indicate a strong emphasis on brotherhood and support among court musicians. In the case of Gganga, his fellow musicians lament his punishment and continue to support him, even though he has committed a crime in the court by going against the rules that the royalty have set in place. They even go as far as composing a song that would hopefully convince the king to pardon him, a process that is neither easy nor secure, as such an attempt could easily backfire on them.

Reorienting our perspective and meaning of justice, the song explores the question of accountability between the king and his people, not only in terms of the leader's capacity to extend punishment but also in the people's reciprocal capacity to confront him. This arrangement is characterized by the philosophy of *ubuntu*, which means one cannot exist as one is without others.[8] This theme parallels other court songs' focus on the king's thoughtfulness and leadership, and it recalls and demonstrates the previously discussed royal court harpist's historical role in giving voice to the people of Buganda by lending advice to the king.

Each interpreter's analysis of "Gganga Had a Narrow Escape" reorients our perspective and meaning of justice, providing a unique spin on the song's connections to this topic with a focus on the related themes of punishment and mercy. Through their readings of the song, we see that the real physical and emotional impacts on people far exceed any one view about these themes. The interpreters' applications of the song's lyrics to politics remind us to avoid war and violence, both of which might leave different kinds of scars (physical, psychological) on the groups of people involved. The commentators, therefore, suggest that leaders of those people must be cautious in how they approach conflict. As we have seen in the previous part of this book, these interpreters continue to morph, hybridize, and revitalize the lyrical content with new contexts and ideas.

---

8   On *ubuntu*, see Eze 2010 and Houshmand 2019.

Part IV

Songs about Loyalty and Duty

Mutual trust, allegiance, and dependability are some of the pillars of power relations that characterize bonds among people inside and outside the royal court in Buganda. Exploring themes of loyalty and duty within these relationships, part 4 explores notions of social debt and reciprocation in the contexts of kingship, national politics, and more proletarian relationships such as those between fellow musicians and family members. The songs express some of the emotions associated with bonds of loyalty in a variety of ways. Each song offers a nuanced glimpse at the inner workings of loyalty and duty in Buganda and Uganda as a whole. Chapter 12 uses the themes of regret and appreciation to frame its discussion of the song "I Would Have Given You a Large Haplochromis" ("Nandikuwadde Enkejje Entulumba"). This song describes the regret one of the king's subjects felt when he was unable to meet the leader's immediate need: offering him a haplochromis, which is a type of fish endemic to some African lakes. It broadly displays the regret that all people feel when unable to express their appreciation toward those who have positively affected their lives. Chapter 13 focuses on the themes of lament and uncertainty in the song "The Flutists' Legal Case" ("Omusango gw'Abalere"), which laments court flutists whom the king removed from duty for disrespectful behavior. Capturing the more somber emotions attached to loyalty and duty, the two songs show us that loyalty has a negative side. Parties may experience lament, regret, loss, missed opportunities, personal failures, and other feelings or experiences that arise from our attachments to others. Although each of these songs explores separate topics and sentiments, their mournful subject matter and sorrowful tones unite them.

The two songs that close part 4 revolve around affection, respect, and subservience, all of which characterize the Baganda's relationship to the king. Beyond the historical accounts and somber retellings of their lyrics, these songs illustrate loyalty through the various affirmations of power and reverence that different kings' subjects (performers and commentators) articulate. Chapter 14 illustrates themes of power and selfishness in the song "The Little Lion" ("Akawologoma"), which effectively depicts the king, while also detailing the loyalty and obligations that his subjects display. Chapter 15 explores themes of reverence and love in the song "The King Is a Lion" ("Kabaka Mpologoma"), which portrays the Ugandan national government in relation to Buganda's king and his right and duty to rule over his own people. Both songs use leonine imagery to outline the kingly aura and the sentiments he inspires in his people. The songs demonstrate a willing devotion toward the king's rule, in addition to the mutuality of the relationship he shares with his subjects and how he reciprocates this love and exercises his power. In the various interpretations that are presented and analyzed in part 4, the lyrics of the songs become a collective dialogue about the contemporary government of Uganda and the relationships held between leaders and their people.

The four songs featured in part 4 are reminders that loyalty and duty permeate all types of relationships, as we see presented in the lyrics, commentaries, and interpretations. Loyalty does not just apply to bonds of friendship and family but typifies broader relationships, between a king and his people, and between a government and its citizens. It is a mutual acknowledgment, a two-way street where both sides of the relationship must exhibit attention and care for each other. As the four chapters of part 4 illustrate, many Baganda put their faith in their king and demonstrate their obedience, and the leader responds to this faithfulness by taking care of them and making the best decisions. The numerous connections that commentators draw on in their readings of the songs further confirm the universality of loyalty. They reimagine the relationships the songs deal with within today's political contexts, applying concepts such as betrayal, attachment, and hardship in the compositions to contemporary situations. Accordingly, they highlight the problems within Uganda's current government and the challenges of proper leadership in the twenty-first century. Through every interpretation, a new permutation of meaning is born, and the analyzed song becomes more significant than the sum of its individual parts.

12

"I Would Have Given You a Large Haplochromis"

Regret and Appreciation

"I Would Have Given You a Large Haplochromis" ("Nandikuwadde Enkejje Entulumba") is primarily a song about a king's subject who regretted his failure to locate a kind of fish the leader desired. Albert Muwanga Ssempeke (ca. 1930–2006), the performer of the version analyzed here, shared the following historical context:

> The court performers of King Jjunju (r. ca. 1780–1797) composed the song "I Would Have Given You a Large Haplochromis" after King Jjunju instructed Gabunga, the official in charge of the boat moorings at his lakes, to go find him a special kind of fish called *enkejje entulumba*, which many considered to be nutritious. Wasting no time, Gabunga set off for the lake. On his way there, however, he contemplated the small size of the fish in question. He wondered if it was appropriate to deliver such a small fish to the king. In his mind, doing so was simply unfitting for the king's greatness. As Gabunga walked toward the lake, talking to himself, he ran into a man with a mental disability. The man asked him why he looked puzzled, why he was talking to himself, and if he needed help. Gabunga explained his dilemma to the stranger. Following his explanation, the man advised him to immediately return to the king and tell him that the kind of fish he wanted was only available during a specific season, when the lake filled up from the rains. For the king to get the fish, he needed to wait until then. Gabunga returned to the king and did as the man advised him. To Gabunga's surprise, the king honored his recommendation. Moreover, the king eventually forgot about the matter, never bringing it up again. This episode in part inspired the song "I Would Have Given You a Large Haplochromis."[1]

---

1   Ssempeke interview, July 27, 2005.

As Ssempeke suggests, "I Would Have Given You a Large Haplochromis" communicates the mutuality inherent in human relationships. It evokes Gabunga's encounter with a common man, where he seeks his advice and they address the conditions of his task, resolving as to what Gabunga should do next. The song demonstrates how their interaction serves as a birthing ground for solving his conundrum. It further illustrates how the man's perspective on the issue grants Gabunga valuable insight that directs him toward a new angle. As a result, despite his desire to go seek out a haplochromis, the man's advice is beneficial, and Gabunga appreciates it.

Ssempeke's performance of "I Would Have Given You a Large Haplochromis" features an accompaniment by the bow harp (*ennanga*), which produces a soft but effervescent buzzing timbre. Like other song presentations using the bow harp described in previous chapters, his performance includes two intertwined instrumental parts: a primary melody played by one hand and a secondary or countermelody played by another hand. These melodic parts collectively support the vocal part, and the three are inseparable. Ssempeke's performance opens with the two instrumental parts interlocking. They are soon joined by his singing. These layers become interwoven, and yet each layer maintains its own rhythmic and melodic character. At times the three parts are in unison. No one part dominates another or receives special prominence. Ssempeke's lyrics and their delivery express a bittersweet mood and emotion that captures the blend of the song's feelings of appreciation and regret. One can feel this tone of appreciation in the song's more effervescent aspects, while its regretful feeling resides in the tone of the performer's vocal delivery. As such, the lyrics sound both forlorn and joyous. While Ssempeke's performance is full of textural brilliance, his reserved singing style and introspective repetition of certain lyrics and instrumentation evokes the text's sorrow. Throughout his performance, Ssempeke emphasizes the tones of the bow harp's low-pitched strings, and his voice tends to remain on certain pitches of the strings for longer than others. Furthermore, his vocal melodies consistently start on high pitches and descend into a lower tonal range over time rather than rising or fluctuating back and forth. These, among other performance techniques, bring out a wistful and forlorn atmosphere. Ssempeke's lyrics appear below:

1 *Nandikuwadde enkejje entulumba, ne weeyanza*
I would have given you a large haplochromis, and you appreciate

2 *Nange nandikuwadde enkejje entulumba, ne weeyokera*
Personally, I would have given you a large haplochromis, and you grill

3 *Wamma nnaamuweera ki? Nange ntegedde nga yankuuma*
Truly, what shall I offer him? For I have come to know that he took care of me

4 *Kitange nnaamuweera ki? Nange ntegedde nga yankuuma*
What shall I offer my father? For I have come to know that he took care of me

[*brief instrumental interlude*]

5 *Mmm, nnaakola ntya? Nnaayita ani?*
Hmm, what shall I do? Whom shall I call?

6 *Bayite omulangira oli, wamma nze omufumbo*
Let them call that prince, truly, I, the married

7 *Mpaata mugonja mpaawo alya*
I peel a *gonja* banana but no one eats

8 *Maama, mpaata mugonja mpaawo alya*
Surely, I peel a *gonja* banana but no one eats

9 *Kyokka bayigganya nze omunaku, babuuze kye baŋŋamba*
But they persecute me, a pauper, ask them what they want from me

10 *Olaba bayigganya nze omunaku, babuuze kye baŋŋamba, emirembe gayaaza*
You see, they persecute me, a pauper, ask them what they want from me, peace breeds laziness

11 *Mmm Mmm, nnaakola ntya? Wamma nze omufumbo*
Hmm hmm, what shall I do? Indeed, I, the married

12 *Bayite omulongo oli, wamma ye nnyini nsi*
Let them invite the other twin, indeed, he is the owner of the country

13 *Nange nnaakola ntya? Nange ntegedde nga wankuuma*
Personally, what shall I do? I have come to know that you took care of me

14 *Olaba baasaze majja, nange ntegedde tebaasoboke*
You see, they made a fresh plot, I have come to know that they will be impossible to handle

[*brief instrumental interlude*]

15 *Ka ŋŋende, kale weeraba, naye eno ensi yaffe yali nnungi*
Let me go, well, goodbye, but this country of ours was good

16 *Ka ŋŋende, ka ŋŋende, naye eno ensi yaffe yali nnungi*
Let me go, let me go, but this nation of ours was good

[*brief instrumental interlude*]

17 *Nnaakola ntya, oo ndimuweera ki? Mmange ntegedde nga yankuuma*
What shall I do, oh what shall I offer her? I have come to know that my mother took care of me

18 *Wamma, nandikuwadde enkejje entulumba, ne weeyokera*
Indeed, I would have given you a large haplochromis, and you grill

19 *Wamma nandikuwadde enkejje entulumba, ggwe eyannamba*
Indeed, I should have given you a large haplochromis, you who told me

20 *Olaba bayigganya nze omunaku, nnaayita ani?*
You see, they persecute me, a pauper, whom shall I call?

21 *Bayite omulongo oli, maama nze omulongo*
Let them call the other twin, indeed, I, the twin

22 *Maama ensi yaffe yali nnungi, emirembe gayaaza*
Indeed, our country was good, peace breeds laziness

In Ssempeke's lyrics, he expresses the pain that arises when one fails to reciprocate another's assistance. He also describes the gift of the haplochromis to express reciprocity, agonizing over his sudden inability to show his appreciation to another (lines 1–2). In referring to the person to whom he owes this favor, the performer often switches between describing his father or mother (lines 4 and 17), even using vague pronouns (line 2 and 13). As a result, the figure whom the singer owes becomes interchangeable. This quality is also true of the singer's identity, as he refers to himself at times as a spouse (lines 6 and 11) or pauper (lines 9–10, and 20), but he only does so during specific sections of the song and is quick to diverge from the tone and message that accompanies those self-identifications. The singer also takes on the identity of "the twin," the king (line 21), a strategy that enables him to switch perspectives between the king and a subject. Overall, "I Would Have Given You a Large Haplochromis" collects multiple unique perspectives on processing the loss of reciprocity, which it articulates through variations in its lyrics. Another key theme in the song is the notion of external actors plotting the singer's downfall (line 14). His regret draws on this fact, as he comes to recognize that the one who had once helped him is no longer there.

As we have seen, the main portion of "I Would Have Given You a Large Haplochromis" laments the singer's failure to fulfill his part of a relationship and thus sever the loop of exchange. However, the singer does not base the song on guilt, instead framing it with a genuine sense of loss, as though his failure to reciprocate has been injurious to his existence in a more profound way. This is not loss in the traditional sense but in that one has lost tandem with a mutually beneficial relationship whereby the singer is no longer able to share and reciprocate the assistance of another. In this way, mutuality is not just a moral demand that people should serve one another because it is the right thing to do, but a relationship that fulfills the servant and recipient alike. It is joyful because this reciprocity is imbued with vitality. The song's form further exemplifies the concepts above, as the singer shuttles between perspectives and meanings. He is a spouse and a kin and a nobody, and those whom he owes are his mother, father, or an unnamed friend. Here, mutuality extends out to everyone in the community, as the composition's perspectives are themselves disseminated. This serves to encourage an interwoven web of interactions, which the performer constructs between the song's multivariate identities.

Regret and Appreciation

The differing interpretations presented in subsequent paragraphs reexamine "I Would Have Given You a Large Haplochromis" in a new light while also evoking universal truths. In their evaluations of the song, many interpreters observe mutuality and reciprocity through the feelings of appreciation and regret. Based on these themes, they discuss the song's connection to issues of political deterioration. Many expand its notion of reciprocity, discussing the obstacles inherent in modern leadership and social, mutual interactions. The way that the song's lyrics switch between identities particularly highlights the two-way, exchanging nature of relationships, which interpreters in turn use as a guide for analyzing and critiquing self-centered leadership practices.

In John Magandaazi Kityo's analysis of "I Would Have Given You a Large Haplochromis," he asserts the importance of appreciating others in the moment for what they have done. Arguing that connections and reciprocity benefit us beyond material or symbolic gain, he explains that the singer's sadness over his failure to reciprocate draws from a sadness at the loss of the relationship itself. Kityo then proceeds to reframe this notion through the lens of modern political governance. He explains how failed reciprocity lets down both sides of the power dynamic, as neither party receives support from the other. People start disliking and criticizing a leader, so much so that they are unlikely to support him even when he is doing good for the people:

> As the opening lyric of the song suggests, those who either choose not to appreciate others or forget to do so are often regretful of it later. One must appreciate the things one receives from others or those who have done well for one. This might be why the singer asks what he shall offer his mother, who gave him security, when he sings: "What shall I do, oh what shall I offer her? I have come to know that my mother took care of me." Appreciation is particularly meaningful because it forms a connection

between two people. People are less likely to forget where they came from or who helped them get where they are today when they actively show their appreciation for what others have done to help them. However, there are also occasions where people only repay others for their good deeds with strife. Much of this arises from forgetfulness, when one does not thank those who have helped one as soon as possible, and rather puts off showing their appreciation for a later date. Eventually, those who helped that person become frustrated, and soon the acknowledgment of their help is all that they focus on. They confront the beneficiary, asking why he or she does not appreciate them for what they have done. This is the situation that Buganda seems to be facing currently and has perhaps faced for the past thirty years politically. It is important for politicians to remember their roots and those who supported them. Here, I am referring to the relationship between President Museveni and the Baganda people, who supported the guerrilla war (the Ugandan Bush War) that made him president. They based their support on the promises he made to them, including reinstating federalism, which would allow Buganda to have political independence and a more active kingship. However, Museveni never kept all his promises. Although he restored traditional political institutions, most of the political power still lies with the central government. In other words, Buganda's kingship remains a passive one.[2]

Kityo's interpretation of "I Would Have Given You a Large Haplochromis" describes reciprocity in more abstract terms, shuttling between perspectives and meanings to provide a clear instance where reciprocity collapses and affects both parties negatively. As with the described relationship between President Museveni and the Baganda, any betrayal of trust results in the progressive, continual decline in the relationship's value. If allowed to continue like this, the moment of exchange might no longer be reciprocal, but a form of negativity and selfishness, with each seeking to acquire the best deal for him- or herself, often at the expense of others. Although a relationship of some kind may remain, it might no longer be rewarding. Instead, a series of calculated and economized negotiations will define it, and both sides will come to loathe it. This is the case with the relationship in question. As Evalisto Muyinda observes, many Baganda continue to desire greater political autonomy due to the kingdom's long history of independent rule, which we can trace back all the way to the beginnings of the fourteenth century.[3]

Edward Ssebunnya Kironde continues Kityo's analysis of the connection between modern politics and the issue of rewards and recompense. His interpretation provides a more detailed look at the singer's predicament. Rather than focusing on failed reciprocity, he examines why the singer

---

2   Kityo interview, December 14, 2019.
3   Muyinda 1991, 2.

cannot reciprocate. He determines that the performer's desire to reciprocate though unable to describes the condition of many Baganda today. According to Kironde, because of their alleged mistreatment by leaders, and the mismanagement of the country, many do not have the resources to help themselves, let alone help others:

> "I Would Have Given You a Large Haplochromis" is from the perspective of someone who would like to reward those who helped him but is unable to. External factors limit that person from showing proper appreciation, but the person wishes to thank them all the same. From a political standpoint, the song paints a picture of a society of oppression, one with a large gap between the haves and the have-nots. Because of their access to better resources that their position in power affords them, some leaders seek help from overseas instead of going to their own health institutions. In contrast, many of their subjects go without any resources due to the lackluster performance of those leaders. Furthermore, many citizens have freedom of speech on paper, but their rights do not carry over to reality. The constitution is too flexible, allowing members of the current administration to simply adapt it to their own whims. Because some people feel like they barely exercise their rights, they believe the nation is no longer the Pearl of Africa as it was once called. Several citizens are proud to be Ugandan and are proud of their country, but they are displeased with the way the failures of the current leadership are holding the nation back.[4]

Kironde distinguishes between being proud of one's country and being upset at being neglected by the government. Here, the Baganda do not feel the same rewarding relationship that they have historically maintained with their king, and this disconnect diminishes their hopes to witness Uganda reclaim glory and prosperity.

Given this situation, many Baganda are hesitant to place their trust in governmental systems, and thus they might withdraw from engaging with those in power. Harriet Kisuule's interpretation is empathetic to this conundrum by recognizing that while exercising such caution is valuable to any type of relationship, it must not be done so with regret but with an optimism that one can achieve a caring, reciprocal bond. She maintains that reciprocity can only occur in an atmosphere of mutual trust and care. She describes, in a similar vein to Kityo, what can happen when that relation degrades. Kisuule explains how a leader who fails to appreciate the people will receive no appreciation in return and elaborates on her stance:

> It is a good thing to remain hesitant at first to give or accept things from others until they have proven themselves worthy of the occasion. The haplochromis (*enkejje*) referenced in the song is valued as a particularly good

---

4   Kironde interview, December 19, 2019.

type of fish. Therefore, the listener can extrapolate that if the king was truly beloved by his people, then his subjects would have offered him the haplochromis. That is partly why it is important to establish mutual respect in politics. People love a good leader, wish him well, follow his instructions, and support whatever he wants them to do. The same cannot be said for a poor leader. For example, people often listen to a king's chief who asks them to work together with him to renovate roads, but they might not do so to a poor national government leader. Returning to President Museveni's leadership over Uganda, it is true that he has done some good things for Ugandans. However, external factors dictate the extent of his ability to do such things. For instance, Ugandans might request the government to provide them with welfare, but it may be impossible or unsustainable due to the size of the population. Just like the performer mentioned in the song, the president may wish to make Ugandans feel appreciated but cannot. Furthermore, during some of the times when he can fulfill his commitments to bettering the nation, people do not always appreciate him. He has constructed roads and schools, but to some, these acts of goodness pale in comparison with the destruction he has done. The key, then, is to look at the whole picture and not make a judgment on him based on a single action.[5]

Although she diverges from the other perspectives on "I Would Have Given You a Large Haplochromis," Kisuule affirms that a reciprocal dynamic between leader and subject depends on the extent to which they share genuine appreciation for each other's role in their lives. When this relationship becomes tainted with animosity, apathy, or a lack of compassion for the other's personal condition, then both sides will come to regret having trusted each other. However, to provide the flip side to this, Kisuule warns that compliments can be dangerous as they may deceptively portray appreciation:

> Sometimes flattery and praise can ruin the quality of leadership. It is therefore important for leaders not to accept such praise blindly. They should think about why and how people are praising them—whether it is genuine or simply for their own benefit, appearing as a fleeting acknowledgment that they reverse quickly. Leaders must do their research, and if they find there is a particular quality that people especially like, it is wise to try and augment it. Anytime a leader has not performed well or made a mistake, he should acknowledge it, correct it, and move on. Leaders need to bolster their weaknesses as well as their strengths and look out for those whom they lead. Moreover, critical thinking and analysis are crucial. For example, if a shopkeeper notices a large influx of customers, it could simply be that the items she is selling are popular. However, she might also realize, after

---

5   Kisuule interview, December 21, 2019.

some careful analysis, that people go to her shop because they are getting more change at the end of the transaction than they are due. Those people might be traveling to the shopkeeper's store knowing that they will get a better deal than at other places. That is why it is important to analyze and understand people's motivations in doing things. These same skills are crucial in politics and leadership, where they help leaders make informed decisions. Leaders must ask themselves why people behave the way they do and consider any ulterior motives they might have. People also need to work hard on their own and not necessarily expect gifts from others. They should not be idle and sit around waiting to receive the brown envelopes of cash that President Museveni sends to his followers. They need to act themselves and listen to their leaders carefully.[6]

Here, Kisuule recognizes that compliments might be disguised ill will and that if one is not skeptical of them or aware of the broader context of the flattery, then one might realize that one who gives a compliment may be trying to extract something from others rather than enjoy in kind with them.

Steven Mukasa Kabugo maintains other interpreters' focus on the present by providing some Kiganda proverbs that reflect both the singer's need for advice and the situation of contemporary youth. His views shed additional light on the significance of reciprocity in guiding one toward a desired goal:

> Seeking advice and assistance from others is particularly helpful, especially for the youths of today. Many strongly dislike having to seek out advice, but as Buganda's ancestors said, *Obuteebuuza, bwe butambuza amazzi emisana n'ekiro* (Failure to consult makes water flow day and night). It flows by without any knowledge of where it is or where it is going, never reaching its destination.[7]

Here, "failure to consult" could mean lack of advice and correction. This philosophy transforms the lyrics of "I Would Have Given You a Large Haplochromis," which in turn demonstrates how the mother and father referenced are more than just stand-ins for people who helped the singer. Their designation as parents takes on more significance as we see that it is not just their material assistance that is important but their guidance and emotional support as well. In this way, we come to appreciate how reciprocity exists in several forms.

Delving into the aspect of "I Would Have Given You a Large Haplochromis" that represents the thoughts of an unappreciated ruler, Kironde explains how subjects might set up leaders to fail from the start due to the nature of the expectations they place on them:

---

6   Ibid.
7   Kabugo interview, December 19, 2019.

The song expresses the irony that no leader can fulfill all his promises during his time in power. No ruler in history has succeeded in making good on all of his claims, and even those who are exceptionally good leaders do not fully succeed. Indeed, those who wanted to extend their influence globally and conquer much of the world, such as Napoleon and Caesar, failed. Therefore, people need to understand that all leaders fail at some point. Forces beyond anyone's control or understanding make it impossible for a leader to be perfect and account for a wide range of people's needs.[8]

Kironde expands on this theme of imperfection:

Every leadership has some form of opposition, either directly or indirectly. There are always a few people who are against a leader's ideologies, reminding us that it is impossible to be a perfect leader. However, while there are some imperfections that people can live with, there are others that they simply cannot. People generally choose leaders who promise to deliver absolute perfection. Many expect leaders to be superhuman. While this task is impossible, no one admits it as such. No one wins an election saying, "I'm a human being just like you, susceptible to mistakes." Instead, everyone must claim that they are grandiose freedom fighters, appealing to the imagined ideal of a perfect political leader.[9]

Kironde's commentary encourages us to understand that failure is not simply a question of individuals being ineffective but that it depends on the many intersecting forces of everyday existence. This perspective offers new insights into the lyrical meaning of "I Would Have Given You a Large Haplochromis," centering on the idea that there are no perfect systems, no "ideal" arrangements. The singer's lament takes an additional concept, the possibility that his sorrow is not an exception but an expectation of living. The song acquires a new context, as it comes to represent a method of coping with suffering when it comes rather than avoiding it. Calling on music's capacity to recuperate and mend mental and physical injury, the song seems to caress the singer and his listeners, comforting them in the face of failure and depression. As for the power relation, expecting perfection from others will keep people from appreciating what they already contribute to their communities.

Peter Kinene and Kironde use "I Would Have Given You a Large Haplochromis" to expound on poverty. Following Kisuule's analysis, they provide additional thoughts on the singer's conundrum, describing how, for instance, poverty causes emotional distress and isolation due to the feelings of failure and incompetence that accompany it. In doing so they

---

8   Kironde interview, December 19, 2019.
9   Ibid.

depict poverty as more than a form of material and existential deprivation. They suggest that the impoverished are deprived of necessities and are thus unable to partake in the rejuvenating, joyful mutuality that is so crucial to life. Kironde comments:

> The lyric "You see, they persecute me, a pauper, ask them what they want from me, peace breeds laziness" (line 10) echoes the struggles that leaders face. However, in truth, leaders also play a role in bringing about this deterioration. Leadership and structural systems tend to stagnate and decay during periods of peace, because there is no stressor to make sure that they are working properly. So even though the country is currently in a state of peace, various members of society are suffering financially. Due to inflation, one US dollar is equivalent to about 3,600 Ugandan shillings. Dreaming of being a millionaire in shillings would not make sense. It simply does not make sense.[10]

In the same vein, and recalling John Lonsdale's observation that naturally, poverty engenders no sense of love or loyalty for one's government,[11] Kinene adds,

> Poverty is an element that can cause people to feel isolated or restricted. It wears down individuals' self-esteem, making them feel perpetually worthless. They want to show their appreciation to those who have helped them but do not have a means to do so. They are stuck in a constant cycle of thoughts, focusing on how the system has not given them the same things that it has given others.[12]

Kinene and Kironde both highlight the singer's conundrum as a unique challenge he must overcome, a constant stressor that he must always mediate as long as he is alive. As we see in the lyrics, the singer's lament is not due to a circumstantial failure on his part. Instead, it is an ever-present question, applied to his mother and his father and anyone else he might encounter throughout his life. However, even as the interpreters reimagine the song to represent the challenges of poverty, it also represents the efforts to overcome it. As evident in the singer's words, there remains a determination to overcome and fulfill his responsibilities. The singer, unable to provide a haplochromis, must search for alternate passages to reciprocate help. Rather than give up, he simply adjusts his aim.

Jimmy Ssenfuka Kibirige demonstrates how "I Would Have Given You a Large Haplochromis" addresses the conundrum of leaders who are not properly rewarded for their service, explaining the impossibility of

---

10   Kironde interview, December 19, 2019.
11   Lonsdale 1992, 449.
12   Kinene interview, December 16, 2019.

satisfactorily returning the value of service. On the other hand, Kibirige also shows how such excellence in leadership is itself inherently unlikely, as it is nearly impossible to find the right person to protect and uplift a collection of good-intentioned people. He describes this delicate balance:

> "I Would Have Given You a Large Haplochromis" expresses the sentiment that there is no perfect candidate, no perfect heir to take on a country filled with people of goodwill. The singer might be afraid that though the nation and society seem to be good, there is no one worthy to properly protect it. Furthermore, there is no reward good enough to properly thank those who have done exceptional service. Additionally, those who find and appoint people of substance often do not receive recognition either. In the end, however, when a leader comes to power, the initial promises they made, which helped them get elected, quickly become obsolete. The fiery statements that excited voters into believing they were electing people willing to enact real change are quickly snuffed out to reveal that they were simply political trivialities with no substance behind them. When leaders get to power, they quickly forget their promises to serve the people uprightly.[13]

Further articulating the dynamic between leaders and citizens, Kibirige adds,

> Leaders should give thanks to the people who bring them into power. It is the will of the people that brings them from grass to grace; when they first come to power, they are nobodies. And yet, as soon as they reach grace, they forget where they came from. The people who raised the leaders up are then bitter that they have not remembered them. Consequently, there is a great deal of strife and disillusionment regarding the relationship between the people and their leaders. Another component that contributes to this strife is the fact that because the leaders recognize they have a limited time in power they spend that time amassing wealth for themselves, instead of serving the people. The discontent that this leadership style fosters in turn becomes a factor that fuels crime, corruption, and wrongdoings, which the leadership can then use as an attempt to justify its behavior.[14]

Kibirige comments on how these obstacles converge to create a cyclic process of emotional negativity, where leaders lie to the people, and the people disregard them. In this vein, "I Would Have Given You a Large Haplochromis" can depict the failed dynamic that exists between current leaders and citizens in Uganda. Each side is partly responsible for this failure in reciprocity.

---

13 Kibirige interview, December 15, 2019.
14 Ibid.

Emphasizing the points of his preceding analysis, Kibirige further stresses the relevance of the song to specific twenty-first-century political contexts. He sheds light on how the damaging actions of leaders have resulted in increased "crime, corruption, and wrongdoing," which in turn function as a justification for leaders to amplify their own greedy, self-serving, and destructive measures:

> The song's message is pertinent because many leaders have forgotten where they came from; they have forgotten the people. Those who make it to power should at least offer their appreciation for what others did to get them there. But, again, that element is missing. Many are ungrateful for the help of others, only focusing on what they did themselves. The irony is that in many instances, some of these leaders have never been to school or made attempts to educate themselves. They are rich fools ruling over those who are much wiser than they are. Intellectuals, including musicians who came to be prophets and major figures in society, are under their control. "I Would Have Given You a Large Haplochromis" expresses these frustrations and relates to modern issues, like those expressed by the People Power political movement led by Bobi Wine.[15]

Here we glimpse another complex blockage that keeps civilians from appreciating those in power. Kibirige suggests that just as the singer's failure resulted in having no one to support him, leaders today burn their bridges with the people, and both suffer as a result. His commentary projects the meaning of "I Would Have Given You a Large Haplochromis" onto the obstacles and conflicts of the modern day. The song and the contemporary context become entwined, creating a new image entirely from the fused parts of the two.

Kibirige's and Kabugo's concluding analyses of "I Would Have Given You a Large Haplochromis" summarize both the reasons why leaders should try their best to support their people, as well as the barrier that personal greed poses against successful leadership. Kibirige notes:

> The leaders beg for whatever they can get, thus mirroring the marauding pauper mentioned in the song. There is a need to appreciate those who do good. It is not productive to only focus on the negatives. Unfortunately, many people do this and are expectant and demanding, unappreciative of those who do not deliver what they want. The difficulty of satisfying the people means that many leaders simply give up trying to do so. They openly admit their wrongdoings and self-serving nature, noting that anyone else in their position would do the same. Therefore, there is a real need to give credit where credit is due and to not forget one's roots. Leaders need to have zeal to protect their people and the systems in place, designed

---

15 Ibid.

to serve future generations. It might even be worthwhile to require that outgoing leaders recommend candidates for elected positions. They need to remember that they are public figures, not comedians. To most of them, it is all a performance. They just want people to see them as saviors. By being so caught up in their own self-importance, many current leaders destroy the initiatives that could enable folks to have prosperous futures.[16]

Kabugo also takes up this theme:

> The opportunists are those who praise leaders and stick by their side only when they have something to give them in return. They feed them all the gossip and flattery that they want, but as soon as the leaders' luck turns, they abandon them. They are nothing more than fair weather friends—hypocrites and opportunists.[17]

These comments further recast "I Would Have Given You a Large Haplochromis" by critiquing self-obsession. Kibirige and Kabugo describe how some contemporary leaders have become too obsessed with their own images, acting like comedians and actors, performers on the national political stage. Kabugo even stresses that it is not just these leaders who are culpable but also those who surround them and feed on their shallowness. Through these perspectives, Kibirige and Kabugo transform the song into a model for self-reflection. They highlight how, in comparison to some of today's leaders, the singer is self-aware and acknowledges his failures. Although he describes pain and lament, his lament is itself the first step in becoming a better leader and a better person. Thus, the song becomes a model for self-overcoming as it describes the first, often painful step in the process of remaking oneself.

Conclusion

"I Would Have Given You a Large Haplochromis" is a musical expression of regret centered on a subject's inability to fulfill his monarch's specific culinary request. The composition transforms a seemingly mundane failed fish acquisition into a deeper examination of the relationship between ruler and subject. It elevates this unfulfilled request for haplochromis to symbolic importance, suggesting that even small failures to meet royal expectations carry significant emotional and potentially political consequences. Through its focus on this specific disappointment, the song illustrates how subjects internalize their responsibility to satisfy royal desires, regardless of how trivial these wishes might appear.

---

16 Ibid.
17 Kabugo interview, December 19, 2019.

"I Would Have Given You a Large Haplochromis" embodies a multitude of perspectives. The song communicates the lamentation a king's subject feels when he is unable to properly express his loyalty and gratitude. On the one hand, the singer represents the thoughts of the king, recalling the court musicians' purpose as a bridge between the common people and Buganda's leader. Accordingly, the song depicts the king's worry over his responsibilities to the people and his desire to fulfill their needs as best he can. On the other hand, the perspective emulates that of the common person, of one who fails to reciprocate their role in a relationship and thus reaps the consequences. In both cases the song is sorrowful over the loss of reciprocity, a tale of forewarning in which we are encouraged to reciprocate and assist others whenever we can, as a sign of good faith and as a way of maintaining good relations with those around us. However, interpreters' analyses of "I Would Have Given You a Large Haplochromis" bring this theme even further.

Some interpreters read the song as a commentary on the impact of poverty, describing how it hurts on more than a materialistic level, instead invading parts of individuals' spiritual and emotional lives as well. Others read the work as a model for leadership, a part in the difficult process of overcoming personal faults. And a few interpret the song as a depiction of the cyclical negativity between leaders and citizens, as both fail to look out for the other, causing both to suffer as a result. These interpreters' comments confirm that the song's lyrical content not only applies to personal relationships but also to interactions between leaders and their subjects. For this reason, "I Would Have Given You a Large Haplochromis" is relevant to many twenty-first-century political contexts, acting as a reminder for politicians to remember their roots and thank their original supporters, among other necessary human functions. Additionally, it laments the inability of Baganda citizens to reciprocate as a result of their own alleged mistreatment by national politicians. To this point, research collaborators argue that although overly high expectations might lead to disappointment, the people must still hold political leaders to certain standards to generate harmony among the masses. They demonstrate that it is through this mutual relationship between leaders and subjects that valuable progress is achievable.

13

"The Flutists' Legal Case"

Lament and Uncertainty

Written by grieving musicians, the song "The Flutists' Legal Case" ("Omusango gw'Abalere") laments the court flutists whom King Ssuuna II (r. ca. 1824–1854) removed from duty for disrespectful behavior. The following context of the song was relayed by Albert Muwanga Ssempeke (ca. 1930–2006), who also performed the rendering examined in this chapter.

> The musicians composed the song following their dismissal from the court. Although the king had an exclusive passion for the flute and its music, he would expel his flutists as a form of punishment after one of them had an affair with a princess. This act was taboo, since the musician was a non-royal. In this song's context, after the ensemble's expulsion, they returned to their home village, Kalungu, Bbira. But when King Ssuuna II (r. ca. 1824–1854) passed away, his son and heir to the throne, King Muteesa I (r. ca. 1856–1884), immediately inquired about the flutists who had previously performed for his father and why they were missing from the court. His officials explained to him that Ssuuna II had dismissed them for committing a crime, but they never specified it. Because of Muteesa I's passion for flute music, he ordered that the flute and drum ensemble members return to the court, and as soon as they arrived, he asked them to perform for him. They performed "The Flutists' Legal Case." Fearing that Muteesa I might reopen the case about why his father dismissed them, the flutists substituted the phrase *Omusango gw'abalere gwegaludde, bantwale e Bbira gye banzaala* (The flutists' legal case has resurfaced, they should take me to Bbira, my birthplace) with the line *Nze ndigenda n'abalere ab'e Kalungu, bantwale e Bbira gye banzaala* (I will go with the flutists of Kalungu, they should take me to Bbira, my birthplace). After the musicians finished performing for the king, he asked them to interpret the lyrics of the tune. In their response, they told him that the statement "I will go with the flutists of Kalungu" expressed that he had chosen them as his personal flutists. The amused king accepted the performers back into the court as the official flutists.[1]

---

1   Ssempeke interview, July 27, 2005.

"Birthplace" means the singer's ancestral home. Stressing the themes of lament and uncertainty, "The Flutists' Legal Case" depicts the sorrow of court musicians encountering the reality of death for the first time. They are lost in thought, as they contemplate missed opportunities, their past, as well as the lonesomeness they are facing. By using the line "I will go with the flutists of Kalungu" instead of "The flutists' legal case has resurfaced," the original lyric, the flutists change the song's meaning to reflect the forgiveness and clemency that the king has given. This transformation shows how the song itself becomes an expression of the situations it describes. At one time, it speaks to the tragedy of experiencing the king's punishments, embodied by fears of death, and regrets over one's lack of kin. But in the court performers' revised rendition, per its historical context, it comes to represent the musicians' redemption from that state, signified by their long-delayed return to the court. In this way, the song becomes a conduit for the contexts that it represents, not only acting as a static depiction of the initial action but also functioning as a living and changing double of the event at hand. The song changes with the flutists, the court, and the world at large. This point is crucial to the themes illuminated throughout this chapter as well as to our exploration of the ways in which "The Flutists' Legal Case" continues to come alive with today's stories and conceptions.

Ssempeke sings the "The Flutists' Legal Case" to the accompaniment of a Kiganda bow harp (*ennanga*). His performance commences with the instrumental part, which includes two subparts plucked by the right and left hands' thumbs and index fingers. The two parts interlock, producing a complex web of buzzing sound. As the instrumental continues, the vocals enter to deliver a sequence of similar melodies, each one starting at generally a high range and then descending into lower notes. While the instrumental part sounds more improvisational and spontaneous, the vocals rely on frequently repeating lines and phrases. The tone of the song's lyrics reflects grief and regret, among other themes; one can hear the resounding lament in the performance's overall sonic qualities as Ssempeke sings the following lyrics:

1 *Anti omusango gw'abalere gwegaludde, bantwale e Bbiru*
Because the flutists' legal case has resurfaced, they should take me to Bbira

2 *Nze nno mpimaapima eddiiro, linsobedde, bwe nsituka nzirawo*
I am imagining the size of the living room, I am baffled, restlessly I get up as I get back down

3 *Gubadde gutya?*
What is the matter?

4 *Ow'omukwano, bantwale e Bbira gye banzaala*
My dear, they should take me to Bbira, my birthplace

5 *Agalifa sizadde nze, bwe ndifa ndigenderera*
As I am to die childless, when I pass away, I shall perish

6 *Agalifa sizadde nze, bwe ndifa ndigenderera*
As I am childless, when I pass away, I shall perish

7 *Wambwa alekerera entujjo n'azina entoli*
Mr. Dog ignores the drumbeat or pulse and dances to the finger snaps

8 *Naawe omukulu ow'ennimi onoolyanga ky'olaba*
And you, the principal of tongues, you will always eat what you see

9 *Bwe ntunuulira taata gye yagenda, amaziga gakunkumuka*
When I look at where father was buried, tears stream down

10 *Bwe ntunuulira mmange gye yagenda, amaziga gakunkumuka*
When I look at where my mother was buried, tears stream down

11 *Agalifa sizadde nze, bwe ndifa ndigenderera*
As I am to die childless, when I pass away, I shall perish

12 *Wambwa alekerera entujjo n'azina entoli*
Mr. Dog ignores the pulse or drumbeat and dances to the finger snaps

13 *Aaaa munnange, linsobedde, bantwale e Bbira*
No, my dear, the living room has puzzled me, they should take me to Bbira

14 *Lino eddiiro linsobedde, bwe nsituka nzirawo*
This living room has perplexed me, restlessly I get up as I get back down

15 *Nange ndigenda bwomu, nze, eby'okufa bigenderera*
Even I, shall go alone, death takes away completely

16 *Ate ndigenda bannange*
And I shall go, my dears

17 *Ssanja eribikka bannaffe, lye bababuza obusolo*
Dry banana leaves that cover our fellows, are the same used to roast animals

18 *Ssanja eribikka bannaffe, abayizzi lye bababuza obusolo*
Dry banana leaves that cover our fellows, are the same hunters use to roast animals

19 *Aaaa munnange, linsobedde, bantwale e Bbira*
No, my dear, the living room has puzzled me, they should take me to Bbira

20 *Gubadde gutya?*
What is the matter?

21 *Anti omusango gw'abalere gwegaludde, bantwale e Bbira*
Because the flutists' legal case has resurfaced, they should take me to Bbira

22 *Anti omusango gw'abalere gunsobedde, bantwale e Bbira*
Because the flutists' legal case has puzzled me, they should take me to Bbira

23 *Gubadde gutya?*
What is the matter?

24 *Omukulu ow'ennimi, onoolyanga ky'olaba*
The principal of tongues, you will always eat what you see

25 *Anti, Mukasa ow'e Zzinga*
You see, Mukasa of Zzinga

26 *Nange ndigenda bwomu nze*
Even I, shall go in solitude

27 *Ssanja eribikka bannaffe, abayizzi lye bababuza obusolo*
Dry banana leaves that cover our fellows, are the same hunters use to roast animals

28 *Anti eribikka bannaffe, abayizzi lye bababuza obusolo*
Because those which cover our fellows, are the same hunters use to roast animals

29 *Gubadde gutya?*
What is the matter?

30 *Maama linsobedde, bantwale e Bbira, omulongo, baze*
Surely, it has baffled me, let me be taken to Bbira, the twin, my husband

"The Flutists' Legal Case" as sung by Ssempeke describes the fear and shock of death in terms of one's own life and the life of another. It does so without providing a specific narrative, instead appearing to emulate the torrent of thoughts that might run through one's mind upon contemplating one's own death. The singer begins by speaking from the perspective of the deceased as he contemplates the life he is leaving behind. One significant lament of this persona is that he does not have a legacy to pass down, no child to extend his experience and desires (lines 5–6, and 11). He describes this absence of legacy differently from his individual death, framing it as extinction. By placing it in this broader conceptualization, the singer's death becomes more than the absence of a heartbeat, as it interacts with the notion of existence itself. The song makes this delineation between death and extinction by relating it to kinship and memory, describing how the two might serve to prevent the former. This point goes beyond describing a symbolic effect of kinship, instead affirming its profound impact in human networks. In this vein, one might accept that death is less severe and final if some part of oneself lives on in another.

Expanding further on this notion of kinship, the singer describes how death forces one to go alone (lines 15 and 26), to leave behind the friends and family that one spent a lifetime caring for. This description and awareness does not diminish the pain that is inherent in death but instead acknowledges that while death may be preferable to total extinction, it is still a great isolation that seems nearly unbearable. This focus on lonesomeness also emphasizes connection over material wealth or ambition, as the song does not lament over the loss of riches or failure to achieve goals. Instead, it laments the loss of friends and family, earthly and human tethers.

Transitioning from the notion of kinship, "The Flutists' Legal Case" also repeatedly depicts a dog who dances without an ear for rhythm (lines 7 and 12). The dog's dancing also seems to reflect the way man lives, ignorant and innocent to the world, unseeing and unfeeling. This theme about Mr. Dog seems to represent some form of reprimand, evoking the importance of remaining mindful in any circumstance. It encourages listeners to tune in to the beat of the song and recognize that the world and individual existence are not separate but intricately woven and interconnected. Simply put, one must hear the beat, the rhythm of life and dance to it. Other lines that suggest reprimand include "And you, the principal of tongues, you will always eat what you see" (line 8) and its variation, "The principal of tongues, you will always eat what you see" (line 24). Both lyrics refer to telltales who repeat what they hear.

"The Flutists' Legal Case" then transitions to the perspective of those who were once friends with the deceased. "Our fellows" (lines 17–18 and 27–28) means deceased friends. The song also describes the multiple uses of banana leaves for both funeral ceremonies and the preparation of small game (lines 17–18 and 27–28). In this way it speaks to the cyclic quality in life, using banana leaves as an allegory for the connection that life and death share. The banana leaves feed the fire that simultaneously consummates one's death while also maintaining another's life by preserving their food source. This circular quality is repeated in the line "This living room has perplexed me, restlessly I get up as I get back down" (line 14). Here, the singer refers to the place where he will be laid for viewing when he dies. He also becomes baffled by the apparent smallness of common life, as demonstrated by the futile repetition of standing and sitting. Furthermore, this line and its variation (line 2) are also a symptom of the singer's confusion. He is unable to cope with his "room" and thus can do no more than repeatedly attempt to stand and repeatedly fail. In this way, the line becomes cyclic and tautological, simultaneously maintaining cause and effect.

Lament and Uncertainty

The interpreters of "The Flutists' Legal Case" referenced in this section put its themes into further political contexts through their multiple readings, each one offering a different perspective on the work's possible meanings and applications. Their interpretations center on notions of leadership, caution, obedience, and justice, among other ideas that this chapter explores through the broader themes of lament and uncertainty. Kinene connects the bafflement that the singer of "The Flutists' Legal Case" expresses in the opening lines to the notion that one needs to be particularly careful when talking about leaders. His analysis highlights the idea of mediating mutuality, as success and failure in politics can result in complications that undermine the trust and reciprocity of a relationship. As he suggests, when a person desperately seeks to hold on to his power, he may tend to lash out against those who threaten that power. As such, any mutual relationship in a power dynamic can easily turn into a dangerous and self-destructive excursion, as one will seek to sabotage the other's success in one's own favor. Thus, it is important to tread warily while in the presence of those who display a particular fear of change or difference. Kinene explains how their panicked attachment to power could be dangerous for any who engages with them:

> It is unwise for subjects to give leaders the slightest chance to convict them of wrongdoing, even if they might believe they have done nothing wrong. In other words, there should be no doubt as to the consequences of a particular action if one has truly thought it through before taking it. The same concept applies to acknowledging mistakes. People should refrain from talking carelessly about leaders because their comments can annoy or anger them and thus cause the responsible parties harm. They should restrain unabashed gossip as much as possible. If it is possible that one's comments will upset and disturb a leader, one should avoid them. One must refrain from this talk because leaders have the power to single out people and punish them. This phenomenon played out during a recent by-election in Lira District. During the event, some people smashed in President Museveni's car with a rock. Assuming it was the act of a member of the opposition, he ordered an attack on the opposition leader, Bobi Wine. Incidentally, the attack never went as planned, as Museveni's bodyguards shot and killed Bobi Wine's driver instead of the leader himself. To reiterate, it is not wise to annoy or anger people in power as they will likely retaliate. However, the potential for leadership and politics to cause problems for others does not just apply to common people—it applies to other civil servants as well. Leaders who feel that those below them threaten them may try to sabotage others. This could be through threats, slander, and blackmail, among other tactics. The goal is to make potential rivals

quit politics entirely due to their lack of career success. Parties undertake most of these schemes at an individual level. A person looks to cause harm to another, targets him, and ultimately causes his arrest and punishment. They plan out a trap for their rivals to fall into, which is why, especially in the world of politics, it is important to not blindly accept what others give to one, lest it be a trick.[2]

Kinene's interpretation of "The Flutists' Legal Case" contemplates the ways the initial singers could have avoided their bitter end. By focusing on the punishment levied on them and the reasons behind it, Kinene articulates the importance of caution when encountering the powerful. Otherwise, one might repeat the mistake of these court flutists. To him, the song becomes a cautionary tale to those who engage with the strong, challenging us to perceive the risks that might arise if one fails to behave thoughtfully.

Kinene then focuses on the bafflement of the singer when he suddenly faces the doors of death, illustrating the vertigo that comes with personal change. As for politics, this realization has supposedly been ignored by Uganda's leaders, as he describes their confusion and frustration with people who wish to oust them from positions of power. Rather than accepting such changes, they become stuck on them, so obsessed that they begin crafting stories as to why a change should not have happened. Such resistance to change is commonplace, as ordinary people are constantly inventing alternate—or "right"—worlds, where things go as expected and as desired, where they can remain in power for as long as they please. For politicians and common people alike, these stories grant them a sense of agency over their lives. For leaders, having such control means retaining power by whatever means they deem necessary. It is a question of priorities, and when their priorities are so far removed from their environment, it means that the leader cannot recognize the problems of the people, let alone solve them. According to Kinene, this is one of many problems tied with incessantly resisting change, for when it does occur, people are unprepared and unable to respond:

> When some leaders leave positions of power, they complain bitterly about how the masses failed to appreciate the good that they did them. However, the leaders should realize that these complaints will only embitter the masses toward them, especially if they ignored and undervalued the people during their time in power. This point also applies to former leaders' comments about their successors. Even if successors might be doing a better job than the former leaders, the previous leaders might bitterly criticize them, showing their inability to accept loss. They fail to grasp that the best course of action after the masses remove them from their positions is to move

---

2   Kinene interview, December 16, 2019.

on. Often, however, they dwell on it, remaining focused on the past in a way that is neither beneficial to themselves nor others. They claim that they have done wonders for the people, never considering that perhaps it is their less than stellar performance that led to their removal. To be more successful, they need to accept the changes that come their way, as well as any criticism that might arise from blunders in their leadership. They need to accept the blame for their wrongdoings.[3]

The concept of lamenting change that Kinene problematizes also reflects the striking value shift that takes place when one encounters the end of life. It stems from the realization that many of the values once cherished no longer matter. Modern leaders, again, highlight this reality, as they are confused and distraught at the thought of losing all that they once fought so hard for. They become unable to love life because they are too focused on the inherently ephemeral and shallow values they cling to. Power and wealth seduce them and blind them to the world of potentialities that exist beyond the reaches of material wealth and influence. They stake their lives on these most shallow values and suffer profoundly as a result. They abandon life in favor of security, safety, and order. These points go beyond moral criticism, as the suffering the leaders in question encounter is not from some otherworldly retaliation for their evil deeds. Instead, this suffering is a direct extension of the deeds and obsessions, as they become lost in themselves and lose the capacity to appreciate life, suffering and all. These dynamics allow the message of "The Flutists' Legal Case" to connect to the way one might come to understand change. It depicts death as the ultimate instance of change, revealing the song as a piece that recognizes and embraces such change for its tragedy and its vivacity. Furthermore, rather than claiming that such events are wrong or should not have happened, the song recognizes them as necessary extensions of every person's fate.

In the same way that a dancing dog only pays attention to what is unimportant (lines 7 and 12), people who are prejudiced allow half-baked conceptions to shape their understanding of entire groups of people. In his interpretation, John Magandaazi Kityo explains how prejudice arises from a fear of otherness and one's ignorance of the inherent interdependence of people:

> Prejudice has resumed among the people of Uganda. Right now, it is possible to have a situation where someone will not get a job offer based on generalizations about them. Perhaps the employer assumes that the Banyoro people are better than the Baganda people, or something of that nature. Some people maintain a grip on the past even when that history is not just. They should remember that a lot has changed and that the

---

3   Ibid.

people of today are not the same as those of the past. "The Flutists' Legal Case" explores this notion further by reminding us that there should be an individual responsibility for sin rather than a group one. The danger in not separating an individual from the group they come from, whether ethnic or economic, is that it is easy to blame them for things that were not their fault but the fault of others or their ancestors. One should not hate a child for the actions of his parents.[4]

In the first sense, John Magandaazi Kityo speaks to how understanding personal nuance is an antidote to prejudice, which arises from attempts to organize the world in a linear manner, as anything nonlinear is considered chaotic or disorderly. Prejudice also attempts to reduce the infinite complexities of life into singular and isolated traits that seek to determine identity. So, like Mr. Dog's only paying attention to the snapping, prejudice can only pay attention to the most superficial and obvious qualities and as such produces caricature-like figures that are always inaccurate. These dynamics mirror the state of some of Uganda's modern leaders when they attempt to make the world coherent when it simply cannot be. Many do so by justifying their own rule and criticizing that of their successors, desperately trying to prove that the present path was not the right one to go down. Overall, prejudice is an agonizing resistance to the natural, changing order of the world.

As Kityo highlights, the generalizations and biases that people produce toward groups lead to unintended consequences, and eventually these prejudices will affect interactions. Steven Mukasa Kabugo also looks at this interpretation but more specifically addresses those whom a musician could face and, indeed, those whom the titular musician of the song faced:

> In the past, if a musician sang something disrespectful and the king found out that he insulted him, the royal soldiers would come for the musician and kill him. Accordingly, "The Flutists' Legal Case" came about as a result of a musician's earnest request to explain himself and his perceived wrongdoings through trial.[5] Drawing on the wisdom of and lesson from this song, many contemporary Baganda elders emphasize to youth that because the future is always uncertain, they should always try and get whatever they need in the present moment. For singers, if there is something they want from a leader, they should praise or flatter him so that they can reach their goal and secure a better future.[6]

---

4   Kityo interview, December 14, 2019.
5   The song "The Handsome Catch a Slight Squint" ("Empujjo Zikwata Balungi"), chapter 4, describes an attempt to assuage King Ssuuna II (r. ca. 1824–1854).
6   Kabugo interview, December 19, 2019.

The future is always uncertain, so it is crucial to mediate circumstances to achieve desired outcomes. One must continue living and growing in the face of uncertainty, learning to maneuver rather than codify it. This view demonstrates the importance of not just throwing oneself into the world blindly and passively but of actively rolling the dice of stepping into fate with both eyes open. These lessons change "The Flutists' Legal Case" as more than a depiction of fate but as a response to it. Thus, the song does not merely describe the singer's circumstance but also his attempts to overcome it, as he seeks to placate the anger of the king who is punishing him. In the case of King Ssuuna II's musicians, their music did not simply describe the situation passively. It was also an active attempt to shape and move the world around them. This act speaks to the song's function as a living and active part of the world. The process of reimagining exemplifies this dynamic. Interpreters continue to reimagine each piece of the song in a way that applies it to a fresh context. They revive it in these instances, renewing its capacity to impact the world in new ways.

Edward Ssebunnya Kironde's reading of "The Flutists' Legal Case" also focuses on the appeals to emotion that the singer makes. These appeals are one way that people may try to get back into the good graces of a leader after having fallen from favor. The singer seems to invoke emotional details to stir the sympathies of the king and reduce his punishment, thus dodging the true consequences of his actions. This process reminds Kironde of contemporary politicians who are constantly posturing to ensure their own success:

> The masses themselves, more than the individual leader, determine the ethos and atmosphere of a particular leadership. In the case of the flutists, they worked to reverse their ousting from the court by praising the king. They always had something good to say about their king to mark themselves as worthy of their positions. In a matter of speaking, they were just like some national politicians in Uganda. The more junior members of the political scene like Kusaasira, Big Eye, and Full Figure are always acting in praise of President Museveni, much as the flutists did for the king. They are concerned with preserving their own positions of power and are willing to manipulate the system to gain from it. In due course, they can convince others of that which they have no real knowledge of. Beyond politicians, often people in general fall into this rut of sycophantic praise, hoping that they will gain something from it. This practice typically happens when dealing with foreigners or sources of money from abroad. Despite a desire to fund projects, such as for a student's tuition costs, from local financial sources, whenever foreign investment or funds become available, fundraisers tend to forget their initial plans entirely. They lose the bigger picture and focus instead on the sheer quantity of money they can get, regardless of where it comes from. They flatter and praise in the same way the flutists did to manipulate others for their own benefit.[7]

---

7   Kironde interview, December 19, 2019.

By comparing the singer's call to pity with the flattery that so many politicians use, Kironde shows the ways manipulation is a crucial part of mediating relationships as well as the participants within them. This perspective diverts from the previous commentary on the importance of mediation and caution when encountering powerful figures. Conversely, this view suggests that such mediation could lead to the downfall of all involved. As is the case in Uganda, attempts at manipulation might lead to corruption, if a person uses slick language to get away with benefiting from public funding. Such actions could also lead to the uplifting of certain leaders regardless of what they do, leading to the result that those in power are more likely to stay in power, regardless of the benefits they provide the people. This is in part because those who work under them exclusively compliment and affirm them instead of criticizing them honestly. This viewpoint provides a caveat to the song that the singer's performance is not purely honest. If he is not careful, his strategy may result in disaster. In other words, the singer's method is high risk, and the listener must treat it with great caution. As we saw with King Ssuuna II, his musicians may have praised and manipulated him, but they only did so as a way of subverting his rule in other ways, hiding their true criticism behind the apparent flattery of the song. However, the politicians that Kironde describes do the opposite. They allegedly praise and flatter those above them with no thought to the good of the people or the senior leaders they praise, instead only seeking benefits for themselves. They throw everyone else under the bus for their own gain.

Turning back to the discussion on death, Kabugo's comments appear to evoke the lyrics of the song about the subject. The singer goes alone, overcome by death because of his lack of children. For someone without children, death is the end of their existence, whereas if they had children, Kabugo explains, they would have passed on their likeness and talents so that parts of them would live on:

> Many people pass down their talents to those who are close to them, especially to their children. When people die and leave this world, it is natural for those who were close to them to experience a variety of emotions, grief and sadness often chief among them. However, if they had children who remain, those they were close to are likely to be less sad, knowing that the children might continue to carry the deceased person's talents even though the deceased him- or herself is gone. The performer of "The Flutists' Legal Case" encourages people to have families of their own so that the people they leave behind will not forget them even after their death. He mentions dry banana leaves as a representation of how people can ignore and neglect those without children when death takes them. If a person is childless, who will truly mourn him or her? The general message is that it is not good for

someone, particularly those with great talent, to die having not brought children into the world first.[8]

Kabugo's discussion of the connections of "The Flutists' Legal Case" to themes of kinship and legacy transform the song into a warning for those who have yet to die. Thus, he shows how it advises people to procure their legacies before they die so that they might live on through those who succeed them. He alludes to the idea that having a legacy softens the blow of death by allowing the deceased to subsist in the figures of those that they leave behind. With Kabugo's analysis, the song becomes an imaginative conception of the self, arguing that life is not merely contained in the body but that it also resonates in the bodies of those it encounters. As Kelly Askew puts it, "The self, then, as a performed character, is not an organic thing that has a specific location, whose fundamental fate is to be born, to mature, and to die; it is a dramatic effect arising diffusely from a scene that is presented."[9] In other words, it exists outside the temporalities of human life. One's conceptions, desires, and instincts come back to life in friends and family, having a profound effect on the way that they conceive of and relate to the world. This perspective also applies to "The Flutists' Legal Case" itself, as the ways its own legacy is born in the interpretations that spring from it become clear. It is a child to its composer in much the same way that this chapter's interpretations are children to it. Each version of the song becomes an extension of its life, a reimagined form that revitalizes it in a new body of meanings.

Kinene continues his earlier comments about twenty-first-century leadership. His thoughts reflect the sentiments that Kironde has already voiced on some contemporary leaders:

> They take as much as they can get, feeling no remorse for those who are left to pick through the scraps. People like this also take things to give them to those who are close to them, especially their children. Sometimes, someone may take something for individualistic, selfish uses which others had planned to use as a communal resource. They are not concerned with the well-being of others and instead only consider their own satisfaction. This happens especially among politicians and leaders. They embezzle funds that the government is supposed to use for healthcare or infrastructure and use them for their personal business. This hypocrisy is evident in "The Flutists' Legal Case" itself, particularly in the lyric "Dry banana leaves that cover our fellows, are the same they use to roast animals" (line 17) as well as its

---

8   Kabugo interview, December 19, 2019.
9   Askew 2002, 20.

variation "Dry banana leaves that cover our fellows, are the same hunters use to roast animals" (line 18). A few leaders use things that are intended to help the masses for personal gains, at the expense of many.[10]

Kinene reframes our understanding of the banana leaves to reflect a criticism of selfishness and greed in modern Uganda and Africa as a whole. He shows how hunters who use the banana leaves, usually meant for funeral ceremonies or covering the ground that shelters the dead, prevent this tradition from happening when they use them to roast their small game. The hunters, despite the relatively low importance of their task, take the leaves for themselves and thus deprive the funeral goers of what they need to send off their friends and loved ones. This practice portrays a model for what happens when one does something at the expense of others and speaks to the dynamic of community and individuality, as we see in "The Flutists' Legal Case." It recasts the song as a commentary on acceptable behavior while still maintaining the philosophical lens around it.

Commenting on the lyric "And you, the principal of tongues, you will always eat what you see" (line 8) and its variation (line 24), Kinene reorients "The Flutists' Legal Case" around the notion of bad behavior and the consequences that arise from it. He particularly explores the damage that those who deceive can do, whether the consequences fall on themselves or others:

> People should avoid gossiping and indiscreetly spreading rumors because these situations may easily turn against them in the end. It is important to never purposefully spread a rumor because sometimes when people interweave words, the repercussions that come along with doing so might not be in their favor. Not supporting or engaging in these sorts of behaviors is important because it ensures one's innocence should anyone accuse them of any wrongdoing. Moreover, people need to work toward unity. Particularly within the political sphere, there is a lot of discord, especially spawned by a failure to acknowledge the assistance that others provide. Even when people are accomplices, they are quick to throw one another under the bus to get ahead. Thus, the saying, *Gw'olya naye enkejje enjokerere; y'akuyita "dduma bikalu"* (One with whom you eat roasted haplochromis; calls you "devourer of hard things"). Some people may engage in unbecoming behavior with others, only to turn around and sell them out when the time comes. Again, their first and foremost interest is protecting themselves. Such bootlickers have caused many problems. Therefore, people need to be wary of those who agree too readily because they are often concealing self-serving behavior.[11]

---

10   Kinene interview, December 16, 2019.
11   Ibid.

Here, "devourer of hard things" means a glutton, which also refers to a person who turns against another. Kinene's commentary transforms "The Flutists' Legal Case" into an advisory tale that encourages listeners to pursue unity and kinship over material wealth and personal ambition, not because it is necessarily the right thing to do but because a deterioration of life might occur within oneself if one does not. Such might have been the case with the singer who, according to the lyrics, no longer could appreciate his life because he had probably given it all up for his own hyper-individualized sense of value and success. In fact, other lyrics suggest that the singer might be standing at the doors of death as a result of living only for selfish purposes. By alienating those around him, he has lost any recourse for his current condition or position. He cannot convince anyone to help him, as he has lived his life only for himself. In much the same way, he will go alone through death and will be without kin to carry on his legacy (lines 5–6, 11, 15, and 26). At the end, he suddenly becomes aware that he misplaced his values throughout his life. He realizes with a sudden rush of regret that he could have avoided his current circumstance if he had carried himself differently. This state suggests an understanding of "The Flutists' Legal Case" that reduces the sympathy one feels for the singer, portraying him as one who is reaping what he has sown rather than one who is struck by an unfortunate and unavoidable circumstance.

Transitioning toward a more spiritual analysis of "The Flutists' Legal Case," Kibirige discusses the significance of the lyric "You see, Mukasa of Zzinga" (line 25). Mukasa is a chief administrator of the gods in traditional Kiganda beliefs. According to Kibirige, this invocation of the supernatural relates to the concept of *cce*—a personal spirit or god—that contributes to the spirituality of the song. In his description of *cce*, Kibirige notes that it appears as a gut instinct, a feeling that directs one in a particular direction without necessarily justifying it with the logical deduction one might find in discursive topics. Flipping the script on the musicians, the interpreter portrays them as manipulators instead of protagonists and the king as a victim of their influence, or more generally, he depicts the leader as one who fails to stick by his *cce*. In relation to "The Flutists' Legal Case," the leader disobeys its advice and guidance by giving the musicians a second chance after it has already warned him not to. Kibirige elaborates on how this reasoning presents the message of the song as an instinctual and inexplicable phenomenon:

> Leaders should attempt to listen to what some Baganda people might call their *cce*, a personal spirit or god. Each person has his or her own unique *cce*, and it is vital to listen to it because disobeying it tends to result in woe. Leaders especially must respect their *cce*. If it calls for someone to be punished, that person should be punished. And if a leader gives someone a second chance, he or she may have given it to the person against the wishes of his

or her *cce*. In the case of the flutists that the song references, they seem to have defied the king's *cce,* thereby manipulating their way back into the court after their initial dismissal. The king might not have listened to his *cce* and no one might have held him accountable for his ignorance of its wisdom. A similar event happened during the reign of a certain king. He dismissed the flutists from the court because he found out that one of them had had sexual relations with a princess. But the musicians came back and pleaded with the king's heir to reinstate them in their positions, and he obliged. They easily manipulated him because he did not stand his ground.[12]

With this interpretation, "The Flutists' Legal Case" becomes an embodied affirmation of spirit. Rather than wielding spirituality in opposition to the body, as a transcendent form against the lowly materiality and impurity of the flesh, it wields the body and spirit as extensions of each other. In addition, Kibirige's analysis flips our interpretation of the singer and the king. Rather than considering them the protagonists of the story and the song, the interpreter presents them as the antagonists who sow dishonesty into the power dynamic. He forces us to recognize the multiplicity that exists in any situation by demonstrating the good and bad in both. Accordingly, we might appreciate how the king's compromise ultimately enabled the bad behavior that first caused his father's decision. This decision reflects poorly on both the king and the flutists, as neither party learns from the situation that previously caused so many problems.

Kibirige comments further on the idea of compromise, extending his discussion about the importance of trusting one's gut in making decisions. He centers on the ways one might overcome manipulation by remaining steadfast in one's will. He suggests that rather than attempting to always accommodate others, it is sometimes best to reject their demands and stand alone:

> Many people today, leaders themselves included, disguise their motives and deceive others. When they appeal to their voters, they appear humble, accountable, and frugal. In reality, they mislead and cheat their supporters and vice versa. The supporters may refuse to listen to their leaders, and the leaders may hide information from their supporters. Both parties should be ready to show good in the face of evil rather than caving and matching that poor behavior with their own, because that evil will eventually catch up with them. For the story of the flutists, it is likely that the unpleasant behavior continued once the king allowed them back into the court. That was the repercussion for the king compromising his father's decision. Leaders need to recognize that they should never compromise the truth, as doing so comes with serious repercussions.[13]

---

12 Kibirige interview, December 18, 2019.
13 Ibid.

This perspective seems to contradict other discussions of the importance of listening to one's advisers or hearing the words of the people.

Harriet Kisuule summarizes the ideas that other interpreters have presented on contemporary leadership, concluding both the analysis of the song and its historical context by reflecting on one of the central themes of the composition's narrative: how to be a good leader. She reinforces the recurring theme about reciprocity. However, whereas the previous instances speak to the cautiousness that is crucial to maintaining mutually beneficial relations, Kisuule speaks to the trust that is similarly vital to those relations. In essence, one must mediate and balance these two attitudes to create an effective and mutually beneficial dynamic. If one aspect substantially dominates the other, the relationship will likely suffer as a result. Kisuule states that it is up to readers to draw for themselves where the line is, where they may best establish trust and caution:

> "The Flutists' Legal Case" details the importance of being careful among leaders and politicians to avoid facing charges. Being careful requires obedience. If there is a situation that calls for one's input, one should listen attentively, attempt to reach an appropriate compromise, and pass good judgment. But leaders must have the ability not only to properly correct and advise their subjects but also to accept corrections and advice in return. A good leader always makes his or her people feel as though he or she has listened to them and considered their voices. He or she sets a good example. If one was not blessed with natural leadership qualities, one should make up for it by attempting to develop them through concise goals and principles. Truthfulness and faithfulness are two of these important characteristics. Leaders who betray the masses lose their love and support, so it is best for them to be truthful. When they preside over disputes, or if they are trying to clarify an agreement between parties, they must be honest with both. They should also be able to share in the triumphs and defeats of their people—they need to be one with the masses, walking along with them, because leadership is ultimately an extension of the people. Leaders and their subjects must move along together.[14]

This position recasts "The Flutists' Legal Case" as a multivalent depiction of reciprocity. Rather than positing a particular trait as the ultimate solution to any circumstance, this contradiction and added perspective show that such silver bullets simply do not exist. Instead, there is a constant process of reimagining, redistributing, and remaking that exists as long as the relationship endures. Much like the banana leaves that the song references, relationships undergo a perpetual cycle of growth, overcoming themselves

---

14 Kisuule interview, December 21, 2019.

as they progress and reconstituting themselves with new parts and new conceptions.

Conclusion

"The Flutists' Legal Case" functions as a musical lament created by Ssuuna II's court musicians mourning their dismissal. The composition transforms the king's disciplinary action against disrespectful flutists into a preserved record of both the punishment and the emotional aftermath it produces among the performers. As a commentary on power dynamics, "The Flutists' Legal Case" illustrates the complexities of interpersonal relationships in the royal court. Not only are personal emotions in the song abundantly evident, but the work also simultaneously expresses and offers a commentary on various sociopolitical themes, including kinship, legacy, death, spirituality, extinction, decay, and deterioration.

Various interpreters explore these topics through the themes of lament and uncertainty, bringing the song far past its initial lone perspective. In particular, they reexamine it, relate its lyrical content to the political situation in twenty-first-century Uganda. Each of them provides a unique spin to the work, transforming it into a critique of selfishness, a commentary on manipulation, and a discourse on spiritual conduct all at the same time. Accordingly, the song acquires a flurry of new potential meanings as different interpreters pull it close and allow parts of themselves to resonate with it.

14

"The Little Lion"

Power and Selfishness

The song "The Little Lion" ("Akawologoma") paints a powerful yet loving image of Buganda's king, while also detailing the loyalty that his subjects display. Reminding us that one of the king's official titles is the lion (*empologoma*), the song employs the lion figure to represent the leader. Albert Muwanga Ssempeke (ca. 1930–2006), the performer of the "The Little Lion" version analyzed in this chapter, offered the following historical context about the song:

> "The Little Lion" expresses the belief that the king is analogous to a lion, cautioning his subjects to handle him carefully, hence, the lyric *Bakakwate mpola balye ebintu* (They should handle him with care so that they can feast). The song recalls a lion that King Muteesa I (ca. 1854–1884) tamed and kept at his court. That lion eventually went feral and ate a child, prompting the king to shoot and kill him. People who walked through the area of the court where the animal lived had to be careful not to agitate him, lest he lash out and cause great harm. In fact, visitors interested in seeing him received special instructions on how to behave around him. With the guidance of court officials, some would feed him animal meat. According to another story, however, "The Little Lion" originally advised people to take a lion cub to the royal court and offer him to the king as a gift. The song's performers advised: *Bakatwale embuga kalye ebintu* (They should take him to the court to feast) and *Bakakwate mpola kalye ebintu* (They should handle him with care so that he can feast).[1]

The historical context Ssempeke presents offers a listening guide for "The Little Lion" and its meanings and alludes to the court musicians' roles as advisers to the king and his subjects, whom, per the performer's comments, the song indirectly advises to handle the king carefully so they can obtain

---

1   Ssempeke interview, July 27, 2005.

good things from him. Accordingly, the lyrical content of "The Little Lion" praises the figure of the little lion, an allusion that we can trace to King Muteesa I. However, even within the context of the song's composition, the lion is a multivocal figure, one whose meanings vary. In a literal sense, the figure could represent the fabled animal that King Muteesa I owned during his kingship, allowing us to understand the song as a historical description. This framing, which portrays the lion as a real animal who is tamed and kept at Muteesa I's court, has multiple implications. First, its position as a historical account means that it exemplifies a revival and reinterpretation of the past. Whereas historical methodologies often center on an obsessive desire to inscribe the past as frozen, linear, and coherent, "The Little Lion" depicts the past as colorful and alive, changing with each instance of performance and with each moment of interpretation. The lion, rather than being an anecdote of Muteesa I's rule, comes to life in the lyrics of the song, dancing atop the rhythms and melodies that the performer weaves. As a result, this lively depiction becomes flexible, allowing the past to come alive and become reapplied in or relevant to the present.

Furthermore, the figure of the lion itself, in relation to the king, poses its own set of messages that we can recast. This literal representation is valuable because it provides another layer to the relation of lion and king explored in this chapter. Now we can see this relationship as more concrete, causing us to think about how the lion should be treated, why the king might have tamed him in the first place, and what to draw from his outburst and subsequent death at the hands of the king. Through a more figurative lens, the little lion may represent the king's power, the relationship between a leader and his people, or the selfish hunger that seems to plague many global political systems today.

Ssempeke performs the lyrics of "The Little Lion" without instrumental accompaniment, singing a series of winding melodies that move abruptly between high and low registers. His lyrics flow swiftly in smooth succession, and his delivery style is somewhat conversational, shifting unpredictably. However, he generally sings with a movement and projection that is confident and tuneful. His voice has a spacious timbre that further portrays the little lion. Ssempeke sings,

1 *Akawologoma, akawologoma*
The little lion, the little lion

2 *Bakatwale embuga kalye ebintu, mukwano gwa bonna*
Let them take him to the court to feast, a friend to all

3 *Akawologoma, nneeyanze, ssebo, akawologoma*
The little lion, I am grateful, sir, the little lion

4 *Sirina googera, nze omundabiranga mukwano gwa bonna*
I lack strength to speak, pay my salutation to the friend to all

5 *Akawologoma, naganza munnange, akawologoma*
The little lion, I betrothed my friend, the little lion

6 *Bakatwale embuga kalye ebintu, ndigenda n'ani?*
Let them take him to the court to feast, with whom shall I go?

7 *Nnaayita ani, jjajjange Ntale, nnaakola ntya?*
Whom shall I entreat, my ancestor Ntale, what shall I do?

8 *Sirina googera, nze omundabiranga nnyinibuyinza*
I lack strength to speak, pay my respects to the owner of authority

9 *Ndigenda n'anjagala, akawologoma*
I shall go with the one who loves me, the little lion

The opening lyrics of "The Little Lion" describe a lion beloved by the singer and the Baganda people (lines 1–2). The performer shares how he wishes for the lion to be taken to the court to be fed, following which he expresses his gratitude to the lion (line 3). The musician states that he lacks the strength to speak and thus asks the listener to pay his salutations to the lion, whom he refers to as "the friend to all" (line 4). Later in the song, the singer addresses him as "the owner of authority," the law maker (line 8) and "the one who loves me" (line 9). At the same time, the performer also expresses uncertainty, asking his ancestors about whom he should go with (line 6) and whom he should entreat (line 7). The singer quickly resolves his questioning, as he concludes that he will go with "the one who loves" him, implying that he will go with the lion (line 9).

The song's depiction of the lion here heavily implies that he is a representation of the king. This is evident not only from the king's preexisting association with the lion as a regal and powerful figure but also because "the lion" is one of his titles, along with various other names that the singer bestows on him. He describes him as "the owner of authority" (the law maker) in one instance, demonstrating that the little lion is not literally a lion but someone of high status, like the king. Furthermore, the sort of praise he provides to the little lion reflects the praise that singers afford the king in other, more direct allegories.

A peculiar aspect about this song is that although the Baganda refer to the king as "the lion of Buganda," the performer never explicitly confirms that the lion figure is the king. Even with the line referring to the lion's authority, one could interpret it as indeed talking about the animal. In this way the singer provides the song with a capacity for interpretation that draws on the imaginations of those who encounter it. Even if the lion clearly represents the king, one can interpret all the descriptors for it creatively to draw out varying meanings. The figure of the lion, being only an indirect reference to the king and kingship in general, is malleable in a way that a more specific allusion to the king could not be. This becomes clear in the various interpretations of "The Little Lion" presented in this chapter, as they all seem to have unique takes on what the song could be portraying.

Power and Selfishness

Different commentators interpret "The Little Lion" as an image of contemporary Uganda, utilizing the "lion" figure to illustrate the unfettered self-centeredness of leaders. The commentators' interpretations reveal views on power and selfishness in varied political spheres. Opening the discussion on power and selfishness, Steven Mukasa Kabugo's assessment of "The Little Lion" provides a different interpretation of the symbolism behind the lion. He regards the lion as more like someone attempting to improve his or her place in the world by appealing to superiors. Doing so is no easy task, however, so one must put in effort to maximize one's chances of gaining recognition, as Kabugo points out:

> A person needs to try hard to find favor with his or her superiors, because those who ingratiate themselves always receive extra rewards. For example, a musician known for his well-arranged compositions and beautiful words would often receive invitations to perform at the court festivities. He gained fame and in turn received invitations to more festivities and permissions to partake in the opulent feasts that accompanied them. Sometimes the king's chief would even reward singers with leadership of villages for their performances when their songs correctly prophesied the future.[2]

This perspective alludes to difficult situations that many musicians face today. They can no longer rely on their skill as musicians but must also pursue the goodwill of those who wield greater influence than they do. Without doing so, they cannot achieve the recognition they need in order to grow; their popularity might thus stagnate or they might disappear entirely. These contexts reframe the intentions behind the lion's friendships. Rather than being friends "to all" (lines 2 and 4) for the sake of it, this analysis explains that lions make friends for the purpose of being fed, to move up and survive in the difficult world that they live in. This point alludes to the importance of mutuality in surviving the unpredictability of life. When one's friends support one, it becomes far easier to manage the unexpected, as that person will be able to pool resources to maximize everyone's ability to overcome

---

2   Kabugo interview, December 19, 2019.

obstacles. Returning to the lion, the life of a predator is often tenuous and stressful. Starvation is always closer than one might like. Situations always force one to fight for one's prey, without any guarantee of success. Just a few failed hunts could result in death, as the lion might no longer have the strength for the chase. However, if the lion is under the care of the court, such worries disappear. The king will feed the lion as needed, and thus the stress of life will decrease.

Focusing on the more popular understanding that the little lion is the king, Harriet Kisuule's interpretation explains the ways a leader should attempt to emulate and, on occasion, avoid the behaviors of a lion. While she identifies the qualities that are crucial to effective leadership, she emphasizes that excessive harshness, although necessary at times, is ineffective in regularity because it drives subjects away, making them too intimidated to view a leader as one of their own. Thus, expanding such a rift between a leader and their people will injure both sides, as the leader will be unaware of the people's qualms and will thus lead blindly. Instead, Kisuule notes, a leader should aim to be friendly and loyal, dedicating himself to his people in the same way that they dedicate themselves to him:

> The lion is always sturdy and unyielding, but these qualities are detrimental if too persistent. To use an example, if leaders become too unyielding and harsh, people will be scared to approach them. A good leader loves his people and listens to their issues. He cares for and wishes them well. He is also just and exemplary, always serving as a fair judge. A good leader is faithful, amicable, and approachable. Additionally, he should be spiritual, so that he does not become too prideful and, instead, remains humble. He needs to be able to descend from the rarified height of leadership to be among the common people.[3]

This point of view articulates a philosophy of leadership where the leader and the led are one. The philosophy was common during the years of King Muteesa II (r. 1939–1966), who, according to some of his musicians, always aimed to treat his people well and listen to their issues. Accordingly, they stood by him faithfully after the fall of his kingdom in 1966. By drawing on the little lion's parallels with a leader and by describing the lion's friendships, Kisuule frames "The Little Lion" as an affirmation of a particularly mutual kind of leadership, one that views the leader as an extension of the people. Contrasting with other commentaries presented in this chapter, she reimagines the lyric detailing the lion's many friends, using it as evidence of the lion's or king's willingness to connect with the people on a personal and reciprocal level.

---

3   Kisuule interview, December 21, 2019.

In his analysis of "The Little Lion," Edward Ssebunnya Kironde sees little lions as members of the leadership. He expands on Kisuule's comments by providing several specific examples of greedy lions at work in the current Uganda government:

> In contemporary times, it is easy to draw the lines or parallels between little lions and greedy political leaders. Leadership hangs in a balance between personal desire and a desire to serve others, between what one wants and what one's purpose is. Leadership issues are so prevalent across the globe in part because the balance is delicate. Most leaders always try to get their hands on their own slices of the cake, so to speak. The people eventually turn against these leaders. The anti-corruption walks that the president organized and participated in recently cost close to forty billion shillings, an absurd amount of money just for a walk. Therefore, even the anti-corruption walk itself was likely a source of corruption that benefited the little lion. Many leaders promise to serve the interests of the people, but of course the benefits they receive are the only thing that motivates them. Such leaders are scarcely better than little lions themselves. All they are interested in is how they can profit from their association with the court. A lion is a lion. It eats everything and goes after anything. But, again, there is a balance at play. Even though they are ambitious predators, they never grow to large numbers. Often, they die premature deaths because they are overly ambitious with their prey. Lions should remember that there are always repercussions for their behavior, even when it feels as if they are going unchecked.[4]

Kironde's reading of "The Little Lion" as a reflection of current leaders allows him to describe the conflict that authority figures face. They must choose between serving their own interests and serving the interests of the people. The little lion figure illustrates the behavior of leaders who have fallen to their more selfish desires. Much like the little lion, they eat their fill with little consideration for others, sometimes even eating those who feed them. In other words, these leaders betray the trust of the people and of their peers by pursuing personal success above all, even sacrificing the well-being of their comrades to do so. A voracious greed much like the lion's own powerful appetite drives this behavior; both can lead to ruin when left unchecked.

Kironde also compares selfishness with a lion's appetite and thus recognizes that greed may be an unavoidable vice. Even if one disciplines oneself to not be so impulsive, selfishness is always something to keep at bay. For most of their lives, people tend to perceive themselves as distinct entities from those around them. They see the self as a discrete form that wins and

---

4   Kironde interview, December 19, 2019.

loses independently from everyone else, and in this logic, living becomes a process of mediating between the solitary "I" and the plural "we." It is not necessarily a matter of whether greed is evil, since it is already embedded within all people; rather, it depends on whether one can recognize oneself in others, form a mutual relationship with them, and thus dedicate one's livelihood to them. This conflict is evident in leaders like Idi Amin and others, who assisted and supported Baganda court musicians even as he was cruelly violating many other people. He saw himself in the musicians but could not see himself elsewhere.

As Kironde further explains, selfishness injures those who embody it as much as those who encounter it. Such is the case with the lion, for when he bit the hand that fed him, he lost a crucial source of food and support. As we saw in the historical background of "The Little Lion," when King Muteesa I's lion ate a child, he swiftly killed him. This decision was only natural, as the lion had proved himself dangerous to the court and the people in it. In much the same way, leaders who reveal their unfettered greed become dangerous to the collective. Although they may maintain their posts for some time through violence and manipulation, they will eventually fall. Here, Kironde wields the figure of the lion to expand on an imaginative discourse of leadership. By rereading the song, he uses the lion to mirror modern leaders, framing their greed and selfishness through the lion's own ferocious hunger.

Kironde expands on his comments about the alleged greed and corruption of modern leaders by providing a specific example in the case of the Buganda government itself:

> Some people have accused the Buganda prime minister, Charles Mayiga, of acting only from his own self-interest. They claimed he embezzled from the Brick (Ettoffaali), a fundraising scheme that the kingdom created to help renovate and restore its royal tombs. He made the scheme more extensive than originally planned, fundraising overseas and in all divisions of the kingdom. Some people said, at the end, he had raised a tidy sum of money. Other people claimed that the work the kingdom's administration did on the tombs was far less than they could have paid for with all the money he collected. He never accounted for his spending, and some members of the committee that oversaw the project suddenly ended up building fabulous houses. What happened was all quite clear.[5]

Other sources challenge Kironde's allegations, however, arguing that the Buganda government handled Ettoffaali funds appropriately. The sources include an online publication by Denis Jjuuko in which he explains that during the early years of his leadership, Mayiga embarked on the ambitious Ettoffaali fundraising campaign, traveling extensively throughout the kingdom. To

---

5   Ibid.

ensure transparency, he appointed business leaders to spearhead the initiative and implemented strict financial accountability measures. He never personally handled any donations: whenever funds were presented to him, he immediately transferred them to the committee. Breaking with tradition, he became the first prime minister who neither signed checks at Mmengo (the location of Buganda's government headquarters) nor had signing authority on the Ettoffaali bank account, leaving contract decisions entirely to the committee. The campaign maintained exceptional financial transparency, publicly declaring all contributions, down to minor expenses such as bank charges. Anyone seeking verification can simply review archives from television stations that documented the Ettoffaali drive. In addition, complete financial records were published by the *Daily Monitor* on July 8, 2014, and remain accessible online. The campaign successfully raised approximately twelve billion Uganda shillings, which funded the construction of a perimeter wall around the sixty-four-acre Kasubi Royal Tombs, as well as developments at Masengere and BBS (Buganda Broadcasting Service) Terefayina, the Kingdom of Buganda's official television station. Ironically, some of the most vocal critics demanding accountability for the Ettoffaali funds are the same politicians whose own contribution checks bounced during the campaign.[6]

Yet Kironde raises concerns about other Buganda government projects that are overseen by allegedly greedy and corrupt officials:

> Another project that many Baganda have stood against is the Title in Hand (Kyapa mu Ngalo) project. The philosophy behind the project is that if someone resides on the king's land, the administration grants them an official title to the land. They lease the title and the land for a time, around forty years or so, following that one can renew it in exchange for a generous financial gift to the kingdom. This arrangement stands in stark contrast to the prior arrangements, which made it impossible for one to buy one's way into such a position. Accordingly, some people are questioning the development and the intentions behind them. Another project that many question is the rule that requires all Baganda to register with their respective clans. Some suspect that this might just be a plot by clan leaders to increase their own standings, so they are hesitant to pursue it. Even something that may be good for the masses or truly serve their interests is now questioned because people are beginning to realize the deception involved with poor leadership. Leaders all come disguised as wolves in sheep's clothing. Although they may not appear dangerous at first, it is best to think of them as lions and to remember that a lion is dangerous no matter its size. The only difference is that some go about their business cautiously, while others dive in to take whatever they can get.[7]

---

6   Jjuuko 2021.
7   Kironde interview, December 19, 2019.

Kironde articulates the effects of rampant greed on the mindsets of common people. As indicated by the example of the allegations regarding Buganda's prime minister, even the most respected positions are susceptible to this alleged greed. As such, the subjects find themselves in a state of uncertainty. They do not know whom to trust because any project or campaign, no matter how good it might sound, could actually just be another elaborate scheme for personal gain. From this uncertainty, Kironde further interprets "The Little Lion" through the lens of manipulation. He explains how its small stature may only serve to obscure its hidden aggression and ferocity. By comparing politicians to lions, he demonstrates the importance of maintaining skepticism, as the politician's "size" provides no true indication of the danger he poses. His "size" could simply be a ruse to distract subjects from his hidden ferocity. This point illuminates the precarious condition that many Ugandans face. The nature of contemporary politics leads some to distrust all individuals in leadership positions, feeling as if at any moment their leaders can abandon or betray them. Given the current mass unemployment issue in Uganda, the already worrisome position of having no available income is only compounded by dishonest and self-interested leaders. Kironde pursues this point even further, taking the precariousness that many Ugandans feel and transforming it into a tool for survival. He reveals that the distrust they feel is crucial to their long-term survival. They must recognize greed's prevalence, and avoid it whenever possible, using their insight to spot the little lions as the dangerous predators they are.

Jimmy Ssenfuka Kibirige expands on Kironde's interpretation of "The Little Lion" by describing how "little lions" exist as a plague throughout governmental systems. He elaborates on the various methods that the allegedly self-serving lions in the Uganda government use, as well as the negative impact that their actions have on the people:

> Evil breeds evil, and a lion is a lion regardless of its size or age. Even the smallest lions can be as fierce as the adult ones. Therefore, it is important to neglect not even the smallest, to not underestimate anything because everything has the capability to possess power. It is the small things, like the little lions, that can be particularly disastrous. They can infect and triumph over one's leadership. The dangerous people embedded in one's leadership systems ultimately cause their downfall. The best way to address such little lions as a leader is to keep away from some of the pleasures that come along with politics. In other words, leaders should stay away from the games that characterize the little lions' behavior—the double-sided nature and shows of cheap popularity. Many leaders use others in pursuit of their own political glory, taking advantage of their naivety. They play on the psyche of those they want to manipulate, convincing them that what they are doing

is for their good. They twist those who follow them into being mindless sycophants, and into abandoning their own morals in favor of petty things. In the end, those who follow them and do their bidding end up digging their own political graves.[8]

This viewpoint presents the little lion as more than an allegory for individuals, as it is a model for a particular philosophy of selfishness that is endemic throughout government. People must be wary of little lions because, despite their lack of obvious power, their nefarious and manipulative strategies can easily result in a country's downfall. Drawing on this point, it is crucial to recognize that lions might manifest beyond the most visible roles in governments. They may be hiding behind their superiors or disguising themselves as advisers, but those superiors should still not ignore the responsibility of such little lions. Thus, it is important to be skeptical, not just of those who are most immediately in power but of anyone in the system. If one recognizes corruption and greed as a plague, it becomes that much easier to recognize its symptoms.

Jessy Ssendawula complements Kibirige's explanation of "The Little Lion." Rather than framing little lions as nefarious and underhanded actors in the national government of Uganda, he illuminates them as fierce figures who may retaliate when provoked with this warning:

> People need to be especially careful with the current leaders of Uganda because they can swiftly become lions, killing and devouring whoever disturbs their peace. A case in point is Dr. Stella Nyanzi. She reminded President Museveni that he had yet to fulfill his promise of making sanitary pads available to female students. He made the promise in the first place because the lack of feminine-care products was documented as one of the major reasons for school dropouts among female students in some rural areas. However, despite the validity of her critique, it partly earned her imprisonment. Ordinary people should know how much they can provoke the lion before it attacks them.[9]

Ssendawula reframes the lion as a sleeping giant: stolid and unmoving but violent and dangerous when irritated. He further expands on this image by providing an example from President Museveni's rule. If someone bothers a national leader today with his or her words, the leader may lash out and imprison the person. As it was for Dr. Nyanzi, even a reasonable comment can be met with violence and force. These responses pose a stark contrast to the king's attitude, discussed in other chapters. Whereas national

---

8   Kibirige interview, December 18, 2019.
9   Ssendawula interview, December 28, 2019. For fuller context of the events that Ssendawula describes, see Nyanzi 2020.

government leaders might be unreceptive and prone to lashing out, the king does his best to listen and acknowledge the people as much as possible. Therefore, Ssendawula's interpretation of the song illuminates the flaws and shortcomings of national government officials while indirectly contrasting them with the king's successes, interpreting both instances through the lion. The former represents the lion's aggression and ferocity, while the latter represents the lion's nobility and strength in the face of danger. Thus, Ssendawula reframes "The Little Lion" to encompass two seemingly contradictory narratives in one interpretation, demonstrating the power of creativity in expanding the possibilities for meaning.

Ssendawula also looks at how Christian missionaries were "little lions" because they damaged the traditional culture and inhabitants of Uganda. He states that the "little lion" could be used to refer to the missionaries who first came to the king's court. They feasted there after their long, harrowing journey to East Africa, as described in David Rubadiri's poem "Stanley Meets Muteesa."[10]

The role of the church and its missionaries in stamping down Kiganda traditions and values requires further discussion. From an artistic perspective, Moses Serwadda documents how the church opposed the continuation of many traditional dances such as the *ndongo* wedding dance, as church-run educational programs actively prevented girls from learning it. Moreover, they forbade wedding receptions in church halls from performing the dance, and tea and cakes replaced the beer traditionally served at these events. Serwadda further indicates that the preservation of the *ndongo* wedding dance and many others like it thus fell to Muslim artists and those who did not affiliate with the church.[11] The court composer-performer Evalisto Muyinda notes how in addition to undermining traditional dancing, the church pushed a campaign to divest the Baganda of their traditional music, a campaign that involved replacing the music's typical pentatonic scale with their own scale, the diatonic scale.[12]

Beyond devaluing dancing and music, Christian groups in Uganda made concentrated efforts to devalue clanship and kinship, substituting themselves as the primary institution of social structure, as Mikael Karlström shows.[13] These various examples, which occurred at the initial arrival of the missionaries Ssendawula mentions, demonstrate the role of Christian actors as little lions. The situation parallels President Museveni's rule with

---

10   Ssendawula interview, December 28, 2019. For the full poem, see Rubadiri 2020.
11   Serwadda 1971, 20–22.
12   Muyinda 1991, 5.
13   Karlström 2004, 600.

the arrival of the Christian missionaries, demonstrating how stories of the past might be reimagined to constitute active and living parts of the present moment. Rather than existing as distant memories, we can reframe them to engage intimately with the present. Accordingly, they become a crucial tool for making sense of the world.

This chapter's analysis of "The Little Lion" ends with a reminder from Peter Kinene that ultimately it is better to put the needs of the people first:

> When a leader is exceptional, even those he leads wish well for him. They praise him, soothe him, and speak well of him due to his great performance as a leader. This sentiment is a recurring theme of many of the other songs we have discussed.[14]

Kinene highlights the inherent benefits of performing well as a leader. Despite the material benefits of selfishness, he asserts that they pale in comparison to the deep satisfaction one receives when the masses praise and love one. This treatment extends beyond physical conveniences into an unspoken realm of spiritual uplifting and gratification. When leaders' subjects despise them, they feel it in their bones. It becomes an existential threat, as their life force withers under the isolation of their greed. Thus, despite their material wealth, the alleged greedy leaders are poor in a far more profound sense. Here, we recognize that selfish individuals ultimately suffer greatly from their actions, just as the lion would if he attacked his supporters or masters. However, this perspective does not seek to explain the suffering through cause and effect but instead articulates it as an inherent aspect of their actions. In other words, the pain that cruel leaders feel is one that they inflict directly onto themselves. They come to hate life without even knowing it. Thus, Kinene's reading of "The Little Lion" emphasizes the importance of mutuality over material gain. He shows us that the food King Muteesa I's court fed to the lion might not have been as important as the mutual support and care that the lion and the court shared. In much the same way, if the lion were to maul one of the court members, the punishment would not necessarily be the loss of food, but instead it would be the loss of a relationship that far exceeded the value a simple meal would provide.

Conclusion

"The Little Lion" balances royal power with affection through its diminutive characterization of the monarch. By employing the term "little" alongside one of the king's official titles, "the lion," the composition creates an

---

14 Kinene interview, December 16, 2019.

intimate representation of authority that simultaneously acknowledges the ruler's might while expressing endearment. Carrying themes of reverence and love, "The Little Lion" provides us with a set of multiple meanings. First, it is a song about the royal court, describing how King Muteesa I tamed and cared for a lion during his reign. Second, it is about the king, equating his greatness to the strength and nobility of a lion. Although he is dominant and powerful, he is also a friend to all, as he works to lead his people and give back to the community. Through this delicate balance, the kingdom thrives and sustains itself. Third, "The Little Lion" is about the court musicians, demonstrating how they influence the court by directing the king throughout his rule. These ideas show how one could view the lion as an allegory for the king, providing the reader the freedom to interpret what aspects of the lion one might adopt to align with those of the king. As in Ssempeke's explanation, it could refer to the care with which one should handle both. However, there are many other possibilities one could extract from this parallel. One listener might understand the lion as ferocious and powerful and thus carry those tendencies over to the king, whereas another might understand the lion as wise and proud and interpret "little" to mean the empathy and humbleness of the king, seeing it as a reference to his tendency to not be overbearing toward his subjects.

However, the poetic and imprecise nature of the metaphor allows those who encounter this song to listen to it differently, emphasizing certain lines over others because specific traits are interesting and insightful to these individuals. The result is a process where listeners constantly remake the song's meanings depending on their personal perspectives. The contributions of the performer of "The Little Lion" and those of the interpreters featured in this chapter all serve to rapidly transform it into an array of varying and sometimes conflicting narratives. Therefore, the song is not simply a commentary on the roles of a leader but also serves as a model of how people view their leaders. Applicable to many political and social contexts, "The Little Lion" eventually becomes about the greed of those leaders, the importance of love over material wealth, and the significance of skepticism in coping with perpetual precarity.

15

"The King Is a Lion"

Reverence and Love

"The King Is a Lion" ("Kabaka Mpologoma"), an original composition by Ssaalongo Kiwanuka Matovu Deziderio (1924–2015), portrays the Uganda national government in relation to Buganda's king and his right to rule over his people. The composer-performer noted,

> "The King Is a Lion" reminds listeners not to tamper with the king. In the same way one would not tamper with the lion, they should not mess with the king. He suffers no fools, and he is incomparable. He is a lion, and the princes are leopards. Those around him must walk gently, not veering from the path, lest they step on the lion. The king is an entity whose importance is reflected throughout the natural world. Even insects have a king. If a king leaves the area that he oversees, everything else in that area perishes. Accordingly, when the queen termite (*nnamunswa*—one of the king's titles) leaves an anthill (*ekiswa*), all the ants die, too. In the context of Uganda's politics, the Kiganda kingship is particularly extraordinary in the way God ordained it.[1]

Deziderio's remarks evoke the differences between the power of the king and the power of political leaders in the national government administration. By revealing the impact that he and his kingdom have had on the political landscape of Uganda, "The King Is a Lion" suggests that the current national government should permit the active involvement of royal politics in political decision-making. When Deziderio asserts that God ordained the king's right to rule, he seems to be suggesting that the king's rule needs no justification. That is, its justification is a transcendent assertion, proved by its natural existence. In comparison, the democratically elected governments of today demonstrate an extractive justification of power. They are only powerful if the masses deem them to be so, and the masses are only powerful to the extent that leaders allow them to be. This relation becomes tautological,

---

1 Deziderio interview, July 15, 2005.

as the powers that the leaders exert seem more theatrical, or performative, than real. Their orders become ways to garner the vote, to justify their own positions, rather than to have an impact. Without a higher purpose imbued in their power, it fails to reach beyond the circular relations that have made them leaders in the first place. Instead, it feeds back into the relations. They come to exert power for the sole purpose of ensuring that power remains with them, ensuring that they get the votes they need to maintain it.

This sort of power does not operate in the same way that power once did, as it exists almost exclusively in a realm of theatrics, of simulated power that players use to articulate certain figures—for example, casting some national politicians as the heroes of the people. The operation of these national government administrators is made possible by their alleged failure to recognize their responsibility to the masses they rule—that is, as individuals that "God has ordained" as the figureheads of the masses. Instead, such leaders exist as mere pawns in the larger system of power that presides over every mode of life. Thus, the power that they wield is not philosophically nor existentially "meaningful" because it only drives them to partake in self-serving activities. When we look at the interwovenness of the king with his kingdom, we understand that as is the case with the natural order, one would collapse without the other. This perfected dynamic, however, arises from a reciprocal reverence and love between a leader and the people.

Typical for performances featuring the tube fiddle, the only two components involved in Deziderio's presentation of "The King Is a Lion" rendition are the solo instrumentation and the singular vocal accompaniment. The performance opens with the tube fiddle playing sharp, brief phrases in quick succession. The vocal accompaniment enters swiftly after, with Deziderio singing in an impassioned fashion and in high register. The instrumental and vocal parts both go through markedly different phases or sections throughout the performance, but their texture does not change. With minimal textural lushness, the performance emphasizes different lyrical themes, with Deziderio telling a story about the relationship between the king and his people. The lyrical content stresses both the mutual intimacy and the unquestionable power of the king, a balance that evokes agreement and respect. One of the most important aspects of kingship is the leader's camaraderie, which court musicians have historically shared; this friendship yields the king's respect and obedience of his subjects. Deziderio's performance accentuates this blend of friendly praise and dutiful respect in the overall lyrics and mood of the song, which are cheerful and serious at the same time. For example, he repeatedly uses the word "comrade" to describe the king, each time with a passion that nearly strains his vocal cords.

Deziderio's chant-like singing style not only is reflective of the strong emotions associated with the king's authority but also evokes the reverence that the king's subjects have for him and his eminence. During some passages, the performer's voice stays monotonously at the same unwavering pitch, occasionally dropping down a few pitches. Other times, he begins his lyrics at the very top of his head voice, reaching high pitches that later drop down. This contrasting blend of monotony and urgency aligns with the portrait of the king's power, which is ubiquitous and widely accepted but nonetheless striking and inspiring. This power, as portrayed in the lyrics, according to the singer, is ultimately justified by God and is evident in the natural world around us. Using animal imagery (the lion and the leopard), Deziderio conveys the idea that these power structures and the sanctity of leaders are inherent even in the laws of nature. His observance of the natural world makes these lyrics more universally applicable and relatable:

1 *Nnina munnange omulongo*
I have a friend of mine, a twin

2 *Nnina munnange, bba bonna*
I have a friend of mine, a husband to all

3 *Bannange abalangira*
Dear princes

4 *Bannange abambejja*
Dear princesses

5 *Kabaka mpologoma, bbaffe, nnantajeemerwa, alimujeemera ani?*
The king is a lion, our husband, one who is never disobeyed, who will ever disobey him?

6 *Kabaka mpologoma, bba, ngo, nnantazannyirwako, alimuzannyisa amanyanga!*
The king is a lion, husband, leopard, one who is never played with, whoever shall mess with him will learn a lesson!

7 *Munnange*
My friend

8 *Nnina munnange, omutanda*
I have my friend, His Majesty

9 *Nnina munnange, bba bonna*
I have my friend, a husband to all

10 *Nnina munnange, eyandeese*
I have my friend, whom I have come to see

11 *Nnina munnange, omulongo y'oyo*
I have my friend, he is that twin

12 *Nze Dezi, abatammanyi*
I am Dezi, for those who do not know me

13 *Kati mubuuze ku bandabako*
Now ask those who have ever seen me

14 *Abange abatammanyi*
Those who do not know me

15 *Bannange, ndikomawo*
My friends, I shall be back

16 *Oba nga temummanyi*
If you do not know me

17 *Munninde ndikomawo*
Keep waiting, I shall be back

18 *Abange ebigambo bye byo*
Friends, those are the words

19 *Otambula mpola, towunjawunja*
Walk cautiously, do not meander

20 *Munnange, tolinnya ku ngo*
My friend, do not trample on the leopard

21 *Olinnyako mpola, towunjawunja*
Tread carefully, do not meander

22 *Kabaka mpologoma, bba, ngo, nnantazannyirwako, alimuzannyisa ani?*
The king is a lion, husband, leopard, one who is never played with, who will ever play with him?

23 *Abange, endagaano kye ki?*
Friends, what is an agreement?

24 *Bannange mubuuze, endagaano y'eyo*
My friends ask, that is an agreement

25 *Endagaano za dda nnyo*
Agreements are from long ago

26 *Nga ne Muteesa Walugembe kw'ali*
When Muteesa Walugembe was reigning

27 *Okumanya nga endagaano za dda*
Because agreements are from long ago

28 *Olaba ne Kisingiri endagaano kw'ali*
Even Kisingiri signed the agreements

29 *Stanis Mugwanya endagaano kw'ali*
Stanis Mugwanya signed the agreements

30 *Olaba ne Bazoogera endagaano kw'ali*
Even Bazoogera signed the agreements

31 *Abange endagaano bw'eba*
Friends, that is usually what an agreement is

32 *Aa! Otuuse, endagaano kye kyo*
Aha! You are right, that is truly an agreement

33 *Abange endagaano ky'ekyo*
Friends, that is truly an agreement

34 *Owange obadde mulungi, endagaano ze zo*
My friend, you have been a good audience, those are the agreements

The lyrics of "The King Is a Lion" focus primarily on the king as a figure that subjects should revere and respect. However, from this reverence comes a familiarity. The song begins with a reference to the king, describing him as a "friend" and a "husband to all" (lines 2 and 9). One of the king's many honorifics, a husband to all (*bba bonna*), reflects the close, almost familial relationship between the leader and his people, and it is the maintenance of this relationship that lies at the core of the Kiganda society. As the composition continues, it becomes clear that the singer's camaraderie with the king is a crucial aspect of the leader's greatness. This greatness is inseparable from his camaraderie with his people, a point that transitions into the other primary theme of the song: the notion that the king is not a leader to be trifled with, as obeying the king (line 5) naturally arises when the power dynamic between leader and subject maintains love and respect for each other. The singer further emphasizes this point when he clarifies that all who disrespect the king learn the consequences soon after (line 6). The statement speaks to the swift backlash that would result from the king's supporters if one were to ever violate his trust. Indeed, the lyrical phrase "who will ever disobey him?" (line 5) is apt because the song enforces that no self-respecting person would do so. After sufficiently praising the king, the song transitions into a discussion of agreements (lines 23–34), emphasizing the long history of mediation in which the king has participated. It describes how the process of finding consensus and making accords is inherent in the kingship, as the parties who made such accords signed them during the reign of rulers from many generations ago. The song concludes by describing that these agreements reflect the greatness of the king himself, good for all who partake in them.

Reverence and Love

Through different interpretations of "The King Is a Lion," the song becomes a collective dialogue concerning the contemporary Ugandan government, the relationships between leaders and their people, and a wealth of other subjects. These and related topics are the focus of this section, which uses themes of reverence and love to examine the song's lyrics. Steven Mukasa Kabugo's interpretation of "The King Is a Lion" evokes the unity that shapes the masses' relations with the king and relations with one another. He suggests that leaders such as kings are not simply figures vying for whatever value they can extract from those they rule but that they are intimately invested in their people's happiness and success:

> "The King Is a Lion" reminds leaders to fulfill what they have promised the masses. Similarly, the song speaks to married couples or anyone in some form of partnership, encouraging them to not betray one another's trust. The song and Kiganda society in general place emphasis on the need to respect the kingship and acknowledge the esteem of the king, whom many Baganda regard as truthful and reliable. As such, he lives in harmony with his people and counts them among his friends.[2]

Kabugo highlights the parallels between personal relationships and political ones. He shows that one cannot limit reciprocity to a particular field, as one of its defining qualities is its application to all spheres of life. The reciprocal exchange of the king with his people does not reflect an exception to such categorization but demonstrates the insufficiency of such a rule outright. It shows that one must embrace the personal in politics, not as a subordinate or extraneous quality but as a crucial part of what constitutes politics outright. This philosophy reimagines "The King Is a Lion" by revealing how reciprocity, a fundamental element of social life, applies to the political sphere, to the Kiganda kingship. The song simultaneously expresses and comments on these two supposedly separate lenses, encountering and engaging with them in tandem.

Building on Kabugo's explanation of the king's good leadership qualities, Harriet Kisuule describes the way the leader handles precarious political situations. As with the king and his people, one should recognize that any mutual relationship extends beyond the sum of its parts, strengthening both parties beyond the mere combination of their already existing abilities. According to Kisuule,

> The king demonstrates the extent of a good leader's determination to face challenges. He kneels for no one, not even the national government, which may

---

2   Kabugo interview, December 19, 2019.

try to deny him the security it is supposed to provide. This is not something that bothers him because he can stand on his own, regardless of the resources the national government makes available to him. He has the support of his people, and they give him the strength to stand tall regardless of the situation. The Baganda are generally unified in their respect and love for the king and as a result of their support, he does not concern himself with the petty behaviors of the national government. Denying him funding barely changes his attitude. For example, when the government took the kingdom's radio, Central Broadcasting Services, off the air in 2009, the king, rather than panicking, remained calm and waited patiently until the government initiated the talks to reinstate the radio station. However, the king might protest to the national government his need for a state car and monthly salary, as is his established right due to his status as a cultural leader. But again, that is not what he truly values. His determination enables him to not compromise the value of his kingdom for personal gains, and in doing so he sets an example for his people.[3]

Kisuule's reading of "The King Is a Lion" demonstrates how the source of the king's strength is not the king alone but also the mutuality between him and his people. Through their support he achieves a determination and stalwartness that far exceeds what would have been possible otherwise. The king is "never played with" (lines 6 and 22) in part because he has the support of his people. This view demonstrates his strength in the face of adversary while also illuminating his popularity among his supporters.

Edward Ssebunnya Kironde expands on the explanation of the king's leadership by focusing not on his tactical ability, as Kisuule does, but on his inherent sovereignty. Kironde also applies this explanation to the power the government affords to modern elected officials, explaining the differences in power under the more recent form of constitutional monarchy:

> The image the lion figure evokes is representative of the king of Buganda in that he is renowned for his power. Thus, many Baganda accord him the same amount of power they accord a lion and give him names such as a man like charcoal that breaks an axe (*ssemandaagamenyembazzi*), signal grass (*ccuucu*), and snake (*musota*). These titles are indicative of the times when the Baganda people were supposed to fear a king rather than revere him; they were supposed to invoke an aura of power and danger, associating them with a leader who has supreme authority. Thus, the people awarded him titles such as the supreme man (*ssaabasajja*); our husband (*bbaffe*), the patriarch of the entire kingdom; and the supreme landowner (*ssaabataka*), for all the land in Buganda is technically his. Therefore, "The King Is a Lion" thoroughly explores the sovereignty of the king.[4]

---

3 Kisuule interview, December 21, 2019.
4 Kironde interview, December 19, 2019.

Ccuucu, also known as signal or Congo signal grass, is a type of tropical male grass that many Baganda describe as spiny and itchy. Because of its nature, they do not use it to thatch traditional shelters or cover the floors of these shelters. The use of *ccuucu* as one the king's titles underscores how he commands a lot of respect and the fact that his subjects never question him. *Ccuucu* and other descriptors referenced by Kironde underscore the king's divine sovereignty in comparison to contemporary elected leaders' more tautological justifications for sovereignty. This reference emphasizes his power, but it does not specify whether the terms for his strength arose independently of his rule or specifically to describe his rule. Thus, we see the fundamental quality of his strength, as even language seems to bend to the impact of his rule. National government leaders, on the other hand, are undeniably subordinate to language, as their position only spawns from language's premeditated validation of their role (through founding documents, legislation, and so forth). This practice, which further demonstrates the linguistic shifts that have taken hold of the world in recent decades, transforms the commentary of "The King Is a Lion" as a reflection on the unique power that the king has historically held. As such, the king's universal and atemporal investment in the world begets the reverence that his people feel for him.

Kironde further elaborates on the king's divine sovereignty in his interpretation. His criticism of contemporary national government leaders responds to the alleged attempts by these officials to arrogate this sovereignty to themselves. However, due to the fundamental differences in their social positions, governmental leaders allegedly place a strain on the general population, demanding wealth and respect for an illusory cause. As a result, says Kironde, many suffer because those in power continuously seek to hoard the power for themselves instead of focusing on benefiting the masses:

> The king is the embodiment of sovereignty, and he is without question at the peak of authority. His subjects follow his commands without hesitation. The difference between the kingships of the past and that of the present, though, is that the current kingship is more of a ceremonial monarchy. There is one problem that the monarch still poses, even a ceremonial one. Due to the inheritance of the throne, it is possible to have a bad king or queen simply because the person in line for the crown is not well suited for the position, but the culture or inheritance requires the person to take it. The one upside to this arrangement is that being a good monarch is the same as being any other leader: good leadership is a skill that one can learn. Compared to the king of Buganda and the ceremonial monarchy he heads, the political leaders who work with the current national government of Uganda are not kings. Some people elect them to their positions as a direct result of their opting out of traditional monarchical rule. Consequently,

they should not feel entitled to the same treatment as members of the royalty. Nevertheless, many leaders behave like kings. Some even expect huge salaries and unjustifiable benefits for the service they give the people. This means that rather than having a single lion at the top, the government now appears to be infested with a whole pride of lions. Nothing seems to change, and Ugandans seem to be listening to the same old story that their country tells repeatedly.[5]

Kironde seems to be suggesting that the number of politicians who are desperate to replicate the power of the king have given political authority a more damaging effect. This desperation juxtaposes "The King Is a Lion" against the "false kingship" that contemporary national government leaders perform. Descriptors such as "one who is never played with" (lines 6 and 22) and "a husband to all" (lines 2 and 9) take on new meaning, forcing us to wonder how there can be so many replicas of one "husband to all" and one "never played with." With this lens, the song becomes an almost satirical commentary on the behavior of elected leaders, as it shows us the cycle of failure that they participate in to achieve their own impossible goals. In the same vein as Kironde, Issiaka Ouattara observes that although individual prestige is strongly associated with ancestral legacy, it is also linked to the active social fabric of the community.[6] In this sense it is possible for a ruler, despite being a descendant of past rulers, to rupture himself from this fabric of the community and be a poor leader. Thus, while leadership depends on universal forces, it also must constantly produce and renew itself in the present moment.

Considering the king's position as the patriarch of the Baganda, Peter Kinene provides further elaboration on the ways the monarch cares for the needs of his people. In his explanation of how the leader is mindful of their needs, Kinene adds that the king conveys himself as approachable and amicable to the masses, whereas national government politicians allegedly isolate themselves from them. Kinene states,

> The king's people listen to him, and he listens to them in return, assisting them with shelter, education, and finances, among other needs. His actions reflect the sentiment that "The King Is a Lion" expresses, that a good king should fend for his people and vice versa. A more specific example of the latter occurred in 2009 when national government politicians prohibited the king from attending the Youth Day Celebrations in Bugerere. This is an annual event celebrating the achievements of youth everywhere, originally organized worldwide by the United Nations in 2000. His people protested his exclusion from the event, and eventually Buganda reached an

---

5   Ibid.
6   Ouattara 2018, 154.

agreement with the central government. Beyond that, the king is simply an approachable figure. If someone is in need, all they must do is go to him and he will attempt to help them however he can. President Museveni, however, believes this approach is too casual and unbecoming of a leader. He remains aloof, separated from the masses rather than interacting with them.[7]

This perspective further illuminates the shifting qualities of power that have been discussed in this chapter. On the one hand, the king interacts with his subjects on an amicable basis because he knows that his rule is not in question. On the other hand, he also knows that an inherent part of that rule is his willingness to represent and embody the people, as it is precisely his ability to combine and reinforce their interests that makes him such an undeniably powerful king. Thus, he is kind, helpful, and approachable, qualities that might make elected leaders jealous and undermine their authority. This difference might be a result of these leaders' power being constantly in question, not only for the way some gained their office (through war, then through election, and then through voter repression and manipulation) but due to their inability to access the divine sovereignty that justifies the king's rule. As a result, elected leaders must always perform their leadership and power to justify their hold on it. Without doing so, their influence may evaporate as quickly as water in the hot sun. This could also explain why, even today, the king allegedly poses a danger to these temporary officials. Despite the king's total lack of political control, the support he carries and the remnants of this divine justification still pose a substantial challenge to the elected politicians' rule. Even as the country moves away from the kingship system, the king himself still holds enough respect to challenge the national government's control of the country.

Echoing Kinene's thoughts on the king's fatherly role, Jimmy Ssenfuka Kibirige confirms that the leader is the householder (*nnannyinimu*) of Buganda and the one who is never despised (*nnantanyoomebwa*), among other honorifics. Kibirige advises national government leaders not to attempt to copy the king's power but to instead attempt to embody the behavior that leads to this power:

> Other leaders should take note of his actions and try to emulate him in their own rule. Many respect him for his success in overseeing the kingdom and as a result always obey him. For example, in 2009, the

---

7   Kinene interview, December 16, 2019. For additional information on the 2009 event, see "Uganda: Investigate 2009 Kampala Riot Killings; One Year Later, No Prosecutions and Failed Parliamentary Inquiry," Human Rights Watch, September 10, 2010, https://www.hrw.org/news/2010/09/10/uganda-investigate-2009-kampala-riot-killings.

national government denied him the right to tour his counties of Kyaggwe and Bugerere. His people were extremely upset at the lack of respect the national government showed him and forced their way into these areas anyway in hopes of seeing him. Tensions began to escalate. However, the king, upon seeing the violence that was arising from the situation, called for his people to stop their protests. He preserved their lives rather than preserving his pride.[8]

This commentary suggests that national leaders' desperation to replicate the king's power only serves as further evidence of their insufficiency and inability to achieve it. If they recognized that embodying reciprocity is what enables divine sovereignty, then they may be able to gain the masses' support and thus gain at least an approximate amount of influence to what the king has historically had. However, doing this would require one to completely rethink one's relationship to leadership and power outright. The king does not make a deliberate decision to support his people in exchange for power. Instead, the act of reciprocity and his attitude of openness come naturally to him. His position as a monarch embodies these qualities just as Deziderio's place as a court musician embodies his reciprocity. Such embodiment, through the lens of "The King Is a Lion," recognizes the importance of the king's position in conjunction with his behavior. Rather than viewing the two as separate phenomena, this point frames the song to emphasize their unity. The king is not all-powerful at one point and independently reciprocal, caring, and open at another; rather, he is both powerful and reciprocal at the same time, in the same way. Each is an expression of the other, and anyone who seeks to replicate a trait must embody the details and idiosyncrasies that produce it.

Focusing on Uganda's current problem of Buganda's pushing for royal autonomy within the existing national governmental structure, Jessy Ssendawula provides a brief overview of the elements that justify royal autonomy in his analysis of "The King Is a Lion." His commentary returns to the previously discussed notion that elected leaders must embody the king's actions if the general public is to respect them like they respect him. In this case, Ssendawula relates this idea to how elected leaders approach the king, pointing out their mistake of underappreciating the influence he still holds. He emphasizes the difference in power between the king and modern elected leaders, recognizing the king's substantial power despite his lack of official political control. He shows us that one should not simply define power by one's ability to enact policy but instead on one's right to define policy. Although the king may not have the literal capacity to make these macropolitical decisions, his justification through his people means

---

8   Kibirige interview, December 19, 2019.

that he wields more power than one assumes. Ssendawula asserts that these dynamics illuminate a unique conception of power by rejecting the common tendency to equate it with political control:

> The king is like a lion in that when people approach him directly, they do it carefully so they do not cause trouble. Many Baganda believe that he is above all men, and before him all subjects submit as if they are children to well-respected parents. However, his power enables him to act not just as a superior but as a friend to the Baganda. His position gives him exclusive rights in Uganda based on the agreements and treaties that Buganda made long ago which provided the foundation for the creation of the country. Therefore, "The King Is a Lion" warns the national government: they should avoid rewriting history and accord the king the respect he deserves. Specifically, they should award him respect by facilitating peaceful negotiations, as Buganda is the origin of most of the agreements that outline Ugandan governance today.[9]

By comparing these periods of agreement-making, Ssendawula emphasizes how "The King Is a Lion" articulates the nature of the king's rule.

John Magandaazi Kityo concludes this analysis of "The King Is a Lion" by providing a full picture of the historical context that led to the decline of royal political power. He focuses on the role of Western colonialism in dismantling this power as he expands on its exploitation of historical agreements with the kingdom:

> The kingship functions as an agreement between the people and the king. The leader demonstrates to the public how to best lead their lives and in return the people expect the king to be an upright leader. Both parties hold each other to the agreement in a way that is similar to other sorts of contracts.[10]

Kityo adds:

Colonizers and the church frequently used these sorts of binding contracts in Uganda. During the beginning of the colonial period of the 1850s to the 1880s, when the British first arrived, their main interactions were with the Baganda.[11]

Kityo's remarks recall the tone of Europeans in their accounts about Buganda. From the Christian writer Constance E. Padwick's (1886–1968) works, one can see that although some European representatives may have seemed friendly, in their reports they ridiculed King Muteesa I

---

9   Ssendawula interview, December 28, 2019.
10 Kityo interview, December 14, 2019.
11 Ibid.

(r. ca. 1854–1884), portraying him as lazy and weak and thus insisting that he was an incompetent leader.[12] Western accounts of Kiganda culture are similarly awash with racist overtones. One narrative from 1863 describes a Kiganda court song as "senseless words, which stand in place of the song to the negroes; for song they have none, being mentally incapacitated for musical composition."[13] Kityo's interpretation of "The King Is a Lion" further problematizes the role of colonialism in deconstructing the power of the king, giving greater context to the sorts of agreements that led to the kingship's decline. In doing so, he shows us what processes ultimately led to the disseminated power we see today and how those processes relate to the present political situation in Uganda:

> Naturally, the rich history of song and composition that has existed in the area for centuries disproves these nonsensical assertions. Despite these untruthful claims, it was these sorts of men who visited the king's court and eventually formed the initiating agreements that came to outline the relationship between the Baganda and the British. However, the time came when those who had first drawn up the agreements died (including the three regents whom Dezidasu mentions in lines 28–30), and soon those who replaced them forgot the amicable spirit of the agreements, replacing them with exploitative practices. Some people hijacked and distorted them to the advantage of the colonizers, from whom they were benefiting. This exploitation wore heavily on the people of Uganda. It was not long before they grew fed up with their treatment at the hands of the British, leading to a struggle that ultimately led to political independence in 1962. This occurred when, acting without much of a plan, Obote and King Muteesa II took power and established a new government. Obote became the first prime minister of Uganda while King Muteesa II became the first president of the country. After overthrowing King Muteesa II and making himself president, Obote established the 1967 constitution that nullified all former agreements. However, a lack of preparation caused a rocky transition, and the country went through a difficult period of anarchy that lasted through the Amin regime. It was through these changes and uncertainties that Uganda struggled, getting to the state it is today under President Museveni.[14]

This history contextualizes the process of colonial exploitation as a shift in the way that parties make agreements. Kibirige describes the initial agreements as being one of mutual support between the king and his people. The decline only happened once parties began to violate the new agreements,

---

12 Padwick 1917, 65.
13 Speke 1909 (1863), 31.
14 Kibirige interview, December 14, 2019.

starting with the colonial powers but continuing through Obote's regime and finally reaching Museveni. The aforementioned historical context, through the framework of "The King Is a Lion," reframes its discussion of agreements in terms of the mishaps one can see in the present. Whereas the song appears to only allude to the agreements of the kingship, Kityo's analysis connects its discussion to the present, contrasting the agreements of the kingship with the exploitative ones of the colonial and postcolonial eras.

Conclusion

"The King Is a Lion" serves as a political statement that Deziderio uses to position Buganda's monarchy within Uganda's contemporary power structure. Unlike traditional royal songs, this composition deliberately addresses the tension between kingship and national governance. Its lyrics describe the king's sovereignty and efficacy as a leader, reflecting the intimate relationship between him and his court musicians as well as the latter's impact on the Buganda kingship. Accordingly, Deziderio uses the concept of social accord to describe the arrangement of reciprocity between the king and the musicians. The song's discussion suggests that the leader is uniquely equipped to manage the challenge of guiding his nation.

Many interpreters of "The King Is a Lion" see the song as a blueprint for how a leader should relate to his people. Per the song's lyrics, there is a certain degree of intimacy and mutuality between the king and his subjects that is ideal which connects them through friendship, trust, and respect. However, interpreters' readings of "The King Is a Lion" do not stop at exploring the domains of kingship and royalty. They also engage with broader themes of reverence and love within the larger national polity, highlighting the importance of mutuality and reciprocity, among other topics that permeate most of the lyrical content and analyses of the songs discussed throughout this book. Some commentators use the notion of social accord to articulate the changing circumstances of the current era, contrasting the historical agreements that "The King Is a Lion" references against those of today. Many frame the song through the context of twenty-first-century national politics, especially in relation to the shifting power dynamics that have shocked the kingdom. One interviewee juxtaposes the song's affirmations of the king against the rule that President Museveni provides, illuminating the new challenges that elected leaders face today and the way they continue to exacerbate such obstacles by refusing to accept the changes that have taken place. Another interpreter describes the song in the context of colonialism and postcolonial governance, articulating how agreements made in this context have transformed the Kingdom of Buganda into an entirely new animal, from a pride of lions serving the collective to a group of stray dogs all fighting for themselves. One interpreter even frames the song as a reflection on the position of the king in twenty-first-century Buganda, using it to explain the leader's substantial influence and power despite his total lack of political recognition from the national government.

Part V

Songs about Mutuality and Cooperation

Within African axiology, the mutuality of interpersonal relationships lies at the heart of societal values and lifestyles. The same arrangement applies to the Buganda royal court, and the musical compositions this institution has produced prove these principles. The reciprocity characterizing all relationships, especially those between the king and his subject, transcends more traditional notions of hierarchy and status, emphasizing the inherent balance between all peoples.

Part V explores these ideas of mutuality and cooperation as an overall approach toward life in Buganda and Uganda. The four songs featured in this part offer intricate, nuanced, and unique portrayals of reciprocity, examining all angles of the subject and in myriad contexts. Chapter 16 analyzes the themes of love, unity, and reciprocity in the first two songs, "They Show Each Other Stumps" ("Balagana Enkonge") and "Mawanda Loves His Men" ("Mawanda Ayagala Abasajja Be"). The songs illustrate these themes in the context of friendship and family relationships but also, more broadly, in the context of the king and his people. "They Show Each Other Stumps" portrays an ideal mutual relationship through a story about two friends warning each other of upcoming obstacles as they walk down a path together. Although the song's subject arises in a specific context, it can apply to various relationships, including twenty-first-century politics. A song about a king who cares for his subjects, "Mawanda Loves His Men" also encourages people to care for one another, an essential component of any healthy, reciprocal relationship. The song particularly celebrates how King Mawanda (r. ca. 1738–1740) displays love for his people.

The other two songs featured in part 5 both embody and reinforce the function of praise in the royal court. They demonstrate how love and respect serve as the basis of the mutuality constantly affirmed and cultivated between a king and his people. Whereas the songs discussed previously demonstrate the way performers utilize false praise to manipulate the fancies of political leaders, the songs discussed in part 5 use praise as a sincere and legitimate affirmation of mutual love between the king and his subjects. Framed around this notion of genuine praise, chapter 17 examines the song "Baamunaanika Hill" ("Akosozi Baamunaanika"). Commending King Muteesa II (r. 1939–1966) and his eminence, the song highlights the symbiotic, loving relationship he has with his subjects. Chapter 18 continues this idea by exploring the love and respect one feels for one's king in the song "We Love the Supreme Man Exceedingly" ("Ssaabasajja Tumwagala Nnyo"). Although closely related in subject matter, each song lends a new angle to the mosaic of mutuality and cooperation that we have touched on in previous parts.

The songs presented in part 5 are unique in their narrative perspective, historical significance, and stylistic qualities. The analyses presented portray the emotions and actions that constitute mutual bonds, which can range from friendships to romantic endeavors to political relationships. This part focuses on the latter, as the lyrics of these songs express the relationship between the king and his subjects. However, through interpreting these lyrics, contemporary Ugandans reimagine the songs, evaluating the kingship and the national government in tandem. As a result, this process adds differing and sometimes conflicting meanings to the ongoing discourse in Uganda's political landscape. Thus, the meaning morphs into something more diverse and malleable. It is in this spirit that the meanings behind the five songs in question take on a vast array of possibilities, inviting a new tangibility to modern political discourse.

16

"Mawanda Loves His Men" and "They Show Each Other Stumps"

Love, Unity, and Reciprocity

Whether shared between a king and his subject or among companions, meaningful and effective personal bonds all embody love, unity, and reciprocity bonds. The two songs examined in this chapter, "Mawanda Loves His Men" ("Mawanda Ayagala Abasajja Be") and "They Show Each Other Stumps" ("Balagana Enkonge"), focus on these connective tissues of relationships. The first song expresses the love between King Mawanda (r. ca. 1738–1740) and his subjects. In a related but less specifically political way, the second song tells the story of two friends warning each other of upcoming tree stumps as they walk along a path. Semeo Ssemambo Ssebuwufu (ca. 1959–2015), who performed the version of "Mawanda Loves His Men" discussed here, was himself a court page. He had this to say about the song's background:

> The song confirms that the king loves his subjects. It recalls the pre-1966 times, when the king took care of his court pages (*abasiige*) and servants (*abagalagala*). They served in the royal court full-time, fulfilling their primary duties. These responsibilities included noting and reporting everything that took place there. It was not easy, say, for someone to steal the king's belongings, because his pages and servants were watching. In essence, they were the eyes and ears of the royal court. King Muteesa II (r. 1939–1966) cared for his pages in specific ways—feeding us, clothing us, and educating us with his own funds.[1]

---

1 Ssebuwufu interview, June 10, 2013.

Ssebuwufu's commentary highlights the king's care for those he leads, not only stemming from his responsibility to them as a ruler but his concern for their well-being as if they were his own children, his spouses, siblings, or friends. Court pages like Ssebuwufu and his contemporaries primarily reciprocated the caring concern of the king by performing music. These deeds reflect the leader's intention to treat his subjects as family.

Ludoviiko Sserwanga (ca. 1932–2013) shared the following background about the version of "They Show Each Other Stumps" he performed for this project:

> When doing something with potentially significant consequences with your friend, you must know he is trustworthy. If you are walking along at night and you are the first to see a stump in the way, you should tell your friend, "Hey, there is a stump—don't bump into it." This means true friendship: you do not want anything to befall your friend that might hurt him. Those types of friends are like kin. They are people who love each other, because they do not want something bad to happen to the other. That song is about loving one another, but it is even applicable to affairs of the kingdom. Even the people the king collaborates with must point out things that may cause him harm.[2]

Sserwanga articulates the connection between pointing out stumps and developing trusting and profound relationships. We come to recognize that it is not the grand gestures and the spectacular pursuits that strengthen relationships but the minute and almost imperceptible movements that occur naturally in each moment, like anticipating obstacles in your way. For instance, the king and his musicians watch out for each other, not to prove themselves nor to make a statement. They do it because they care for each other, as each sees the other as an extension of themselves, belonging to the shared fabric of the kingdom. In addition, the imagery of two friends cautioning each other to watch out for upcoming stumps as they walk along a path highlights the intimate rapport that is typical of this relationship between this leader and his subjects.

Ssebuwufu's performance of "Mawanda Loves His Men" uses a style similar to that of "Gganga Had a Narrow Escape" (chapter 11), as he and I accompany his singing with two interlocking parts that we play on a seventeen-slab xylophone known as *akadinda*. Our performance begins with the initiator (*omunazi*) part, unaccompanied for one full cycle. Ssebuwufu plays all the notes featured in this cycle on the downbeat. After the one-cycle solo progression, I join him with the complementary divider (*omwawuzi*) part. This part differs structurally from the divider parts of other xylophone songs covered in this book: I fill the spaces between Ssebuwufu's notes with

---

2   Sserwanga interview, July 15, 2005.

two quick notes instead of a single note, a technique that creates a lilting feel with triplets. The song maintains this feel throughout our performance, with the initiator and divider parts playing off each other in perfect, syncopated equilibrium. Following the entry of my divider part, Ssebuwufu begins to sing. Over the sound of the xylophone, his vocal part repeats the titular phrase:

1 *Mawanda ayagala basajja be*
Mawanda loves his men

The singer repeats this phrase in a similar fashion several times during the last quarter of each cycle, adding a minor modification in each iteration. At one point, he performs vocables that mimic the initiator melody. Ssebuwufu's vocal delivery is strong and impassioned, with many of his vocal phrases ending on its highest notes. Closely listening to the relationship between the vocal and instrumental parts reveals an ongoing conversation, as longer sections of the overall instrumental part make calls to which short vocal phrases respond. Our performance concludes with a coda comprising about a cycle and a half of Ssebuwufu's initiator part joined by a few seconds of my divider part at the very end.

The king and his people share a strong sense of interdependence, thus mutuality, and this is the primary topic of "Mawanda Loves His Men," which stresses the king's love for his subjects. The song's themes of generosity, interdependence, and collaboration all permeate its performance, which captures our joyous emotion and expression and other sonic aspects, including bouncy rhythms, cheerful tone, quick tempo, and rich texture. The themes of interdependence and collaboration emerge from the interlocking of the initiator and divider parts of the xylophone, as the notes we play are harmonically consonant together and maintain a steady rhythm. As a result, we contribute equally to creating a whole functional piece, and neither part can function without the other.

Another example of a mutual relationship within the sonic framework of the song is the call-and-response structuring of the instrumental and vocal parts mentioned earlier. The multiple interdependent relationships firing at once throughout our performance also reflect the way court musicians have historically relied on each other as a body of creative artists, who together serve the king in and out of the royal court. Our performance of "Mawanda Loves His Men" captures many aspects of their relationships and those they help sustain, both in performance and its historical context.

In his performance of "They Show Each Other Stumps," Sserwanga uses his voice and hands synchronously, singing modestly as he claps along. Although the overall performance is celebratory and cheerful, his singing sounds casual, carrying an almost improvisational sensibility. This is in part because Sserwanga's performance also serves as an interpretation of the instrumental version of "They Show Each Other Stumps," which he performs on the notched flute (*endere*) a few minutes before presenting the vocal version. When a group of singers performs the song, they may present each line of the lyrics below in a call-and-response style, with the leader singing the initial phrase and the respondents singing the subsequent phrase. Sserwanga sings both melodic phrases, which he punctuates with a brief pause that lend each lyric its conversational essence. Occasionally, the subsequent phrases feature vocables that sound very similar to some of the flute lines played in group performance. Sserwanga's performance lasts only half a minute, and he ends as abruptly as he begins.

1 *Bajja balagana enkonge, ye wuuyo Omulangira Kikulwe!*
They came showing each other stumps, there he comes, Prince Kikulwe!

2 *Maama, balagana enkonge, ye wuuyo Omulangira Kimera*
Oh, they show each other stumps, there he comes, Prince Kimera

3 *Abajja balagana, abalagana enkonge, mmm*
Those who came showing each other, those who show each other stumps, mhm

4 *Atudde mu kibuga n'alamula, mmm*
He is seated in the city, judging the affairs of his nation, mhm

5 *Kabaka atudde mu lubiri n'alamula ensi ye, ee*
The king is seated in the royal court, judging the affairs of his nation, eh

6 *Kabaka atudde mu ntebe n'alamula ensi ye, ee*
The king is seated on the throne, judging the affairs of his nation, eh

7 *Tteere ddere ddere*
Tteere ddere ddere

8 *Abajja balagana, abalagana enkonge!*
Those who came showing each other, those who show each other stumps!

Focusing on relationships between friends, the king and his subjects, and kin, among other groups, the song "They Show Each Other Stumps" serves as a celebration of love, unity, and reciprocity. Sserwanga's singing opens with lyrics that describe the friendship between Prince Kikulwe and Prince Kimera, explaining how the two show each other stumps (lines 1–3). These lyrics draw our attention to the quality of the royals' relationship. The seemingly benign act of pointing out a stump indicates a unique kind of intimacy where both parties keep an eye out for the other, not for any reason besides a desire to save the other from trouble or pain. The reciprocity between them, then, is not forced but one sustained by a mutual and natural trust. The song's subsequent transition to the king's rule, which the singer describes as "judging the affairs of his nation" (lines 4–6), further cements this message. "They Show Each Other Stumps" reveals to us how simple acts, like the ones that the two princes shared, might translate into far more complex circumstances, such as the rule of a kingdom. The lyrics teach us that such small actions eventually build a foundation of trust that enables Buganda to operate.

Love, Unity, and Reciprocity

The interpretations of "Mawanda Loves His Men" and "They Show Each Other Stumps" presented in this section reveal how mutual love, unity, and reciprocity provide the contour of functional relationships. The interpretations explore these themes, framing them through varied contemporary settings.

As we have pointed out, taking care of one another and upholding a sense of mutual support make up the relationship between the kings of Buganda and those who serve them in the royal court and beyond. Peter Kinene's interpretation of "Mawanda Loves His Men" recalls this system of trust by explaining how people should protect those they are close to. On this point, he stresses the value of warning others of imminent danger. This wisdom underscores how selflessness minimizes conflict in relationships:

> In politics and leadership, there are always traps to fall into; tricky situations that can ruin one's career. It is important to avoid these traps and to warn our friends about them. One must tell them to continue slowly or to take a different approach, for instance. When people do not do this, even the most senior of leadership can fail. One particularly effective strategy for finding good advice is to examine the past. Looking at the solutions one's forefathers or past leaders used, as well as the challenges they faced, can help in determining the best way to remedy current issues. Furthermore, it can also give a good indication of other problems that could arise in the future. Consequently, it is important for leaders to take the warnings and advice of those closest to them seriously. This is critical for continuing their rule and maintaining the stability of their public image. Failure to do so could mean economic and developmental failure. Even those who are not in grand positions of power should take this approach and heed the advice of their friends, for it is a way to ensure personal peace.[3]

---

3   Kinene interview, December 16, 2019.

By comparing listening to a friend's advice with seeking guidance from one's forefathers, Kinene demonstrates how mutuality might cross our perceived temporal boundaries. For example, a king's love does not merely extend to his contemporaries but also affects his descendants and future subjects. This conception challenges the primacy of linear time by posing an alternative framework where the past and present can converge and interact with each other, in turn determining the phenomena of the future.[4] In doing so, Kinene enhances our ability to creatively imagine how the king shows his love.

In his analysis, Edward Ssebunnya Kironde offers thoughts on the various difficulties and high expectations leaders face. He is sympathetic to them, recognizing that anyone who takes a political position will have some weakness in their skills and knowledge. However, he emphasizes that such a thing is not tragedy, as any good ruler ought to be able to rely on and support others to strengthen the quality of his or her leadership. This relates to an earlier discussion of the court music institution and its various ensembles, where a similar idea served as the backbone of their performance practice. These similarities emerge in the decentering of the individual so that a collective's members can cooperate fluidly, as Kironde suggests:

> Even though people may be leaders, it does not mean they have everything figured out. This is to say that no elected leader will really be the full package. That is why it is critical for leaders to embrace the advice of others, particularly on matters they have no expertise in. For instance, President Museveni, though he has his faults, recently appointed a woman nicknamed Full Figure to help him resolve issues like poverty and crime in the ghettos of major cities. The fact that a leader who has been in power for over thirty years seeks advice from young people confirms that all people, no matter how experienced they are, do well to heed the advice of others. No leader can say he or she really has it figured out. Everyone needs the guidance of others in some sense, so no one can claim to be a worthy leader based purely on experience. President Museveni claims he went to the bush to fight for peace, but the effort was not his alone. The support from other freedom fighters and even other countries equally helped him win the war. However, at the same time, politicians like him criticize Bobi Wine for not being knowledgeable about certain things while hypocritically claiming they are better. Indeed, leaders should not have to be perfect or have everything figured out. They are fallible human beings just like the rest of those they lead. This is not to say that people should not hold them to high standards but instead that they should focus a little more on character than on experience when choosing our leaders. If one has a heart to serve, one can do well as a leader.[5]

---

4   See also Ouattara 2018, 151.
5   Kironde interview, December 19, 2019.

As Kironde argues, it is each person's individual ability to trust and work with others that results in successful leadership, just as in the case of a musical performance. From the perspective of "Mawanda Loves His Men," this process demonstrates how the notions of love and mutuality might apply to current political contexts. Where historically one might see mutuality with the kingship, people today often obscure this behavior from view, as if it is somehow negative to seek out the aid of others.

Similar to "Mawanda Loves His Men," "They Show Each Other Stumps" highlights principles of ideal leadership, and many interpreters see the song's message as advice to contemporary politicians. Several comment on how the general message of the song relates to today's leadership, including John Magandaazi Kityo, who advises how leaders could more effectively engage with their opponents:

> It is wise for leaders to listen to others, especially those with opposing views. In most cases, it is the opposition that can point out their shortcomings and stumbling points; they are easily able to notice faults. If they engage in a dialogue with one another and point out the other's problems, it is likely they will address those problems more quickly. They help you see the stumps before you hit them. This might also be why some of today's leaders have managed to maintain their power for so long. Perhaps they realized early on that members of the opposition are not enemies, but rather people who can help the leaders see their own "stumps." Being mature and able to accept criticism from others is a major factor in their longevity as leaders, due to their ability to admit to and then subsequently work to correct their mistakes.[6]

Kityo's analysis tips the message of "They Show Each Other Stumps" toward the criticisms that two opposing groups share. Rather than depicting opposing relationships as mutually destructive, Kityo frames the message of the song to reimagine the opposition as an ally. He shows us how conflict itself can constitute a mutual relationship. Beyond a commentary on the importance of mutuality between allies, Kityo suggests that one can deconstruct and reimagine what constitutes an ally in the first place.

Addressing a list of wrongdoings committed by current leaders, Jimmy Ssenfuka Kibirige explains how self-centeredness will riddle a society and asserts that humility and foresight are crucial remedies to this problem:

> An ideal society is humble and possesses the foresight to anticipate and solve any potential problems. Today, however, bad intentions (*amakuuli*) plague society, particularly among the leadership. It would be much better off with leaders who could appropriately accept criticism.[7]

---

6   Kityo interview, December 14, 2019.
7   Kibirige interview, December 19, 2019.

Kibirige suggests how contemporary leaders define politics in terms of self-centered and corrosive relationships between actors. Everyone involved loses, as these actors replace mutual support with strategic sabotage.

Kibirige ends this chapter's analysis of "They Show Each Other Stumps" by claiming that harnessing unity is necessary to attain prosperity in a community. He spends less time indicting leaders, however, saying,

> It also confirms that good leadership is possible when the people are unified in their support of a campaign. When the people are one, good leadership is inevitable. There is no propaganda, no attempts to ridicule the leadership, because there are no lines of division to incite disagreement and protest. Therefore, "They Show Each Other Stumps" describes those who show themselves their own paths and point out the obstacles that block it. The song could also be about standing against a fellow leader who becomes an obstacle to the progress of society. The difference is that unlike today, the past leaders mentioned in the song were trying their best to be mutually aligned and create peace for one another. Leadership used to be about complementarity, about working together to create a model society. But current people are simply against one another. Today it is about ridiculing one leader for the benefit of another.[8]

This interpretation points up the fact that seeking unity is something we often fail to do today. Kibirige reminds us that dissent in the population often grows from an initial disregard of the people's wishes. To this point, he emphasizes the importance of accounting for one's relationships when pursuing a leadership role. Neglecting even one rapport, especially one as important as one's relationship with the masses, can result in disaster. Kibirige transforms "They Show Each Other Stumps" into a commentary on how we should conceive of contemporary politics. Rather than encouraging us to simply criticize and reject one leader for another, he explains the importance of rising above electoral politics to pursue the more important goal of uplifting the country. This framing recognizes the importance of mutuality, as it demonstrates that consensus is still achievable amid disagreement.

Conclusion

The songs "Mawanda Loves His Men" and "They Show Each Other Stumps" celebrate the love, unity, and reciprocity between friends, the king and his subjects, and kin, among other relationships. "Mawanda Loves His Men" humanizes royal governance by focusing on affective bonds rather than mere power dynamics. By transforming the relationship between king

---

8   Kibirige interview, December 19, 2019.

and subject from authority to emotional connection, the song suggests that effective rulership requires genuine care for those being governed. Its focus on King Mawanda's love for his men allows it to establish reciprocal attachment as essential to political stability. In parallel, "They Show Each Other Stumps" functions as a more intimate examination of mutual care through its narrative of friends warning each other about obstacles on their shared path. The song elevates this simple act of looking out for one another into a broader metaphor for how personal relationships function through reciprocal vigilance and protection.

Despite the apparently simple nature of "Mawanda Loves His Men," performers and listeners reimagine it in a variety of new contexts, wielding unique ideas, through which they interpret and reconceive its lyrics. Beyond acting as a commentary on the mutual relationship between the king and his subjects, the song becomes a criticism of the individual focus of twenty-first-century politicians and a reflection on how mutuality more fluidly can emerge today. With "They Show Each Other Stumps" as an example, one finds that although pointing out a stump to assist one's friend is rather banal, it is an act that emerges from a deeply established basis of love. In this way, focusing on friendship and mutuality, the song highlights how unity comes from exercising love. These instances speak to the prevalence of reciprocity as an inherent Kiganda social norm. Some interpreters explore this theme in terms of a relationship between opposing politicians, while others explain it as a backdrop or contrast to the alleged greed and self-centeredness of a national government politician. Others yet frame it in terms of the multiplicity of relationships that exist in everyday life.

17

"Baamunaanika Hill"

Genuine Praise

Whereas praise can be given to leaders as a deceptive tool for fulfilling self-interest, genuine praise still does occur in the power dynamic, reaffirming the positive aspects of relationships within the royal court and other political settings. The song "Baamunaanika Hill" ("Akasozi Baamunaanika") praises the hill on which one of Buganda's primary royal courts sits. King Ccwa II (1897–1939) chose the court to be his resort, evoking the resonant power of place to emphasize the intimacy and care practiced between a leader and his subjects.[1] Ludoviiko Sserwanga (ca. 1932–2013), explained the historical context of "Baamunaanika Hill":

> The song primarily praises the hill in question because of its importance, illustrating how the Baganda have historically cherished it as a landmark. In fact, court performers initially composed and performed it to commemorate the construction of the Baamunaanika court. There, a number of kings took good care of their subjects, especially those who served them personally. Adopting "Baamunaanika Hill" as part of Kiganda court music repertoire, court performers then used the song to praise the king for his leadership and support.
>
> King Muteesa II (r. 1939–1966), for whom we performed regularly, remunerated many of his musicians with plots of land. More than that, his government made some of this gifted land nontaxable. During the musicians' time at the court, they also received food and clothing from the king's government, which handled their general upkeep and that of their musical instruments. In this manner, the king supported his musicians as some of the song's lyrics poetically reflect. Some musicians would serve at the court for a given term, thus in their own sense settling for a time, as other lyrics confirm.

---

1 See also Muyinda 1991, 7.

For musicians who were not pages, the king's administration would separate them into groups, each of which would work at the court for a specific time, sometimes several months. When that period had passed, the next group of musicians would come in and take their place. It was only after a given group of musicians had completed their terms that the king would reward them land or other forms of gratuity. The cycle continued as the year went on so that there were always musical performances within the court. Some musicians would bring along apprentices to serve with them at the court and learn the skills necessary to be a court musician. Their intent, as always, was to serve their king as best they could. Unsurprisingly, every song in the court music repertoire at least mentions his majesty, the king, and he is the primary subject of many, as well. Even when musicians would reference external, seemingly unrelated elements, the primary subject they sang about would still be the king or, sometimes, the officials who worked closely with him.[2]

In his narration of the historical context of "Baamunaanika Hill," Semeo Ssemambo Ssebuwufu (ca. 1959–2015), a former page of King Muteesa II (r. 1939–1966), also elaborated on how the king reciprocated the effort of his young pages at Baamunaanika:

> Although the king spent most of his time at the Mmengo court, he visited Baamunaanika periodically. If he was going to visit there, it was the responsibility of selected pages who served at the Mmengo court to arrive ahead of the king to clean the Baamunaanika court. These sentiments are partly captured by several lyrics, including *Baamunaanika baakakola nnyo!* (They fashioned Baamunaanika very well); *Alina bingi by'alowooza, ow'e Mmengo* (He has a lot on his mind, the one of Mmengo); and *Tumwagala nnyo, bamundabire* (We love him very much, may they convey my regards to him).[3]

Sserwanga's remarks confirm that the king supported musicians within spaces like the Baamunaanika court in a mutually beneficial fashion. He provided for their needs, and they informed, entertained, and advised him. Similarly, apprenticeships within the court were not simply extractive or transactional relationship; instead, they were mutual exchanges, with experienced court musicians providing their knowledge and skills, while their apprentices provided the opportunity for their mentors to sustain and grow their craft while serving the king. Ssebuwufu's observations recall how the king occasionally moved between his musicians' shelters within the court. With this context, the creation of Baamunaanika Hill is not a single event but an ongoing process of preparation that continues as long as the king

---

2   Sserwanga interview, July 6, 2005.
3   Ssebuwufu interview, June 6, 2013.

continues moving. For Sserwanga and Ssebufuwu, "Baamunaanika Hill" relates to their personal connection with King Muteesa II. Although they focus on different aspects, their commentaries emphasize similar themes. For instance, in Ssebuwufu's version, he does not describe the pages' role of cleaning the court ahead of the king's arrival as unquestioned service to the king; instead, he qualifies it with lyrics such as "He has a lot on his mind, the one of Mmengo." In this way, Ssebuwufu's variation gives "Baamunaanika Hill" another meaning, indicating that the king did not receive the labor of his pages carelessly. Instead, he reciprocated their effort by thoughtfully leading the kingdom and fulfilling his responsibilities to the best of his ability.

Sserwanga opens his performance of "Baamunaanika Hill" by softly bowing the tube fiddle (*endingidi*) to produce a melody of rapid notes in triple meter. After briefly introducing this instrumental material, he begins to sing lyrics loudly in a chanting style. For the most part, he sings in the higher end of his vocal range, occasionally reaching the highest pitches with his head voice, sounding like roaring cries. Most of his vocal phrases differ from one another, and he punctuates them with pauses of instrumental material. Sserwanga's tube fiddle playing grows more frantic as the piece goes on, until the end, when it mellows out into silence. In the course of his performance, he brings out the song's joyous lyrical content with his energetic playing, only staying on a couple of notes and alternating between them to create a healthy balance of tension and release. In addition to the song's cheerful instrumentation, the vocal part is equally impassioned, given its exploration of high notes. Such an energetic performance reflects the love that the singer feels for the king. Sserwanga's lyrics appear below:

1 *Kasozi Baamunaanika keeyagaza nnyo!*
Baamunaanika Hill is a source of great pleasure!

2 *Baamunaanika baakakola nnyo!*
They fashioned Baamunaanika very well!

3 *Akasozi Baamunaanika keeyagaza nnyo!*
Baamunaanika Hill is a source of much pleasure!

4 *Omutanda gy'ali, omutanda, nnannyinimu!*
His Majesty is there, His Majesty, householder!

5 *Bukya mmusenga, siryanga ku dduma!*
From the time I settled near him, I have never eaten food without sauce!

6 *Bukya mmusenga, sitemanga mmuli!*
From the time I settled near him, I have never had to cut down reeds!

7 *Omutanda gy'ali, omulongo, nnannyinimu!*
His Majesty is there, the twin, householder!

8 *Nnaabeera wano, omulongo w'abeera!*
I will settle here, where the twin lives!

9 *Nnaatuula eyo, omutanda gy'abeera!*
I will sit there, where His Majesty lives!

10 *Omulongo y'oyo! Luwangula*
That is the twin! Conqueror

11 *Omulongo y'oyo, omulongo, nnannyinimu!*
He is the twin, the twin, householder!

12 *Nnaatuula wano, omutanda w'atudde*
I shall sit here, close to where His Majesty is seated

13 *Alina bingi by'alowooza, kabaka waffe!*
He has a lot on his mind, our king!

14 *Alina bingi eby'amatendo, kabaka waffe!*
He has a lot that is splendid, our king!

15 *Mwattu bw'obanga omulabye, omundabiranga!*
Should you happen to see my dear, convey to him my respects!

16 *Nayagala munnange, siriyagala mulala!*
I loved my dear, I will never love any other!

17 *Omulongo y'oyo, Luwangula Mutebi*
That is the twin, Conqueror Mutebi

18 *Akasozi Baamunaanika baakakola!*
They fashioned Baamunaanika Hill!

19 *Akasozi Baamunaanika baakakola!*
They fashioned Baamunaanika Hill!

20 *Omutanda gy'abeera*
Where His Majesty resides

21 *Baamunaanika keeyagaza nnyo!*
Baamunaanika is a source of great pleasure!

22 *Mwattu bw'obanga ogenze, omundabiranga!*
Should you go visit my dear, convey to him my respects!

23 *Omulongo y'oyo, omulongo, nnannyinimu!*
That is the twin, the twin, householder!

24 *Alina bingi by'alowooza, omulongo, baze!*
He has a lot on his mind, the twin, my husband!

25 *Alina bingi, ow'omukwano*
He possesses a lot, the beloved

26 *Nnaatuula wano, omukulu w'atudde*
I shall sit here, close to where the leader is seated

27 *Nayagala munnange siriyagala mulala!*
I loved my dear, I will never love any other!

28 *Omulongo y'oyo, Luwangula Mutebi!*
That is the twin, Conqueror Mutebi!

29 *Alina bingi by'alowooza!*
He has a lot on his mind!

30 *Alina bingi, oweekitiibwa, omulongo y'oyo*
He possesses a lot, the honorable, that is the twin

31 *Kyokka empologoma, ngo! Omutanda gy'abeera*
But the lion, leopard! Where His Majesty lives

32 *Omutanda mw'ali, ffenna tumwagala nnyo!*
His Majesty is in, we all love him very much!

33 *Anaakwata mpola, agira abaayo*
He will handle with care, let him continue reigning

34 *Kyokka akwatanga mpola ebigambo*
But he is to handle matters with care

35 *Anaakwata mpola, afuge!*
He will handle carefully, let him reign!

The lyrics of "Baamunaanika Hill" show how celebrating the site in question comes from the composer's love for the king: because the leader is there, the hill becomes the object of his praise (lines 1, 3, and 18–19). The singer also praises the king because he is great and generous, describing how when he is there, the food is plentiful (line 5) and the work is pleasant (line 6). "I have never had to cut down reeds" refers to collecting materials for constructing and maintaining the court enclosure, which is traditionally made of reeds. The song repeats that the singer will stay at Baamunaanika (lines 8–9), implying his loyalty to the king and recognizing how he benefits from serving him. During the performance, it becomes clear that the singer is not merely a subordinate to the leader but a type of equal. The king's service to the people is not simply to rule over them but to guide them, to handle matters "carefully" and to rule with wisdom (lines 33–35). In response to the king's generosity, his subjects and the court musicians must give back with their own loyalty and dedication (line 32). The latter part of the song focuses less on the people's duty to the king, prioritizing the leader's service to his people.

Genuine Praise

Following Sserwanga and Ssebuwufu's perspectives, the interpreters of "Baamunaanika Hill" explore how genuine praise and related themes apply to twenty-first-century political contexts. For example, Harriet Kisuule offers her thoughts on the rewards and results of the caring leadership that Buganda's king exemplifies. Expanding on the notion of reciprocity, she stresses that leaders will only be able to attain love and care from their people when they demonstrate it themselves. In particular, she compares the alleged behavior of President Museveni with that of King Mutebi II (r. 1993–present), articulating how the king takes his responsibility to his people more seriously than the president. Kisuule alleges that the president is lacking in his sense of responsibility to the masses:

> People love a leader who leads well. A leader who accepts advice, judges the subjects fairly, and cares for them genuinely. These are some of the qualities of Buganda's current king and the reason for which many Baganda love him. They are satisfied with his leadership and do not complain about him. People in other leadership positions should take note of his attributes and try to emulate them within their own positions. President Museveni, for example, could be more popular among the masses if he paid close attention to why they love the king or tried himself to emulate the king's ways. The king handles his duties with care and caution, especially by taking the time to listen to his people. Elected leaders should use listening as a strategy to help them secure second terms in office. These habits enable the king to be a successful leader. His popularity is derived from the exemplary leadership he offers. Finally, to be good and successful, leaders should not superimpose themselves in situations where heavy-handed leadership is unnecessary. This is another strength of the king of Buganda.[4]

In supplying current examples that fit the historical contexts of "Baamunaanika Hill," Kisuule reimagines the song as a work with messages that Ugandans can use to address the political challenges of today. She suggests that leaders may only receive genuine praise when their labor warrants it. Such a conundrum seems to beg for a more reciprocal and caring power dynamic.

Explaining the benefits that come from closely associating with leaders, Peter Kinene compares the care that court musicians such as Sserwanga and

---

4   Kisuule interview, December 21, 2019.

Ssebuwufu once received from King Muteesa II (food, housing, land) to the promotions and gifts that those who support national politicians receive. He points to the singer's confession that he has profited from being in the proximity of the king, warning that such opportunities might inspire manipulation and greed rather than integrity. As self-interest constantly shifts, it behooves people in a leader's close circle to know that manipulation and greed can be the near enemy of a wholesome relationship. In this vein, Kinene points to specific figures in the national government:

> When President Museveni put forward a motion to abolish the upper age limit for the presidency, some people supported the motion and tabled the proposal. In return, he made some of those people cabinet ministers. Aligning themselves with the president opened up a variety of privileges and opportunities for them. This is the order of the day in the contemporary Ugandan political scene. Those who make it their goal to help leaders consolidate and retain their power are those who profit the most. Therefore, being close to leaders tends to invoke personal change, as people profit due to their proximity to them.[5]

Kinene's commentary highlights an alternative understanding of the relationship that "Baamunaanika Hill" describes. Rather than imagining a positive and virtuous exchange between leaders and subjects, he shows us the flip side, that of a near enemy. He reveals how the benefits that the singer gains could be at the expense of the masses. By highlighting the risks of this relationship, Kinene equips us with a more critical stance on such encounters, avoiding the lofty idealism that might suffuse one's praise of leadership. Furthermore, Kinene demonstrates how authority based on a transactional model might lead to the "purchase" of empty praise and conditional loyalty.

Kinene then compares the advantages that Uganda's president provides to his followers with those that Buganda's king has provided to his people. He suggests that the main difference between the two is that the king does not offer rewards for loyalty but acts of kindness that flow into the reciprocal nature of the power dynamic. According to Kinene, "Baamunaanika Hill" alludes to how King Muteesa II provided for his people, and it also evokes how King Mutebi II invests in programs that uplift and benefit the population:

> The king spearheads programs for education, literacy, healthcare, and economic growth.[6] One program currently in place is called Coffee Does Not Disappoint (Emmwanyi Terimba). Focusing on encouraging financial development and healthy saving habits through coffee production, this movement has received a lot of support from the masses and the prime

---

5 Kinene interview, December 16, 2019.

6 For examples of these programs, see Matovu 2023.

minister's office. Because of this and other programs, as well as the support they receive from the king's government, many Baganda are always thinking about the good that their king does for them. In other words, people recognize the benefits they receive from him, and because of that, they choose to remain under his rule.[7]

Kinene's point shows how the king operates with the implicit knowledge that he serves the people with a loving and persistent dedication.

Further elaborating on the love and respect shared between the king and the Baganda people, Kinene delves deeper into what exactly constitutes their mutuality, referencing the lyric "Should you happen to see my dear, convey to him my respects" (line 15) to emphasize that this love is not merely superficial or transactional:

> Good leadership and the love of the people are part of a self-reinforcing cycle. The Baganda people generally have freedom, they eat well, and they are happy. That is partly why they respect the king and support him to remain in power, carrying out his administrative responsibilities from one of his seats at Baamunaanika. Freedom, liberty, and peace—all being elements that are so desirable to a people—spring from the leadership itself, which is why the king's subjects praise and support him, as Sserwanga sings. If the king was not an effective leader, the musicians, and the other people he leads would not be praising him in the manner they do. His subjects trust him so that even when there are difficulties, they will not lose hope. Because the king handles matters with care, the people let him rule and they always have hope in him.[8]

By examining the finer details of the song's lyrics, Kinene offers a new conception to apply to this power dynamic, allowing us to see and appreciate how the love that many people feel for the king exemplifies a profound sense of respect. Their mutuality is a model for sustainable leadership.

Continuing with this theme, Steven Mukasa Kabugo articulates that this power dynamic has a familial nature, noting that it "behooves the Baganda to praise and speak well of the king and queen, whom they love, just as with their own wives and husbands."[9] He adds that some Baganda "exalt the king and queen over anyone else. There is a sense of familial respect, which applies equally to the king and queen as it would to a father-in-law or mother-in-law, both of whom are important figures in Buganda."[10] This familial reverence for royalty evokes the love that one might hold for

---

7   Kinene interview, December 16, 2019.
8   Ibid.
9   Kabugo interview, December 19, 2019.
10 Ibid.

one's kin. Accordingly, we can illuminate the macropolitical realm with micropolitical, interpersonal phenomena.

Kisuule then flips the script, delving into the darker reality of what might happen when leaders refuse to govern with a sense of love and respect. To help us understand this danger, Kisuule explains that the king's rule depends on the people's love and respect for him, while the admiration of national politicians might rely too heavily on coercion and threats of retribution. According to Kisuule, the result is that national politicians tend to impose a facade of power rather than allowing the people to naturally grant it to them:

> Effective leaders win the love and respect of the masses by listening to their needs. An interest in their well-being, rather than a simple desire to rule over them, is critical. Otherwise, a descent into terror tactics and despotism is likely. It seems like President Museveni has fallen into the latter category. Sometimes he incites fear by saying he came to power through violence and harsh tactics and that the next president will only remove him from power by similar methods. People have begun to realize that he will only leave office through death or war. It is clear he is not ready to have an open dialogue about changes to the presidency. He has replaced the love people had for him in their hearts with fear and hate and has lost the trust of the electorate. True leaders need to prove their love and care for their people. It is by being patriotic and ready to serve the nation, as opposed to thinking only of one's own needs, that a leader can thrive in his position.[11]

In this interpretation, Kisuule imagines "Baamunaanika Hill" not in terms of its praise but of the flip side where the negative effects arise when one rejects one's responsibilities to the people. As a result, she gives us a more nuanced perspective on both Uganda's political situation and the song.

Conclusion

"Baamunaanika Hill" serves as a geographical tribute that uses place as proxy for praising monarchical relationships. By celebrating the specific hill where King Ccwa II established his court retreat, the song creates a musical association between physical location and royal governance. Similarly, by evoking themes of kinship and family ties, "Baamunaanika Hill" portrays an ideal image of the king's relationship to his subjects. Although one might assume that a king would be a leech on his people, extorting their production and loyalty through monarchical position, this song illustrates how he earns his people's respect through his service to them, his responsibility to care for

---

11   Kisuule interview, December 21, 2019.

their needs, and support for them. By following through on these duties, the king arouses genuine praise.

A leader's ability to fulfill his responsibilities and meet his subjects' expectations by exercising mutuality and reciprocity are recurrent themes in a variety of interpretations. The details that Sserwanga and Ssebuwufu provide about working in the royal court imbue the song with a sense of eminence and relevance. They transform "Baamunaanika Hill" from a simple, poetic praise to a musical record of life with the king. These performers' personal accounts address how the role of court musicians supports successful leadership, as their work is inherently reciprocal. Other interpretations illuminate the song's intersections with national politics, greed, and kinship. On the one hand, the song suggests that belonging to a leader's close advisory circle may result in succumbing to greed. On the other hand, it shows that one's love for the king is like one's love for one's father. Thus, whether closeness begets corruption depends on the values and trust that one brings to the power dynamic. Most important, research collaborators reveal how the principles from Buganda's royal court apply to today's Uganda. When this happens, one will find that these principles are universal and temporal, as the same passions from decades or centuries ago will both enlighten or corrupt today's political wellness.

18

"We Love the Supreme Man Exceedingly"

Love and Respect

The song "We Love the Supreme Man Exceedingly" ("Ssaabasajja Tumwagala Nnyo") centers on the struggles of the king in fulfilling the duties of his office. Its lyrics state that the king does this rather well, and thus he rightly belongs on the throne. Whether referring to the king's travels through all the counties in Buganda, making diplomatic excursions to Europe, or returning to the kingdom to restore its greatness, the performer Ludoviiko Sserwanga (ca. 1932–2013) affirms that these pursuits befit a king, indicating his wisdom and strong presence as a ruler. Sserwanga shared the following historical context about "We Love the Supreme Man Exceedingly" when he performed his version:

> During the reign of the late King Sir Edward Muteesa II (r. 1939–1966), many of his royal court musicians were quite young. However, there were still those at the court who had served under his father, the late King Daudi Ccwa II (r. 1897–1939). When King Muteesa II ascended the throne, the Buganda government brought forth those musicians to assist with his reign. They narrated the history of his father's rule to him so that he might be better equipped to handle the challenges of leadership. The king listened attentively to all their advice, which was essential in constructing the foundation of his rule. This process was reminiscent of the coronation process that occurred in 1993, when Muteesa II's son Ronald Mutebi II (r. 1993–present) took the throne described in some of the lyrics of the song.
>
> Muteesa II was exiled by colonial administrators in the United Kingdom in 1953 after he called for Buganda to be separated from the rest of Uganda. As soon as Governor Andrew Cohen sent the king into exile, clan heads across Buganda took the case to court. The clan heads

succeeded in their challenge to Cohen, with the verdict of the case confirming that the king had been wrongfully exiled.[1] After learning of his win, the king returned to Buganda in 1955. He was like a new man, renewed with strength. This was the period when my brother Ssempeke and I began working as court musicians and was also the time when the king's son, then Prince Mutebi II, the current king of Buganda, was born.

Despite King Muteesa II's return in 1955 and the subsequent rejuvenation of Kiganda court music, such joyful happenings were not to last. This is because after eleven years, in 1966, a war broke out that resulted in an attack on Muteesa II's court. Consequently, the central government overthrew King Muteesa II, forcing him and his family to flee once more to the United Kingdom, where the king remained in exile until his death in 1969. His exile plunged Buganda back into silence once more. This silence continued through the return of his body from abroad and the eventual enthronement of King Mutebi II. During Mutebi II's reign, court music has been restored, as I describe in some of the lyrics. The trip to Europe I mention in the song was one for diplomatic purposes after Mutebi II's coronation, but it still references the royal family's initial exile to the United Kingdom. The travel and displacement of the king are the subjects of some of the other lyrics.

Despite the chaos and destruction caused by the 1966 attack on the royal court, some of the original court instruments survived and are still in use today. When the central government seized the court, the musicians who were able to escape to safety took the musical instruments that they could with them. They hid and protected them until the current administration restored the kingship under King Mutebi II. A call went out for those who had fled to come back to the court so that the musical instruments and the musicians who played them might be of service to their king once more. This is how the government of Buganda restored some of the instruments originally used in the court.[2]

The advisory and commentator roles of court musicians that Sserwanga explains here shed light on how the Kingdom of Buganda has historically tasked musicians with informing and guiding new kings during and beyond their coronations. In this sense, we can understand "We Love the Supreme Man Exceedingly" as an informative piece on the history of the kingdom. Sserwanga's narrative further demonstrates how Buganda never forgot the relationship of mutuality despite the overthrow of her kingship. These dynamics contrast with the current regime as well as with King Ssuuna II's rule discussed in previous chapters. In both instances, the people were unhappy with their rulers and wished for their deaths. After Ssuuna II

---

1   See also Kafumbe 2018, 7.
2   Sserwanga interview, July 6, 2005.

died, they celebrated his passing subtly. With Muteesa II's kingship, on the other hand, his musicians maintained ultimate loyalty to the king. Court performers functioned as extensions of both the people and the king. They felt this social responsibility so deeply in their work that after the 1966 attack on the court, they rushed to protect their instruments. Simply put, preserving the fabric of the kingdom meant preserving the music. This context allows us to understand "We Love the Supreme Man Exceedingly" as a model for governance that leaders might draw on to better contextualize contemporary governmental practices. Whereas we might expect a kingship to be coercive system with the king's followers obeying him out of either passivity or greed, in Buganda we see that even after the king's fall, many civilians remained deeply loyal to the kingship. Therefore, the rule that Muteesa II provided was mutual and, in several ways, more democratic than the rule that today's elected leaders enact. Despite Muteesa II's hereditary right to leadership, the people still legitimized, or "negotiated consent," to his rule.[3]

Some of the lyrics that Sserwanga references in his account evoke multiple meanings related to different contexts. For instance, lyrics about the king's displacement describe a diplomatic excursion to Europe, while at the same time suggesting the exile to Europe that the royal family also experienced. Pier confirms how lyrics that allude to the king's displacement are popular in Kiganda songs, not only to express royalty but also to voice complaints of the issues unfurled during the current national regime, many of which result from unregulated economic policies.[4] Lyrics and commentaries on the kingdom's restoration also carry with them a dual meaning: in the same moment that they refer to the kingdom's own revival, they also evoke the revival that is crucial to the practice of interpretation. These and other lyrics speak to the multiplicity of meanings within the text of "We Love the Supreme Man Exceedingly" and the ways that listeners might reimagine the song.

Sserwanga's performance of "We Love the Supreme Man Exceedingly" features him playing a tube fiddle (*endingidi*) with which he bows a rapid melody. Over this background, the performer intersperses his vocals between pauses that he leaves for instrumental excerpts. His voice generally stays in a middle range and delivers lyrics at average volume. The performance pauses after a half minute and then begins again. Like many of the other fiddle performances discussed in this book, "We Love the Supreme Man Exceedingly" has a joyous tone, though Sserwanga's lyrics blend different moods, evoking how one can experience success and adversity simultaneously. Despite a lack

---

[3] I borrow the idea of "negotiated consent" from Lonsdale 1992, 281.
[4] Pier 2017, 16.

of percussion instruments, the song maintains a danceable feel with its polyrhythmic texture. Sserwanga sings,

> 1 *Ssaabasajja tumwagala nnyo, ow'omukwano!*
> We love the supreme man so much, the beloved!
>
> 2 *Tumwagala nnyo, ow'omukwano!*
> We love him so much, the beloved!
>
> 3 *Ssaabasajja yawoomerwa obwakabaka n'abumanya*
> The kingship suited the supreme man and he got to know it
>
> 4 *Baamutikkira engule ye, obwakabaka n'abumanya!*
> They crowned him with his crown, and he got to know the kingship!
>
> 5 *Baamutikkira engule ye, obwakabaka n'abumanya, tumwagala nnyo!*
> They crowned him with his crown, and he got to know the kingship, we love him so much!
>
> 6 *Yawoomerwa engoye ze, ssaabasajja, nnandigobe*
> His clothes suited him, the supreme man, the *nnandigobe* banana
>
> 7 *Yalambula nnyo, n'e Bugerere mu mbwa!*
> He toured widely, and even reached Bugerere—infested with simulim black flies!
>
> 8 *Eyangayaaza*
> He who pampered me
>
> 9 *Alina munne amwagala*
> One who has a friend loves him or her
>
> 10 *Tumwagala munnange, ssaabasajja tumwagala nnyo!*
> We love him, my dear, we love the supreme man so much!
>
> 11 *Omwana wa Nabijjano, tumwagala nnyo!*
> Son of Nabijjano, we love him so much!
>
> 12 *Yawoomera engule, n'obwakabaka n'abumanya!*
> His crown suited him, and he got to know the kingship!
>
> 13 *Obwakabaka buwoomera abantu, obwa Muteesa bwamuwasa*
> The kingship suits people, Muteesa II's throne married him
>
> 14 *Buwoomera ababulya, ne Mutebi nnamba emu!*
> It suits those who are crowned, and Mutebi II is number one!
>
> 15 *Omwoyo, omwoyo gwa munnange gunnuma!*
> The soul, the soul's longing for my beloved is distressing!
>
> 16 *Mwagala, ndigenda n'owange, ow'ekitiibwa*
> I love him, I will forever go with my friend, the honorable

17 *Muyogeeyoge, wamma muyogeeyoge okusaba!*
Congratulations to you all, indeed, congratulations to you all on praying!

18 *Muyogeeyoge, muyogeeyoge wamma!*
Congratulations to you all, congratulations to you all, indeed!

19 *Mwebale kuwonga, obwakabaka buzzeewo!*
Thank you for praying, the kingship is restored!

20 *Mwebale kuwonga, obwakabaka buzze buto*
Thank you for praying, the kingship is revived

21 *Eyangayaaza*
The one who pampered me

22 *Alina munne amuwaana*
One who has a friend praises him or her

23 *Ssaabasajja yalambula nnyo!*
The supreme man toured widely!

24 *Era bwe yalambula amasaza, ne mu Kyaggwe n'atuuka*
And when he toured the counties, he even reached Kyaggwe

25 *Yalambula nnyo, n'e Bugerere wansi*
He toured widely, even down in Bugerere

26 *Yalambula amasaza, ne mu Busiro n'atuuka*
He toured the counties, and even reached Busiro

27 *Bamundabire, ndigenda n'owange, ow'ekitiibwa*
May they convey my regards to him, I will go with my friend, the honorable

28 *Bamundabire, ndibeera n'omu oyo, ow'omukwano*
May they convey my regards to him, I will be with only him, the beloved

29 *Tonjooganga!*
You should never despise me!

30 *Temunjooganga, obwakabaka buzzeewo*
You all should never despise me, the kingship is restored

31 *Omwoyo, ndigenda n'owange, ow'ekitiibwa*
The soul, I will go with my friend, the honorable

32 *Omwoyo, ndibeera n'omu oyo, eyangayaaza!*
The soul, I will be with only him, the one who pampered me!

33 *Mwebale kuwonga, obwakabaka buzzeewo!*
Thank you all for praying, the kingship is restored!

34 *Ateredde mu etuuka, ey'emitwalo, gye nnyimba!*
He is comfortable in the suitable [chair], one worth tens of thousands, I sing about it!

35 *Entebe ateredde mu emyansa, ey'emitwalo, gye nnyimba!*
He is comfortable in a glorious chair, one worth tens of thousands, I sing about it!

36 *Ssaabasajja, yawangula engule, obwakabaka n'abumanya!*
The supreme man succeeded the crown, and he got to know the kingship!

[*brief instrumental interlude*]

37 *Ye wuuyo omwana wa Nabijjano, tumwagala nnyo!*
There he comes, son of Nnabijjano, we love him so much!

38 *Ye wuuyo omwana wa Nnabijjano, omwoyo, omwoyo!*
There he comes, son of Nnabijjano, the soul, the soul!

39 *Nze nno omwoyo gunnumye kiro ŋŋenda, tumukkirizza!*
But my soul's longing for my friend has smitten me at night, so I am departing, we have accepted him!

40 *Yalambula amasaza, ne mu Kyaggwe n'atuuka*
He toured the counties, and he also reached Kyaggwe

41 *Yalambula nnyo, yalambula amasaza, n'e Bulaaya n'atuuka*
He toured widely, he toured the counties, and he even reached Europe

42 *Olw'e Bulaaya lubeera lwa bigere, n'abasajja twandirabye*
Had the trip to Europe been made on foot, we, his men, would have faced challenges

43 *Lwalyoka ne luba lwa mmotoka, n'ebikajjo twandimenye!*
It was fortunately a car trip, or else we would even have had to cut down sugarcanes to survive!

44 *Eyangayaaza!*
He who pampered me!

[*brief instrumental interlude*]

45 *Omwoyo, omwoyo gwa munnange, ow'enkima!*
The soul, the soul's longing for my friend, the one of the Monkey Clan!

46 *Omwoyo, omwoyo gwa munnange, ow'omukwano!*
The soul, the soul's longing for my friend, the beloved!

47 *Tumwagala nnyo, ow'ekitiibwa, gwe nnyimba!*
We adore him so much, the honorable, I sing about him!

48 *Ssaabasajja tumwagala nnyo, yeebale, afuge abantu!*
We love the supreme man so much, thanks to him, let him govern the people!

49 *Awangaale!*
May he live long!

"We Love the Supreme Man Exceedingly" describes various key events, including the loss and subsequent restoration of the Kingdom of Buganda and King Muteesa II's travels and exiles across the globe. The song describes these events not merely to narrate the past but also to use dedication and loss to dually drive the celebratory nature of Sserwanga's performance. Detailing the virtues and good deeds of King Muteesa II and his son, the current king, Mutebi II, the composition also demonstrates why the Baganda love and respect their king. The piece alludes to stories from significant historical moments of the Kingdom of Buganda, including the coronation of Muteesa II and Mutebi II, the former's times in exile, and the tradition of using clan heritage to determine a king's honorifics. That the king derives his power from a vibrant lineage of predecessors suggests that the past is indeed a vital aspect of the present. It is always in dialogue with those who are alive today, and they are always bringing new change.

"We Love the Supreme Man Exceedingly" qualifies the singer's praise for the king by using epithets of respect such as the *nnandigobe* banana (line 6) and by recognizing the strife he has endured. In one lyric, the singer reveals that while traveling to different counties within Buganda, the leader had to traverse swarms of stinging insects to reach Bugerere (line 7). The lyric suggests that he was willing to sacrifice his health and comfort for the sake of his people. Another line (41) tells how the king went beyond his prescribed role and took a long journey to Europe. Although it was extensive and difficult, he still did this task to establish diplomacy between the kingdom and the rest of the world. This determination to serve his kingdom is evident in another lyric, where the singer suggests that the king made this journey with particular haste so that he could return to support his people again as soon as possible (line 42). These descriptions emphasize the king's constant dedication to helping his subjects. This responsibility to his people is clear in yet another lyric where the singer rejoices at the kingship's restoration (lines 19, 30, and 33). Here, we see that despite the dangers of this pursuit, the king still returned for the good of his people. The singer describes this victory as an answered prayer. In these ways, "We Love the Supreme Man Exceedingly" consistently frames the king's greatness in terms of his dedication to his subjects. As the song's lyrics confirm, it is not simply the kingship's prestige that earns praise but his selfless behavior and willingness to fill his leadership role.

Whereas a more restrictive relationship might end up being painful and draining, with the kingship we see how a joy and mutuality rejuvenates people. The kingship's restoration allowed the Baganda to heal their relationship with their king and thus with one another. This idea of reviving the kingdom's life force also evokes notions of spirituality, life, and death, as leaders with an uncaring and violent nature might not only harm the material self but will also inflict existential transgressions.

By touring the counties of Buganda as a newly enthroned king, described in several lines (7, 23–26, and 40–41), Mutebi II was following the example of his late father, King Muteesa II. Mutebi II and Muteesa II demonstrated their responsibility to the kingdom in a more literal sense when they visited all the counties in the kingdom. The song's lyrics illustrate that such an extensive tour was considered impressive (line 40). Places such as Busiro and Bugerere were particularly distant from the more accessible parts of the kingdom (lines 25–26). These lines illustrate the king's dedication to the people, showing that he is willing to pursue a long tour just so he can see how everyone in his kingdom is faring, beyond his own court. This theme allows us to read "We Love the Supreme Man Exceedingly" more literally. More than simply traveling the world, the king visits his various domains and pays special attention to them. Thus, he follows through on his more local, interpersonal responsibilities.

Love and Respect

The various interpretations of "We Love the Supreme Man Exceedingly" that follow expand our understanding of cooperation as a process of give and take, among other subjects that encompass love and respect. In this vein, Edward Ssebunnya Kironde's analysis of the song looks at how the Baganda show their love and respect for their king, even for his faults:

> They deeply cherish and praise him extensively. Those who are particularly invested in the kingdom and its culture even hang his photos in their homes to demonstrate their love for his leadership. As a good leader, the king does not buy the love he receives from his people. They love him naturally, wholly, acknowledging his mistakes as well as his accomplishments. These sentiments are captured in the lyric, "We love him, my dear, we love the supreme man so much!" (line 10).[5]

By pointing out how subjects love the king despite his faults, Kironde implies a far more tolerant kingdom where even though the masses' love

---

5 Kironde interview, December 19, 2019.

depends on the king's merits, subjects exercise patience when evaluating royal performance and are willing to endure adversity to maintain the social contract of the kingdom. This style of relationship recalls how some court musicians responded to the adversity of King Muteesa II's 1953–1955 exile. Rather than abandoning their duties to prioritize their own safety, they risked defending the royal court instruments, which some brought to their homes for safekeeping. When the king finally returned from exile, they revealed their loyalty by returning the musical instruments and rededicating themselves to the kingship. This choice demonstrates how court musicians maintained a deep love for the king despite whatever risks their dedication presented.

Mirroring Kironde's comments, Peter Kinene's reading of "We Love the Supreme Man Exceedingly" describes another angle of the relationship between the king and his subjects by focusing on how he demonstrates his love for them. He articulates the importance of reciprocity, detailing that while subjects must evaluate the king critically, he must also perform his duties earnestly to gain their positive evaluation. The lyrics of the song explain that the people do not simply praise the king for his political prestige; they also recognize his ability to make sacrifices to ensure the well-being of his kingdom. According to Kinene, this includes traveling throughout the region to see for himself what his people experience or feel:

> People never forget good leaders and their leadership never dies. Such leaders rarely abandon their people and always reach out to them to express their support. The king of Buganda exemplifies this spirit by making regular visits to the different counties of the kingdom. He makes inquiries about current issues and does his best to fix any problems that may have arisen. Never in want, his people are satisfied with his leadership because he addresses their needs with genuine care.[6]

Here, Kinene identifies political responsibilities as acts of "genuine care," as the king's tours are not just bureaucratic boxes to check but expressions of affection for those who depend on his just leadership. In other words, he does not pose these tours as pleasant vacations; rather, he invests in them as opportunities to generate a broader sense of wellness in the kingdom.

Jimmy Ssenfuka Kibirige continues Kinene's explanation of the king's valor, stressing the necessity of upholding common values in fulfilling the position of king. However, he reframes this discussion, noting that valor does not have to do with power or individual strength but with one's willingness to perform one's duties. This viewpoint reveals how Kinene's reading of "We Love the Supreme Man Exceedingly" might deconstruct preconceived notions about what constitutes leadership, namely:

---

6   Kinene interview, December 16, 2019.

18: "WE LOVE THE SUPREME MAN EXCEEDINGLY" 🔹 233

A good leader fits his position. He does not appear foolish, and he upholds the values of those he serves first, unlike some leaders of today. His favor does not depend on his strength but on how he serves his people, and he remains informed of their needs. The king of Buganda does this by personally checking on the various royal enclosures—courts and royal tombs—to ensure that everything is as it should be. In time the king will pass these traits down to his successor, continuing the cycle of hereditary leadership that has existed since the kingdom's beginning.[7]

Kibirige suggests that the kingship is an inherently cooperative position that draws on the actions of past and present figures. The king can collaborate with the heads of the kingdom's various sectors to uphold its well-being all the same. Kibirige's affirmation that any good king must prioritize upholding the kingdom before his own pride further suggests that weaknesses or shortcomings will be acceptable, endearing even, if the king has good intentions.

Stepping aside from the relationship between ruler and subject for a moment, Jessy Ssendawula's interpretation reminds us of what happens when a third party tries to hinder such a deep and abiding social fabric. He comments on the consequences that occur when the central government restricts or violates the relationship between the king and his people, showing us how power might fall into different hands than one might expect due to diverging loyalties. Ssendawula adds that despite the central government's material domination of Uganda, their attempts to control the king still end in failure and chaos because they cannot fathom the love the people have for the king:

"We Love the Supreme Man Exceedingly" cautions the central government to respect the Baganda's culture and history of hereditary leadership to maintain harmony. When it challenges those elements, tensions rise, as was the case with the 2009 restrictions on the king's access to Kayunga district. In 2009, King Ronald Mutebi II (1993–present) was touring through the counties of Buganda. Before he could reach Kayunga, however, the central government, led by President Museveni, blocked his journey, citing fears of violence. This decision resulted in a great deal of backlash, including multiple days of rioting and unrest. To maintain regional balances, a leader should make regular visits to the entire country to ensure that everyone feels listened to and cared for.[8]

Ssendawula flips a more traditional understanding of power. He shows us how the king's might does not lie in military strength or political-legal legitimacy; instead, it lies in the trust and loyalty of his people, something that

---

7   Kibirige interview, December 18, 2019.
8   Ssendawula interview, December 28, 2019.

will seem especially dangerous to a government that knows it might have abused the people's trust.

This 2009 incident is just one event in the ongoing ideological conflict between the kingship and the national government. As David Pier observes, there is a significant royalist contingent in Buganda that continues to push for the restoration of the kingdom's semi-autonomous status that it held through the colonial period. Opponents of this position argue that the kingship's success would be counterproductive to Uganda's mission to develop into a diverse democratic nation-state.[9] In fact, much of the ongoing political tension between the national government and Buganda is centered on the issue of Buganda's importance in the national democratic context. Ali Mazrui asserts that without the cooperation and representation of the Baganda, it will be impossible for Uganda to reach fully structured electoral democracy.[10] Knowing the power that Buganda holds over the rest of the country may be why President Museveni has allegedly remained so unyielding on this issue. Court performers and musicians are inextricably involved in this debate. According to Pier, some performers use court regalia and music as cultural justification for the return to the kingship.[11] Indeed, as Kelly Askew reminds us, culture is what defines the spirit of a nation; as such proponents and conveyers of culture, musicians are inherently involved in the process of state-building.[12]

Returning to the depiction of the relationship between the Baganda and their king, Ssendawula notes some of the ways they express appreciation for their ruler. He demonstrates how the king might mobilize the love for his people to achieve support for various projects, including the renovation of the Kasubi royal tombs. In March 2010, a fire that broke out near one of the structures of the tombs partially destroyed them. The project to reconstruct them, which the Japanese government partially funded, began in 2014 and still continues as of 2025.[13] According to Ssendawula,

> Sserwanga's performance of "We Love the Supreme Man Exceedingly" not only expresses the joy the public felt for the restoration of the kingship but also attests to the love the Baganda have for their king. Manifestations of this love include the people's eager support for festivities or projects of any kind that the king and his administration organize. An example is the Brick

---

9   Pier 2017, 6.
10 Mazrui 1974, 9.
11 Pier 2017, 7.
12 Askew 2002, 272.
13 See "Reconstruction of the Tombs of the Buganda Kings Begins," UNESCO World Heritage Convention, May 13, 2014, https://whc.unesco.org/en/news/1124/.

(Ettoffaali), a project that seeks to restore the kingdom's royal tombs that recently got burned down.[14]

By using his influence to accomplish his goals, the king provides a counternarrative to the assumption that he is merely a cultural figurehead, a title imposed on him by the central government. He is a leader in a more profound sense than many elected leaders could ever be. However, this is not due to his material or political strength but because he models the qualities of an exemplary leader, to lead thoughtfully and with interpersonal care.

Kinene's analysis of "We Love the Supreme Man Exceedingly" further justifies why people appreciate the institution of the kingship. He reimagines the lyrics of the song in terms of the king's connection to his ancestors. This approach might refer to his place as an extension of a long line of leaders, whose wisdom all emerges in the current king's reign. Kinene explains that "The kingship suited the supreme man and he got to know it" (line 12) hints at this convergence, as the king's knowledge of the kingship might refer to his intimate connection to the work of previous rulers:

> Buganda's king has more than one hundred official names that the Baganda people designed to accord him the utmost praise and respect. However, beyond just his various titles and hereditary inheritance, he stands out as a deserving leader due to his willingness to carry out the myriad responsibilities of the job and to succeed at it. He fights for his people and for the honor of his position. Accordingly, he truly deserves the honor of that position. Generally, the king's leadership endures because he builds on the wisdom that his predecessor passed on to him, and his successor—the next hereditary leader—does the same. This process highlights the advantages of hereditary rule in that the newest leader will always utilize the experiences and advice of the previous leaders—his ancestors—as guidelines. The system awards positions of power to those who display their ancestors' skills of leadership, ensuring the success of their constituency.[15]

This commentary suggests that rather than taking the history of a kingdom as a frozen memory, the king conceives of it as a constantly shifting, living form. It is a leadership that cannot end, as it survives in all the leaders who follow. This reading of history benefits the kingdom, as it allows people to infuse the songs of the past with the vitality of the present. Much like what Kinene and his contemporaries are doing with "We Love the Supreme Man Exceedingly," the king is constantly reimagining the past to create new and rich possibilities for the present. When we understand this ancestral focus,

---

14 Ibid.
15 Kinene interview, December 16, 2019.

we come to appreciate a spiritual power that runs deeper than that which elected leaders might wield.

Finally, Kinene interprets the song in terms of its relation to international diplomacy. The various lyrics' description of the king's diplomatic journeys to Europe suggest this point (lines 41–43). Kinene not only shows us how state-level politics are relevant to politics on an international scale but also speaks to the importance of the kingship as a leader in far-reaching global initiatives:

> Ultimately, the results of the good leadership detailed throughout "We Love the Supreme Man Exceedingly" is the prosperity of the kingdom, both at a national and international level. The song as a victory piece that commemorates the restoration of the kingship after the abolition of kings in Uganda under the 1967 Republican Constitution. Thus, "We Love the Supreme Man Exceedingly" praises the king for his commitment to remain connected with his people. It also comments on his increased worldly knowledge during the time he spent living in Europe. It discusses the need for leaders to work for a higher quality of life for their people. Smooth leadership and an established place in the international community are distinctive markers of the nation's prosperity in this area.[16]

By demonstrating the virtues of the king through the lens of international engagement, Kinene reminds us how the kingship has adapted to the changes of the international stage beyond Uganda's political borders. He illuminates that the kingship's traditions of interpersonal dedication and responsibility are valuable to consider in the current era, yet he also suggests that those same traditions must change and adapt to the modern circumstances that surround them. Kinene does not argue for a complete return to the precolonial Kiganda kingship system but instead points to it as a model that one might draw on and rethink to conceive of a new government entirely.

Conclusion

As the lyrics of "We Love the Supreme Man Exceedingly" demonstrate, the song venerates royalty through musical celebration that highlights the king's glory. The performer chooses to reveal this glory by drawing attention to the sacrifices the king made and the obstacles he faced, a process that lends itself to the song's serious and sorrowful tones. As the composition's lyrics evoke images of exile and return, or dedication and loss, we come to see a delicate balance between triumph and tragedy. Although the king worked to serve his people, he had to traverse significant adversity. As suggested earlier,

---

16   Ibid.

this song ideates between the positive and negative emotions of ruling. It functions as a testimony to royal competence through its lyrics' focus on the king's fulfillment of his governing responsibilities rather than merely celebrating his status. Therefore, the composition creates a performance-based framework for evaluating monarchical effectiveness, suggesting that the king's right to rule stems from demonstrable actions rather than divine right alone.

"We Love the Supreme Man Exceedingly" expresses the past in its lyrics, constituting a history that reinvigorates this past and activates it in the present rather than freezing or monumentalizing it. This process is evident in the interpretations of commentators, whose analyses of the song connect its lyrics to twenty-first-century contexts. For example, as we have seen, King Muteesa II's musicians concluded that he was a good ruler. In contrast, many Ugandans see elected politicians, despite their democratic rise, as leaders who allegedly use various methods of manipulation and coercion to maintain their place in power. This viewpoint, which is a recurring theme in various interpretations of "We Love the Supreme Man Exceedingly," leads us to reevaluate our assumptions about monarchy and democracy by flipping the positions that the two forms of government occupy. Whereas the Baganda's love and respect for the king is the basis for the mutuality and cooperation that holds the Kingdom of Buganda together, many might not say the same of their relationship with the current national regime.

Part VI

Songs about Conflict and Loss

Death and warfare are universal, but the way each nation, culture, and individual experiences these hardships is unique. Part 6 focuses on themes of conflict and loss. The five songs featured in this part elaborate on the Kiganda ways of living in response to life's unpredictable dangers. The first three songs explore the more physical, corporeal aspects of conflict and loss with a focus on the bloodshed that results from war. Chapter 19 looks at war and fate via the song "Ssematimba and Kikwabanga" ("Ssematimba ne Kikwabanga"), which recounts the tragedy of two brothers who die in battle before they can enjoy the goats they were saving to eat later. The song has multiple lessons: first, it reminds us to be thankful for each living moment; second, it advises us to not count our chickens before they hatch; third, it illustrates the tragedy of wasted potential and the senselessness of violent conflict. Chapter 20 looks at "Poland" ("Polanda") via the related themes of war and imperialism. The lyrics and analyses of this song compare the events of World War II to power dynamics of Ugandan politics, demonstrating how political conflict is often a transnational, universal experience. Chapter 21 looks at two renditions of "The Battle of Nsinsi" ("Olutalo olw'e Nsinsi") to understand the causes and occurrences of civil war. It recounts a civil war between two kingdoms, Buganda and Bunyoro, again highlighting the ubiquitous nature of violence.

The next two songs examine the more spiritual, immaterial side of conflict and loss. Chapter 22 looks at the themes of disagreement and invocation in the song "Let Me Plod with a Stick Close to Kibuuka" ("Ka Nsimbe Omuggo awali Kibuuka"), which focuses on the complex dynamics in disagreements between family members, men and women, and other relationships. Chapter 23 investigates mortality and spirituality in "The Pebble Is Breaking Me" ("Akayinja Kammenya"). This song expresses regretful sentiments from the perspective of a deceased person who pities the living for their lack of gratitude. It calls into question the universal themes of morality and legacy, and it highlights how life in Buganda functions in the context of conflict and loss.

The five songs featured in part 6 make for a fitting final installment, as each one deals with heavy topics such as violence, war, and death. Applying a variety of political lenses to the songs, interpreters explore the potential of each song to serve as a statement about the end of a political dynasty, a social movement, or a lineage of people. Many explore the concept of legacy, both in the context of national leadership and in kinship, thus extracting a wealth of meanings from each narrative.

19
"Ssematimba and Kikwabanga"

War and Fate

The song "Ssematimba and Kikwabanga" ("Ssematimba ne Kikwabanga") narrates the story of two brother warriors, known for their prowess on the battlefield, who were killed during their final battle. According to Peter Cooke and Klaus Wachsmann, Ssematimba was the first to fall, speared through by an enemy, and Kikwabanga followed shortly thereafter.[1] Albert Ssempeke Bisaso (b. 1979) performed the version of "Ssematimba and Kikwabanga" analyzed in this chapter. His paternal uncle Ludoviiko Sserwanga (ca. 1932–2013), who performed an instrumental rendition on the notched flute (*endere*), shared the following account about the song's history:

> Ssematimba and Kikwabanga were two brothers. Historically, some Baganda believe that the brothers lived during the reign of King Ssuuna II (r. ca. 1832–1857). The time came when the king appointed them to go to war. Before they left, Kikwabanga asked Ssematimba how they would celebrate when they returned. Ssematimba suggested they feast on their goats, adding that it was a wise idea not to butcher them before their departure. In other words, he suggested they save the goats for their return from battle. The two brothers then tethered their goats, hoping to butcher them and celebrate the end of the war. But as the saying goes, going to battle is different from going to visit friends. What the brothers expected was not what they got. They never returned from war because it devoured them. In response to these events, court musicians composed "Ssematimba and Kikwabanga" and warned, *Abasiba embuzi musibira bwereere; mulabire ku Ssematimba ne Kikwabanga* (Those who tether goats do so in vain; take the example of Ssematimba and Kikwabanga). The song advises people to do things now instead of postponing them. It encourages them to never put off things until tomorrow if they can do them today.

---

1   Cooke and Wachsmann 2003, 12–13.

However, the song is also about valuing other people and not taking them for granted. Regarding musicians, it may challenge the people they serve to value their importance by taking care of them, for it is when people acknowledge the importance of musicians and their skills that they can deliver the most resounding performances.[2]

Sserwanga remarks how "Ssematimba and Kikwabanga" comments on reciprocity as a practice of mutual growth and overcoming rather than a matter of give and take. That is, the value that two people place on each other can mold into a unified appreciation. His remarks also affirm an eminent relationship to the present, acknowledge the risks of everyday experience, and embrace gratitude while simultaneously critiquing cyclical violence.

Bisaso's performance of "Ssematimba and Kikwabanga" begins with inchoate ramblings on the bow harp (*ennanga*), which quickly gain momentum and settle into an intricate pattern of plucking. Like previously discussed performances featuring the bow harp, the instrumental part of "Ssematimba and Kikwabanga" consist of two complementary melodies played by either hand of the performer in an interlocking fashion. The bow harp part, performed in triple meter, sets the song's rhythmic framework. Soon after the establishment of this instrumental part, Bisaso's vocals commence in a slightly timid way, which continues throughout the performance. He maintains a balance between the instrumental and vocal parts. The rapid rises and falls in intonation portray the conversational quality of the vocal part, with some sections sounding more like dialogue than melodic lyrics. The overall structuring of "Ssematimba and Kikwabanga" is a reminder that multiple musicians can perform the song in a call-and-response style. Sometimes Bisaso employs repetition—for instance, mentioning the two brothers' names, Ssematimba and Kikwabanga, at the end of every vocal phrase. Although he performs the song at a fast tempo, the piece is generally somber and reflective. His low, quiet mood, which the buzzy timbre of the bow harp instrumental enhances, brings out the sentiments of the song's lyrics. So does the performer's slow lyrical delivery and overall sorrowful tone, which bestows a sense of sadness and regret to his performance. After a few minutes, Bisaso's performance unfurls into a nonmusical banter as swiftly as the music stops. Bisaso sings the following lyrics:

1 *Ssebo, Kikwabanga*
Sir, Kikwabanga

2 *Abasiba embuzi musibira bwereere, laba Ssematimba*
Those who tether goats you do so in vain, see what befell Ssematimba

3 *Abaali abangi, nsigadde mu bbanga, ssebo, Kikwabanga*
We were many, but I am left in a vacuum, sir, Kikwabanga

---

2   Sserwanga interview, July 6, 2005.

4 *Lwe ndiva kuno, ndigenda wa Kaggo, baana battu, Kikwabanga*
When I leave this world, I will go to Kaggo's, dear ones, Kikwabanga

5 *Abasiba embuzi musibira bwereere, laba Ssematimba*
Those who tether goats you do so in vain, see what befell Ssematimba

6 *Ogidde onkyawe, olikyawa n'omwana, ogwange gwakubye dda*
Now that you have abandoned me, you will also abandon the child, my heart is already racing

7 *Ogidde onkyawe, olikyawa n'omukulu, laba Ssematimba ne Kikwabanga*
Now that you have abandoned me, you will also abandon the elder, see what befell Ssematimba and Kikwabanga

8 *Abasiba embuzi musibira bwereere, ssebo, Kikwabanga*
Those who tether goats you do so in vain, sir, Kikwabanga

9 *Bwe ndiva kuno, ndigenda wa Kaggo, baana battu, Kikwabanga*
When I leave this world I will go to Kaggo's, dear ones, Kikwabanga

10 *Lwe ndiva kuno ndigenda wa maama, baana battu, Kikwabanga*
The day I will leave this place, I will go to my mother's, dear ones, Kikwabanga

11 *Wamma, ndigenda n'ani nze? Baana battu, Kikwabanga*
Indeed, with whom shall I go? My dears, Kikwabanga

12 *Wamma, ndigenda ne taata, ssebo, Kikwabanga*
Indeed, I will go with father, sir, Kikwabanga

13 *Abasiba embuzi musibira bwereere*
Those who tether goats you do so in vain

14 *Abaali abangi, nsigadde mu bbanga*
We were many, but I am left in a vacuum

15 *Abaali abangi, nsigadde bw'omu nze, laba Ssematimba*
We were many, but I am left alone, see what befell Ssematimba

16 *Olijja emisana, olinsanga mu ddiiro, ogwange gwakubye dda*
When you come during the day, you will find me laid in the living room, having breathed my last

17 *Olijja emisana, olisanga mu ddiiro, nga nze nneegolodde, Kikwabanga*
You will come during day, only to find me laid in the living room, when I am straightened, Kikwabanga

18 *Wamma, ndigenda n'ani nze? Baana battu, Kikwabanga*
Indeed, with whom shall I go? My dears, Kikwabanga

19 *Wamma, ndigenda ne taata, ssebo, Kikwabanga*
Indeed, I shall go with father, sir, Kikwabanga

20 *Abasiba embuzi musibira bwereere, Kikwabanga*
Those who tether goats you do so in vain, Kikwabanga

21 *Bwe ndiva kuno, ndigenda wa Kaggo*
When I leave this world, I will go to Kaggo's

22 *Anti ndigenda ne maama, gy'abeera*
But I shall also go with mother, where she now stays

23 *Abantu ba kuno, ndigenda n'ani nze? Laba Ssematimba ne Kikwabanga*
Residents, with whom shall I go? See what befell Ssematimba and Kikwabanga

24 *Abasiba embuzi musibira bwereere*
Those who tether goats you do so in vain

25 *Anti ndigenda ne taata, gy'abeera*
But I shall go with father, where he now stays

"Ssematimba and Kikwabanga" highlights the distress of the singer, who, reeling at the thought of death, begins to contemplate his life. Beyond the goats that Ssematimba and Kikwabanga raise but cannot enjoy, the lyrics portray the distress of losing one's kin and dying alone. The singer describes this separation as being jilted, as a rejection by his beloved brother that reverberates beyond his own life to impact his child. Repeating the phrase "Those who tether goats you do so in vain" (lines 2, 5, 8, 13, 20, and 24), he recognizes death as a leveler, emphasizing that one's earthly plans no longer matter once death arrives. (Here, "tether goats" could also refer to raising and accumulating the animals.) However, the singer does not necessarily despair at the concept of death itself but at the thought of dying alone. This sorrow about being alone implies that the quality of Ssematimba and Kikwabanga's bond was not one of individually conceived lives but of a mutual strength that they found in each other.

"Ssematimba and Kikwabanga" emphasizes that we are always surrounded by risk and uncertainty in both war and quotidian life. In the case of the brothers in question, they assume they will survive the battle, and thus they choose to postpone enjoying the goats. However, they both die and lose the opportunity for a final meal. With this point, "Ssematimba and Kikwabanga" becomes a narrative about reaffirming one's commitment to the present moment. Rather than thinking that we subsist through the expectation of future success and planning accordingly, we should live life wholesomely and grasp opportunities in the moment. In other words, we should not put things off.

These ideas tie in to expressing gratitude. As Sserwanga earlier explains, valuing others is more than simply appreciating them for their provisions, as one must reciprocate their efforts. In this instance, "valuing" refers to the various ways individuals might exchange with one another, giving and taking until one reimagines one's "values" in the framework of the other's already preexisting set. This applies to twenty-first-century Uganda: whereas the conflicts of the precolonial past no longer torment them, people must now overcome the issue of exploitation among their leaders. Thus, Uganda's issue today might depend on reinstating this logic "valuing" that includes reciprocity, as some of the analysis in the following section demonstrates.

War and Fate

Reading "Ssematimba and Kikwabanga" in a twenty-first-century context, several interpreters engage with its topics via the themes of war and fate, applying them to politics and social life.

For example, they speak about how the song advises leaders to make changes in the moment and to avoid harping too much on the past or the future. Jimmy Ssenfuka Kibirige explains "Ssematimba and Kikwabanga" in terms of two interwoven factors, the first being the notion that violence is reciprocal by nature. Whatever cruelty the brothers inflicted would always come back to them. Kibirige notes that the goats, a plunder that they acquired during battle, were ill gotten because they came at the expense of others. In a karmic sense, the brothers were not able to enjoy them, instead receiving a taste of their own medicine:

> Ssematimba and Kikwabanga's goats were plunder from their previous battles. However, because plunder brings about misfortune, the brothers were probably cursed to never enjoy feasting on the goats. People should never celebrate that which has brought others misfortune. The brothers' feast was meant to be a celebration, but stolen items never bring about anything good. Therefore, it is unwise to celebrate something that is obtained so unscrupulously. Could this be one of the reasons why the brothers died?[3]

Kibirige' second factor here is about living in the moment and appreciating the present. He explains that the brothers lost the chance to enjoy their plunder because they hesitated to do so while they could, instead putting it off under the assumption of a joyful, more resolved future. This

---

3   Kibirige interview, December 18, 2019.

decision was ineffective because the brothers never recognized the possibility of death, as a result failing to appreciate the abundance of their living. Kibirige continues:

> Additionally, it is unwise to put things off until the future given that there is no guarantee one will be around to see it. Kikwabanga and his brother left behind a feast to go to war. They put it off until the future but never came back. They anticipated a tomorrow that never came. Current political leaders should take heed of this lesson and not rush to think of the future. If they have the opportunity to accomplish something, they should do it then.[4]

Kibirige's two points act as an interwoven reframing that demonstrates a multilayered understanding of "Ssematimba and Kikwabanga." Their interconnectedness challenges us to recognize that reciprocity factors into present-mindedness, as one should express gratitude as soon as possible lest some unforeseen event, like a karmic reaction to seizing an enemy's goats, interrupt it. Indeed, those who inflict violence on others earn punishment in turn.

In Steven Mukasa Kabugo's interpretation, he expands on Kibirige's ideas on fate and timing by demonstrating how the song recognizes life's uncertainty. He extends the point to apply to the idea of security. Specifically, he adds more to our discussion on present-mindedness, highlighting the impulses one may have to predict the unknown and to protect oneself. These tendencies dominate the experiences of many individuals, and Kabugo argues that this pursuit will falter at one point or another, for even those with great power or foresight can fail:

> "Ssematimba and Kikwabanga" signifies that even if one does everything in one's power to prevent misfortunes, they will eventually come to pass. An individual can have personal power, but the time will come when someone else will beat or outsmart him or her.[5]

According to Kabugo's analysis, the first step in affirming life is to accept its cruelty and confusion and to love it anyway. Otherwise, an obsession with security only undermines one's ability to enjoy life, while providing insufficient power to fully protect one from danger.

Jessy Ssendawula's interpretation extends the conversation on death and living in the moment by calling to mind examples from popular literature and how they can serve as advice for leaders. Synthesizing the message from "Ssematimba and Kikwabanga" with the content of Chinua Achebe's book *Things Fall Apart* (1958), he draws parallels between the story of the two

---

4 Ibid.
5 Kabugo interview, December 19, 2019.

brothers' deaths and the philosophy of a character in the book known as Unoka. Ssendawula argues that death arrives seamlessly and unexpectedly and that one should, as Unoka put it, eat one's fill while one can:

> The song "Ssematimba and Kikwabanga" reminds me of the philosophy of Unoka, a character from Chinua Achebe's *Things Fall Apart*. Unoka says that whenever he looked at the mouth of a dead man, he realized the folly of people not eating their fill when they had the chance. In this life, what counts more is the present; people never have assurance of tomorrow. Therefore, political leaders should avoid making promises for the future. They should take action now, in the present moment. It is better to accomplish something small in the present than to promise something big in the future. Whenever people have the time to enjoy themselves, they should take advantage of it. They never know if they will be alive tomorrow, regardless of their strength in the past. This song is also a song of disappointment scoffing at saving everything good for the future for which people have no guarantee. It instructs them to use the moment for all they can do, because they never know what tomorrow will bring.[6]

By relating these two stories, Ssendawula uses the image of the mouth of a dead man to express how we should be grateful while we are alive, especially for simple, daily functions like eating.

Adding to the idea that violence is karmically reciprocal, Peter Kinene illustrates the ways that forces tend to feed back on themselves. As he explains, just because one puts one's action in a particular direction does not mean it will stay that way, as the action could come back to bite one later or may have an indirect consequence. For example, a leader might try to rile up his supporters to criticize an opponent, but those same supporters could, once energized, come back to criticize this very leader. Kinene suggests that one cannot assume that telos (purpose) perfectly translates to its effect. Telos only reflects on intention, and once it has begun, Kinene observes, numerous external factors can intersect with this originating force to override such intention:

> Ssematimba and Kikwabanga gained their wealth through war. It is likely the grief and pain of those they killed and robbed contributed to the death of the warrior brothers. They probably died like those they used to attack. The song therefore cautions listeners to be careful, because the sorrows of those they harm may eventually become their own. In politics, for example, politicians may upset and hurt the public or harass one another. Eventually, though, the pain they inflict on others will come back to be inflicted on them.[7]

---

6   Ssendawula interview, December 28, 2019.
7   Kinene interview, December 16, 2019.

Kinene's reimagination of "Ssematimba and Kikwabanga" shows how the brothers' actions and subsequent death were connected, intricately woven aspects of a larger story that the song's text had not yet stated explicitly. His commentary also illuminates the brothers' death as more than mere randomness. By attributing it to their actions, he frames the events of the song not only as a tragedy but as a cautionary tale.

Edward Ssebunnya Kironde uses "Ssematimba and Kikwabanga" to elaborate on how violence and harm manifest today in Uganda. He specifically claims that it reveals how some leaders overstep their rule. He claims that similar to how the brothers acquired their plunder through force, contemporary national leaders supposedly gain some of their riches through political manipulation and social repression. However, says Kironde, these gains may ultimately be subject to retribution because they are ill-obtained:

> Cycles of fighting and looting never end. President Museveni questions why people are calling for him to leave the presidential office when he has discovered oil in Uganda and done other good things for the country. Everything he talks about tends to be in possessive language even when referring to public property: "My country," etc. He forgets that it is not his oil and that he never created it; it is for the nation. He risks being like Ssematimba and Kikwabanga, both of whom never made it back home and who were perhaps too used to victory. They would fight and take people's things, but in the end they died. A hero can so easily turn into the villain. Although it is unclear that this will be the case with President Museveni, many people are already thinking that he is a fallen hero. He liberated Ugandans, but right now, things are not good for most of them. His contemporaries and former heroes or liberators who became corrupt, such as Omar al-Bashir of Sudan and Colonel Muammar Gaddafi of Libya, came to terrible ends. Many Nigerians, too, are praying for the day their president will die. These examples should be a reminder to President Museveni that a leader should not overstay in power. The longer he stays, the more his faults will accumulate. Soon people will no longer focus on the good politicians did in the past and switch their attention to the harm they are doing in the present.[8]

Kironde's statement reveals how the actions of the national leaders and the brothers in "Ssematimba and Kikwabanga" reflect each other and how those of leaders will not go unremembered. Both hopeful and critical, the commentary gives a unique look at the current regime and political situation of Uganda and of Africa at large.

Kironde continues his analysis by remarking that current leaders will eventually have to answer for what they have done, using the image of the

---

8   Kironde interview, December 19, 2019.

two warriors to emphasize that leaders falling from power is inevitable, as their tactics (manipulating the masses to maintain power) are unsustainable:

> Some current leaders of Uganda have reached the same point as Ssematimba and Kikwabanga. Therefore, the time for them to leave is approaching. Even though some might win elections now or spout ideology, the time is coming when they will run out of tactics. It is troubling that some people—mainly pastors—have already declared that President Museveni will win the 2021 election. Many people believe that he will rig the election, and this is obvious in part because he has never lost an election since he has been in office. In some areas, especially those where he is unpopular, ballots do not usually arrive until late afternoon. Other times, districts produce votes that outnumber their populations. Eventually, these and other tactics will backfire.[9]

Kironde projects the two brothers as skilled and renowned warriors while projecting politicians as crafty and manipulative. His presentation of these two related yet differing traits reminds us that great leaders might fall badly when their actions continue to hurt those they lead. In particular, the people in power will eventually have to answer for what they have done, much in the same way the two warriors did.

Affirming the importance of mutuality in lending quality to life, Ssendawula offers an insight about interdependence and why it is crucial for maintaining well-being. He suggests that one's existence is only possible through one's interaction with the surrounding world—with friends, family, and larger social groups. Such interdependence nourishes us, as life is not just a physiological concept or any material marker of individual prowess and achievement (such as rearing and accumulating goats) but a celebration of joyful living with those who are important to us. As he points out,

> People should always have access to some form of entertainment or revelry to celebrate their labors. Celebration and festivities are some of the things that give human lives meaning. Without them, people are little more than clay, set to break and crumble to dust when they die. Again, it is what friends and family share that nourishes them in this world. When death comes, we go with nothing.[10]

Through this analysis, "Ssematimba and Kikwabanga" delivers a philosophy of what constitutes life. If one lives resentfully, enforcing harm for material gain, it is not only one's moral standing that suffers but the fabric of one's being. By rejecting mutual care, living against (instead of for) others, one damages one's own spirit.

---

9   Kironde interview, December 19, 2019.
10 Ssendawula personal communication, April 8, 2020.

In another reading, Kinene criticizes attempts to subdue and predict the future, rejecting common attitudes that attempt to confirm existence as holding a codifiable essence. Instead, he affirms an appreciation of life as it occurs (thus, changes) and embraces both the joy and the suffering associated with it. As he observes,

> Regardless of personal wealth, everyone leaves the same, taking nothing with him or her. Even when someone has a lot of wealth, it cannot provide any security over death. Furthermore, no one is ever certain of when their time will come. For both those reasons, it is important to appreciate the good things in life as they come, as opposed to waiting for some eventual period of total bliss that may never come. This also applies to sharing one's success or rewards with family and friends. People need to do honorable deeds in the present rather than pushing them to the future, which, once more, is inherently uncertain.[11]

As Kinene suggests, no one can achieve transcendent beauty or joy, as that would be a refusal of the existence that we face—a world that can be so cruel, yet so beautiful and worldly. In this way, it is important to appreciate life as it comes. From this perspective, rearing goats comes to represent an over-obsession with maximizing value, of achieving "total bliss." He also seems to imply that if we focus less on accumulating wealth (tethering goats) and more on appreciating family and friends, we will experience less friction at the time of death. In other words, when we embrace, value, and share what we have in the present moment, we might not become like the singer who lamented his isolation, lonesomeness, and loss.

According to Ssendawula, death's inevitability is what makes human life so valuable, and he advises that politicians treat it as such:

> The song reminds leaders that death is a universal force. It comes to the commoner just as it comes to warriors and dignitaries. This inevitability of death, this finite nature, is what defines the preciousness of human life. Leaders should therefore focus their efforts not on engaging in violence or war, but on investing in the health and lives of their people. They should do this both by investing in healthcare and by working to reduce violence and crime, so that as many people as possible can lead long and healthy lives.[12]

Ssendawula's alternate reading of "Ssematimba and Kikwabanga" suggests that the profundity of death, and thus of life, informs political decision-making. With a mindset that embraces this ultimate truth, politicians may be able to enable the joys of existence across a greater swath of their population. Doing so will benefit them, since they will abandon their own exacerbated

---

11   Kinene interview, December 16, 2019.
12   Ssendawula personal communication, April 8, 2020.

preoccupations with preserving themselves and encourage those who keep them in power to support and fondly engage with them.

In her additional comments on "Ssematimba and Kikwabanga," Harriet Kisuule reminds us that leaders must fulfill their social responsibilities to their people, just as parents must do for their children. In this sense, responding to duty plays a key role in achieving a fulfilling life. By refusing to compromise their values for greed, people will uplift themselves and those around them. Applying this idea to leaders, citizens, and warriors, Kisuule reimagines duty as serving to satisfy one's sense of care and presence in the world. These qualities far outweigh the significance of any amount of money or power, as Kisuule explains:

> Ssematimba and Kikwabanga, great warrior brothers who protected their lands, should inspire and teach modern Ugandans to fight with determination. Many need to stand up and protect not only their land, as was the case with the brothers, but their right to truth and fairness. They should do so as the brothers did, being willing to do whatever is necessary to fulfill their role, in this case not as warriors but as active citizens. The same should also apply to leaders. They need to be able to demonstrate that they are committed to fulfilling their role as protectors of the people, rather than succumbing to corruption and damaging the country instead of improving it. So it is important to execute one's duties, regardless of external factors.[13]

Kisuule puts a spin on "Ssematimba and Kikwabanga" that reconciles the disjunction between the roles of leaders and the reality of their actions. She reminds us how death serves as a prerequisite to life. At the moment of death, all that remains is the value in one's life, one's duty, joy, appreciation, and excitement. If one lives a life where one often forgoes such pursuits, always rejecting them in favor of security, safety, uniformity, and stagnation, then one might be surprised to find a particular sensation of emptiness in one's final moments.

Pivoting from other commentators' positions, Kisuule further argues that self-preservation, though often taken to anxious levels, is important given the increasing danger of the world. Drawing on the idea that Ssematimba and Kikwabanga could have avoided death if they had been more careful about which conflicts they were involved in, she suggests that pursuing conflict can unnecessarily lead to death. Even if life is unpredictable, there are still ways to mitigate danger without becoming consumed by concerns for security. Everyone still needs to eat and drink to survive, and in today's world, money is often necessary to acquire sustenance, Kisuule points out:

---

13   Kisuule interview, December 21, 2019.

It is important for leaders to listen to and respect other people's views; they do not have to make decisions like despots. Instead, it is better for them to engage with the community to determine what is best for them. Also, the average person should not try to engage in battles that do not benefit him or her. For example, if the government arrests Bobi Wine, as much as one might believe in him as a leader, it is simply not worth it for ordinary citizens to put their livelihoods at risk by protesting Wine's imprisonment. These people have to work every day for their food and sustenance. In other words, the majority of other people's battles do not and should not concern those not directly involved. Though this may seem callous or uncompassionate, it is necessary to have these sorts of principles and strong will for self-preservation in an increasingly uncertain world.[14]

Kisuule provides a sobering perspective that self-preservation sometimes ought to come before preserving an ideal. The crucial thing, then, is deciding when to save oneself or save another. To this point, she stresses that it is not wise for people to impose their presence onto situations they need not be involved in (like war), as such an action might be risky, arrogant, and self-fulfilling.

Ssendawula draws on his prior discussion of death's inevitability to underscore the importance of cultivating a legacy to persevere after one's death, encouraging politicians to prioritize more humanitarian policies. He argues that if there is something to achieve, then pursuing a sound legacy will constructively impact communities; as in death, people will memorialize someone on the basis of what they leave behind. If one has caused suffering in one's lifetime, one is also likely to dwell on that in one's final moments, just as Ssematimba and Kikwabanga faced their own emotional discomfort. Ssendawula notes:

> Cultivating a legacy that will continue on long past their death should be a goal for all leaders. By serving their people well, their deeds can eclipse their death when it eventually comes, and society will revere them for their leadership the way figures such as Nelson Mandela and Julius Nyerere are.[15]

Ssendawula's meditation on the legacies of twenty-first-century leaders reminds us that only a proud legacy can ward off total annihilation, as it will carry one's memory into generations to come.

---

14 Ibid.
15 Ssendawula personal communication, April 8, 2020.

Conclusion

As a musical memorial, "Ssematimba ne Kikwabanga" transforms two brother warriors' battlefield deaths into cultural legacy. The song documents these brothers' military excellence and ultimate sacrifice, creating a balanced narrative that acknowledges both their triumph and tragedy. "Ssematimba ne Kikwabanga" touches on various topics (life, service, discipline, determination, mindfulness, and reciprocity, among others), all in conjunction with the story of the deaths of the brothers and in relation to the composition's focus on the themes of war and fate. The song's lyrics lament the dead and the inability to fully enjoy life's fruits, demonstrating the ephemerality of life and its material rewards. The lyrics also stress the value of relationships versus financial success. Beyond commenting on the risks of war and relationships between kin and friends, "Ssematimba and Kikwabanga" problematizes notions of conducting one's life. Its lyrics affirm an eminent relationship to the present: acknowledge the risks that occur daily and embrace gratitude, while simultaneously critiquing cyclical violence.

The lyrical content of the song can apply to multiple situations in part because it stresses the well-being of others. Performers and commentators demonstrate this applicability through their analyses, connecting the song's themes to twenty-first-century contexts, including political and social settings. Rendering them as representations of politicians, some interpreters project the failures and vices of the two warriors onto the alleged greedy tendencies of corrupt national government leaders. Some commentators go further, reading the raising of goats as a representation of one's legacy on the one hand and a depiction of material wealth on the other hand. In some discussions of political leadership, the song's analyses shed light on a humanitarian approach to policy, reminding powerful leaders to focus on the health and connectedness of their people rather than their own selfish desires. Ultimately, "Ssematimba and Kikwabanga" serves as a cautionary tale and a prediction for the future.

20

"Poland"

War and Imperialism

The song "Poland" ("Polanda") connects a major event of World War II to Kiganda history by exploring the power dynamics and consequences of tyranny and imperial domination. Thus, it contributes to ongoing discourse about peacemaking and governance in wartime. Ssaalongo Kiwanuka Matovu Deziderio (1924–2015), the performer of the rendition we will discuss, shared the following details about the song's history:

> "Poland" was one of the new songs I learned from my uncle Matyansi Kibirige Baazibumbira in the late 1940s, when I was about twelve years old. Around that time, Buganda sent troops to participate in World War II, which, along with other global events, inspired local musicians to compose and perform songs. Many musicians saw their performances of such songs as a means of participating in conversations about global events.[1]

Edward Ssebunnya Kironde further explained the historical context behind "Poland," as well as the creative liberties that its composers took when writing it:

> Germany invaded Poland in 1939, thereby starting World War II. The invaders occupied the country in a matter of days. The Poles put up a great fight but eventually succumbed to Hitler's forces. At that time, most African countries were still under control of European forces. This meant they were conscripted into the armed forces of their respective colonizers to go fight in the war. For Buganda and the rest of Uganda, Great Britain was the colonizing power for which they fought.
>
> The whole event, World War II, might seem so far removed from the reality of today, something one could hardly imagine happening now, and as such remaining imbued with a historical mystique as many continue to remember it through the ages. But the song "Poland," which draws on

---

[1] Deziderio interview, July 15, 2005.

these events, explores some deep topics that are relevant to current times. For example, the composer equates the whole country of Poland to a city, a comparison he makes perhaps because of the speed with which people can occupy a city. It is hard to visualize the occupation of Poland occurring as quickly as it did, knowing it was an entire country. By describing it as a city, a smaller region, is the singer trivializing the invasion? If so, what is he telling us?[2]

Contextualizing "Poland" in World War II, Deziderio presents the song as a response to the British colonial government's decision to draft Ugandans to fight in the war effort. From this perspective, the song speaks to the hapless violence of colonialism that result in such injustices as the conscription of Ugandans to fight in World War II. The context that Deziderio offers demonstrates the role court musicians have in explaining and making sense of current events within and beyond Buganda. They can distill any sort of political event into a common theme that the Baganda people might witness daily. This practice allows listeners to craft imaginaries between more localized, indigenous regions and European nations, which tend to garner most of the popular focus of the international stage.

Kironde's account also recalls the process by which global politics can filter into Kiganda court music traditions. The commentary reshapes our understanding of what might be "relevant" to these musicians. It also speaks to the musicians' involvement and presence under the colonial rule of the British and highlights the irony of Britain's decisions to claim the moral high ground against Germany while they were conscripting Ugandans to fight in the war. With this background in mind, we come to understand how the lyrics of "Poland" can implicate colonial hypocrisies, even when the performer abstains from explicitly mentioning them.

Deziderio opens his performance of "Poland" with a short instrumental section featuring gentle bowing of the tube fiddle (*endingidi*). Each melodic phrase starts on the same pitch, blossoming upward into higher notes before falling back down into lower pitches as the next measure begins. These phrases also end on the same note. After this opening excerpt, the vocal accompaniment begins. Deziderio repeats several vocal phrases, each one similar in melodic form, rhythmic framework, and overall duration. This repetition of similar melodies evokes the cyclical, redundant nature of violence in political dynasties. The texture of the piece, with the lead melody sung over the accompanying tube fiddle line, remains heterophonic throughout Deziderio's presentation. Toward the end of the performance, he sustains a lyrical phrase of much longer duration without pausing. Shortly afterward,

---

2   Kironde interview, December 19, 2019.

the performance ends abruptly with a final lyric. The tempo and key remains the same throughout Deziderio's brief performance as he sings:

1 *Polanda kyava dda*
Poland goes far back

2 *Ekibuga ekirungi Polanda*
The beautiful city Poland

3 *Ekyalwanyisa abazungu okuttiiŋŋana*
Which caused white men to kill each other

4 *Bw'obaleka balwana, baliwummula*
If you let them fight, they will eventually rest

5 *Ebyali eby'okuteesa bivaamu nnyago*
What seemed to be like peace talks result in shafts

6 *Ggwe ate olaba omukwano gw'abasajja guvaamu nnyago*
You see, even the friendship of men culminates in shafts

7 *Nabo baleke balwane, baliwummula*
Let them fight also, they will eventually tire

Michel Foucault has observed that warfare is not prevented by the rule of law; rather, systemic rules enable the violence that they are supposed to protect against.[3] Thus, colonial systems of thought may be responsible for creating a tendency for civil war, just as they justify the subjugation of peoples. As a rejection of this colonial mindset "Poland" explains that the Europeans fighting in Poland should be left to their sovereign pursuits, knowing that their conflict will eventually pass (lines 4 and 7); "rest" and "tire" imply that the fighters will ultimately resolve their battle. In fact, the wording of the lyrics suggests that such fighting is inevitable and that even comradeship has the chance of dissolving into such animosity (line 6). To borrow Beverley Diamond's framing, the song does not merely mark a historical event but in addition is a testimony.[4] Deziderio sustains a complex phrase toward the end of the song to bring it to an emotional climax. He states, "What seemed to be like peace talks result in shafts" (line 5), where "shafts" means fights. This line and the next one, "You see, even the friendship of men culminates in shafts," demonstrate the eventual yet futile nature of war—that conflict arises, but it is never worthwhile to make a war out of it. Directly after this climax, he repeats the final sentiment—"Let them fight also, they will eventually tire" (line 7)—and the song ends abruptly, leaving the listener to ponder its message.

---

3   Foucault 1977, 151.
4   Diamond 2013, 160.

In the lyrics of "Poland" resides a discourse on the power of neutrality as an option for engaging in conflict. It suggests that conflict is inevitable, a natural part of living that arises on both large and small scales, between friends and enemies alike. Accordingly, one can accept this truth and choose to avoid feeding into the mindlessness that turns conflict into war. Rather than seeing conflict as something to fight or avoid, the song imagines it as a wave of energy that can be managed. When we learn to manage these waves, we avoid inflicting senseless damage.

War and Imperialism

The broad thematic coverage of "Poland" allows interpreters to relate the song to current political contexts. Their comments confirm that its moral lessons lend much clarity to understanding war and imperialism. Overall, they highlight how the song is a wise criticism of injustice and offers a philosophical resolution to this violence. Focusing on the loss that arises in conflict, Peter Kinene explores the negative consequences of enacting violence at individual and cross-national levels. He affirms the notion that acting ruthlessly begets violence, and engaging in such violence might result in a greater loss than what might have occurred with a more mindful consideration. Kinene relates this to materialism:

> People should avoid inciting violence and death over material possessions that are limited to the realm of this earth. Though many toil many hours for those possessions or love them deeply, death eventually and irrevocably separates them. Therefore, killing another human being over such impermanent items makes no sense. People should treasure life above material gains and, whenever possible, avoid the dissolution of friendship or partnership. When either party in a relationship does not feel that the other appreciates him or her equally, they both become resentful and may turn against each other. If it is friends who work alongside one another, they might begin competing and sometimes the tension may erupt into violence. This dynamic exists in many African countries, which may have originally promised to share certain resources or partner up as allies, but soon those promises dissolve when the states become ruthless and attempt to benefit only their people no matter how the process hurts the people of other countries. Once again, though, those countries and their occupants will soon leave the land and other resources over which they might be fighting. People naively believe they are invincible, but "Poland" cautions against pretending to be what one is not.[5]

---

5 Kinene interview, December 16, 2019.

Kinene suggests a way of living that prioritizes amicability and reciprocity over attempting to satisfy depravity with material wealth. Rather than focusing on the exact World War II context of the song, Kinene's commentary draws on its deeper themes to elucidate this philosophical claim.

Jessy Ssendawula amplifies Kinene's thoughts, emphasizing the need to be careful and considerate in one's relationships with others. He extends this notion by suggesting ways that governments can attain amicable relations between each other:

> The song "Poland" praises the beauty of Poland and the initial friendship that existed among the nations associated with it but cautions that the friendliness of men can devolve into fighting or threats of violence. The song shows that when dialogue fails, conflict and war take the lead and as a result people die and lose property. It cautions leaders to be careful in their relations with leaders of other countries because inconsiderate foreign policy may lead to war with the neighbors. It also encourages dialogue as the most effective and peaceful way of resolving conflicts.[6]

Ssendawula argues that the events of World War II came from a failed attempt to communicate, and he accordingly warns against repeating this mistake. Thus, he reimagines conflict as something that depends on how its actors manage dialogue.

Edward Ssebunnya Kironde offers an additional perspective on the idea of the futility of war by seeing it through the eyes of leaders who hold millions of lives in the balance. As we saw in World War II, the carelessness of leaders resulted in many "indirect" war casualties, as happened to Ugandans because they were subject to the British government. Just as there was little care between the powers that began World War II, the colonial leaders failed to attend to the needs of those whom they colonized, a disinterest that, Kironde charges, ignored the physical, social, and cultural well-being of Ugandans:

> Leaders should not involve their countries in war unnecessarily. It is a harsh reality that many engage in war without even knowing why the war started in the first place. Unfortunately, this will continue as long as there are those who take joy in seeing other people's pain and suffering. Such people incite conflict just so they can sit back and watch the world burn in front of them. Again, leaders should not get involved in wars that they have no backing in or do not understand the causes behind. Yet many feel entitled to engage themselves in almost everything, in any dispute no matter how small. Unless they understand the intentions of a conflict, onlookers should in no way involve themselves. People are loath to heed this advice and tend to follow what others are doing without question. This problem is

---

6   Ssendawula interview, December 28, 2019.

compounded by the fact that there, sadly, are many who involve themselves in war while holding on to their own ulterior motives. They fight battles that do not belong to them to push their political agendas through, and in the process, others get caught up in the fray. Furthermore, leaders who do not heed the advice of others, particularly of their own people, partly breed the grounds for war. They may shrug off the advice of younger generations due to youth's inexperience. This is the case in Uganda, where the older leaders who fought during the liberation war constantly discount the ideas of the younger, able-bodied generation. They cannot let go of their power and are not willing to let the younger people begin the process of leading the nation.[7]

These points recall the quality of dehumanization that infests colonial and neoliberal politics. Such colonial ideation continues to reverberate in current African dictatorial administrations, particularly with the way they sacrifice the well-being of the masses for their own sake, treating them as mere resources to be disposed of and exploited. When people regard others as objects, as pieces of value that they can manipulate, it results in ontological forms of violence that proliferate beyond the more situational violence one might observe between and among individuals. When dictators distance themselves so thoroughly from their people, they succumb to illusions about their diplomatic responsibility, that they can no longer recognize its value. This separation begets ignorance, further begetting violence whereby the pretenses of political strategy have obscured the empathy that leaders might actually prefer to rule with. In this sense, decision-making becomes about resource extraction—the vapid, calculated sense of gain and loss, for bodies of power who obsess about their sovereignty that they render themselves insular.

John Magandaazi Kityo discusses "Poland" by reasoning through the struggles between President Museveni and opposition leaders. He emphasizes the relationship between Museveni and one figure, Colonel Dr. Besigye. The two were once allies, but their relationship has gradually descended into a bitter conflict today. Kityo points to this relationship to argue that failing to resolve one's baggage and disagreements will result in greater resentment:

> Dr. Besigye and President Museveni, though now in total opposition, used to work together in a united front. Those who do not know would never guess that they used to have an amicable relationship, given the intensity with which they attack one another today. Besigye used to be Museveni's physician, and though many wonder what drove a doctor and a patient to engage one another with such animosity, they realize that the question is a

---

7   Kironde interview, December 19, 2019.

moot point. Knowing each other closely previously has made their rivalry more bitter, to a point where it is futile to implore them to unite. People who are outside the two politicians' immediate circles might have no effect on helping them to reconcile. The responsibility lies with them alone to try and repair the situation, to recognize that enough is enough. Meanwhile, everyone else must stand back and watch. As the lyric of "Poland" says, "Let them fight also, they will eventually tire."[8]

Using the relationship between Museveni and Besigye to make a more encompassing point about relationships, Kityo interprets the meaning of "Poland" as something of a theatrical performance of the two protagonists, as if they are characters on a stage dramatizing their conflict. Seen this way, the song takes on a new quality, becoming intertwined with the people (the audience) who are impacted by these theatrics.

Conclusion

"Polanda" explores the intersection of global and local history, using Poland's WWII experience as a lens for examining and comparing different power structures. By establishing conceptual bridges between European imperial domination and Ugandan experiences of tyranny, the song creates cross-cultural dialogue through lyrical narrative. Deziderio uses it as a political analysis tool, employing a distant European conflict to explore sensitive local themes of oppression and resistance in Uganda. By focusing on Poland—geographically and culturally removed from Uganda—"Poland" creates intellectual space to consider universal aspects of power abuse without directly criticizing specific local authorities.

At first glance, "Poland" appears to discuss the inevitability of conflict and the importance of avoiding unnecessary interventions into other people's conflicts. Its interpreters analyze it to describe the conflict between twenty-first-century politicians as they vie for power and make power grabs, commenting on how some leaders are unwilling to cede power to the younger generations or to more qualified people. Ultimately, this points to a discussion on the importance of maintaining dialogue in order to keep conflicts from turning violent.

The composer of "Poland" created it not as a linear and coherent description of the war itself but as a creative reimagining that seeks to elicit new thoughts in the minds of the listeners. Just as the song moved its historical audiences to conceive of it in their own context, it succeeds in encouraging us to continue doing so today.

---

8   Kityo interview, December 14, 2019.

21
"The Battle of Nsinsi"

Civil War

In this chapter we explore the theme of civil war by looking at two versions of the song "The Battle of Nsinsi" ("Olutalo olw'e Nsinsi"): a longer version, performed by Ssaalongo Ssennoga Majwala (b. 1953), and a shorter version, performed by Albert Ssempeke Bisaso (b. 1979). The song tells the story of a conflict between the Kingdoms of Buganda and Bunyoro during the reign of King Jjunju (r. ca. 1780–1797) and gives fresh insights into the tragedy of loss. Bisaso, whose account of the civil war in question simultaneously complements and digresses from subsequent accounts, said the following after performing his version of "The Battle of Nsinsi":

> In precolonial Buganda, the kingdom had many strong young men, with tough muscles, who would serve as warriors. The king's officials mobilized many of them across various villages to fight in the war that the song references. The war was between Buganda and Bunyoro, two kingdoms that often engaged in battles with their surrounding kingdoms. During some of these wars, participants looted property and captured people. Most of the young men who participated in the dreadful war died, including the soldiers of Kabalega (the official title of the king of Bunyoro), which explains the line *Amafumu ag'e Nsinsi gatta Abaleega* (The spears used during the Battle of Nsinsi claimed the lives of Kabalega's men).[1]

A supplementary account of the history of "The Battle of Nsinsi" came from the interpreter Edward Ssebunnya Kironde, who identified one of the individuals who died during the conflict and the subsequent story of his status following his death and through the ages:

> Kibuuka was a great fighter. In fact, during his time he was the commander in chief of the Kiganda army fighting against the Kingdom of Bunyoro and the Kabalega. When he died, the Baganda preserved his jaw and his spear,

---

1   Bisaso interview, September 14, 2003.

both of which are cultural artifacts on display in the Uganda Museum. Today, many people regard him as a deity (*lubaale*), summoning him to intervene in many things with hopes that the strength that served him during his life as a warrior will be of use to them as well.[2]

Another interpreter, Jessy Ssendawula, elaborated on this history:

> The song records the incident of a disastrous battle from the history of Buganda. By the end of the battle, the death rates were extreme, especially among the Banyoro (people from the Kingdom of Bunyoro). Almost everyone who witnessed it died in the process, hence the lyric, *Abaalulabako baafa* (Those who witnessed it died). The death rates were so high because warriors used rudimentary but effective spears at the time, which were particularly deadly and laid waste to thousands. The warriors used such weapons as an answer to the societal call to redress the afflictions they were facing. The actions of the warriors expressed their willingness to sacrifice their lives to protect the interests of their community.[3]

Joseph Kyagambiddwa offers a detailed historical context on the conflict that "The Battle of Nsinsi" references, noting that King Jjunju (r. ca. 1780–1797) was unmatched in his warlike nature among all previous kings of Buganda and second only to Kintu in bravery. Driven partly by a desire to reunify the fragmented kingdom and partly by a natural affinity for combat, he transformed warfare into the nation's primary occupation, viewing peacetime as mere idleness. His greatest accomplishment came when he conquered the wealthy county of Buddu from Bunyoro—a territory his predecessors had repeatedly failed to annex through both military campaigns and diplomatic negotiations. The only battle Jjunju ever lost was one he did not initiate; his brother, Prince Ssemakookiro, staged a rebellion and marched against him with an army of loyal followers. The decisive confrontation occurred at Nsinsi, where after brutal fighting the king's forces were defeated, Jjunju himself was killed, and his victorious brother ascended to the throne of Buganda, ruling from approximately 1797 to 1814. In the aftermath of this civil war, musicians composed "The Battle of Nsinsi" to preserve the memory of this bloody conflict for future generations—a battle so fierce that some of the stubbornly defiant vanquished soldiers became wanderers who eventually emerged as a new tribe known as the Abakunta people.[4]

These accounts offer diverse insights into the dynamics as well as immediate and lasting effects of the civil war that "The Battle of Nsinsi" commemorates. For example, Ssendawula's discussion articulates the frame

---

[2] Kironde interview, December 18, 2019.
[3] Ssendawula personal communication, April 8, 2020.
[4] Kyagambiddwa 1955, 121.

of mind that drives the warriors of Buganda to fight and ultimately to die in Nsinsi. Of course, none of these people desire death, but in recognizing their social duty as warriors, they lay down their lives. In considering themselves extensions of their communities, the warriors sacrifice themselves for the good of the whole. Rather than being obsessed with maintaining themselves, they are willing to give that up for the sake of those they care about. This complex imbues civil war with new meanings of dedication and selflessness. Rather than lamenting the warriors' deaths, Ssendawula's comments recognize and contemplate the willpower that precedes those deaths, thus illustrating the dedication with which the people of Buganda serve their kingdom. This point of view is especially relevant to national politicians, as we frequently encounter in them the opposite approach to struggle—self-centered avoidance. The trend implies that contemporary office holders might benefit from beginning to fulfill the duties of the office, as the warriors mentioned in "The Battle of Nsinsi" do.

In addition, Kironde's explanation of the enduring presence of Kibuuka, the Baganda's god of war, shows that violent conflict is still "alive" in the sense that it remains in the lore of the people. Just as living figures change with their environment, so does the perception of this battle. It melds to fit the demands and desires of those who engage with it. Kibuuka is a prime example, for recognizing him as a spirit represents the literal life that he carries as an idea persisting through generations. An idea, although ephemeral, is nonetheless real, as it affects the world around it, and that world affects it in return. This philosophy reshapes our understanding of what it means to die. It shows us that the battle at Nsinsi still affects us today, through pieces and scraps of remembrance that reverberate throughout time, as we see in "The Battle of Nsinsi." The warriors themselves live on, too, as spirits and conceptions that inform how we experience and encounter the world.

In Majwala's and Bisaso's performances of "The Battle of Nsinsi," both musicians accompany their singing with the bow harp (*ennanga*), but each musician uses unique aspects of his creative power to express the themes of the song's lyrics. The bow harp produces a soft, buzzy timbre, and its instrumental part features two interlocking melodies that support the performer's vocal melody. These three melodies are inextricable and complementary. Both Majwala and Bisaso commence their performances with brief instrumental passages that gradually speed up before they sing wistfully. Both renditions also feature bouncy rhythms in triple meter, with vocal melodies trickling sparsely over the instrumentals. Majwala conveys the lyrical content with a unique style of vocal phrasing. He begins each phrase on a higher note and, after a brief sustain, descends into a lower range before ending completely. In other instances, a select few phrases ascend again. This and other features evoke different emotions associated with war and conflict, which Majwala and Bisaso express through an intimate and spontaneous fashion, including chant-like singing that personalizes the delivery of the text. Majwala's lyrics appear below:

1 *Olutalo olw'e Nsinsi lwatta Abaleega*
The Battle of Nsinsi claimed lives of Kabalega's men

2 *Olutalo olw'e Nsinsi lwatta abantu*
The Battle of Nsinsi claimed lives of people

3 *Sitwalulaba, twali bato*
We did not witness it, we were young

4 *Sitwalulaba, twali bato, twali wala nnyo*
We did not witness it, we were young, we were very far away

5 *Olutalo olw'e Nsinsi*
The Battle of Nsinsi

6 *Abaalulabako baafa*
Those who witnessed it died

7 *Abaalulabako baafa, olw'e Nsinsi*
Those who witnessed it died, the Battle of Nsinsi

8 *Abaalulabako jjuuzi, olw'e Nsinsi, lwatta Abaleega*
Those who witnessed it recently, the Battle of Nsinsi, it claimed the lives of Kabalega's men

9 *Amafumu ag'e Nsinsi gatta abantu*
The spears used during the Battle of Nsinsi killed people

10 *Sandizze wa Nsanso, ggwe nno ondeese*
I would not have come to Nsanso, it is you who has lured me here

11 *Sandizze wa Nsanso, ye nno [y']andeese*
I would not have come to Nsanso, he has lured me here

12 *Azze, sandizze wa Nsanso, ye nno [y']andeese*
He has come, I would not have come to Nsanso, he has lured me here

Majwala's version reveals that the singer was too young to participate in the battle (lines 3–4) and, as a result, did not share the gruesome fate that the conflict meant for those who fought there. At the end of the song, the singer expresses a reluctance to go with a colleague named Nsanso (lines 10–12), suggesting his distaste for war and his preference to avoid going into conflict if possible. The singer indirectly criticizes political decision-making that lusts for conflict more than it seeks consensus. Using Nsinsi as an example, he emphasizes that the main thing that comes from violent conflict is loss. Rather than describing the political advantage that some may have achieved from the battle, he illustrates that regardless of the outcome, people died (lines 6–7). In the later section of the song, when the singer describes his youth at the time of the battle (lines 3–4), he advocates for learning from past mistakes. Having survived this violence, he seeks to ensure that people do not repeat history's mistakes.

Bisaso's performance of "The Battle of Nsinsi" is much briefer—just two lines. His vocals sound mellow and reserved, carrying a mournful weight that reflects the negative impacts of war:

1 *Olutalo olw'e Nsinsi lwatta abantu*
The Battle of Nsinsi claimed lives of people

2 *Amafumu ag'e Nsinsi gatta Abaleega*
The spears of Nsinsi claimed lives of Kabalega's men

These two lines, this simple assertion, emphasize the certainty of mortality in war, something that can be avoided by more sensible and compassionate political decision-making.

Civil War

Interpreters look at "The Battle of Nsinsi" to revive and rework its ideas about civil war, discerning their hope for the future and applying thoughts to national politics in Uganda. Relating the song's lyrical content to today's conflicts, Jessy Ssendawula notes the importance of diplomatic skills in avoiding political violence. Although he recognizes justifiable occasions for conflict, he emphasizes that war, which is the proliferation of conflict, ultimately leads to negative outcomes for many, and thus it is never worth it. Ssendawula does not outright condemn conflict as a political action, however, stating:

> Leaders should focus on avoiding wars, encouraging dialogue, and only entering a conflict when there is no other alternative. This is necessary because war is a double-edged sword; it leads to the destruction of life and property on both sides. An example of this more diplomatic style of leadership is how the Uganda government tried numerous times to engage in talks rather than battle to end the conflict in northern Uganda with the Lord's Resistance Army rebel group. This is not to say that war is useless. Sometimes it is necessary to engage in violence or take drastic measures to restore peace within a community. Everything good requires some sacrifice, and in cases such as those, leaders need to be prepared to accept the bloodshed and loss of life that come with their decisions.[5]

---

5   Ssendawula personal communication, April 8, 2020.

These perspectives reposition the topic and purpose of "The Battle of Nsinsi," reflecting on a new set of circumstances. By projecting the song's message onto the decisions of contemporary politicians, we might consider the problems and failures of the past as wisdom to face present challenges.

Ssendawula also explains the way common people suffer from war's violence. Since the people are subject to the whims of their leaders, he suggests that leaders should exercise great empathy and consideration for their subjects, rather than treating them as disposable. He specifically points to the king of Bunyoro: by engaging in the battle at Nsinsi, he did not conceive of himself as an extension of his people. Instead, he operated as some current elected leaders supposedly do, separating himself from the profound sense of grief that the masses feel during and after violent times. As Ssendawula stresses,

> When leaders engage in war, it is not them but the soldiers and common people who suffer defeat and loss of life. Using the example of the story that "The Battle of Nsinsi" is based on, Omukama Kabalega, king of Bunyoro at that time, directed the war from the comfort of his royal court, letting his soldiers die on the battlefield while he remained in safety. As the saying goes, where two elephants fight, it is the grass that suffers.[6]

Ssendawula implies here that an unfair advantage of being in a position of leadership is that one can remove oneself from the tactical and emotional suffering of war. Whereas a politician might argue that it is a unique struggle to balance interests and seek peace in power relations between peoples and nations, such deliberations seem like a frivolous game where human lives become disposable for the sake of winning. In these ways, "The Battle of Nsinsi" becomes a subtle criticism of the blinding effect that power has on a leader's ability to see the value of human life.

In his analysis of "The Battle of Nsinsi," Jimmy Ssenfuka Kibirige extends Ssendawula's ideas by providing an example of how people in Uganda currently suffer from the decisions that leaders make. In particular, he criticizes the vapid grabs for political power that leaders might make. Kibirige suggests that in election cycles, self-interested ambition often precedes the interests of those whom one must lead and support:

> Leaders today attain positions not knowing what tomorrow is going to be like. Granted, they have their inner intentions, but regardless, those intentions rarely result in their desired outcomes. The president recently published his new cabinet list, which followed a reshuffle of many good candidates whom he robbed of their positions. Also, an *Opera News* (a Uganda news site) article I read referenced three members of parliament

---

6   Ibid.

who had raised 300 million shillings in an effort to boost their campaigns for cabinet positions, only for them to lose the races. Such behavior is pointless. Those politicians were already high up in the government, but still they wanted more. They should have been satisfied with their positions and not robbed the people of money that they could have used to actually solve their problems rather than wasting it on fruitless campaigns. In the guise of helping the public, many politicians actually take from them. Leaders ought to turn a new leaf and start putting the people first. It is the only way to truly achieve a model society.[7]

Kibirige's words indicate that pursuing self-interested politics leads to a great deal of pain that could have been avoided.

Ssendawula concludes his interpretation by looking at the lessons from the song that he believes are most relevant for current leaders and civilians. Meditating on selflessness and bravery, he argues that leaders must not regard their country as a separate and exploitable resource but as an extension of their own livelihood. He draws parallels between the dedicated leaders and the warriors in "The Battle of Nsinsi," as both parties aim to enlighten and enrich the communities that shape their world. In this sense, Ssendawula elaborates, they are willing to sacrifice their lives and their pay, among other things, for the sake of their country, which is a responsibility that they do not take lightly:

For both leaders and regular members of society, this involves breaking from the status quo to do what they believe to be best for society. Leaders should take a lesson from the soldiers that "The Battle of Nsinsi" describes and dedicate their lives to the benefit of their society. Despite the odds the soldiers faced, they knew they needed to fight against the problems that were plaguing their community. According to the account of the battle, even King Jjunju died in the fight for his people. Leaders must fully dedicate themselves to curbing the problems that their societies face. Indeed, some leaders have taken up this cause, like President Uhuru Kenyatta, who gave up 80 percent of his monthly salary to give more funds to the ongoing fight against the coronavirus in Kenya, or like President Paul Kagame of Rwanda, who asked all public servants to forgo their salaries to buy food for those who are unemployed during the lockdown that the pandemic caused. Their dedication and self-sacrifice are true patriotism.

The other lesson that listeners can glean from "The Battle of Nsinsi" is about bravery and courage. None of the soldiers at the battle in question deserted, even though they valued their lives and would have preferred not to fight. Modern individuals should recognize and try to emulate the courage of these fighters in facing the hardest of challenges for the

---

7   Kibirige interview, December 18, 2019.

good of their community. Again, some people have taken this message to heart, with a few opposition leaders in Uganda having disobeyed President Museveni's order to not donate food items to the needy during the coronavirus pandemic. They risk imprisonment and trial but continue to contribute to the national task force to help fight the virus.[8]

Ssendawula's closing remarks nourish "The Battle of Nsinsi" with fresh meaning that directs our perspective toward the bravery and determination that the warriors who sacrificed themselves for the sake of the kingdom expressed. In this way, the song comes to articulate a particular loyalty to the kingdom that even the threat of death cannot challenge.

Conclusion

"The Battle of Nsinsi" depicts a historical conflict between the Kingdoms of Bunyoro and Buganda and the violence and death that resulted from it. The composition functions as a historical record preserved in multiple versions, with each rendition offering different dimensions of the same inter-kingdom conflict. Through Majwala's extended rendering and Bisaso's condensed performance, the song demonstrates how a single historical narrative can be transmitted with varying emphasis across generations.

On further examination we come to understand how this story behind "The Battle of Nsinsi" evokes themes in twenty-first-century Ugandan politics. The interpretations presented in this chapter underscore many of the topics that research collaborators engage with in their contributions, such as violence, death, lament, deterioration, tragedy, suffering, and loss, among others. The contextual information that Majwala, Bisaso, and a handful of interpreters provide, as well as the interpreters' analyses, connect the song to the obstacles and conflicts of the current era. One interpreter frames the song in terms of the model behavior that the warriors of Nsinsi demonstrate, suggesting that one should expect such conduct from contemporary politicians. Another interpreter frames it through the losses that frequently arise from unnecessary conflict, highlighting the notion that current leaders should avoid conflict whenever possible. These topics relate explicitly to contemporary political landscapes where leaders are responsible for carrying out decisions about whether to engage in violent conflict. Through interpreters' various analyses, we come to see how the value of "The Battle of Nsinsi" evolves into multiple layers of meaning.

---

8   Ssendawula personal communication, April 8, 2020.

22

"Let Me Plod with a Stick Close to Kibuuka"

Disagreement and Invocation

"Let Me Plod with a Stick Close to Kibuuka" ("Ka Nsimbe Omuggo awali Kibuuka") is about the troubles that arise in marriage, for which the song's protagonist turns to spiritual powers for help. Visceral and metaphysical dimensions of conflict and loss are manifested in this song. Albert Muwanga Ssempeke (ca. 1930–2006), the performer of the lyrics analyzed in this chapter, expands our understanding of the song by recounting this background story:

> There was once a man who lived with his wife. However, his wife decided to divorce him; she left his homestead, and returned to her childhood home. The ex-husband followed her and tried to reconcile with her so that she would return to him, but she refused. He insisted that eventually she would return because of their child. The man went back and forth between his homestead and the ex-wife's childhood home several times, each time asking the woman to return, but each time he got the same response. He even took the matter to his mother-in-law, reporting to her that her daughter had vowed not to return home. At one point he asked to have his child, but the ex-wife would not agree to give the child to him. The man was never able to move the mother-in-law, who said she never wished to get involved in their matters. The man became angry and said that he would leave, but he would walk slowly with a stick close to Kibuuka, the god of war in Buganda, to pray to him. He assured the ex-wife that she would eventually return their child to him. The ex-wife had been making the divorce unnecessarily difficult for him by not letting him have custody of their child. The man, feeling cheated, turned to supernatural power. When he returned home, he took out a stick and began plodding along, singing, *Ka nsimbe omuggo awali Kibuuka* (Let me plod with a stick close

to Kibuuka). He put matters into the hands of Kibuuka, whom many believe to have great power, hoping that he would soften the ex-wife's heart so that their child could return to the man's home. He prayed for this and hoped that with luck and time, her mind would change.[1]

Per Ssempeke's account, in "Let Me Plod with a Stick Close to Kibuuka" we encounter a confluence of kinship, spirituality, and sociality. The first idea the singer examines is the kinship ties of the family. The main source of conflict is the contentious relationship between husband and wife, but the mother-in-law also plays a crucial role, serving as a mediator between the disagreeing parents. Mediation is beneficial in any mutual relationship, and mediation by a third party is also a foundational principle of the Kiganda kinship system. Beyond lamenting this conflict, the singer laments the loss of his child. Finally, the evocation of Kibuuka reflects the importance of spirituality when mediating conflict. The singer calls on Kibuuka to assist him, hoping that the deity's power will sway things in his favor. However, Kibuuka does not exert power in an obvious way, through brute force and coercion. Instead, the performer seeks out Kibuuka to convince his mother-in-law to change her mind and return his child to him of her own accord. Thus, the song's spiritual invocation avoids spectacular miracles and explosive movements, instead asking for slight and subtle shifts that, in this case, have a greater effect.

Some Baganda perform "Let Me Plod with a Stick Close to Kibuuka" in ritual contexts that involve summoning different kinds of spirits. Peter Hoesing has shown how, through such contexts, one may better understand the pantheon of Kiganda spirits and epistemological structures.[2] These spirits may include territorial spirits, working spirits, and the spirits of ancestors.[3] John Janzen shows that when they are called upon during spirit mediumship (*okusamira*), they vary in their specificity and function as well as their temperament.[4] David L. Schoenbrun further suggests that this practice is part of a broader set of healing practices called *ŋgòmà*, which are used to understand how physical maladies relate to various supernatural forces. Affected persons come together in healing ceremonies that rely heavily on ritual music, engaging in conversation with healers and supporters through singing, drumming, and dancing.[5] In this way, musical performance serves as a tool for social and spiritual redress. "Let Me Plod with a Stick Close to

---

1 Ssempeke interview, July 11, 2005.
2 Hoesing 2019, 97.
3 Ibid.
4 Janzen 1992, 94–95.
5 Schoenbrun 2006, 1419–1420.

Kibuuka" evokes the feeling of these practices, as it invokes a supernatural being to facilitate social redress.

In Ssempeke's performance of "Let Me Plod with a Stick Close to Kibuuka," which he shared after a presentation of its instrumental version on the notched flute (*endere*), he sings variations of the same melody, unaccompanied by instrumentation. After his voice ascends and descends through the melody, he ends each phrase on the root note, establishing the song's key. Ssempeke intersperses his performance with quick slides and brief inflections. His timid and forlorn singing evokes the feeling of the contentious relationship between the couple in question. He also brings out the song's spiritual aspects by repeating several lyrics, minimizing development of melodic material, and delivering the lyrics in an introspective, meditative fashion. His performance ebbs and flows with tranquility, suggesting associations with solace and faith. Overall, Ssempeke's melodic and lyrical delivery captures the song's focus on determination. He sings,

1 *Ka nsimbe omuggo awali Kibuuka*
Let me plod with a stick close to Kibuuka

2 *Ka nsimbe omuggo, baganda bange*
Let me plod with a stick, my brethren

3 *Ka nsimbe omuggo awali Kibuuka*
Let me plod with a stick close to Kibuuka

4 *Ka ŋŋende, nnadda, nnyazaala wange*
Let me leave, I shall be back, my mother-in-law

5 *Omwana owange mulimuleeta*
You will return my child in the future

6 *Emirembe n'ennaku sirina googera*
For generations and days, I lack strength to speak

7 *Omwana owange mulimuleeta, ee*
You will bring my child in the future, eh

8 *Ka nsimbe omuggo, nnyazaala wange, oo wa?*
Let me plod with a stick, my mother-in-law, oh where?

9 *Ka nsimbe omuggo awali Kibuuka, oo!*
Let me plod with a stick close to Kibuuka, oh!

10 *Ka ŋŋende ewaffe, nnyazaala wange*
Let me go to my homeland, my mother-in-law

11 *Ekikutte obudde kiributa edda*
What seems to be holding, time will eventually release it

Throughout the lyrics of "Let Me Plod with a Stick Close to Kibuuka," the singer invokes the spirit Kibuuka, wielding the name as a threat or warning to his mother-in-law. The husband wishes she would return his child and warns her that she must do so in time (lines 5, 7, and 11). Although the singer never addresses Kibuuka directly, instead appearing to speak to the mother-in-law, the line "Let me plod with a stick close to Kibuuka" implies that he is entreating Kibuuka to assist in his objective, to overrule the decision of the mother-in-law in the process. Interestingly, there is no mention of force or coercion in the lyrics. The singer does not describe Kibuuka as taking the child and giving it to him. Instead, he expects the mother-in-law to return the child herself, painting Kibuuka as an indirect and subtle actor, one who produces results without directly participating in the process. Overall, "Let Me Plod with a Stick Close to Kibuuka" signifies a failed instance of reciprocity: neither side of the relationship confronts their disagreements to seek a resolution. Instead, the ex-wife decides to let it taper off. Furthermore, although the mother-in-law refuses to help the son-in-law and decides not to take a position on the issues between him and her daughter, her passivity still impacts the couple's relationship. Her lack of action is still an action, a force, intersecting in the relationship from a third stream. This behavior imbues "Let Me Plod with a Stick Close to Kibuuka" with fresh meaning as a demonstration of how marriage—typically represented as a bond between two people—becomes striated by relationships that supposedly exist outside of the marital arrangement. Thus, we cannot reduce interchangeability to instances of exchange that are immediately visible, but we must recognize that relationships take on invisible, subtextual forms. Invoking Kibuuka affirms this idea again, as it begets another type of subliminal reciprocity in the relationship. Kibuuka's intervention stands parallel to the mother-in-law's own neutrality, as both appear to act by their nonaction and move with stillness.

Disagreement and Spiritual Invocation

Interpreters engage with "Let Me Plod with a Stick Close to Kibuuka" through the themes of disagreement and spiritual invocation, shaping the song's meanings into insights on trade, politics, and other subjects. Harriet Kisuule draws connections between the ex-husband in the song and two modern Ugandan politicians, Bobi Wine and Colonel Dr. Kiiza Besigye, who have been attempting to win an uphill effort against the recurring incumbent president, Yoweri Kaguta Museveni. Kisuule underscores the husband's persistence in getting his son back, presenting the song as a model for how one might respond to any obstacles that lie in the path of realizing one's ambitions. She then connects this point to how national political leaders, like President Museveni, present as formidable incumbents to opposing leaders, who must remain steadfast if they want to win:

> Plodding or pressing on with a stick demonstrates the determination to hold fast to something. The singer presents the idea that holding fast to what one values is the way to achieve success and victory. This determination is the same force that has driven Besigye, one of the political opponents of President Museveni. The police have sprayed him with tear gas and attacked him, but he has still continued. He has been persistent even though he has not become president. He has recognized that he may never come to power, but he has said that his main agenda is to get Museveni out of office. He is willing to fight for what he desires. The same is true of Bobi Wine. During the times that the police surrounded his house to prevent him from leaving it to campaign, sometimes he was already in the city center, campaigning regardless. He demonstrated his determination to fight for his cause. The Baganda people should try to emulate such determination, to listen and persist on the issues that are important to them. The more vocal they are, the easier it will be for their leaders to determine what they should focus and act on.[6]

Kisuule suggests that the primary goal of President Museveni's opponents is to dissolve the relationship that he has allegedly locked his people into and to form a new one. His opponents, by attempting to push him out of power and thus allowing the possibilities for a new leader to emerge, display an unrelenting drive to overcome obstacles and form new connections whenever necessary. Such a willingness to establish fresh relations allows nations and people to succeed.

Continuing with the idea of struggle and failure, Edward Ssebunnya Kironde addresses the frequent failures of contemporary politics in his interpretation, recognizing that failure is a crucial aspect of life. Kironde explains that no matter how hard one works, failure can always happen. Drawing from the husband's call to Kibuuka, he explains that in times of failure, some may turn to spiritual forces in a final attempt to achieve what they desire:

> People try to seek out those they believe can help them, but the current system turns them down, sometimes making it clear that there are no other avenues to pursue. They often believe they have done their best, but they still receive no good news from their efforts. They might even drop to their knees to pray to God, having given up completely. In their desperation, they put their fate in His hands, hoping for some divine intervention. To some, it may appear that the only thing that could change their fortune

---

6 Kisuule interview, December 21, 2019.

is a miracle. This is the case in contemporary Uganda, where people are unsure whether leadership will change hands soon. The situation is tense, and many believe that only God can save the people. There is bitterness on both sides, the government and the opposition, and nobody has any idea how to fix the problems at hand.

Before President Museveni first came to power, no one could have predicted that he would have been able to oust the Obote regime. But he succeeded in using bush warfare tactics to depose Obote from power, thus surprising many. Similarly, today no one has any idea who will oust Museveni from the presidency. To many, even a prominent opposition figure like Bobi Wine is unlikely to stand a chance because when the elections come, Museveni is sure to use the army to intimidate voters at the polls. He is clearly of the mindset that he came to power by the gun and therefore cannot leave it by the ballot. Democracy in Uganda suffers because of this. However, someday Museveni will leave office.

Although it seems that the current political state will not end anytime soon, there is hope among opposition leaders. Thus, Bobi Wine has composed and performed songs such as "It's the Right Amount of Sugar" ("Kassukaali Ke Ko") and "We Shall Wear a Crown" ("Tuliyambala Engule"). Yet, it seems like the only crown the Baganda might be wearing by the end of the upcoming January (2021) elections is the same one that has been in place for the past several decades. The state of things is escalating, and many hope that it does not reach the extent reached in Libya. Gaddafi's dictatorial regime killed those who preached against him and his ideologies, and the people of Libya never realized that his plan was to be a lifetime president until it was too late. It took "a Kibuuka" to uproot him. With the way things are going in Uganda, they too may need a figure like Kibuuka to perform a miracle.[7]

To Kironde, "Let Me Plod with a Stick Close to Kibuuka" acknowledges life's unpredictability. Without recognizing this, one could easily fall back into the static idealism that is so prevalent today. One who cannot cope with the unexpected and will only view the world through a calculated and orderly framework that does not account for human irregularity. Unpredictability can have both negative and positive impacts, so it might be helpful to see all the ways it might manifest. In "Let Me Plod with a Stick Close to Kibuuka," the ex-husband bases his actions on his acceptance of life's unknowns. His call to Kibuuka is not a direct summons to a deity but a plea to the unknown that hopes for a phenomenal shift. In this way, the ex-husband is casting himself on fate, calling on the Kibuuka spirit fully aware that the spirit might not respond.

---

7   Kironde interview, December 19, 2019.

Transitioning from national politics, Steven Mukasa Kabugo points out that "Let Me Plod with a Stick Close to Kibuuka" focuses on a different kind of power dynamic. The ex-wife stalwartly refuses to return home, which leaves her ex-husband speechless: "Let me leave, I shall be back, my mother-in-law" (line 4); "You will return my child in the future" (line 5); "For generations and days, I lack strength to speak" (line 6). Focusing on mediation, Kabugo speaks to how investing too heavily in self-interest can muddle a relationship. As a result, one must not only subscribe to mutuality but tactically engage in it, as relations can often deteriorate into disregard and loathing if mismanaged. In this sense, "Let Me Plod with a Stick Close to Kibuuka" suggests that the ex-husband was not prepared to respond to conflict because he had forgotten to stay connected to his ex-wife's interests. Shocked when his fantasy of perfection failed, he was unable to think of what to do and resorted to calling on Kibuuka:

> The man is unable to properly express his emotions or come up with a convincing argument to win back his ex-wife. This challenge is a reminder that words and rhetoric have significance for contemporary Uganda, say when it comes to lending money. Transparency is the best practice when people are interacting with those from whom they have borrowed or to whom they have lent money. Lenders must be clear and firm. If a lender is trying to collect a loan of five million Ugandan shillings from a borrower, for instance, that borrower might pay the lender an installment of two million. After that, he might get cold feet and start lying about the repayment of the balance. If the lender is not careful, the borrower could even accuse the lender of extortion or another crime to get the person imprisoned. In other words, the borrower may plot against the lender, trying to dupe him out of his money. For this reason, the lender needs to approach the issue with great tact.
>
> There are several proverbs that address the game of cat and mouse between debtor and lender mentioned earlier. They include *Ensigalira; ebanjibwa mugezi* (The outstanding balance of a debt is collected by a shrewd person); *Ekiyita waggulu, otegera wansi; empungu terya bire* (Whatever flies in the sky, you trap it on the ground; the eagle does not eat, live in, the clouds); and *Ky'owola otudde; okibanja oyimiridde* (Whatever you lend out while seated, you demand it while you are standing).
>
> The first proverb reminds us that finances and agreements often test people who believe that they are clever, and that one should demand repayment wisely to avoid the borrower's taking advantage of one.
>
> The second proverb specifically advises people to act calmly in the face of obstinance when seeking redress for their payment. The person they loaned to may be shouting to the skies, vowing not to repay their money. But if they are clever, they will quietly seek the redress of the law and serve a subpoena against the offending party. They would approach at ground

level to address the one who was swelling in the sky and, in doing so, reduce their pride and lofty airs.

The third proverb expresses the outcome of what happens when frustrations arise from not receiving payment, particularly when parties made the initial loan agreement informally. One may lend someone a sum of money, expecting it back within a certain time, and trust the borrower's word that she will repay it. However, the time for repayment might come and pass, causing the lender to remind the borrower of the agreement. Then, because of the absence of a written record of the transaction, the borrower may try to claim that it never happened or that the amount she owes is less than what the lender is demanding. The frustration of this predicament might cause the lender to lose his temper, and as a result he might demand harshly what he once gave away calmly.[8]

The first proverb that Kabugo shares in this analysis connects the ex-husband's story to the dynamic between lenders and borrowers. These parallels between the proverb and "Let Me Plod with a Stick Close to Kibuuka" demonstrate the importance of keeping fingers on the pulse of one's relationships. One must be clever, thus cognizant, with one's decisions to avoid escalating an already tenuous circumstance. To this point, the ex-husband takes time to call on Kibuuka, wishing for some indirect help to ease the tensions between him and his ex-wife. Rather than doing something rash such as calling the police or attempting to take his son back by force, the ex-husband steps back and takes the time to contemplate the events and request assistance.

The second proverb further frames "Let Me Plod with a Stick Close to Kibuuka" through a more general idea of conflict. Using images of sky and ground, man and eagle, the proverb shows us the importance of staying "grounded" to overcome precarious situations. It speaks to the importance of acting thoughtfully when faced with disagreement rather than succumbing to blustering and anger. In this sense, the ex-husband becomes the one who must begin mediating his relationship with his ex-wife. After getting no solution from his mother-in-law, he turns to Kibuuka in hopes of resolving the situation. Here, we have two ways to interpret this situation: one person could argue that the ex-husband is unprepared, as his initial course of action fails; another might argue that his appeal to Kibuuka represents some degree of mindfulness as he bides his time, allowing himself and his ex-wife some space to reflect and clarify where the points of tension lie in their disagreement.

The third proverb reimagines the meaning of "Let Me Plod with a Stick Close to Kibuuka" by showing what might happen when one fails to heed the

---

8 Kabugo interview, December 19, 2019.

advice of the previous two wisdoms. When the relationship between a lender and borrower (or a giver and taker) begins to break down, this may force the lender to demand his money rashly, dropping the level-headedness that he might have previously retained. In the heat of these hot emotions, one ought to work through one's scenario more cautiously. Rather than simply trusting someone blindly, one should consider how much the borrower needs the money and how trustworthy he or she is. In "Let Me Plod with a Stick Close to Kibuuka," the mother-in-law presents this precise dynamic. Rather than blindly agreeing with her daughter's ex-husband and encouraging the daughter to return to him, she decides to step back and see how things play out. By encouraging her daughter's ex-husband to take his time, she enables the actors in this distraught relationship to focus on reconnecting their commitments to each other rather than seeking retribution or forcing an outcome.

Jimmy Ssenfuka Kibirige relates the song's portrait of a marital relationship to political relationships as well, such as those between a leader and his country. He interprets "Let Me Plod with a Stick Close to Kibuuka" by connecting the stress of the romantic relationship it conveys to the stress of political ones. His view diverges from those of other commentators in that he sees the ex-husband's perseverance as a rigid and unyielding stance against change. Kibirige also argues that the ex-wife's obstinance means that the ex-husband's hapless efforts are more injurious than beneficial. Kibirige is making an argument about fluidity and flexibility:

> When a relationship falls through, it is best to maintain one's dignity and move on. If one's wife has left one, one should let her be and go search for a new partner. But as the song shows, the ex-husband was unwilling to let his ex-wife go. He plodded with a stick so many times, making trips back and forth to his ex-wife's childhood home to woo her back into his life. He put time and effort into a fruitless situation. We should all learn from his hardships and learn to let things go once it becomes apparent that they cannot be resolved. Current leaders should learn the same lesson. No one is permanently planted into leadership. And yet, they do everything in their power to make it so, even invoking deities to come and intervene on their behalf. Indeed, over the course of history it has become common for some leaders to keep diviners on retainer so that they can consult and harness the power of spirits. Some have consulted pastors about maintaining their positions in society. They should learn to let go when things have failed, when their time has ended, and give other people a chance to serve in their positions. They should not be like the ex-husband the song mentions, pressing on with his walking sticks or pleading for another chance. Instead, they should move on and try their hand at something else. They should use their talents to find success in the changing world. They should not remain

rigid and unyielding to change, as it will only serve to hurt and fatigue them further.⁹

The foregoing analysis confirms that destruction and decay are a crucial part of existence and that one must accept unpleasant change when it comes. This point contrasts with the commentaries on perseverance that others have provided regarding President Museveni's opposition. This diverging perspective gives the song greater nuance in terms of our understanding of both positions. On the one hand, this nuance allows us to recognize the importance of perseverance. On the other hand, it enables us to recognize the value of letting go and accepting our defeat when we lose a cause. The interplay of these two conflicting points gives us an opportunity to combine seemingly contradictory views into multivariable arguments.

Kibirige also claims that leaders are too unyielding to change. The point he raises further expands on previous views about letting go, stressing that doing so may benefit said politicians:

> When they lose elections, they demand a recount or waste taxpayer money to organize other elections, only to lose again. Some feel they have gone through too much to lead for only a three-year term, so they might take bribes to stay in their positions. They have not learned to let go and are totally unwilling to allow new blood into the system despite the societal transformations that have taken place. When President Museveni recently released the list of new cabinet ministers, the first thing people noticed was the lack of change. A post went viral on WhatsApp comparing the list to that of Finland. The Finnish prime minister was thirty-three years old at the time and was the oldest in the cabinet. The finance minister was only thirty years old. The comparison to the cabinet of Uganda was quite stark. The Ugandan prime minister was seventy-six years old, forty-three years older than his Finnish counterpart. According to a saying, a new broom sweeps clean, but an old broom knows the corners. Uganda has reached the point where all its leaders are old brooms. They only sweep the corners. However, the masses want to see clean ground. They want new brooms to come in.
>
> So leaders should not be rigid about change. When granted authority, upcoming leaders should not become overzealous or have large expectations as current leaders do. Some abuse their authority by manipulating others to do their dirty work. They sweet-talk and use others, elevating their status before ripping the ladder out from underneath them and leaving them hanging in midair. All the sycophants who serve them eventually lose direction and fall, having dug their own graves. An applicable saying is, "One who cares less reaps misery." Most current leaders do not care

---

9 Kibirige interview, December 18, 2019.

for their people, and so in the end they are buried with their own misery. They deserve to leave the world and let the current generation prepare for future leadership and generations.[10]

Kibirige argues that letting go requires us to facilitate and embrace change. In this way, the ex-husband in "Let Me Plod with a Stick Close to Kibuuka" represents both sides of this spectrum, facilitating change even as he sticks to the old. On the one hand, he calls on Kibuuka to assist him, putting his faith into the hands of a powerful deity and thus releasing his own desperate grasp on the situation. On the other hand, he is still asking for Kibuuka's aid so that he might preserve his relationship with his ex-wife, refusing to accept the end. This idea speaks to the contradictions that exist within every person, the alternative pursuits that converge over even the smallest actions. It also speaks to how opposition leaders differ from government leaders. Although both are tightly grasping their positions, the former pursue major change, grasping for a new world, even at the expense of their own lives. The administration is, on the other hand, haplessly grasping for the old, holding on to a position that cannot last forever.

Peter Kinene's interpretation comments on struggle and the spiritual notion that everything occurs exactly when it needs to. These sentiments assure those endeavoring for change in Uganda that they will eventually achieve their goal. More specifically, Kinene suggests that he trusts in fate, which serves to bolster the points that other interpreters have made:

> People earn good things after a persistent struggle. The song's refrain of "plod with a stick" is indicative of a persistent trek, a long-lasting struggle to attain that which one is working toward. It requires one to keep in transit day after day until one reaches success. Repetitive action brings success. It all connects back to the proverb *Atya omusana; talya bwami* (One who is afraid of the scorching sun does not become a chief). Everything has its own timing. When the appropriate time comes, nothing can stand in its way. Though the ex-husband mentioned in "Let Me Plod with a Stick Close to Kibuuka" never achieved what he set out to do, the song encourages us that with time everything will pass. If it was meant to happen, it does so at the right time.[11]

Claiming that change is an inherent quality of life, Kinene seems to argue that one must jump headfirst into the dangers and confusion that such change presents. Rather than attempting to secure and freeze life, Kinene recommends that we let chance lift us away, which will allow us to appreciate life for both its joys and sufferings. In this he paints "Let Me Plod with a

---

10   Ibid.
11   Kinene interview, December 16, 2019.

Stick Close to Kibuuka" as a tragic celebration of living. The ex-husband's desperate pleas to Kibuuka and his lament over the loss of his wife both reflect the pain and desire of daily life. His situation forces him to reckon with his pain, while he also rolls the dice to see what else Kibuuka has in store for him.

Conclusion

Typically performed in ritual contexts that address such topics as kinship, spirituality, and determination, "Let Me Plod with a Stick Close to Kibuuka" presents the perspective of a frustrated husband whose ex-wife has left with his child. As a result, he invokes the Baganda's war god Kibuuka to persuade his mother-in-law to mediate this couple's conflict and bring back the child. By presenting the complexities of this divorce, the song demonstrates how intricate relationships can be, as the husband's marriage is not just between him and his wife but also intersects with his mother-in-law, his son, and the deity Kibuuka. Accordingly, "Let Me Plod with a Stick Close to Kibuuka" operates as a musical narrative exploring the intersection of marriage difficulties and spiritual intervention. It transforms personal marital struggles into a framework for understanding how individuals seek supernatural assistance during relationship crises. This process further illustrates how spiritual resources may be integrated into addressing intimate relationship problems in Buganda. The imagery of "plodding with a stick," which suggests a difficult journey toward spiritual assistance, emphasizes both the desperation and determination involved in seeking supernatural intervention.

Reimagining "Let Me Plod with a Stick Close to Kibuuka" through a twenty-first-century political framework, interpreters reevaluate the song further. Many focus on how the ex-husband in the song expresses spiritual determination to overcome his disagreement with the ex-wife. As these interpreters demonstrate, his longing for his child represents a grander desire for a strong kinship network and a legacy of offspring that can relate to many political leaders of the world, particularly those who wish to continue their violent conflict. Conversely, the idea that one can determine and control the variability of one's life applies equally to leaders holding on to their power and those who wish to challenge these power-hungry leaders. Interpreters draw on Kiganda proverbs, national politics, and various conceptions of reciprocity to proliferate imaginative possibilities.

23

"The Pebble Is Breaking Me"

Mortality and Spirituality

Death and decay are recurring themes in "The Pebble Is Breaking Me" ("Akayinja Kammenya"). The song juxtaposes the world of the living with the world of the dead from the perspective of someone who is dead. It laments the living, whose lack of appreciation for the gift of life disdains the dead. The song also highlights how mortality reveals the ultimate brevity of political regimes, relating this brevity to the materialism and violence prevalent in contemporary life. In this spiritual discourse, notions of rebirth and revitalization reveal the deeper values of Buganda that focus on conflict and loss. Ssaalongo Ssennoga Majwala (b. 1953), who performed the version of "The Pebble Is Breaking Me" analyzed in this chapter, elaborates on the composition's background:

> Long ago, before the invention of coffins, when people died, their relatives wrapped them in bark cloth, dug graves, and placed the bodies in them. Immediately after they had buried them, they piled a lot of soil on the graves so that it was higher than the ground around it. To ensure that the mound of soil stayed intact, and to show that they had buried someone in a place, they placed stones on his or her grave.
>
> As mentioned earlier, stones often serve as an allusion to death in Kiganda songs. Many living Baganda believe that their deceased relatives never actually die. Rather, they move from the natural world to the supernatural world, a transition that surviving relatives facilitate by helping the deceased to rest in the ground. The living cannot see them there after the burials, which is in part the cause of the sadness of the occasion.[1]

Demonstrating the intersection of loss and spirituality, Majwala's account describes death as an extension of life rather than a separate realm. This intimacy with death is what allows the song's performer to embody it so well, as

---

1   Majwala interview, September 22, 2003.

we see how the singer uses his oratorical skill to vividly describe the sensation of being buried and entering the world of the dead. Such oration impacts the way we listen to and comprehend the song: instead of being a mere description of events, it creatively encompasses the spiritual and psychological aspects that constitute mortality.

At the start of Majwala's performance of "The Pebble Is Breaking Me," he plays a brief excerpt that features a gentle plucking of the bow harp (*ennanga*). The tempo of the buzzing instrumental part begins to pick up, quickly falling into a tight, consistent rhythm. Like bow harp songs presented in previous chapters, this part features two interlocking melodies that support the vocal lines when played together. When Majwala's vocals enter, they grow louder and more passionate. His words express the regret and lament of a dead person, who pities the living who fail to appreciate the beauty and wonder of their existence. Majwala brings out these emotions in his performance by repeating and accentuating specific bow harp notes in a way that renders the song mellow and sorrowful.

"The Pebble Is Breaking Me" is slower than the tempos of other bow harp songs, and Majwala's performance successfully evokes a dejection and introspection that we might not associate with more energetic or cheerful songs. Many of his phrases end with loud inflections, where his voice rises significantly to cry out, almost as though he is in pain or is dying. Other times he employs a loud sustain at the end of the vocable *waalaalaa* or its variation *waalaalaala*, wordless for the sake of emotional expression and often used to express alarm. These vocalizations lend passion to the lyrics that emphasize the text's meaning. It is as if they are calling out to the living, to deliver deep reflections from beyond the grave, reminding those alive to be grateful for their opportunity. While Majwala sometimes sounds as though he is crying out, at other times he rapidly vocalizes sequences of syllables. In the middle of his performance, he chooses to hum a continuous stream of notes in unison with the instrumental melody. He then repeats several lyrics in a row. Toward the end of the performance, the bow harp drops out as his voice carries on, only rejoining after a few seconds of the solo vocal performance. The two eventually fade out: the vocals lessen in intensity, and the bow harp flows into silence. Overall, Majwala's performance of "The Pebble Is Breaking Me" expresses death and decay in its stylistic elements, evoking other possible experiences of deterioration, such as that of a friendship, an edifice, or Buganda's cultural and musical institutions.

1 *Akayinja kammenya*
The pebble is breaking me

2 *Baana battu, akayinja kammenya, nze*
Dear children, the pebble is breaking me

3 *Eee, akayinja ka nnyabo*
Eh, mother's pebble

4 *Ndigenda bw'omu, baaba, emagombe*
I will go alone, older sibling, into the grave

5 *Ndigenda bwe nti, baaba, emagombe*
I will go by myself, older sibling, into the grave

6 *Emagombe, emagombe, baaba, emagombe tejjula*
The grave, the grave, older sibling, the grave does not get filled up

7 *Emagombe, emagombe, baaba, emagombe tejjula*
The grave, the grave, older sibling, the grave does not get filled up

8 *Emagombe, emagombe, ee, emagombe*
The grave, the grave, eh, the grave

9 *Ndigenda bwomu*
I shall go alone

[*brief instrumental interlude*]

10 *Akayinja kammenya*
The pebble is breaking me

11 *Baana battu, akayinja ka nnyabo*
Dear children, mother's pebble

12 *Akayinja ka ssebo*
Father's pebble

13 *Ee, akayinja kammenya*
Eh, the pebble is breaking me

14 *Waalaalaa, akayinja ka nnyabo*
Waalaalaa, madam's pebble

15 *Tuyonja empya, baaba, bateeka ku bbali*
We clean and clear courtyards, older sibling, but we are laid at the outskirts

16 *Tuyonja ennyumba, ssebo, bateeka mu lusuku*
We clean and adorn houses, sir, but we are buried in the plantation

17 *Nga tugejjera empewo, ffe, nga ekitembe*
We fatten up for no reason, like *ekitembe*, a wild banana plant

18 *Okwebikka omuddo, nga essalambwa*
Covering ourselves with grass, like a puff adder

19 *Babikka amayinja, baaba, tuliwo*
They cover with stones, older sibling, there we are

20 *Babikka amayinja, baaba, mmm*
They cover with stones, older sibling, mhm

21 *Mmm . . .*
Mhm . . .

22 *Mmm . . .*
Mhm . . .

23 *Mmm . . .*
Mhm . . .

24 *Akayinja, akayinja, ssebo, akayinja*
The pebble, the pebble, sir, the pebble

25 *Akayinja ka nnyabo*
Mother's pebble

26 *Tulaba abalungi, magombe*
We see the beautiful, death

27 *Eee, tulaba abagagga, magombe*
Eh, we see the wealthy, death

28 *Ssebo, emagombe tejjula*
Sir, the grave does not get filled up

29 *Emagombe, emagombe, baaba, emagombe tejjula*
The grave, the grave, older sibling, the grave does not get filled up

30 *Laba, laba, laba, ggwe*
Look, look, look, you

31 *Laba, laba, laba eno, amagombe*
Look, look, look here, death

32 *Emirembe, emirembe, baaba, emirembe giggwa*
Regimes, regimes, older sibling, regimes cease

33 *Emirembe, emirembe, baaba, emirembe giggwa*
Regimes, regimes, older sibling, regimes cease

34 *N'ogwa Amin*
Even that of Amin

35 *N'ogwa Muteesa, ssebo, omulembe*
And that of Muteesa, sir, the regime

36 *N'ogwa Muteesa, baaba, omulembe*
Even the one of Muteesa, older sibling, the regime

37 *N'ogwa Museveni, ssebo, omulembe*
Even the one of Museveni, sir, the regime

38 *Aliba ani oyo, atalifa aliva wa?*
Who will he be, who will escape death, where will she come from?

39 *Aliva wa ggwe, atalifa, aliba ani?*
Where will he come from, who will escape death, who will she be?

40 *Laba, laba, laba, ggwe, aliba ani?*
Look, look, look, you, who will he be?

41 *Oliva wa eyo, olibeera ani?*
Where will you come from, who will you be?

42 *Aliba ani oyo, aliva wa eyo?*
Who will he be; where will she come from?

43 *Laba, laba, laba, ggwe, amagombe*
Look, look, look, you, death

44 *Waalaalaala, amagombe, amagombe, ssebo, emagombe*
Waalaalaala, death, death, sir, the grave

45 *Emagombe, emagombe, emagombe*
The grave, the grave, the grave

[*brief instrumental interlude*]

46 *Terimwa lumonde*
There is no growing sweet potatoes there

47 *Eee, terimwa lumonde*
Eh, there is no growing sweet potatoes

[*brief instrumental interlude*]

48 *Laba professor, ssebo, amagombe*
Look at a professor, sir, death

49 *Laba professor, amagombe*
Look at a professor, death

50 *Abaganda n'Abalango, amagombe*
The Baganda and the Langi, death

51 *Abacholi n'Abalango, amagombe*
The Acholi and the Langi, death

52 *Ee, aliba ani oyo, ee, aliva wa eyo?*
Eh, who will he be, eh, where will she come from?

53 *Aliba ani oyo, aliba ani oyo?*
Who will he be, who will she be?

54 *Oliba oli awo, nga luntwala*
You will be off guard, when it takes me

55 *Olibeera eyo, nga luntutte*
You will be far away, when it takes me

56 *Majwala, Majwala, baaba, omulanga*
Majwala, Majwala, older sibling, the harpist

57 *Baana battu, Majwala, Majwala*
Dear children, Majwala, Majwala

58 *Ee*
Eh

59 *Ee, laba ndaaga*
Eh, look, I am suffering

60 *Tuyonja empya, ssebo, bateeka ku bbali*
We clean and adorn courtyards, sir, they put us at the outskirts

61 *Tuyonja ennyumba, ssebo, bateeka mu nsuku*
We clean and adorn houses, sir, they bury us in plantations

62 *Tugejjera empewo ffe, nga ekitembe*
We fatten for no reason, like *ekitembe*, a wild banana plant

63 *Beebikka omuddo, nga e ssalambwa*
They cover themselves with grass, like a puff adder

64 *Babikka amayinja, baaba, tuliwo*
They cover with stones, older sibling, there we are

65 *Babikka amayinja, ssebo, tuliwo*
They cover with stones, sir, there we are

66 *Beebikka amayinja, baaba*
They cover themselves with stones, older sibling

67 *Ee aliba ani oyo, aliba ani oyo?*
Eh, who will he be, who will she be?

68 *Aliva wa oyo, aliba ani oyo?*
Where will he come from, who will she be?

69 *Laba ndaaga, ndiba ndaaga, ee*
Look, I am suffering, I will be suffering, eh

These lyrics imagine personal annihilation not just as an incipient moment but as a phase taking place in a vaster environment of life and death. Multigenerational references highlight the universality of death. In Buganda, the world of the living and that of the dead are interconnected. Accordingly, referencing stones or rocks is common in Kiganda songs about death because they allude to the traditional burial practices of the Baganda, who wrap their dead in bark cloth before covering the grave with stones. References to "the pebble" (lines 1–3, 10–14, and 24–25) and "stones" (lines 19–20 and 64–66) in Majwala's lyrics serve as a metonym where pebbles and stones represent the burial mounds that they make up and the bodies that they conceal. "The pebble is breaking me" (lines 1–2, and 10) means "death is weighing on me," "mother's pebble" (lines 3 and 11) implies "mother's death," and references to cleaning and adorning the house (lines 15–16 and 60–61) refer to obsession with material possessions that one leaves behind after death. Those listening to "The Pebble Is Breaking Me" might also associate breaking pebbles with fracturing kinship and company. Throughout the song, the singer addresses someone using the title *baaba* (lines 4–7, 15, 19–20, 29, 32–33, 36, 56, 64, and 66), which means "older sibling" but could also suggest "dear." He also uses the expression *baana battu* (lines 2, 11, and 57), which translates as "dear children." Moreover, he consistently uses words that simultaneously evoke consanguineous and filial kin. "Sir" could also mean "father," "madam" could also mean "mother," and "dear" could also mean "child." At the same time, the singer describes the loneliness associated with death, saying that he will go just alone (lines 4 and 9) into the grave. Thus, he highlights the importance of both biological and social kin in one's contemplation of life and its end. On the one hand, the singer's speech might allude to his desperation to maintain bonds, as he begins to refer to the listener using intimate language. On the other hand, his words may refer to the role that family and friends play in a person's funeral rites, as they see their deceased off.

The phrase "the grave does not get filled up" (lines 6–7 and 28–29) imagines death as a spatial landscape that far exceeds the amount of people that have ever died. This is also to say that the vast expanse of death is unavoidable, as it remains inherently open to newly freed spirits. This idea places the ordinary pursuits of living beings in a greater context, for whatever life one builds for oneself will cease someday. The lyrics compare humanity's efforts to *ekitembe* (lines 17 and 62), a wild plant that seems to grow bananas but whose fruit is inedible. Commonly found in forests, it looks similar to—and is sometimes mistaken for—the staple banana plant called *ekitooke*, which produces edible bananas generically called *amatooke*. *Ekitembe* comes across as attractive and perhaps nutritious at first sight, but it is not edible. The singer compares it to a person who fattens "for no reason" or grows to die (lines 17 and 62). These points divert away from human concerns like achieving material wealth or attaining honorable behavior, instead recognizing that death is final. The points are not nihilistic; instead, they reflect a way of embracing life unattached to material obsession. The singer develops this commentary even further when he evokes the death of a professor (lines 48–49), suggesting that knowledge, too, dissipates in death. In this sense, knowledge is as contingent as material wealth, only predicated on the idiosyncrasies of the age. Despite the professor's beliefs, truth cannot exist in and of itself. It is a human conception, and so it requires a human being to believe in it. It falls apart just as quickly as the professor's body, falling into the great existential fog.

At this point the song transitions to discuss regimes (lines 32–37), applying the inevitability of death to the end of government administrations. It abstracts death, positing it as just a moment along a greater existential scheme of change, accomplishing this when the singer simultaneously embraces the interdependent forces of creation and cessation. By asking "who" will come and defy this law of existence (lines 38–42, 52–53, and 67–68), the singer demonstrates imminence—the feeling that something is about to occur. In this sense, life is always in a process of becoming. From the perspective of social institutions, the process of becoming and change is lying in wait for the next great leader or regime that will seek to defy death. "The Pebble Is Breaking Me" does not reject these pursuits entirely, but it does recognize that the failure of such attempts is inevitable.

At last Majwala faces his own mortality, recognizing that his own investment in its conundrum is futile and subject to the fickle whims of existence (lines 56–57). At the same time, he affirms and accepts his existence in its utter vulnerability.

Emphasizing the fleeting nature of life, Majwala's lyrics generally suggest that one must reevaluate values that prioritize material success and wealth over personal relationships. Because life is fleeting, accrual of material value is futile in comparison to the fruitful, lively connections people make with others. He mentions different family members to demonstrate how mortality affects these kin networks. For example, when one person dies, his or her death ripples outward through a fabric of loved ones. This is partly why the singer encourages the living to appreciate their fleeting surroundings. Seen through this lens, we might instead approach death with a faith that things will all work out in the end.

The ideas and emotions expressed in "The Pebble Is Breaking Me" also apply to political leadership. Again, Majwala reminds us that all dynasties will become dust eventually and that these ends are not necessarily tragedies, for the end of one political regime will allow the fruit of another's to bloom. The song thus suggests that politics can follow a cycle of rebirth and revitalization. As we have seen, the singer himself illustrates how political administrations follow one other, constantly dying and being reborn simultaneously. Furthermore, the song draws parallels between the temporality and flexibility of lived experience and that of political power and control. In this sense any regime that resists the fact of its eventual death might face a meaner death than it would prefer to have.

Mortality and Spirituality

Jessy Ssendawula's interpretation of "The Pebble Is Breaking Me" advances the discussion of mortality and spirituality by focusing on these themes in relation to materialism and politics. In his account of the song's various meanings, he expounds on the inevitability of death, noting that the composition talks about the belief that when one's time comes, one must succumb to human mortality and the fate of death. When people die, surviving relatives and friends place them in graves, and though their loss might weigh heavily on the survivors' hearts, the deceased will remain as stone, unmoving.[2] He then expands on the song's refutation of materialism and emphasis on temporality:

> Death renders all earthly pleasures useless. The big barns, parlors, courtyards, or compounds that are cleaned daily do not house the dead who paid for them. The only place for the dead is at the demarcation lines, at the margins of their land, where their relatives bury them. The dead leave their decorated houses, and grass covers their bodies as though they were puff adders. Surviving relatives and friends rain stones upon those who once enjoyed the spaces they built, and place them in plantations; the dead will never walk their compounds again.[3]

While focusing on the song's conception of death, Ssendawula also reflects on how such inescapable destruction mediates social relations. Death wrenches people from the relations they may have occupied in life, as human selves will ultimately transition from being a focal point in a complex set of relations to having their bodies displaced to the corners of property, at the peripheries of their relatives' thoughts and spaces. Thus, death displaces people's relationship to the world—not necessarily erasing it but relocating it so that it lies in the margins of social, political, and spatial life. This observation allows "The Pebble Is Breaking Me" to become a framework

---

2   Ssendawula personal communication, April 8, 2020.
3   Ibid.

for discussing death as a type of status shift that shapes people's positionality in the world. With this degree of nuance, Ssendawula's perspective accounts for how death is a matter of relationality.

Connecting this song to politics, Ssendawula extrapolates a message that current leaders might be able to glean from it. Relating the realities of modern leadership with the inescapability of death, he reminds them of their vulnerability and how they will be unable to take their worldly pleasures to the grave:

> Leaders who overstay their welcome and wish destruction on their opponents should take this song as a reminder that no man can conquer death. Regimes and generations come and go, and as the singer notes, the reigns of President Amin and King Muteesa II both ended. Similarly, that of President Museveni will, too. Those in power should avoid hubris and the mistreatment of their subjects, for humans are all but clay, themselves included. One day they will be the same as even the most common of citizens.
>
> Many times, leaders amass wealth by stealing from government coffers and failing to provide the proper services to the people they lead. They do not care about the consequences of this gap in service, as they and their families can go abroad to receive better treatment whenever they want. But when death visits, it does not care who you are. It is like a disease. It isolates people from their loved ones and will take them if it so chooses, regardless of their possessions.[4]

Ssendawula's comments reflect the fragility and temporality of life, suggesting that one should make the most of its highs and lows, embracing it for what it is rather than desperately securing and protecting it. By comparing people to clay, he implies that they are evanescent and malleable, subject to nature's ultimate ability to remake or reshape or dissolve them. It also affirms the idea that people should not treat life as something that they can freeze and protect indefinitely but instead as something that they can joyfully mold. This perspective helps us understand "The Pebble Is Breaking Me" through philosophies that encourage us to accept our ultimate fate.

In this vein Ssendawula further encourages leaders to avoid blindly accumulating material wealth. He asserts that death does not discriminate, regardless of the riches and land someone has hoarded. When their relatives bury them, they will not leave them in their great houses or with their riches but will bury them off at the edge of their land, which is what happens to ordinary Baganda. Such fleeting riches do not transfer to the next world. Consequently, Ssendawula argues, leaders should spend their time finding

---

4   Ibid.

ways to engage with life more profoundly and subtly; relentless pursuit of self-interest is not worth the self-deterioration that accompanies it:

> It is not worth sacrificing personal morals for the sake of mere impermanent success. Leaders who favor their kinsmen for important government positions should learn from "The Pebble Is Breaking Me" that no matter one's status, when one dies one's relatives will not bury one in the bungalows, cars, or yards they bought during a life of excess and wealth. Rather, they will take them down to the deserted plantations. President Museveni needs to refrain from his nepotistic tendencies because no matter what, all those whom he favors will eventually die. Death knows no tribe. There is no one who can conquer death. People are simply standing in its path, waiting for it to knock them down. When that happens, the earth and stones will cover them when their relatives bury them as though they had no significance to anyone in this world. It does not matter one's status or tribe; death is the great equalizer.[5]

This philosophy centers our focus on the notion of death as a challenge to contemporary political contingencies, showing us how "The Pebble Is Breaking Me" relates to current leaders and points to the value of death because it ultimately equalizes us.

Conclusion

"The Pebble Is Breaking Me" functions as a musical memento mori that speaks from beyond the grave, using a deceased narrator to create perspective on life's transience. The song's lyrics focus on death and its relationship to life, exploring this phenomenon in several different contexts (politics, kinship, performance) and emphasizing its universality, affecting the rich, the wise, and the hardworking alike. In one interpreter's analysis of the song, he connects these themes intimately to the conundrums and obstacles of contemporary sociopolitical life. He first discusses the theme of death, highlighting its capacity to reposition people from the center of their social relations to the periphery. Then he frames this same concept of death as an extension of the claylike quality of life as both malleable and temporary. Last, he uses these two interpretations to reexamine the song as a critique of the alleged nepotistic practices that Ugandan politicians follow, describing how their hoarding and selfishness will ultimately come to naught.

With its plurality of perspectives, "The Pebble Is Breaking Me" becomes a wide-ranging commentary on life and death. It transforms death from an abstract concept to an immediate voice, allowing listeners to experience,

---

5   Ibid.

through a human voice, the reality of mortality and the meaning it gives to human life. The song's lyrics serve as spiritual commentary on contemporary values, with the dead narrator lamenting how the living waste their precious time through materialism and violence rather than appreciating life's temporary gift. This vantage point establishes a framework for evaluating both individual priorities and broader political systems.

Author Interviews

Anderson, Lois. Personal communication, November 20, 2005.

Bisaso, Albert Ssempeke. Interviewed September 14, 2003, Kamwokya town, Kampala District.

Deziderio, Ssaalongo Kiwanuka Matovu. Interviewed July 15, 2005, Kamwokya town, Kampala District.

Kabugo, Steven Mukasa. Interviewed December 19, 2019, Buwambo village, Wakiso District.

Kabwama, Ssaalongo Paulo. Interviewed July 20, 2005, Katende village, Mpigi District.

Kafeero, Mukasa. Interviewed July 28, 2005, Nakasero town, Kampala District.

Kibirige, Jimmy Ssenfuka. Interviewed December 14, 2019, Buwagga village, Wakiso District.

———. Interviewed December 15, 2019, Buwagga village, Wakiso District.

———. Interviewed December 18, 2019, Buwagga village, Wakiso District.

———. Interviewed December 19, 2019, Buwagga village, Wakiso District.

Kinene, Peter. Interviewed December 16, 2019, Bulamu-Gayaza town, Wakiso District.

Kironde, Edward Ssebunnya. Interviewed December 19, 2019, Kanyanya town, Kampala District.

Kisuule, Harriet. Interviewed December 21, 2019, Nalusugga village, Wakiso District.

Kityo, John Magandaazi. Interviewed December 14, 2019, Namugongo town, Wakiso District.

Majwala, Ssaalongo Ssennoga. Interviewed September 22, 2003, Kyambogo town, Kampala District.

———. Interviewed October 1, 2003, Kyambogo town, Kampala District.

Ssebuwufu, Semeo Ssemambo. Interviewed June 23, 2009, Kigoowa town, Kampala District.

———. Interviewed June 4, 2013, Kyambogo town, Kampala District.

———. Interviewed June 6, 2013, Kyambogo town, Kampala District.

———. Interviewed June 10, 2013, Kyambogo town, Kampala District.

Ssempeke, Albert Muwanga. Interviewed July 27, 2003, Kamwokya town, Kampala District.

———. Interviewed July 28, 2003, Kamwokya town, Kampala District.

———. Interviewed July 11, 2005, Kamwokya town, Kampala District.
———. Interviewed July 12, 2005, Kamwokya town, Kampala District.
Ssendawula, Jessy. Interviewed December 28, 2019, Kasozi village, Wakiso District.
———. Personal communication, April 8, 2020.
Sserwanga, Ludoviiko. Interviewed July 6, 2005, Kamwokya town, Kampala District.
———. Interviewed July 7, 2005, Kamwokya town, Kampala District.
———. Interviewed July 15, 2005, Kamwokya town, Kampala District.

Works Cited

Adima, Faustine Otum Anualia. 2004. "The Role of Duluka Dance among the Lugbara in Northern Uganda (West Nile Region)." Bachelor's thesis. Makerere University.
Agawu, Victor Kofi. 2016. *The African Imagination in Music*. New York: Oxford University Press.
Ampene, Kwasi. 2020. *Asante Court Music and Verbal Arts in Ghana: The Porcupine and the Gold Stool*. New York: Routledge.
———. 2021. "Power and Responsibility: Royalty and the Performing Arts in Asante-Ghana." *African Studies Review* 64 (3): 523–546.
Anderson, Lois. 1968. "The Miko Modal System of Kiganda Xylophone Music." PhD diss., University of California, Los Angeles.
Askew, Kelly. 2002. *Performing the Nation: Swahili Music and Cultural Politics in Tanzania*. Chicago: University of Chicago Press.
Atim, Teddy, et al. 2018. *The Effect of the Lord's Resistance Army's Violence on Victims from Northern Uganda in* Prosecutor V. Dominic Ongwen. Abstract of Feinstein International Center Report. Tufts University, Feinstein International Center. https://fic.tufts.edu/publication-item/prosecutor-v-dominic-ongwen/.
Bakan, Michael. 2007. *World Music: Traditions and Transformations*. New York: McGraw-Hill.
Balabarca, Lisette. 2013. "Social Denunciation of the Politics of Fear: Rock Music through the Eighties in Argentina, Chile, and Peru." In *Song and Social Change in Latin America*, edited by Lauren Shaw, 77–90. Plymouth, UK: Lexington Books.
Barbalet, Jack M. 1985. "Power and Resistance." *British Journal of Sociology* 36 (4): 531–548.
Barz, Gregory F. 2001. "Meaning in *Benga* Music of Western Kenya." *British Journal of Ethnomusicology* 10 (1): 107–115.
Baskerville, G. K., and G. L. Pilkington. 1896. *The Gospel in Uganda*. London: Church Missionary Society.
Campbell, John. 2006. "Who Are the Luo? Oral Tradition and Disciplinary Practices in Anthropology and History." *Journal of African Cultural Studies* 18 (1): 73–87.

Cheeseman, Nic, David M. Anderson, and Andrea Scheibler, eds. 2015. *Routledge Handbook of African Politics*. New York: Routledge.
Chikowero, Mhoze. 2015. *African Power, Music, and Being in Colonial Zimbabwe*. Bloomington: Indiana University Press.
Ciantar, Philip. 2013. "The Process of Musical Translation: Composing a Maltese Festa Band March from Libyan Ma'luf Music." *Ethnomusicology* 57 (1): 1–33.
Cooke, Andrew, and James Micklem. 1999. "Ennanga Harp Songs of Buganda: Temutewo Mukasa's '*Gganga Alula*.'" *Journal of International Library of African Music* 7 (4): 47–65.
Cooke, Peter. 1988. "Track Listing, Texts & Translations." Liner notes, Albert Ssempeke, *Ssempeke!* CD. Recorded 1988. University of Edinburgh.
———. 1994. "A Reply to Ulrich Wegner." *Ethnomusicology* 38 (3): 475–479.
———. 1996. "Music in a Ugandan Court." *Early Music* 24 (3): 439–452.
Cooke, Peter, and Sam Kasule. 1999. "The Musical Scene in Uganda: Views from Without and Within." *Journal of International Library of African Music* 7 (4): 6–21.
Cooke, Peter, and Klaus Wachsmann. 2003. Program notes to *The King's Musicians: Royalist Music of Buganda-Uganda*. Performed by various artists. CD. Topic Records, British Library Sound Archive.
Dave, Nomi. 2014. "The Politics of Silence: Music, Violence and Protest in Guinea." *Ethnomusicology* 58 (1): 1–29.
Diamond, Beverley. 2013. "Native American Ways of (Music) History." In *The Cambridge History of World Music*, edited by Philip V. Bohlman, 155–180. Cambridge: Cambridge University Press.
Dungu, Solomy Katasi. 1993. "The Influence of Music Analysis on the Students' Understanding of Music in Selected Secondary Schools." Master's thesis, Makerere University.
Eze, Michael Onyebuchi. 2010. *Intellectual History in Contemporary South Africa*. New York: Palgrave Macmillan.
Feld, Steven. 2012. *Jazz Cosmopolitanism in Accra: Five Musical Years in Ghana*. Durham, NC: Duke University Press.
Foucault, Michel. 1977. "Nietzsche, Genealogy, History." In *Language, Counter-Memory, Practice: Selected Essays and Interviews*, edited by D. F. Bouchard, 139–164. Ithaca: Cornell University Press.
Frolova-Walker, Marina. 1998. "'National in Form, Socialist in Content': Musical Nation-Building in the Soviet Republics." *Journal of the American Musicological Society* 51 (4): 331–371.
Garratt, James. 2018. *Music and Politics: A Critical Introduction*. Cambridge: Cambridge University Press.

Gilman, Lisa. 2009. *The Dance of Politics: Gender, Performance, and Democratization in Malawi.* Philadelphia: Temple University Press.

Hanna, Judith Lynne, and William John Hanna. 1968. "Heart Beat of Uganda." *African Arts* 1 (3): 42–45, 85.

Hoesing, Peter. 2019. *Kusamira: Ritual Music in Uganda: Spirit Mediumship and Ritual Healing.* Urbana: University of Illinois Press.

Hoffman, Barbara G. 2017. "The Roles of the Griot in the Future of Mali: A Twenty-First-Century Institutionalization of a Thirteenth-Century Traditional Institution." *African Studies Review* 60 (1): 101–122.

Houshmand, Zara. 2019. "Ubuntu: A Philosophy of Dialogue." In *Mind & Life Digital Dialogue.* Charlottesville: The Mind and Life Institute. https://ubuntudialogue.org/ubuntu-philosophy-of-dialogue/.

Janzen, John M. 1992. *Ngoma: Discourses of Healing in Central and Southern Africa.* Oakland: University of California Press.

Jjuuko, Denis. 2021. "Hidden Facts about Katikiro Mayiga's Mansion in Lweza, Shocking Details!" *Homeland*, May 12. https://www.homelandmedia.co.ug/news/hidden-facts-about-katikiro-mayigas-mansion-in-lweza-shocking-details/.

Kafumbe, Damascus. 2004. "The Continuity and Change of the Nnanga among the Baganda People of Central Uganda." Bachelor's thesis (music), Makerere University.

———. 2006. "The Kabaka's Royal Musicians of Buganda-Uganda: Their Role and Significance during Ssekabaka Sir Edward Frederick Muteesa II's Reign (1939–1966)." Master's thesis, Florida State University.

———. 2011. "The Kawuugulu Royal Drums: Musical Regalia, History, and Social Organization among the Baganda People of Uganda." PhD diss., Florida State University.

———. 2018. *Tuning the Kingdom: Kawuugulu Musical Performance, Politics, and Storytelling in Buganda.* Rochester, NY: University of Rochester Press.

Kaminski, Joseph S. 2012. *Asante Ntahera Trumpets in Ghana: Culture, Tradition, and Sound Barrage.* Burlington, VT: Ashgate.

Karlström, Mikael. 2004. "Modernity and Its Aspirants: Moral Community and Developmental Eutopianism in Buganda." *Current Anthropology* 45 (5): 595–619.

Katamba, Francis, and Peter Cooke. 1987. "Ssematimba ne Kikwabanga: The Music and Poetry of a Ganda Historical Song." *World of Music* 29 (2): 49–68.

Kodesh, Neil. 2010. *Beyond the Royal Gaze: Clanship and Public Healing in Buganda.* Charlottesville: University of Virginia Press.

Kubik, Gerhard. 1998. "Intra-African Streams of Influence." In *The Garland Encyclopedia of World Music. Volume 1: Africa*, edited by Ruth M. Stone, 293–326. New York: Garland.

———. 2010. *Theory of African Music (Volume I)*. Chicago: University of Chicago Press.

Kyagambiddwa, Joseph. 1955. *African Music from the Source of the Nile*. New York: Praeger.

Langlois, Tony. 2009. "Music and Politics in North Africa." In *Music and the Play of Power in the Middle East, North Africa and Central Asia*, edited by Laudan Nooshin, 207–227. New York: Routledge.

Lohman, Laura. 2016. "'The Artist of the People in the Battle': Umm Kulthūm's Concerts for Egypt in Political Context." In *Music and the Play of Power in the Middle East, North Africa and Central Asia*, edited by Laudan Nooshin, 33–53. New York: Routledge.

Lonsdale, John. 1992. "The Moral Economy of Mau Mau: The Problem." In *Unhappy Valley: Conflict in Kenya and Africa, Book Two: Violence and Ethnicity*, edited by Bruce Berman and John Lonsdale. Athens: Ohio Univeristy Press.

Mackinlay, Elizabeth. 2016. "Dear SEM." *SEM{Student News}* 12 (2): 15–16.

Makubuya, James. 2000. "'Endingidi' (Tube Fiddle) of Uganda: Its Adaptation and Significance among the Bagand a." *Galpin Society Journal* 53:140–155.

Martin, Denis-Constant. 2013. *Sounding the Cape Music, Identity and Politics in South Africa*. Somerset West, South Africa: African Minds.

Martin, James, S.J. 2011. "The Story of the Ugandan Martyrs." *America: The Jesuit Review* (online magazine), June 3. https://www.americamagazine.org/content/all-things/story-ugandan-martyrs.

Matovu, Muhamadi. 2023. "Buganda Kingdom Looks for Development Projects to Modernise All Ssaza, Gombolola Land," *NilePost*, February 19. https://nilepost.co.ug/2023/02/19/buganda-kingdom-looks-for-development-projects-to-modernise-all-ssaza-gombolola-land/.

Mazrui, Ali. 1974. "The Social Origins of Ugandan Presidents: From King to Peasant Warrior." *Canadian Journal of African Studies* 8 (1): 3–23.

Mirela 2024. "8 Main Types of Translation," *Poeditor*, April 18. https://poeditor.com/blog/types-of-translation/.

Moorehead, Alan. 1971. *The White Nile*. 2nd ed. New York: Harper & Row.

Mutebi, Golooba. "Bring Back the G-Tax; without It the Village Men Are Nothing, Have Nothing," *East African*, March 3, 2012 (Updated on July 26, 2020). https://www.theeastafrican.co.ke/tea/oped/comment/bring-back-the-g-tax-without-it-the-village-men-are-nothing-have-nothing--1307362.

Muyinda, Evalisto. 1991. Liner notes, *Traditional Music of the Baganda as Formerly Played at the Court of the Kabaka*. CD. Berlin, Germany: PAN Records (3).
Nannyonga, Sylvia. 1995. "Selected Traditional Secular and Sacred Music of the Baganda People: A Comparative Study." Master's thesis, Makerere University.
Nannyonga-Tamusuza, Sylvia. 2002. "Gender, Ethnicity and Politics in Kadongo-Kamu Music of Uganda: Analysing the Song Kayanda." In *Playing with Identities in Contemporary Music in Africa*, edited by Mai Palmberg and Annemette Kirkegaard, 134–148. Uppsala: Nordiska Afrikainstitutet.
Nannyonga-Tamusuza, Sylvia A. 2005. *Baakisimba: Gender in the Music and Dance of the Baganda People of Uganda*. New York: Taylor & Francis.
Nketia, J. H. Kwabena. 1962. "The Problem of Meaning in African Music." *Ethnomusicology* 6 (1): 1–7.
———. 1975. *The Music of Africa*. New York: Norton.
Nooshin, Laudan. 2005. "Subversion and Countersubversion: Power, Control, and Meaning in the New Iranian Pop Music." In *Music, Power, and Politics*, edited by Annie J. Randall, 231–272. New York: Routledge.
Nsimbi, M. B. 1956. *Amannya Amaganda n'Ennono Zaago* [Kiganda names and their origins]. Kampala: East African Literature Bureau.
Nyanzi, Stella. 2020. "Personal Narrative: Bloody Precarious Activism in Uganda," *The Palgrave Handbook of Critical Menstruation Studies*, July 25. https://www.ncbi.nlm.nih.gov/books/NBK565635/.
Omojola, Bode. 2009. "Politics, Identity, and Nostalgia in Nigerian Music: A Study of Victor Olaiya's Highlife." *Ethnomusicology* 53 (2): 249–276.
———. 2012. *Yorùbá Music in the Twentieth Century: Identity, Agency, and Performance Practice*. Rochester, NY: University of Rochester Press.
Ouattara, Issiaka. 2018. "The Griots of West Africa: Oral Tradition and Ancestral Knowledge." In *Constructing the Pluriverse: The Geopolitics of Knowledge*, edited by Bernd Reiter, 151–167. Durham, NC: Duke University Press.
Padwick, Constance E. 1917. *Mackay of the Great Lake*. New York: Oxford University Press.
Peterson, Derek. 2012. *Ethnic Patriotism and the East African Revival*. Cambridge: Cambridge University Press.
Pier, David. 2017. "Song for a King's Exile: Royalism and Popular Music in Postcolonial Uganda." *Popular Music and Society* 40 (1): 5–21.
Politz, Sarah. 2018. "'People of Allada, This Is Our Return': Indexicality, Multiple Temporalities, and Resonance in the Music of the Gangbé Brass Band of Benin." *Ethnomusicology* 62 (1): 28–57.
Przybylski, Liz. 2016. "Dear SEM." *SEM{Student News}* 12 (2): 14–15.

Pun, Sara Hong-Yeung. 2016. "Thoughts from the Field." *SEM{Student News}* 12 (2): 11.

Qashu, Leila. 2019. "Singing as Justice: *Ateetee*, an Arsi Oromo Women's Sung Dispute Resolution Ritual in Ethiopia." *Ethnomusicology* 63 (2): 247–278.

Reed, Daniel B. 2016. *Abidjan USA: Music, Dance, and Mobility in the Lives of Four Ivorian Immigrants*. Bloomington: Indiana University Press.

Robinson, Dylan. 2020. *Hungry Listening: Resonant Theory for Indigenous Sound Studies*. Minneapolis: University of Minnesota Press.

Rubadiri, David. 2020. "Stanley Meets Mutesa." Poem. *Poetry Nook*, https://www.poetrynook.com/poem/stanley-meets-mutesa.

Sanga, Imani. 2008. "Music and Nationalism in Tanzania: Dynamics of National Space in *Muziki wa Injili* in Dar es Salaam." *Ethnomusicology* 52 (1): 52–84.

Schoenbrun, David L. 2006. "Conjuring the Modern in Africa: Durability and Rupture in Histories of Public Healing between the Great Lakes of East Africa." *American Historical Review* 111 (5): 1403–1439.

Serwadda, Moses. 1971. "Ndongo, a Wedding-Dance of the Baganda of Uganda," Diploma thesis, University of Ghana.

Speke, John Hanning. 1908 (1863). *Journal of the Discovery of the Source of the Nile*. New York: E. P. Button.

Steingo, Gavin. 2007. "The Politicization of 'Kwaito': From the 'Party Politic' to Party Politics." *Black Music Research Journal* 27 (1): 23–44.

Tracey, Andrew, and Hugh Tracey. 1998. Liner notes, Michael Baird, *Royal Court Music from Uganda 1950 & 1952*. CD. Sharp Wood Productions.

Wachsmann, Klaus P. 1953. "The Sound Instruments." In *Tribal Crafts of Uganda*, edited by Margaret Trowell and Klaus P. Wachsmann, 311–415. London: Oxford University Press.

Walser, Ferdinand. 1982. *Luganda Proverbs*. London: Mill Hill Missionaries.

Wiggins, Trevor. 2005. "An Interview with J. H. Kwabena Nketia: Perspectives on Tradition and Modernity." *Ethnomusicology Forum* 14 (1): 57–81.

Index

abagalagala (servants), 205
Abakunta people, 262
abasiige. See court pages (*abasiige*)
Achebe, Chinua, 246–47
Adima, Faustine, 48
adungu. See bow harp (*adungu*)
advice
  failure to heed, 94, 103, 107–8, 171, 173, 209, 258–59, 276–77
  knowledge as, xix
  to leaders, 103, 105–14, 209–11, 215, 219, 223, 224, 225, 235, 246, 250, 259
  value of, 30, 83, 106–14, 137, 139, 144, 150–51
Agawu, Kofi, 6, 33, 37
Ahmed Bin Ibrahim, 52
akabbiro (secondary totem), 70
akadinda. See xylophones (*akadinda* and *amadinda*)
akogo. See lamellaphone (*akogo*)
al-Bashir, Omar, 248
amadinda. See xylophones (*akadinda* and *amadinda*)
amakuuli (bad intentions), 211
amatooke (bananas), 287
Amin, Idi, 4, 82, 181, 200, 290
"Amount of Sugar Is Just Right, The" ("Kassukaali Ke Ko") (B. Wine), 66
Ampene, Kwasi, 40
Anderson, Lois, 37
animal horn (*eŋŋombe*)
  Bisaso as performer, 12
  Majwala as performer, 14

animal symbolism
  clan totems, 69, 70, 77
  in "Federalism," 87–88, 93
  in "The King Is a Lion," 188, 190–92
  in "The Little Lion," 142, 175–202
  of Mr. Dog in "The Flutists' Legal Case," 162, 165, 166
  snake as symbol of greed, 82, 83–84, 85
animosity, 103, 115–27, 150, 256, 259
appreciation
  expressions of, 234–35, 242, 245, 257
  false, 150–51
  lack of, 281; by leaders, 149, 155, 164; for leaders, 149, 153–54, 155, 164
  of life as it occurs, 246, 247, 250, 251
  poverty limiting, 153
  reciprocity and, 242
  regret and, 141, 143–57
Arab traders in Buganda, 3, 52, 56
"As He Plucked Them" ("Bwe Yazimaanya")
  greed and selfishness in, 49–50, 69–78
  historical context, 69–70
  interpretations of, 71–78
  Kafeero's performance of, 9
  Kamaanya criticized in, 49–50
  musical elements, 70
  song text, 70
Askew, Kelly, 120, 169, 234

baaba (older sibling; endearment), 287
baakisimba (Kiganda drum or music and dance genre), 14, 16
"Baamunaanika Hill" ("Akasozi Baamunaanika"), 10
  genuine praise in, 204, 214–23
  historical context, 214–15, 219
  interpretations of, 219–23
  musical elements, 216
  song text, 216–18
  Sserwanga's performance of, 10
baana battu (endearment), 287
Baazibumbira, Matyansi Kibirige, 13, 254
Badongo Dancers, 22
Baganda (defined), xi. *See also specific terms and topics*
Bakan, Michael, 6
Balabarca, Lisette, 42
Bantu clans, 3
Bantu languages, xii
Barbalet, Jack M., 42, 44
Barz, Greg, 40
"Battle of Nsinsi, The" ("Olutalo olw'e Nsinsi"), 15
  Bisaso's performance of, 13
  civil war in, 239, 261–68
  historical context, 30, 261–62
  interpretations of, 265–68
  musical elements, 263–64
  song text, 264
bba bonna (king's honorific), 192
bbaffe (king's honorific), 194
Beliveau, Annie, 17–18
Besigye, Kizza, 17, 72, 119, 259–60, 272–73
Better Education Less Labor project, 123
Binaisa, Godfrey, 4

Binks, Emma, 17–18
Bisaso, Albert Ssempeke, 8–9, 23
  author and, 22
  biography of, 12–13
  bow harp performances, 12, 22
  on historical context of "The Battle of Nsinsi," 261
  instruments played by, 12
  performance of "The Battle of Nsinsi," 261, 263–64, 268
  performance of "Ssematimba and Kikwabanga," 241–44
  performance of "They Chopped Off His Fingers," 131, 133, 135–36, 138
  Ssempeke's and Sserwanga's legacies continued by, 13
bow harp (*adungu*), 12
bow harp (*ennanga*), 12, 22
  Bisaso as performer, 12, 22, 242, 263–64
  Gganga as performer, 128–31
  harmonic tunings of, 38
  Majwala as performer, 14, 22, 263–64, 282
  performance logistics of, 39
  role of king's private harpist, 28–29, 42
  Ssempeke as performer, 22, 144, 159
bowl lyre (*endongo*)
  Bisaso as performer, 12
  Kabwama as performer, 115–17
  Majwala as performer, 14
  symbolism of, 121
  variable tuning for, 38
bravery and courage, 134, 262, 267–68
Brick (Ettoffaali) fundraising scheme, 95, 181–82, 234–35

INDEX   303

Buganda, Kingdom of. *See also* court musicians; court songs in Buganda; *specific kings*
  Christian missionaries in, 3, 134–35, 185–86
  clan heritage, 230
  clan structure in, 70, 182
  conflicts with Bunyoro Kingdom, 30, 239, 261–65, 268
  court music in colonial, 9, 199–200
  court music in postcolonial, 4–6, 9–15, 225
  court musicians supported by Amin, 181
  court songs as living history, 36, 40, 46–48, 235–37, 263
  decline of royal political power, 199–200, 201–2
  dissolution of, 103
  education in, 123–24
  familial reverence for royalty in, 221–22
  female court musicians, 15–17
  female dancers, 15
  foreign cultural products in, 5–6
  history and political landscape, 3–4
  Kasubi tombs rebuilding project, 95–96, 181–82, 234
  Kiganda worldview, 20–21
  king's love for subjects, 205–13
  king's titles and honorifics, 81, 192, 194–95, 197–98, 230
  kings' tours of counties, 230–31, 232, 233
  kingship differences between past and present, 115–17
  leonine imagery of king, 142, 175–78, 188–92, 194–95, 199
  Mmengo court, 9, 10–12, 13, 14, 82, 88, 182, 215–16
  palace attack, 1966, 4, 10, 12, 13, 82, 225, 226
  post-1993 kingship restoration, 4–8, 9, 14, 87, 93, 233, 236
  post-independence social structure deterioration, 7
  pre-1966 tax arrangements, 88
  recent initiatives, 123–24, 220–21, 234–35
  regional rights demanded by, 87–101
  status within Uganda, 3, 4, 6–7, 188–92, 233–34
  Wamala court, 9
Buganda ku Ntikko (Buganda at the Peak) project, 123
bulungi bwansi (communal work), 88
Bunyoro, Kingdom of
  conflicts with Buganda Kingdom, 30, 239, 261–65, 268
  history of, 3
burial practices, Baganda traditional, 287

Cady, Elizabeth, 17–18
Campbell, John, 48
caution
  central government and, 233
  in dealing with leaders, 163–64, 168, 175–78, 192, 258
  karma and, 247
  leaders' need for, 54, 103, 105–14, 173, 206, 219
  trust and, 66–67, 183
  value of, 149–50, 248, 253, 257
  wisdom and, 62
cce (personal spirit or god), 171–72
ccuucu (signal grass), 194, 195
Cheeseman, Nic, 34
Chikowero, Mhoze, 43
Christian missionaries
  in Buganda, 3, 134–35, 185, 199–200
  in Uganda, 185–86

Ciantar, Philip, 33
Coffee Does Not Disappoint (Emmwanyi Terimba) program, 220–21
Cohen, Andrew, 3, 224–25
collaboration. *See also* cooperation
  benefits of, xvii, xix, 31
  interdependence and, 207
  leadership and, 109
  power dynamics and, 31, 33–35
colonial dynamics in ethnographic research, 33–35, 46–47
colonialism and colonial rule
  colonial mindset, 256
  European monarchical social norms, 6, 91–92
  nineteenth-century, 3
  power relations in, 42, 199–200, 201–2, 224–25
commentary, songs about, 43, 49–101
Como-Mosconi, Angelina, 17–18
compromise, 172–73, 194, 251
conflict, songs about, 239–92. *See also* domestic disputes; violence; war
connection. *See also* cooperation; mutuality
  importance of, xvi–xvii, 78, 147–48, 162
  between king and subjects, 7, 9, 92–93, 231–37,
  performer-audience, 41
Cooke, Andrew, 35, 36
Cooke, Peter, 35, 37, 82, 241
cooperation, 54–55, 75–76. *See also* mutuality; reciprocity
  songs about, 45, 203–37
corruption. *See* greed
courage. *See* bravery and courage
court musicians. *See also* specific kings; specific performers' names
  court pages (*abasiige*), 10, 134, 205–6, 214–16

  cultural importance of, 54–55
  dangers to, 7, 51–53, 54–55, 103, 128–39, 158–74
  featured in book, 8–15
  flattery of king, 49–50, 51–59, 60–68, 77
  guidance of king, 45, 69, 70–71, 105–9, 224–26
  instruments' importance to, 116–17
  instruments protected by after 1986 attack, 4, 225, 226, 232
  as intermediaries between court and public, 28–29, 49–50, 79–80, 82–83, 175–76
  intimacy with king, 117, 198, 214–16, 218–19
  king's private harpist, 28–29, 42, 128–39
  non-royal performances of, 5
  plots of land given by King Muteesa II to, 214–18
  role in explaining current events, 255
  tension between singers and leadership, 25
court pages (*abasiige*), 10, 134, 205–6, 215–16
court songs in Buganda. *See also* *specific performers or rulers*; *specific song titles*; *specific topics*
  biased views in lyrical interpretations, 27–28
  composer-performers of, 8–15, 22–23
  defining, 28–30
  ethical considerations and interpretive process, 25–27, 31
  instruments' use in, 37–39
  interpreters, working with, 17–18, 21–22, 23–25
  musical meaning, 39–41
  performance opportunities after 1993, 7

popular decline of, 5
power relations in, 41–46
rarity of current performance, 6
recasting (or reimagining) process
　in interpretation of, xviii–xix, 18,
　21, 32, 34–35, 40–41, 50
recontextualization of, 4–5, 17, 18,
　20–21, 22, 23–25, 32
repertoire of, 5, 28, 29, 36–37, 215
research methods and approaches to
　lyrical interpretation, 20–31
song text components, 36
songs about conflict and loss,
　239–92
songs about leadership and
　responsibility, 103–139
songs about loyalty and duty,
　141–202
songs about mutuality and
　cooperation, 203–37
songs about political engagement,
　criticism, and commentary,
　49–101
Criminal Investigations Directorate
　(CID), 25
criticism
　direct, 49–50, 66, 79–86
　indirect, 61, 69–78, 85, 131
　modes of, 43
　self-correction and, 109–11
　songs about, 49–101

Daily Monitor, 182
Daudi Ccwa II, King, 214, 222–23
　court musicians of, 9, 13, 14, 224
Dave, Nomi, 43
Dawuda, 11
death
　avoiding sentence of, 53, 54, 56,
　　128, 131, 133, 135, 136
　betrayal and, 122
　change and, 45–46, 288

　as extension of life, 281–92
　facing reality of, 159, 161–62, 164
　inevitability of, 288, 289
　of King Muteesa II, 111–12
　legacy and, 161–62, 168–69, 171,
　　174, 244
　mourning and ridicule, 50, 79–86
　as prerequisite to life, 251
　profundity of informing decision-
　　making, 250–51
　as ultimate instance of change, 165
　universality of, 287, 290–92
deceit, 49, 51, 57, 60, 62–68, 170,
　172–73
"deep Luganda," 41, 85–86
deliberation, 103, 115–27, 133, 266
determination
　of King Muteesa II, 230
　of leaders, 124, 193–94
　spirituality and, 271, 273, 280
　of warriors, 251, 253, 268
Deziderio, Ssaalongo Kiwanuka
　Matovu, 8–9, 22–23
　author and, 22
　biography of, 13
　as composer of "Federalism,"
　　87–101
　on context of "Federalism," 87–88
　on context of "The King Is a Lion,"
　　188–89
　on context of "Unadvisable
　　Kayemba," 105–6
　as court musician, 198
　on historical context of "Poland,"
　　254–57, 260
　performance of "Federalism," 87–89
　performance of "The King Is a
　　Lion," 189–92, 200, 201
　performance of "Poland," 255–56
　performance of "Unadvisable
　　Kayemba," 106, 114
Diamond, Beverley, 33, 46–47, 256

disagreement
  complex dynamics in, 239, 269–80
  reconciling differences, 120–21, 212
domestic disputes, xx–xxi, 30, 269–70, 272, 275–76, 277, 279, 280
Drum Making as a Way of Life in Southern Uganda (film), 18
drums, Kiganda, 14
  as conduits for speech, 38
  female performers, 15, 16–17
  gendering of, 16
Dungu, Solomy Katasi, 36
duty
  justice and, 103
  of leaders, 71, 75
  mutuality and, 44–45, 113
  power relations and, 44–45
  serving the king not viewed as, 117
  songs about, 141–202
  of subjects, 103

ebika (clans), 70
ebisoko (idioms), 60
Egypt, 43
ekiswa (anthill), 188
ekitembe (wild, inedible banana plant), 287–88
ekitooke (banana plant), 287
ekkanzu (tunic), 52
Elephant (Njovu) Clan, 10
embuutu (also *mbuutu*; Kiganda drum), 14, 38
emibala (melo-rhythmic beats with associated textual phrases), 38
empologoma (king's title "lion"), 175
empuunyi (Kiganda drum), 14
endere. See notched flute (*endere*)
endingidi. See tube fiddle (*endingidi*)
endongo. See bowl lyre (*endongo*)
engalabi (Kiganda drum), 14
enjobe (antelope), 87

enkejje (haplochromis), 143, 149–50
enkenku (stale beer), 24
ennaka. See white ants, harvesting
ennanga. See bow harp (*ennanga*)
eŋŋombe. See animal horn (*eŋŋombe*)
ensaasi (gourd shakers), 14
envubu (hippopotamus), 87
Ethiopia, 45
ettale (meadow), 87
Ettoffaali fundraising scheme, 95, 181–82, 234–35
exploitation, 87–101
  by colonial powers, 199–202
  by leaders, 96, 99–100, 113, 245, 259, 267

"Fair-Skinned" ("Kabirinnage")
  continuing relevance of, 67–68
  flattery, deceit, and satire in, 49, 60–68
  historical context, 60–61
  interpretations of, 62–67
  Kafeero's performance of, 9
  musical elements, 61
  song text, 61, 67
false praise. *See also* flattery; manipulation
  critiquing through, 66–67
  of King Ssuuna II, 49, 50, 51–59
  manipulation through, 150–51, 166–68, 203
fate
  accepting, 290
  of death, 289
  of Gganga, 103, 133, 134, 136
  spirituality and, 273, 274, 279
  uncertainty of, 166–67
  war and, 239, 241–53
"Federalism" ("Federo")
  animal symbolism in, 87–88, 93

as Buganda Kingdom's unofficial anthem, 100
Deziderio's performance of, 13, 87–93
engagement with national politics, 30, 87–101
interpretations of, 93–101
manipulation, exploitation, and reciprocity in, 50, 87–101
musical elements, 88–89
political context, 87–88, 91–92
private group performance of, 30
song text, 89–91
text analysis, 91–93
Feld, Steven, 46
fiddle, tube. *See* tube fiddle (*endingidi*)
flattery
false praise and, 45, 49, 52–53, 58, 77, 150–51
manipulation through, 60–68, 166–68, 178–79
mockery disguised as, 49
by opportunists, 156
self-worth and, 62
by wedding performers, 63
flute. *See* notched flute (*endere*)
"Flutists' Legal Case, The" ("Omusango gw'Abalere"), 55
historical context, 158–59
interpretations of, 163–74
lament and uncertainty in, 141, 158–74
musical elements, 159
song text, 159–61
Ssempeke's performance of, 10
Flutists of the King (Abalere ba Kabaka) ensemble, 11
Foucault, Michel, 46, 65, 256
"Freedom" ("Ddembe") (B. Wine), 66
friendship. *See also* mutuality
dissolution of, 257

love, unity, and reciprocity in, 203, 205–13
purposes of, 178–79, 189, 201
value of, 73, 206–9, 213, 257–58
Frolova-Walker, Marina, 44–45
Full Figure, 64–65, 167, 210

Gabunga, 143–44
Gaddafi, Muammar, 248, 274
Garratt, James, 43
gender and court music performance, 15–17
"Get Up" ("Situka") (B. Wine), 66
"Gganga Had a Narrow Escape" ("Gganga Alula"). *See also* "They Chopped Off His Fingers" ("Baamutemako Engalo")
historical context, 128–31, 136–37
interpretations of, 134–39
musical elements, 129, 130
punishment and mercy in, 103, 128–39
song text, 129–30, 131–33
Ssebuwufu's performance of, 10, 128–31, 206
versions compared, 133
Ghana, 43
Gilman, Lisa, 37
Gombe, Kabenge, 17
gourd shakers (*ensaasi*), 14
Grasshopper (Nseenene) Clan, 69, 70, 77
gratitude, 76, 157, 177, 239–40, 242, 245–47, 253
greed
avoiding, 170–71
gluttony associated with, 76
of leaders, 49–50, 69–78, 92–93, 96, 117, 155–56, 180–87, 213, 253
of leaders' associates, 220, 223, 226, 266–67

greed (*cont'd*)
　leonine imagery, 180–86
　in modern Uganda and Africa as a whole, 170
　refusing, 251
　serpentine imagery, 82, 83–84, 85
　uplift rejecting, 251
ground bows (*ssekitulege*), 39
Guinea, 43

"Hand Him Over to Kyagulanyi" ("Mukwase Kyagulanyi") (B. Wine), 66
"Handsome Catch a Slight Squint, The" ("Empujjo Zikwata Balungi"), 166n5
　false praise in, 49, 51–59
　historical context, 51–54
　interpretations of, 54–58, 64
　Kafeero's performance of, 9
　musical elements, 53–54
　song text, 53
Hanna, Judith Lynne, 35
Hanna, William John, 35
Hannington, James, 134
harp. *See* bow harp (*ennanga*)
"Harvester of White Ants, The" ("Omussi w'Enswa"), xvi–xviii
"He Has a Lot on His Mind" (Alina Bingi By'Alowooza")
　deliberation and animosity in, 103, 115–27
　interpretations of, 117–26
　Kabwama's performance of, 14, 115–17
　musical elements, 115
　sociopolitical contexts, 29
　song text, 115–16
healing ceremonies, Kiganda, 270
Hoesing, Peter, 270
Hoffman, Barbara G., 43

horn, animal. *See* animal horn (*eŋŋombe*)
householder (*nnannyinimu*), 81, 83, 92, 137, 197
"Householder" ("Nnannyinimu")
　continuing relevance of, 86
　cultural imagery in, 50, 84–86
　historical context, 79–80
　interpretations of, 81–86
　Kafeero's performance of, 9
　mourning and ridicule in, 50, 79–86
　musical elements, 80
　song text, 80–81

"I Am Fed Up with Them" ("Mbakooye) (Kenzo song), 66
"I Would Have Given You a Large Haplochromis" ("Nandikuwadde Enkejje Entulumba")
　historical context, 143–44
　interpretations of, 147–57
　musical elements, 144
　regret and appreciation in, 141, 143–57
　song text, 144–46
　Ssempeke's performance of, 10
imperialism, 30, 239, 254–60
inanga. *See* trough zither (*inanga*)
Institutional Review Board (IRB), 25
instruments, Kiganda court. *See also specific types*
　differences in agency and creative freedom for, 38–39
　performance of songs on, 37–39
　political power of, 116–17
　post-attack survival of, 4, 225, 226, 232
　vocal accompaniment for, 39
invocation, spiritual, 171, 239, 269–80
Islam in Buganda, 3

Janzen, John, 270
Jjunju, King
   court musicians of, 143–44
   war with the Bunyoro Kingdom, 261–65, 267
Jjuuko, Denis, 181–82
Johnson, Boris, 126

kabaka (Buganda king), 36, 70, 82
Kabaka Education Fund, 123
Kabalega, Omukama, King of Bunyoro, 266
Kabugo, Steven Mukasa, 17
   alternative version of King Kayemba's death, 107
   interpretation of "As He Plucked Them," 76–77
   interpretation of "Baamunaanika Hill," 221–22
   interpretation of "Fair-Skinned," 63
   interpretation of "Federalism," 94–95
   interpretation of "The Flutists' Legal Case," 166–67
   interpretation of "Gganga Had a Narrow Escape," 137
   interpretation of "The Handsome Catch a Slight Squint," 55
   interpretation of "Householder," 84–85
   interpretation of "I Would Have Given You a Large Haplochromis," 151
   interpretation of "The King Is a Lion," 193
   interpretation of "Let Me Plod with a Stick Close to Kibuuka," 275–77
   interpretation of "The Little Lion," 178–79
   interpretation of "Ssematimba and Kikwabanga," 246
   interpretation of "Unadvisable Kayemba," 107
Kabwama, Kayondo, 14
Kabwama, Ssaalongo Paulo, 8–9, 23
   biography of, 14
   performance of "He Has a Lot on His Mind," 115–17, 125, 127
Kafeero, Mukasa, 23
   biography of, 9
   on historical context of "As He Plucked Them," 69–70
   on historical context of "Fair-Skinned," 60–61
   on historical context of "The Handsome Catch a Slight Squint," 51–53
   on historical context of "Householder," 79–80
   performance of "As He Plucked Them," 70
   performance of "Fair-Skinned," 61
   performance of "The Handsome Catch a Slight Squint," 53–54
   performance of "Householder," 80
   performance style of, 9
   on Ssuuna II, 44
Kafumbe, Damascus, xi, 4, 22n1, 23n2, 70n2, 224–25n1
Kagame, Paul, 135, 267
Kakumba, Mark, 134
Kalyagonja, Yowaana Maswanku, 10
Kamaanya, King
   compared to current Ugandan leadership, 72–74, 76
   court musicians of, 45, 69–78
   dislike of music, 44, 60, 61
   failure as leader, 76
   life and reign of, 9
   temperament of, 51, 53, 69, 70–71
Kaminski, Joseph, 43
Kamya, Betty, 119
Karlström, Mikael, 7, 185

Kasubi tombs rebuilding project, 95–96, 181, 182, 234–35
Kasule, Sam, 82
Kato Ruhuuga (Kato Kintu), 3
Kayemba, King
  arrogance of, 108–9
  attempted assassination of, 67, 103, 105–14
  court musicians of, 106, 107
Kenya, 267
Kenyatta, Uhuru, 267
Kenzo, Eddy, 66
Khachaturian, Aram, 44–45
Kibirige, Jimmy Ssenfuka, 17
  interpretation of "As He Plucked Them," 71, 75
  interpretation of "The Battle of Nsinsi," 266–67
  interpretation of "Fair-Skinned," 63–65
  interpretation of "Federalism," 97–98, 99
  interpretation of "The Flutists' Legal Case," 171–73
  interpretation of "The Handsome Catch a Slight Squint," 56–58
  interpretation of "He Has a Lot on His Mind," 122–24
  interpretation of "Householder," 83–84
  interpretation of "I Would Have Given You a Large Haplochromis," 153–56
  interpretation of "The King Is a Lion," 197–98, 200–201
  interpretation of "Let Me Plod with a Stick Close to Kibuuka," 277–79
  interpretation of "The Little Lion," 183–84
  interpretation of "Ssematimba and Kikwabanga," 245–46
  interpretation of "They Show Each Other Stumps," 211–12
  interpretation of "Unadvisable Kayemba," 108–9
  interpretation of "We Love the Supreme Man Exceedingly," 232–33
Kibirige (court flutist), 11
Kibuuka (warrior god), 30, 261–62, 263, 269–70, 272, 273–74, 275, 276, 279, 280
Kiganda conception of history, 47
Kiganda (defined), xi
Kiganda drums. *See* drums, Kiganda; *specific names*
Kiganda musical instruments, 10–14, 22. *See also* instruments, Kiganda court
Kiganda song, 35–39. *See also* court songs in Buganda
  ambiguity in, 40–41
  Luganda language of, 35, 37
  lyric components in, 36
  musical elements in, 35–36
  purposes of, 36–37
Kinene, Peter, 17
  on harvesting white ants in Buganda, xv–xviii
  interpretation of "As He Plucked Them," 73, 76
  interpretation of "Baamunaanika Hill," 219–21
  interpretation of "Fair-Skinned," 66–67
  interpretation of "Federalism," 95–96
  interpretation of "The Flutists' Legal Case," 163–65, 169–71
  interpretation of "Gganga Had a Narrow Escape," 134–35
  interpretation of "He Has a Lot on His Mind," 121–22, 124–25

interpretation of "I Would
  Have Given You a Large
  Haplochromis," 152–53
interpretation of "The King Is a
  Lion," 196–97
interpretation of "Let Me Plod
  with a Stick Close to Kibuuka,"
  279–80
interpretation of "The Little Lion,"
  186
interpretation of "Poland," 257–58
interpretation of "Ssematimba and
  Kikwabanga," 247–48, 250
interpretation of "They Show Each
  Other Stumps," 209–10
interpretation of "Unadvisable
  Kayemba," 111–13
interpretation of "We Love the
  Supreme Man Exceedingly," 232,
  235–36
"King Is a Lion, The" ("Kabaka
  Mpologoma")
  Deziderio's performance of, 13,
    188–202
  interpretations of, 193–202
  musical elements, 189–90
  reverence and love in, 142, 188–202
  song text, 190–92
kinship
  Buganda social structure, 4
  conflict and, 270
  deterioration of Buganda social
    structure, 7
  fracturing, 287, 291
  idea image of king as family, 222,
    223
  legacy and, 161–62, 169, 171, 174,
    235–36, 240, 244, 280
  missionaries' devaluation of, 185
  white ants story and, xvii
Kironde, Edward Ssebunnya, 17,
  258–59

on historical context of "The Battle
  of Nsinsi," 261–62
on historical context of "Poland,"
  254–56
interpretation of "As He Plucked
  Them," 73–74
interpretation of "The Flutists' Legal
  Case," 167–68
interpretation of "He Has a Lot on
  His Mind," 119–22, 125–26
interpretation of "Householder,"
  81–82
interpretation of "I Would
  Have Given You a Large
  Haplochromis," 148–49, 151–53
interpretation of "The King Is a
  Lion," 194–96
interpretation of "Let Me Plod
  with a Stick Close to Kibuuka,"
  273–74
interpretation of "The Little Lion,"
  180–83
interpretation of "Mawanda Loves
  His Men," 210–11
interpretation of "Ssematimba and
  Kikwabanga," 248–49
interpretation of "Unadvisable
  Kayemba," 109
interpretation of "We Love the
  Supreme Man Exceedingly,"
  231–32
Kisuule, Harriet, 17
interpretation of "As He Plucked
  Them," 72, 75–76
interpretation of "Baamunaanika
  Hill," 219, 222
interpretation of "Fair-Skinned,"
  62–63
interpretation of "The Flutists' Legal
  Case," 173–74
interpretation of "He Has a Lot on
  His Mind," 117–19

Kisuule, Harriet (cont'd)
  interpretation of "I Would
    Have Given You a Large
    Haplochromis," 149–51
  interpretation of "The King Is a
    Lion," 193–94
  interpretation of "Let Me Plod
    with a Stick Close to Kibuuka,"
    272–73
  interpretation of "The Little Lion,"
    179
  interpretation of "Ssematimba and
    Kikwabanga," 251–52
  interpretation of "Unadvisable
    Kayemba," 109–11
  interpretation of "We Love the
    Supreme Man Exceedingly,"
    24–25
Kityo, John Magandaazi, 17
  interpretation of "Federalism,"
    93–94, 99–100
  interpretation of "The Flutists' Legal
    Case," 165–66
  interpretation of "The Handsome
    Catch a Slight Squint," 55
  interpretation of "Householder," 84
  interpretation of "I Would
    Have Given You a Large
    Haplochromis," 147–48
  interpretation of "The King Is a
    Lion," 199–200, 201
  interpretation of "Poland," 259–60
  interpretation of "They Show Each
    Other Stumps," 211–12
  interpretation of "Unadvisable
    Kayemba," 107–8
  interpretation of "We Love the
    Supreme Man Exceedingly," 25
Kkunsa, 52–53, 54
Kodesh, Neil, 6
Kony, 65–66

Kubik, Gerhard, 6
Kulthūm, Umm, 43
kwaito music, 43
Kyagambiddwa, Joseph, 37–38
  on historical context of "The Battle
    of Nsinsi," 262

lamellaphone (*akogo*), 12
lament
  lack of legacy and, 161–62
  of living, 281–82
  over failed relationship, 280
  regret and, 253
  sarcastic, 79, 83
  self-reflection and, 152, 153, 156
  uncertainty and, 141, 158–74
Langlois, Tony, 40
leadership
  adaptable and solution-based,
    122–23
  advice and caution, 103, 105–14,
    150–51, 173, 175–80, 210–11,
    219
  appreciation between citizens and,
    150, 153–55, 157, 219, 234
  arrogance and self-centeredness, 73,
    74, 92, 108–10, 119, 147, 178,
    211–12, 213, 263
  carelessness of, 258–59
  change and, 288–89, 290
  conflict avoidance, 264–66, 268
  court songs links to, 49
  deliberation and animosity, 103,
    117–24
  empathy and, 187, 259, 266
  failed reciprocity in, 147–49, 157
  flexibility in, 277–79, 289
  follow-through and, 24–25, 123
  forgiveness in, 158–59
  greed and, 92–93
  lack of appreciation for, 153–54

listening and dialogue as qualities of good, 44, 56–57, 108–11, 118, 171–72, 219, 251–252, 260
"little lions" in governmental systems, 180–85
morality and, 290–91
mutuality and, 57–58, 109–10
oppressive, 81–85, 109–14
overwork and, 126
persistence and, 124, 272–73, 279
profundity of death informing decision-making, 250–51
proverbs on, 124–25
punishment and mercy, 103, 128–39
qualities of good, 179, 186
resistance to change and, 163–66
responsibility and, 44, 62–63, 71–72, 75, 83, 98, 103–39, 155–56
selfishness and, 71, 73, 74–75, 92, 178, 211–13, 263
self-obsession of, 156, 157
social responsibilities of, 251–52
songs about, 103–39
thoughtless, 123–24
trust and, 173–74
unrealistic expectations for, 151–52
legacy
ancestral, 196
cultivating a, 252–53
kinship and, 161–62, 168–69, 171, 174, 235–36, 240, 280
"Let Me Plod with a Stick Close to Kibuuka" ("Ka Nsimbe Omuggo awali Kibuuka")
background story, 269–70
disagreement and invocation in, 239, 269–80
familial and marital conflicts in, 30
interpretations of, 272–80
musical elements, 270–71
song text, 271–72

Ssempeke's performance of, 10
"Little Lion, The" ("Akawologoma")
historical context, 175–76
interpretations of, 178–87
musical elements, 176
power and selfishness in, 142, 175–87
song text, 176–77
Ssempeke's performance of, 10
living in the moment, 29, 239, 241, 244–46, 247, 253, 290
Lohman, Laura, 43
Lonsdale, John, 92, 118, 153, 226
Lord's Resistance Army, 66, 135, 265
loss
denial of, 98
inability to accept, 164
intersection with spirituality, 281–82
isolation and, 162, 186, 250
mutual, 97
of mutuality, 117
poor leadership and, 121–22
of reciprocity, 146, 157
songs about, 239–92
tragedy of, 261–62, 264–65
love. *See also* loyalty; reverence
death and, 288, 290
for friends, 206, 208–9, 212–13
for king, 188–237
of the king for his subjects, 142, 207, 212–13
for lion owned by king, 175–78, 186–87
loyalty
to king, 36, 153, 157, 218, 220–21, 222–23, 226, 232–34, 268
of leaders, 71, 179
negative side to, 141
power relations and, 44–45, 122
songs about, 141–202
universality of, 142
lubaale (deity), 262

Luganda language
  "deep Luganda," 41, 85–86
  defined, xi–xiii
Lule, Yusuf, 4
Lumoonyere (King Ssuuna II's flute), 51
Lwanga, Charles, 134
lyre, bowl. *See* bowl lyre (*endongo*)
lyrical interpretation. *See also specific songs and interpreters*
  biased views in, 27–28
  defined, 21
  ethical considerations and interpretive process, 25–27
  indigenous representation in, 33–35, 46–47
  recasting (or reimagining) process in, xviii–xix, xxi–xxii, 18, 21, 32, 34–35, 40–41, 50
  working with composer-performers, 22–23
  working with interpreters of songs' meanings, 23–25

Mackinlay, Elizabeth, 33
Magoba, Waalabyeki, 17
Majwala, Ssaalongo Ssennoga, 9, 23
  on advisory role of king's private harpist, 28
  on background of "The Pebble Is Breaking Me," 281–82
  biography of, 14–15
  bow harp performances, 14, 22
  performance of "The Battle of Nsinsi," 261, 263–65, 268
  performance of "The Pebble Is Breaking Me," 282–88
Makubuya, James, 116
Malawi, 37
Mali, 43
manipulation
  breakdown of trust through, 97, 118, 183
  ingratiation through, 178–79
  by leaders, 50, 54, 87–101, 181, 237, 278
  of leaders, 54–58, 60, 64–65, 94, 171–72, 174, 203–4, 220
  mediating relationships through, 168
  of subordinates, 112
  of system, 167–68, 183–84, 197, 220, 237, 248–49, 259
Martin, James, 134
materialism, 257–58, 281, 288–92
Mawanda, King, 203, 205–13
"Mawanda Loves His Men" ("Mawanda Ayagala Abasajja Be")
  historical context, 205–6
  interpretations of, 209–13
  love, unity, and reciprocity in, 203, 205–13
  musical elements, 207–8
  song text, 207–8
  Ssebuwufu's performance of, 10
Mayiga, Charles Peter, 17, 95, 181–82
Mayinja, Ronald, 66
Mazrui, Ali, 234
mercy, 54, 59, 103, 128–39
Micklem, James, 35–36
mindset, 7, 34, 120, 183, 274, 250
mortality, 45, 239–40, 265, 281–92. *See also* death
mourning, 50, 79–86
Mukasa, Joseph, 134
Mukasa (chief administrator of the gods), 171
Museveni, Yoweri Kaguta
  commentaries referencing, 17, 24–25
  disappointment with, 100
  eventual death of, 290–91

"Federalism" and, 87–101
flattery of, 167
Full Figure and, 64–65, 210
government oppression under, 83, 184, 185–86, 222, 248–49
isolation of, 72, 110, 196–97
leadership of, 104, 114, 118, 148, 150, 151, 200–201, 220
opposition to, 119–20, 163, 259–60, 268, 272–73, 274, 278
party system dissolution under, 8
power seizure, 1986, 4
reign longevity of, 7–8, 58, 274
restoration of kingdoms, 87
satirical song about, 65–66
self-centeredness of, 74, 92, 97–98
support for, 66
treatment of Buganda King Sir Mutebi II, 62, 194, 196–97, 219, 233, 234
as a young leader, 111
Mushroom (Butiko) Clan, 17
Musicians of the King (Abadongo ba Kabaka) court ensemble, 11, 13
musota (snake), 194
Mutebi II, King Ronald
commentaries referencing, 17
coronation of, 4, 224, 230
court musicians of, 10, 225
cross-county tour of, 230–31, 233
Deziderio's performance of "Federalism" for, 88
father's influence on, 231
initiatives of, 124, 220–21, 234–35
Museveni's treatment of, 62, 194, 196–97, 219, 233, 234
praise of, 230–31
Muteesa I, King
court musicians of, 158
European ridicule of, 199–200
lion at court of, 175–76, 181, 186, 187

Muteesa II, King Sir Edward
court musicians of, 9–14, 22, 26, 205–6, 214–18, 220–21, 224–25, 232, 237
death of, 4, 111–12, 225, 290
example to son, 231
first exile of, 3, 224–25, 230, 232
loyalty of subjects, 179
praise of, 204, 224–31
return from exile, 16
second exile of, 4, 12, 225, 230
Ssebuwufu as court page for, 10, 205–6
university named after, 123
as Uganda's first president, 3–4, 88, 200
mutuality. *See also* reciprocity
between allies, 211
as core African societal value, 45–46, 203
amid disagreement, 212
extra-temporal, 210, 230, 235–36
friendship and, 213
between government and the people, 120–21
in human relationships, 143–44, 146–47, 153, 178–79, 248–49, 253
in Kiganda performance practices, 39
between king and aides, 53
between king and court musicians, 116–17, 158–74, 214–37, 224–37
between king and subjects, 45–46, 64, 97, 106, 186, 210–11, 231, 237
between leaders and their people, 57–58, 109–11, 118–19, 142, 151–53, 157, 179, 193–94, 196–97, 200–201, 207, 220–23, 232–33
mediating, 163–64, 192, 270, 275–77

mutuality (*cont'd*)
  rejuvenation of people through, 231
  between rulers and opposition, 120–21, 211, 259–60
  songs about, 203–37
  of trust, 141
  between wildlife species, 93
Muyinda, Evaristo, 12, 148, 185
Mwanga II, King
  court musicians of, 128–39
  Uganda Martyrs and, 134–35

Nakachwa, Francisca, 17
nankasa (also *namunjoloba;* Kiganda drum), 14
Nannyonga, Sylvia, 36
Nannyonga-Tamusuza, Sylvia, 15, 16, 41
National Resistance Movement (NRM), 7, 72–74, 87, 118
ndongo (wedding dance), 185
nepotism, 76–77
ngòmà (healing ceremony), 270
Nishikubo, Ryo, 18
Njabala, tale of, xix–xxii
Nketia, J. H. Kwabena, 6, 39, 40–41
Nnakuzaabasajja, Antanansi, 10
nnamunswa (queen), 188
nnannyinimu. See householder (*nnannyinimu*)
"Nnannyinimu" ("Householder"). *See* "Householder" ("Nnannyinimu")
nnandigobe (banana), 230
nnantanyoomebwa (leader's honorific), 197
Nooshin, Laudan, 42, 44
notched flute (*endere*), 11–12, 39
  Bisaso as performer, 12
  Ssempeke as performer, 271
  Sserwanga as performer, 208, 241
  Ssuuna II as performer, 51–52
Nyanzi, Stella, 184–85

Obote, Apollo Milton, 3–4, 7, 82, 200–201, 274
  Museveni's defeat of, 7
obusuulu (land tax), 88
"Officer, I Do Not Fight with You" ("Afande Sirwana Naawe") (B. Wine), 66
okulanga (to announce), 28
okusamira (spirit mediumship), 270
okuyimba (to sing), 39
olubiri (Buganda's royal court), 28
olusa (marsh), 87
oluwa (the giver), 52
oluwalo (land tax), 88
Omojola, Bode, 34–35, 41
omulanga (king's private harpist), 28–29
omumbowa (royal bodyguard), 52
omunazi (xylophone primary melody player), 129, 206–7
omusiige (court page). *See* court pages
omuziro (primary totem), 70
omwawuzi (xylophone secondary melody player), 129, 206–7
Opera News, 266
oral traditions, studying, 46–48
Oromo, Arsi, 45
Otafiire, Kahinda, 17, 74
Ouattara, Issiaka, 196

Padwick, Constance E., 199–200
"Pebble Is Breaking Me, The" ("Akayinja Kammenya"), 15
  effects of death in, 30
  historical context, 281
  interpretations of, 289–92
  mortality and spirituality in, 239–40, 281–92
  musical elements, 282
  song text, 282–89
People Power Movement, 64, 155
Peterson, Derek, 6–7

Pier, David, 41, 85, 226, 234
Players of Akadinda Xylophones (Abaakadinda) court ensemble, 10
"Poland" ("Polanda")
   Deziderio's performance of, 13, 255–56
   historical context, 29–30, 254–55
   interpretations of, 257–60
   musical elements, 255–56
   song text, 256
   war and imperialism in, 239, 254–60
political engagement, songs about, 43, 49–101. *See also specific leaders and institutions*
Politz, Sarah, 65
poverty, 92, 96, 99, 137, 149, 152–53, 157, 210
power relations, 41–46
   advice and caution in, 105–14, 163–64
   collaboration and, 31, 33–34
   between composer-performers and audience, 25
   between court musicians and king, 45, 51–55, 69, 70–71, 77–78, 106–9, 116–17, 138, 158–74, 187, 189–90, 214–37
   between court musicians and public, 28–29, 49–50, 175–76
   decolonizing, 33–35
   discovering and discussing, 27–28
   ethnography and, 31
   failed reciprocity and, 147
   flattery and, 45, 178–79
   of king vs. power of national political leaders, 188–89, 195–202, 237
   loyalty and duty in, 44–45
   lyrical interpretations of, 24–25, 26–27, 30, 32
   music as a medium for, 41–42
   musical artists under authoritarian regimes, 42–45
   mutuality and, 275–77
   opposition's methods, 119–23
   pillars of, 141
   posturing in, 167–68
   respect and, 44, 45
   role of king's private harpist, 28–29, 42
   selfishness and, 142, 175–87
   transnational, 239
   trust and, 45, 112–13, 233–34
   violence and, 45–46, 264–65
praise, genuine, 204, 214–23. *See also false praise*
prejudice, fear of otherness and, 165–67
proverbs and sayings, Kiganda
   on advice, 151
   on betrayal, 170
   on caution, 111–12
   on debtor-lender relations, 275–77
   on excessiveness, 24
   on fresh leadership, 278–79
   on generosity, 76
   on industriousness and leadership, 124–25
   insights gained from, 78
   on knowledge, xix
   on lack of follow-through, 24–25
   on need for advice, 151
   on nepotism, 77
   on persistence, 279
   on personal efforts, 113
   on physical appearance, 63
   on success and friendship, 73
   on war, 241, 266
Przybylski, Liz, 33
Pun, Sara Hong-Yeung, 33
punishment
   of Christian martyrs, 134–35
   consequences of, 170, 186
   of court musicians, 55, 103, 128–39, 158–74
   karma and, 246
   subtlety avoiding, 85–86

Qashu, Leila, 45

reciprocity. *See also* mutuality
 appreciation and, 150–51
 conceptions of, 280
 failed, 50, 93–100, 146–51, 154, 157, 163, 272
 in human relations, 76
 importance of, 232
 in human relations, 76
 between king and court musicians, 44, 106, 117–18
 of King Muteesa II, 215–16
 between leaders and subjects, 12, 57, 137, 139, 142, 179, 189, 193, 198, 201, 203, 205, 208–13, 219–20, 223
 mindfulness and, 245–46, 253
 multivalent depiction of, 173–74
 between musicians, 39
 notion of, 147
 between opposing political actors, 120–21, 211
 as practice of mutual growth, 242, 245
 present-mindedness and, 246
 prioritizing, 258
 of punishment and mercy, 138
 search for, 153
 selective, 98–99
 subliminal, 272
 trust and, 208–10
 of violence, 245, 247–48
 in white ants' harvesting procedure, xvii, xviii
Reed, Daniel, 47
regret, 159, 239, 242, 282
 appreciation and, 141, 143–57, 164
 fate and, 171
respect
 consequences of disrespect, 55, 137, 141, 158, 166, 171, 174, 192
 for king, 141–42, 189, 192–202, 203–4, 221–22, 224–37
 mutual, 113, 150
 for others, 95–96
 by rulers for subjects, 44, 45, 53, 59, 109, 252
responsibility
 lack of, by president, 219
 of leaders for victims of violence, 136–37
 leaders' rejection of, 222
 of leaders to subjects, 44, 62–63, 71–72, 75, 83, 98, 103–39, 189, 206, 216, 221, 223, 230, 231, 232, 235–37, 252, 267
 of subjects to leaders, 156, 205, 215, 226
 songs about, 103–39
reverence. *See also* love
 familiarity and, 192, 221
 for king, 142, 187, 188–202, 214–23
ridicule
 of Buganda's king by Westerners, 199–200
 of leadership, 212
 mourning and, 50, 79–86
Robinson, Dylan, 34
Rubadiri, David, 185
Rugarama, Joseph, 134
Rwanda, 267

Sanga, Imani, 34, 54–55
sarcasm, 52, 61, 66–68, 79–80, 81
satire, 49, 56, 61, 62–68, 196
sayings, Kiganda. *See* proverbs and sayings, Kiganda
Schoenbrun, David L., 270
selfishness
 avoiding, 183–84, 253
 of leaders, 49–50, 69–78, 98, 117–20, 122, 169–71, 174, 180–81, 267, 291

power and, 142, 175–87, 189
reciprocity and, 148
in Ugandan society, 95
selflessness, 76, 209, 230, 263, 267–68
self-preservation, 123, 251–52
Serwadda, Moses, 185
Serwanga, Noah, 134
Siblings in Love (Abooluganda Kwagalana) ensemble, 12, 22
Sorbo, Brett, 18
South Africa, 43
sovereignty, king's, 194–98, 201
ignorance of, 92
spirituality, 101, 231, 239–40, 270–74, 280, 281–92
ssaabasajja (king's honorific), 194
ssaabataka (supreme landowner; king's honorific), 194
Ssebuwufu, Musisi, 10
Ssebuwufu, Semeo Ssemambo
on background of "Baamunaanika Hill," 215–16
on background of "Mawanda Loves His Men," 205–7
biography of, 9–10
on history of "Gganga Had a Narrow Escape," 128–31, 133
interpretation of "The Harvester of White Ants," xviii
performance of "Gganga Had a Narrow Escape," 129–31, 133, 135–36, 206
performance of "Mawanda Loves His Men," 205–8
as resident page, 10, 205–6, 215–16, 219–21
as xylophonist, 9, 129
ssekitulege. *See* ground bows (*ssekitulege*)

Ssemakookiro, Prince, 262
ssemandaagamenyembazzi (a man like charcoal that breaks an axe), 194
"Ssematimba and Kikwabanga" ("Ssematimba ne Kikwabanga")
Bisaso's performance of, 13, 241, 242
historical context, 29, 241–42
interpretations of, 245–53
musical elements, 242
song text, 242–44
Sserwanga's performance of, 10
war and fate in, 239, 241–53
Ssempeke, Albert Muwanga, 8–9, 23
author and, 22
biography of, 10–12
Bisaso as son of, 12
bow harp performances, 22
on context of "Let Me Plod with a Stick Close to Kibuuka," 269–70
as court musician, 225
on historical context of "The Flutists' Legal Case," 158–59
on historical context of "I Would Have Given You a Large Haplochromis," 143–44
on historical context of "The Little Lion," 175–76, 187
legacy continued by Bisaso, 13
performance of "The Flutists' Legal Case," 159
performance of "I Would Have Given You a Large Haplochromis," 144–46
performance of "Let Me Plod with a Stick Close to Kibuuka," 271
performance of "The Little Lion," 176
sound recording by, 36

Ssendawula, Jessy, 17
   on historical context of "The Battle of Nsinsi," 262–63
   interpretation of "As He Plucked Them," 72–73
   interpretation of "The Battle of Nsinsi," 265–66, 267, 268
   interpretation of "Fair-Skinned," 65–66
   interpretation of "Federalism," 96–97
   interpretation of "Gganga Had a Narrow Escape," 135–37
   interpretation of "The Handsome Catch a Slight Squint," 54–55
   interpretation of "Householder," 83
   interpretation of "The King Is a Lion," 198–99
   interpretation of "The Little Lion," 184–86
   interpretation of "The Pebble Is Breaking Me," 289–91
   interpretation of "Poland," 258
   interpretation of "Ssematimba and Kikwabanga," 246–47, 249–51, 252
   interpretation of "Unadvisable Kayemba," 113–14
   interpretation of "We Love the Supreme Man Exceedingly," 233–35
Ssentamu, Robert Kyagulanyi. *See* Wine, Bobi
Sserwanga, Ludoviiko, 8–9, 23
   author and, 22
   on background of "Ssematimba and Kikwabanga," 241–42, 245
   on background of "They Show Each Other Stumps," 206
   on background of "We Love the Supreme Man Exceedingly," 224–25
   biography of, 10–12
   Bisaso as nephew of, 12
   on celebrations marking Muteesa II's return from exile, 16
   as court musician, 219–21, 223–26
   on historical context of "Baamunaanika Hill," 214–15
   legacy continued by Bisaso, 13
   performance of "Baamunaanika Hill," 216–18
   performance of "They Show Each Other Stumps," 207–9
   performance of "We Love the Supreme Man Exceedingly," 226–30, 234
Ssuuna II, King
   appearance of, 52, 60–61, 63–64
   court musicians of, 51–68, 158, 167, 168, 174
   death of, 50, 79–86, 225–26
   "The Flutists' Legal Case" and, 158–74
   "The Handsome Catch a Slight Squint" and, 49, 51–59, 166n5
   "Householder" and, 50, 79–86
   life and reign of, 9
   as musician and music lover, 44, 51–52, 53, 60–61, 158
   oppression under, 79–86, 225–26
   similarity of current leaders to, 65–66
   "Ssematimba and Kikwabanga" and, 29
   temperament of, 51–52, 53, 56, 57, 58, 60
   vanity of, 49, 52–53, 55, 60
   war under, 241–42
Stalin regime, 44–45
Steingo, Gavin, 43
storytelling sessions, xix–xxii
subalternity, resistance and, 42–43
Supple, Vaughan, 17–18

telos, 247–48
temporality, concepts of, 46–48
termites, xvi–xviii
"They Are Repeating Themselves" ("Bizzeemu") (Mayinja song), 66
"They Chopped Off His Fingers" ("Baamutemako Engalo"), 128. *See also* "Gganga Had a Narrow Escape" ("Gganga Alula")
    Bisaso's performance of, 131–33
    interpretations of, 134–39
    musical elements, 130–31
    punishment and mercy in, 103, 128–39
    song text, 131–33
    versions compared, 133
"They Show Each Other Stumps" ("Balagana Enkonge")
    historical context, 206
    interpretations of, 209–13
    love, unity, and reciprocity in, 203, 205–13
    musical elements, 207–9
    song text, 208
    Sserwanga's performance of, 10, 207–9
Things Fall Apart (Achebe), 246–47
thumb piano. *See* lamellaphone (*akogo*)
Title in Hand (Kyapa mu Ngalo) project, 182
Tracey, Andrew, 82
Tracey, Hugh, 82
trough zither (*inanga*), 12
trust
    betrayal of, 111–13, 121–22, 148, 163, 180, 192, 193, 234, 276
    caution and, 66, 111–12, 149–50, 173, 183
    of court musicians by king, 53, 56–57, 223
    cultivating, 44–45, 99, 211, 221, 223
    losing, 222
    mutual, 141, 201, 208–10, 233–34
    in one's guts to make decisions, 172
tube fiddle (*endingidi*)
    Bisaso as performer, 12
    Deziderio as performer, 13, 88–89, 189–90, 255–56
    Kabwama as performer, 14
    Sserwanga as performer, 216, 226

Uganda. *See also* Buganda, Kingdom of; *specific leaders*
    as British protectorate, 3, 91–92, 254–56
    constitutional changes, 119
    constitutional referendum, 2005, 8, 87
    ethnic nationalism in, 6–7, 120, 121–22, 234, 265
    federalism rejected by ruling government, 4, 87–101, 148
    independence of, 3–4
    kingdoms' reinstatement, 1993, 7–8, 93
    kingdoms' status and power in, 3, 4, 6–7, 188–202, 233–34
    Lugbara people of, 48
    post-1996 political landscape, 7–8, 17, 22, 23–25, 27–28, 32, 50, 58 (*See also specific public figures, initiatives, and events*)
    post-independence leadership, 4
    regional inequality in, 98–100
Uganda Agreement of 1900, 3, 4, 6
Uganda Martyrs, 134–35
Uganda Museum (Kampala), 12, 262
Uganda National Examinations Board, 15
Uganda National Theatre, 12

Uganda People's Congress, 4
Ugandan Bush War, 24, 64, 72, 74, 148
"Unadvisable Kayemba" ("Kayemba Nantabuulirirwa"), 67n11
  advice and caution in, 103, 105–14
  Deziderio's performance of, 13
  historical context, 105–6
  interpretations of, 107–14
  musical elements, 106
  song text, 106
uncertainty
  expectations and, 244, 246
  fate and, 246
  greed and, 183
  honor and, 250
  lament and, 141, 158–74
  political, 137, 200
  self-preservation and, 252
  of vocation, 82–83
unity. *See also* mutuality; reciprocity
  between king and subjects, 198, 203
  lack of, 92, 123
  prosperity and, 212
  working toward, 170–71, 205–13

violence
  avoiding through wise leadership, 198–99, 250
  colonialism and, 255
  in contemporary politics, 84, 85, 163–64, 184–85, 222
  cyclical, 242, 253, 255
  evading through manipulation, 51, 54
  impact of, 103, 134–37
  materialism and, 257–59, 260, 281, 292
  power relations and, 45–46
  reciprocal, 245–48
  resulting from poor leadership, 105, 231, 233
  senselessness of, 135, 239, 264–66
  ubiquitous nature of, 30, 239

Wachsmann, Klaus, 37, 241
war. *See also* violence
  civil, 66, 239, 256, 261–68
  futility of, 256–57
  imperialism and, 239, 254–60
  tragedy of, 239, 241–53, 264–65, 268
  uncertainty in, 244–45
"We Love the Supreme Man Exceedingly" ("Ssaabasajja Tumwagala Nnyo")
  historical context, 224–26, 230
  interpretations of, 24–25, 231–37
  love and respect in, 204, 224–37
  musical elements, 226–27
  song text, 227–30
  Sserwanga's performance of, 10
"We Shall Wear the Crown" ("Tuliyambala Engule") (B. Wine), 66
"We Stand with You" ("Tubonga Naawe) (joint song), 66
weddings
  Christian missionaries' interference in Kiganda traditions, 185
  court musicians' performances, 11, 13, 22
  flattery of bride, 63
white ants, harvesting, xv–xviii
Wine, Bobi
  commentaries referencing, 17, 25, 58, 66, 110–11, 119, 155, 210, 252, 272–73, 274
  Museveni's attempted assassination of, 163
  songs by, 66, 274

World War II, 29–30, 239, 254–56, 258, 260

xylophones (*akadinda* and *amadinda*)
   Bisaso as performer, 12
   interlocking parts, 39, 129, 206–7
   Majwala as performer, 14
   at Mmengo court, 10
   music for, 37, 38
   Ssebuwufu as performer, 10, 129, 206–7

zither, trough. *See* trough zither (*inanga*)

www.ingramcontent.com/pod-product-compliance
Lightning Source LLC
Chambersburg PA
CBHW070233240426
43673CB00044B/1769